D1604461

English Glass

ENGLISH DECORATIVE ARTS

Series editor: Hugh Wakefield

ENGLISH GLASS   R. J. Charleston
ENGLISH SILVER   Philippa Glanville
ENGLISH JEWELLERY   Shirley Bury

ENGLISH DECORATIVE ARTS

Series editor: Hugh Wakefield

English Glass

and the glass used in England, *circa* 400–1940

R. J. CHARLESTON

Formerly Keeper of the Department of
Ceramics and Glass in the Victoria
and Albert Museum

London
GEORGE ALLEN AND UNWIN
Boston   Sydney

George Allen & Unwin (Publishers) Ltd,
40 Museum Street, London WC1A 1LU, UK

George Allen & Unwin (Publishers) Ltd,
Park Lane, Hemel Hempstead, Herts HP2 4TE, UK

Allen & Unwin Inc.,
9 Winchester Terrace, Winchester, Mass 01890, USA

George Allen & Unwin Australia Pty Ltd,
8 Napier Street, North Sydney, NSW 2060, Australia

First published in 1984

British Library Cataloguing in Publication Data

Charleston, R. J.
    English glass. – (English decorative arts)
1. Glass manufacture – England – History
2. Glass trade – England – History
I. Title   II. Series
338.4'76661'0942   HD9623.G72
ISBN 0–04–748003–3

Set in 11 on 12 point Bembo by Nene Phototypesetters Ltd
and printed in Great Britain by Mackays of Chatham

*This book is dedicated to the
members of The Glass Circle,
and to the memory of their first President,
William Arnold Thorpe.*

Contents

Contents

List of Illustrations

Plates

Line Drawings

List of Abbreviations

B.M.	British Museum
cm	centimetre(s)
D.	diameter
H.	height
in.	inch(es)
L.	length
V.A.M.	Victoria and Albert Museum
W.	width

(A further list of abbreviations, relating to the Notes and Bibliography only, will be found at the start of the Notes section, on pages 232–3.)

Foreword

More than half a century has passed since the late W. A. Thorpe produced in 1929 his authoritative *History of English and Irish Glass*, followed by his shorter *English Glass* in 1935. Since that time a great deal of new information has been gleaned from various sources and published in a variety of specialist journals. Clearly it is high time that the threads of English glass history should be drawn together again and interpreted for a new generation. Robert Charleston is uniquely capable of performing this task. He possesses an encyclopaedic knowledge of recent research, much of it carried out by himself, particularly in regard to the critical period of the seventeenth and eighteenth centuries. For many years, until his retirement, he was Keeper of the Department of Ceramics and Glass in the Victoria and Albert Museum. He has maintained an intimate connection with British collectors through his presidency of the Glass Circle (formerly known as the Circle of Glass Collectors) which he took over from W. A. Thorpe in 1957. His stature in the international field is implicit in his chairmanship of the Fellows of the Corning Museum of Glass, the principal American centre of glass studies.

Robert Charleston's book is the first in a series on the general subject of the 'English Decorative Arts', which is planned to deal eventually with all the main disciplines. The books will be published, however, only as and when they can each be written by one of the very few leading authorities. All can be expected to reflect the changes of emphasis which have affected interest and research during the past half century. We can now embrace the story of the arts in the nineteenth and early twentieth centuries; we can not only look at the objects of art themselves but also assess their social and domestic implications; and, above all, we can see, more clearly than before, the English arts in their international context. In all these respects Robert Charleston's book is an ideal prototype for the series.

Hugh Wakefield

Acknowledgements

It is an author's pleasant duty to acknowledge the help of those who have contributed to the making of his book, and in a certain view indeed there seems to be very little that he has done himself. The help comes in varying measures – from those who have shared in the planning at all stages to those who have helped in practical ways to put it into execution. Of the former, it is an especial pleasure to acknowledge the role of Hugh Wakefield, the editor of the new series, who has not only read the whole text at least once and advised on its scope and reshaping where necessary, but has done so with a sensitive regard for the author's feelings, exerting the necessary pressure but exerting it unobtrusively. A comparable diplomacy has been displayed by my publisher, Mr John Newth, who showed great forbearance throughout the prolonged gestatory period of this book. Of those who particularly helped me in its execution I should especially like to thank my daughter, Mrs J. Stringer, who carried out the drawings with a sensitive regard to the needs of the book as well as to the qualities of the glasses concerned; and Miss Eileen Robinson, who typed, re-typed and sometimes re-retyped my manuscript, often at times inconvenient to herself.

Dr D. B. Harden gave me the benefit of his advice on parts of Chapter 1, and Martin Mortimer read through and criticised, perhaps too kindly, the original draft of Chapter 4, while Hugh Wakefield's views on Chapter 5 were expert and invaluable. The faults that remain are entirely my own.

The author of a book of this kind is always beholden to a number of people who put information in his way, and I am happy to acknowledge such contributions from Mr Roy Edwards, who has investigated the industrial establishments of the seventeenth and eighteenth centuries at Vauxhall; Mrs Arlene Palmer-Schwind, who supplied the important reference to an engraver working near London Bridge in 1776; to my former colleague, Miss Nathalie Rothstein, who supplied many references to glass-workers and glass-dealers from her researches in the insurance records; and to Mrs Nancy Valpy, who did the same from London newspapers; to

Major J. F. G. Terry, and to Mr Ralph Walker, who made me free of his work on George Ravenscroft.

I am particularly grateful to Mr and Mrs C. G. Benson, who not only allowed me the choice of a number of pieces in their collection, but provided the photographs; and to Mrs Robert Tritton for the use of her photograph for Pl. 34a and for permission to publish it.

Most books on aspects of material culture owe a great deal to the staffs of museums and libraries who answer queries and set in train the provision of photographs. I should like to single out for thanks in this connection Mr Charles Hajdamach, of the Broadfield House Glass Museum at Dudley; Mrs Rosemary Weinstein, of the Museum of London; and Mr Charles Truman and Miss Moira Thunder, of my old Department at the Victoria and Albert Museum.

Last and most important, I owe to my wife the fact that this book was ever completed. She never let me forget it at times when my attention was tempted into other channels. *Finis coronat opus.*

R. J. Charleston

Glossary

aventurine	Glittering metallic enclosures in the substance of a glass, caused by the crystallisation of metallic copper under reducing furnace conditions.
baluster	A stem narrow above and swelling below (fig. 23), an 'inverted baluster' reversing this order; 'baluster' also used of the whole style of simple substantial stems of the early eighteenth century.
balustroid	A later development of the 'baluster' stem, usually lighter and more slender.
base ring	Usually the rim of a foot made by pushing in the base of a paraison, creating a double thickness, with a hollow edge enclosing the trapped air.
'beech-nut moulding'	A diaper design of raised pointed lozenge motifs produced by mould-blowing.
cames	Lead channels, of 'H' section, used to hold pieces of window-glass and joined by soldering.
capstan	A section of a wine-glass stem swelling at both ends.
chain-circuit	Two (sometimes three) threads laid horizontally round a glass and pinched together at intervals.
chair	A production team centred on a master or 'gaffer', who usually worked seated in a chair with long arms on which to trundle his irons.
cigar stem	A tall hollow-blown stem usually slightly wider at the top.
crannog	An ancient Celtic lake dwelling.
'crizzling'	A defect in glass caused by an imbalance between its alkali and calcium constituents, producing surface roughness, internal hair-cracking, and ultimate disintegration.

cullet	Broken or waste glass re-used with other materials in a glass 'batch' for melting.
cup top	The upper part of a wine-glass bowl spreading towards the rim in a cup-like formation.
flux	Chemical constituent of a glass lowering its melting-point.
folded foot	Disc foot, the edge of which is folded (usually under) to form a welt of double thickness.
frigger	An object, often of a fanciful character, made by a glass-blower in his spare time, from material remaining in the pots.
gadrooning	A calyx of raised ribs, normally mould-blown, round the lower part of a bowl or analogous form.
grisaille	Grey or black fired pigment used, normally on stained glass, for the drawing of outlines, hatching, etc.
grozing	Use of a slotted glazier's iron to nibble the edge of a glass panel to the required shape after preliminary division by a hot iron or diamond-point.
Hyalith	An opaque glass, coloured sealing-wax red or black.
kick	Normally conical re-entrant in the base of a cylindrical or spherical vessel, to ensure stability.
knop	A normally spherical component of a stem (see fig. 23 for varieties) .
ladder stem	A hollow-blown stem having vertical panels patterned with horizontal bars recalling the rungs of a ladder.
lattimo	Italian word (derived from *latte* = milk) denoting an opaque-white glass.
lehr	Derived from the Italian *l'era*, used of a secondary furnace, normally implying an annealing furnace.
lenticular cutting	Cutting to produce a pattern of slender ovals.
lion-mask stem	A hollow-blown stem, produced in a two-part mould, each half patterned with a lion's mask; garlands usually hang down between the two masks.
Lithyalin	An opaque coloured glass patterned to resemble the markings of natural stones.

marvered Smoothed externally and consolidated by rolling on a flat slab of iron (originally of marble, whence the name), as a preliminary to further working.

merese A flat solid disc interposed between the main components of a stem.

metal Traditionally used of the glass material, usually when molten in the pot.

milled cordon A thread of glass laid horizontally round a glass, the ends overlapping, and the resultant ring being notched with the edges of the 'pucellas' (glass-maker's tongs) or milled with a rigaree (q.v.).

muff Cylinder of glass to be slit lengthways and opened out to form a rectangular sheet, normally in window manufacture.

ogee-bowl Wine-glass bowl where the line of bowl and stem forms an ogee (or double) curve.

paraison The gather of glass enclosing the air-bubble of first inflation and ready for further working.

polycandelon A wheel-shaped lighting fixture for suspension, usually consisting of a flat metal ring pierced to take the conical stems of glass lamps.

pontil (punty) A solid iron rod for affixing by a 'wad' (or blob) of hot glass to the base of a blown vessel, thus enabling the worker to continue the work of shaping the neck, rim, etc.

printie A circular disc-like cut on glass.

prunt A blob of glass usually affixed to the wall of a vessel and made more decorative by tooling or impressing with a patterned stamp.

putti Small boys, sometimes winged, represented in classical or classicising scenes.

quarries (from French *carré*) Small panes of glass, normally rectangular or lozenge-shaped, used in plain overall patterns of window-glazing.

ratafia 'A cordial or liqueur flavoured with certain fruits or their kernels, usually almonds or peach-, apricot- and cherry-kernels' (N.E.D.)

rhyton A drinking-vessel, of roughly horn shape, usually fashioned as an animal's head, and often unstable.

rigaree   A tool resembling a pastry cook's wheel, with notched circumference, for imparting a milled design to an applied thread of glass.

rim-fold   A double thickness of glass obtained by folding over the rim of a glass.

rod-handle   A loop handle obtained by applying a solid thick thread of glass to the wall of a vessel.

Roemer   A drinking-glass (usually for Rhenish white wine) with ovoid bowl made in one piece with the hollow cylindrical stem, usually mounted on a conical foot made of a single spiral of glass thread. The stem is usually decorated with prunts (q.v.).

second gather   A supplementary gather often only partially covering the paraison (q.v.) obtained from the first gather: this was often done to provide the necessary substance for mould-blowing ribbed designs (see 'gadrooning').

Sharawadgi   Exotic word deriving 'either from the Chinese *Sa-ro-(k)wai-chi*, which signifies graceful disorder, or from the Japanese *sorawaji*, "not being regular" . . .' (H. Honour *Chinoiserie*, London (1961), 145).

slips   Strips of glass for covering the joins between mirror-plates.

string rim   An applied horizontal thread, usually below the rim of a bottle, for anchoring the pack-thread or wire used in securing the cork.

trailing   Pulling out a thread of glass and applying it to the surface of a vessel in spiral or other designs.

'wrythen'   Spirally twisted, usually used of ribbing.

Introduction

This book attempts a general history of glass in England from Anglo-Saxon times until the relatively recent past, including not merely glass made in England, but glass made abroad and used in England in periods when home production could not meet demand.

We all stand upon the shoulders of our predecessors. Anyone who interests himself in the history of English glass inevitably finds himself turning to the books of Albert Hartshorne, Francis Buckley and W. A. Thorpe, and ultimately using them as the basis of his own work. Hartshorne (1897), however, dealt with far more than merely English glass and took nearly 500 large quarto pages to do it. The core of Francis Buckley's *A History of Old English Glass* (1925) was its invaluable collection of contemporary references to glass in the late seventeenth and eighteenth centuries; otherwise, its arbitrary arrangement and lack of an index make it a difficult book in which to seek a 'round unvarnish'd tale'.

Thorpe's great *History of English and Irish Glasses* (1929), although taking a brief glance back in history before dealing at length with the period from the sixteenth to the early nineteenth centuries, had illustrations of a mere half-dozen glasses dating from before 1600. In his shorter and more general work, *English Glass* (first published in 1935), he redressed the imbalance by dealing at length with Roman and Saxon times, but taking almost a third of his total text to do so. It is hoped in this book to give a more balanced survey, not only in the space allocated to different periods, but in the attempt to show glass in its domestic context without sacrificing the historical and morphological aspects of the subject so faithfully handled by Hartshorne and Thorpe, each according to his lights in his own generation.

No uniform treatment of the subject is strictly possible, for until we come to relatively recent times the surviving evidence is partial and unevenly balanced. Thus for the pagan Saxon period we have a relative abundance of intact glasses from burials and thus an exact idea of the glasses used; whereas from the later Saxon era it is only possible to interpret the sparse fragments from occupation sites by

comparison with the intact vessels surviving from pagan Scandinavia. Of documentary evidence there is virtually nothing. In the
post-Conquest period before 1200 there is effectively a total blank.
From that point onwards the resources of modern archaeology have
brought to light an increasing body of material evidence, including
the physical remains of some of the glasshouses which are known
to have existed in the Surrey/Sussex Weald and elsewhere. Particularly important for our ideas about the glass used in the Middle
Ages has been the discovery, in securely dated thirteenth- to fourteenth-century contexts, of fine glasses made in a virtually colourless material, hitherto regarded as impossible before the middle of
the fifteenth century in Venice. Furthermore, this material was
worked into graceful forms of extreme fragility, though it was
almost certainly not of English manufacture. It has, nevertheless,
seemed imperative to include this evidence so that the reader may
be able to visualise what manner of glasses graced the tables of the
wealthy and powerful at a time when the English glasshouses
themselves were capable of producing no more than utilitarian
wares – bottles, lamps, urinals, distilling equipment and second-
grade window-glass – in a technically imperfect green 'forest' glass.

For some reason, the material evidence of the glass used in the
fifteenth century is less prolific; but, in compensation, the written
records begin to multiply. We are reasonably well informed of conditions in the English industry in the sixteenth and seventeenth centuries, thanks mainly to the exhaustive work carried out among the
British archives by an American scholar, Mrs Eleanor Godfrey,
whose *The Development of English Glassmaking 1560–1640* (1975) is
probably the most important book on English glass to appear since
the Second World War. For the first time, the documentary
evidence seems to outstrip the archaeological, although this is far
from defective and includes important revelations concerning
glass-making in England itself during this crucial period. Whereas
we have at least a dozen identifiable English glasses in the Venetian
tradition from the reign of Queen Elizabeth I, not a single intact
glass (or at best one) appears to have survived above ground from
the reigns of her two immediate successors. It is necessary to piece
the record together from relatively ambiguous archaeological
evidence. The period of the Civil War too is a virtual blank, and
only with the Restoration of Charles II in 1660 can we finally feel
solid ground under our feet. From that time onwards the problem
is not one of finding evidence but of selecting it to keep the narra-
tive within bounds.

With the final decade of the seventeenth century the collector's period really begins, although financial stringency restrains most contemporary collectors from cultivating the field before 1700. The collector's interest to some extent provided the impetus for the books published in the 1920s and 1930s, which accordingly mapped out the field for the benefit of the collector – who conferred the reciprocal benefit of bringing together series of glasses for study. The upsurge of 'investment collecting' in a post-war period of incessant inflation has spawned a whole generation of collectors' books which have, with honourable exceptions, based themselves uncritically on their pre-war forerunners, perpetuating old myths and sometimes downright errors in the publishing scramble to exploit this promising vein. New discoveries and reappraisals of old evidence have often been brushed aside and obscured in the process.

Since the war, the scope of collecting has been greatly expanded in response to the economic forces already referred to, which have begun to make the collecting of even eighteenth-century glass prohibitively expensive. The subject of Victorian glass was first put squarely on the map by the Exhibition of Victorian and Edwardian Decorative Arts mounted by the Victoria and Albert Museum in 1952. In this, however, glass played only a part, and the subject was first formally exposed in its entirety by Hugh Wakefield in his *Nineteenth Century British Glass*, published in 1961. It has since been expanded, but not radically altered, by a number of more detailed studies. The documentation for this period is enormous and is still in process of sifting. Here selection is the critical problem, and an effort has been made to preserve the main lines of the story without sacrificing too much detail.

Just as the texture of a book is affected by the patchiness of evidence falling unevenly in different places, so is it affected by the character of the books which have previously covered the same ground. In passages where the present book may seem to skim rather cursorily over a particular subject, the reason may be that it has already been treated at length, if not *ad nauseam*, in an earlier work. Where it goes into detail over a theme which may seem of relative unimportance, this may be because the topic is one hitherto afforded less attention than it deserves. An attempt has been made in the notes to indicate earlier works in which a certain topic has received special treatment. Thus the spread of the glass industry in different areas has been only tangentially discussed, except in the earlier period, before 1700, when the industry was finally establishing itself firmly in the hierarchy of those commercial undertakings on which Great Britain's industrial success in the eighteenth and nineteenth centuries was based. Nor has any endeavour been made to discuss the inwardness of Jacobite and anti-Jacobite propaganda on glass – it has a literature of its own in which the glasses themselves seem to play a somewhat subordinate role. Hints may be gleaned in the bibliography. On the other hand, what may seem to some an inordinate amount of space has been devoted to the development of wheel-engraving and cutting in the eighteenth century, or to the evolution of gilding and enamelling on coloured and opaque-white glasses in the same period. This allocation of space follows a sense of the aesthetic or technical importance of the types of glass concerned; or of the inadequacy of their treatment in earlier books.

An effort has also been made to touch on those more mundane types of glass on which at least the comforts of civilisation have come more and more to depend – windows, bottles and mirrors – although it has been impossible to do more than sketch their development. The improvements described for one period may be assumed to underlie those in succeeding centuries.

CHAPTER 1

Conquest and Assimilation: The Anglo-Saxon Period
(c. 400–1066)

*The Anglo-Saxon conquest and Germanic Taste, 1 – Pagan
early period glasses, 3 – Middle and late period glasses, 9 –
Christian period, 11 – Window-glass, 12 – Late Saxon glass,
14 – Mosaic glass and secondary working, 14*

Roman glass is commonly found in the territories which consti-
tuted the Roman province of Britannia, and there are even traces of
glass-making on half a dozen sites in England; but a discussion of
the long and complicated developments of Roman glass history is
inappropriate in a book devoted essentially to the making and use
of English glass. Logically the tale takes up when, after the departure of the legions in the early years of the fifth century AD and with
the increasing inroads of the peoples whom we know inexactly as
the Anglo-Saxons, England began to emerge as an entity. The
precise composition of this loose confederation of tribes is uncertain, as is their relationship with the Frankish tribes who overran
the former Roman province of Gaul. Many of the bands who
formed these tribes had had experience as auxiliaries in the Roman
army, or the armies of successor-states, and the tradition relating to
the Anglo-Saxons casts them in a similar role. From the middle of
the fourth century onwards Britain had been plagued by raids from
northern tribes generically called Saxons, but at some time after 450
these casual raids were replaced by a regular occupation of the
Kentish coast by bands of Jutes (cognates of the Anglo-Saxons),
who probably came from the same general area of Schleswig-
Holstein and northern Germany. According to tradition they had
been called in by a local king to help defend Britain against their

marauding cousins. The Venerable Bede (672/3–735) wrote of these events, which happened more than 200 years before his time: 'Those who came over were of the three most powerful nations in Germany – Saxons, Angles, and Jutes. From the Jutes are descended the people of Kent and the Isle of Wight and those in the province of the West Saxons who are to this day called Jutes, seated opposite to the Isle of Wight.' Great obscurity surrounds the formation of the Saxon kingdoms but one of the richest enclaves of Saxon culture, especially in so far as glass is concerned, was that built up in Kent. The splendour of the gold and garnet jewellery found in the Kentish graves is legendary, and of some 250 surviving glasses of the fifth to seventh centuries found in England, no less than 170 come from Kent.

In considering the glasses themselves, it should be stressed at once that there is no clear break between the glass-making of the late Roman fourth century and that of the Germanic fifth century and later. Only a gradual impoverishment (or concentration) of techniques and styles, and an adaptation of shapes and decoration to suit 'barbarian' needs and tastes, can be discerned. Although Roman glass-making centres existed in eastern France and Belgium, Cologne had been the most brilliant centre of the craft in northern Europe during the third and fourth centuries, capable of producing as sophisticated and luxurious glassware as anywhere else in the Roman Empire – 'gold sandwich glasses'; enamelled glasses; glasses with brilliant polychrome threading; and glasses that were wheel-cut and wheel-engraved in the most elaborate styles. In the Frankish period all these techniques were abandoned, and the glassmakers reverted to the use of the blowpipe, the simplest of moulds, and all the resources of threaded decoration. Almost all colour was foresworn except the tones of green, yellow and brown which resulted from the iron impurities of the presumably local sands employed, and from the firing conditions within the furnace. The capacity, or the will, to produce colourless glass – perhaps unpleasing to the Frankish taste – was gradually lost. Exceptionally, cobalt-blue glass was made, and towards the end of the period a material coloured or streaked with copper-red was produced. Of all the specialised opaque glasses used in the heyday of Cologne, only opaque-white continued in use, no doubt imported from the south (?Italy), just as the soda used to flux the glass had to be imported from the Mediterranean.

Glass-making probably ceased in Cologne soon after AD 400, but it is unlikely that the break was sudden or complete. The art probably drifted gradually away from towns to be near supplies of fuel. The medieval glasshouses of northern Europe are almost invariably found in wooded areas, and at least one Merovingian glass-making site in modern Belgium is located in a great woodland area, the source thereafter of fuel for local glass-making.[1]

Just as there was no abrupt break in glass-making style after the German irruptions, so there is no clear-cut demarcation between late Roman and Dark Age glasses found in Anglo-Saxon burials. Apart from carefully preserved heirlooms, such as a mould-blown beaker of a well-known first-century type from Newport Pagnell, it is often difficult to distinguish between glasses – particularly conical beakers and bowls – which are fourth-century survivals and those which were fairly new when buried. There is no positive evidence for glass-making in Britain in the fourth century or later, although its existence cannot be discounted. On the whole it seems more likely that glasses of this or fifth- and sixth-century date were imports from the Continent – whether brought as treasured possessions by the invaders, or imported in the course of trade thereafter. The difficulties posed by these imponderables are illustrated by a cache of eleven glasses found in an early fifth-century context at Burgh Castle, Suffolk. This group contained two footed bowls and two handled flasks of certainly late Roman type, but also two short-stemmed goblets which are one-piece glasses, with stem and foot made by pushing in the base, a feature which distinguishes them from most Roman glasses of this general shape and strongly suggests a Teutonic origin. More doubtful were five truncated conical beakers, two shorter examples betraying by their knocked-off, rough rims their affinity with late Roman glasses, while the three taller beakers had smoothed rims, a normal Frankish feature.

Although the archaeological record is confused, the glasses of the pagan Anglo-Saxon period seem to fall roughly into three chronological groups – Early (approximately fifth to early sixth century); Middle (sixth century); and Late (late sixth to seventh century). This period is reasonably well documented by the many glasses, often intact, found in graves. With the Christian conversion of the seventh century, the old pagan custom of burying grave-goods with the dead was discouraged, and by the beginning of the eighth century had ceased. Direct archaeological evidence for the period after about 700 is therefore restricted to finds from occupation sites, invariably in the form of (often very small) fragments. Some light, however, is thrown obliquely by more complete finds from other northern countries where paganism survived.

The glasses from the earliest period of pagan Anglo-Saxon England, apart possibly from a very few bowls, were devoted to drinking or, in the case of the occasional rare flask, to the storage of liquor. Virtually all have affinities with the late Roman glasses made in the large area of northern Europe neatly epitomised by W. A. Thorpe in the phrase 'Seine-Rhine'. Like them, the early English-found glasses are often of greenish-colourless glass, contrasting with the pronounced green of later vessels; and are frequently decorated with opaque-white threading, sometimes dragged into arcaded designs, marvered flush with the surface. Mention has already been made of a footed cylindrical beaker with body, stem and foot made of a single paraison. Two short-stemmed examples have been found in cemeteries at Croydon and Howletts (Kent) respectively (Pl. 1a), both with several turns of self-coloured threading below the out-turned lip. A third example – from High Down, Sussex – has this feature with a second zone towards the base executed in the opaque-white glass already noted as a trait of Frankish glasses in the fifth and sixth centuries.[2] This glass has a slightly taller stem than the first two, and its shape is significant as foreshadowing the elaborate 'claw-beakers' (pp. 5–7).

One of the notable features of Dark Age glass in the West is the propensity of drinking-glasses to become unstable. This is already to be remarked in the fourth century, no doubt because northern tastes were making themselves felt in the centres of late Roman glass-making. The trend continued through the fifth and sixth centuries, and no doubt reflected Teutonic drinking habits. Although it is dangerous to argue from later to earlier circumstances, passages from the Anglo-Saxon poem of *Beowulf*, committed to writing about AD 1000 but probably reflecting conditions 300 years earlier, may illuminate these customs. When Beowulf went to pay his respects to King Hrothgar in his great hall, 'Now and then before the high courtiers, Hrothgar's daughter bare the ale cup to the nobles from end to end. I heard those sitting in the hall call her Freawaru, as she presented the studded vessel to the heroes.' It was incumbent on the host, either personally or through a relative or servant, to welcome his guest with a glass of ale and to retrieve it from him for replenishment. There was no necessity for it to rest on the table in front of him, and when done with it could be set rim-down on the serving-table (cf. Pl. 2b).

Most Anglo-Saxon drinking-glasses tend in fact to have a vestigial foot or a narrow, flat base and can usually, with care, be stood up. They are, however, top-heavy and since they were presumably valued possessions, they would not lightly have been put at risk in this way. Of one type, however, not even this can be said. In its earliest form this 'bell-beaker' is cylindrical, flaring slightly at the rim and drawing in to an applied knob at the base which makes it categorically unstable. This knob, and the trails with which these beakers are usually decorated, are frequently of opaque-white glass. Although uncommon in English finds they are frequently found on the Continent, notably in France; and fragments from a Merovingian furnace site at Macquenoise in modern Belgium suggest that some at least were made there.[3] The shape changes, perhaps in the early years of the sixth century, into a waisted form, normally decorated like its predecessor (Pl. 1b). Fragments of this type too were found at Macquenoise.[4]

Other kinds of drinking-glass show in their marvered, opaque-white trails an affinity with the 'early' glasses already discussed. They include a plain, tapering 'cone-beaker' with an arcading of white threads round its mid-point, of which three examples have come to light in England, but many more on the Continent. Others are decorated with a spiral of white glass below the rim and may equally be of late fifth- to early sixth-century date. Differing in ornament, although parallel in shape, is a considerable series of cone-beakers named after the most famous of the type, that found at Kempston in Bedfordshire (Pl. 4a).[5] This series, of which some twenty-two examples are recorded, is characterised by trailed self-coloured threads, with a zone of horizontal trailing below the flared rim, complementing vertical loops on the lower two-thirds of the glass. This vertical emphasis, underlining the generally elongated character of the glasses themselves, gives them an extreme elegance and places them among the most beautiful glasses ever made. The English examples appear to belong to the fifth or early sixth century. Occasionally, however, association with later objects suggests that a glass was a carefully preserved heirloom. Comparable glasses on the Continent are similarly dated, and their distribution suggests that they were made on the Meuse or perhaps the middle Rhine. There are almost as many specimens in England as there are in Germany, Holland, Belgium and France combined, and there are two outliers in Czechoslovakia, facts which suggest that this was an export type. A series of beakers with the same decoration, but thicker and of a different shape with a vestigial foot, was made during the same period for the Scandinavian market.[6]

By far the most spectacular drinking-glass of the Anglo-Saxon period was the claw-beaker (Pls. 1d, 3a). This was characterised by the decorative addition of usually two rows of hollow-blown, trunk-like 'claws' applied over horizontal trailing. There has been much discussion of the technique by which these complicated glasses were produced, the most convincing being that propounded by the late W. A. Thorpe.[7] The glass was worked predominantly on the blowing-iron. First the trailing was applied and the foot formed. Then the glass was cooled slightly and the gaffer's assistant would apply a blob of far hotter glass. This would melt the wall of the vessel where it touched and the gaffer would blow so that the blob became a hollow subsidiary paraison, while the assistant pulled it downwards with a hooked instrument to join the vessel wall below. The marks of this process are often visible on the lower part of the claw and, perhaps to conceal these, decorative ribbons were trailed over them and embellished with notching. When the requisite number of claws had been made, the pontil would be affixed to the base, the paraison knocked off, and the rim finished. Altogether, these beakers represent a *tour de force* of the craftsman; and nothing so complicated would be seen again in Europe until the Renaissance. The claw-beakers offered the added attraction that their contents could be seen to ebb and flow in the hollow appendages, no doubt with corresponding aural effects.

The claw-beaker derived from the footed beaker with trailed decoration, a feature retained in the claw-beaker, perhaps because it heightened the mystery of how the glass was made. The technique, however, like all those used on Dark Age glass, had its roots in fourth-century Roman practice. A number of elaborate goblets found in Germany are decorated with hollow fish, snails and shells made in the same way.[8] By about AD 400 these had become unrecognisable as marine creatures but the claw motif, corresponding to the body of the fish or snail, survived in its non-representational decorative role. A beaker from Wickham in Kent has a row of circular, hollow-blown projections above its claws to remind us of the earlier phase of this decoration. In recent years a single example of the elaborate goblet with hollow claws hitherto known only from the Rhineland has been found in England. It is a light green piece from Mucking in Essex, decorated with two superimposed rows of claws below a horizontal zigzag border – a typical fourth-century motif. The glass probably dates from the early fifth century. A true claw-beaker of comparable date, found at Dumpton Park, Broadstairs, follows exactly the form of the footed beaker but is extended vertically to allow for two rows of claws. The next development seems to be a reduction of the clearly defined foot to a flat, basal disc, together with a flexing of the outline of the beaker to produce a bulge where the claws are applied, and a narrower neck. In a field where there is much uncertainty as to dates and origins, it is impossible to know what diagnostic weight to attach to the widely differing features characteristic of claw-beakers. By about AD 500 the claws seem.to increase in size and number while still grouped in two horizontal rows, the makers reaching an apogee of skill in blowing the claws hollow almost to their tips and in disposing them to best effect (Pl. 1d). During the sixth century the claws tend to sink, the upper part of the beaker being occupied by a deep zone of trailing. The later development of the form will be discussed below (p. 9).

Last, but certainly not least, among drinking-vessels come the horns, well known on the continent of Europe but only relatively recently found in England.[9] Rhytons have a long history in glass-making, but realistic copies of animal horns only seemed to develop in response to the demands of the northern peoples from the third century onwards. Again evidence from a later age may help to throw light backwards. In the eleventh century Harold Hardrada, King of Norway, 'like the old kings before him, used to drink from an animal's horn and himself bear the ale from the high seat about the fire to empty the cup of remembrance with those whom he would honour' (cf. Pl. 2b). The transference of this shape into glass was an obvious step and seems to have occurred in the third century. In 1937 a pair of glass horns was found near Rainham in Essex (Pl. 2a) and these remain the only two English finds, apart from a small tip-fragment found in Rutland. They were decorated with a cross-notched ribbon applied a little below the rim, and with a second cordon dragged downwards at intervals to form an arcade, long vertical threads then descending from the lower points of this arcading as far as the tips. The horns, of olive-green bubbly glass, had been curved in one plane and slightly twisted in another to simulate with elegant skill the curvature of a natural horn. The continental analogues to the Rainham horns are datable between the late fifth and the late sixth century, although the snapped-off rims of the Rainham horns recall late Roman glasses finished in this way, and suggest the beginning of this time-span as the period of their manufacture. The tip of a comparable horn has been found at Macquenoise.[10] Since horns of this type are not found in the general area of Cologne but occur elsewhere in Germany, France and Yugoslavia, it is reasonable to suppose that the main centre of production may have been in Belgium.

Only two bottles of Anglo-Saxon date have been found in England – a fragmentary example from Bifrons and an intact piece from the sixth-century cemetery at Lyminge (Pl. 3a),[11] both in Kent. The former, which lacks its neck-rim, is cylindrical with a sharply spreading base, a shape with parallels in the Rhineland; the latter lacks the spreading base, but retains its slightly tapering neck with flaring rim above.

Finally there are a few small bowls of unknown use which come from Anglo-Saxon cemeteries and, in one instance, from a stone-built tomb in York. This last piece has a shallow, hemispherical form and is decorated with a thread spiral under the slightly out-turned lip, beneath which there are vertically trailed loops – a formula corresponding with that of the cone-beakers of 'Kempston' type (Pl. 4a). With these the bowls are presumably co-eval. Apart from the York piece and one from Faversham, the remaining examples come from Islip in Northamptonshire, and from Lackford in Suffolk – an unusual distribution pattern for these early glasses. A second type of bowl has virtually straight sides sloping out from a flat slightly 'kicked' base, and is normally decorated with opaque-white or self-coloured trails, or occasionally with mould-blown decoration. The opaque-white trails and the thin, fine 'metal' both point to an early date. An example from High Down cemetery in Sussex has marvered white threads dragged with a point into a quatrefoil design in the base, a feature occurring on pieces found in Belgium, Holland and the Rhineland, the Dutch example coming from a late fourth- to fifth-century context.[12] The English finds come from High Down, an early site (two examples), and Westbere in Kent (three examples).

A third type of bowl, which was previously thought to be late Roman now appears, from its occurrence in the cemetery at Mucking, to be of Anglo-Saxon date. It is roughly hemispherical, drawn in slightly below the rim to present an 'S' profile, and is decorated with fine trailing below the rim. An example found at Alfriston cemetery in Sussex[13] has the rim trail in opaque-white and mould-blown vertical ribbing on the body, a rare feature also found on a similar bowl of yellowish-brown colour found at the Macquenoise glasshouse.[14] A third piece, from the Howletts cemetery, has the threading combined with a plain body.

Lastly, mould-blown ribbing, slightly 'wrythen' to give sloping lines, occurs on a bucket-shaped green vessel found recently in the Westgarth Gardens cemetery at Bury St Edmunds. The 'bucket' (some 12 cm (4¾ in.) high) has loops applied on the rim, probably to take a 'bail' handle, and is decorated top and bottom with opaque-white spirals – a strong indication of the 'early' nature of this unique vessel, confirmed by the probable fifth-century date of an accompanying spear.

The sixth century seems to have been mainly a period of slow evolution and consolidation. The bell-beaker loses some of its crispness of shape and, though retaining the constriction above the foot, loses its basal button and threaded decoration, often replaced by vertical mould-blown corrugation (Pl. 1c). Like many contemporary beaker-type glasses it tends to increase in height relative to its diameter. Although common on the Continent, only four examples are known in England. Fragments of two bases excavated at Macquenoise suggest that the type originated in the Meuse area.[15] The cone-beakers of 'Kempston' type are joined by others with mould-blown ribbing, sometimes vertical and sometimes wrythen, usually accompanied by threading below the out-splayed rim. In this period the claw-beaker appears to gain in height in the trailed zone below the rim and the claws, although well formed, seem to settle into the lower part of the beaker. This, however, is not a clearly defined progression and doubt will probably always surround the dating of a given example.

The remaining 'early' forms appear to die out in the sixth century, their places being taken by two new shapes which, by their squat proportions, contrast with the growing height of the drinking-beakers already enumerated. These new shapes are the squat jar (Pl. 3b) and the palm-cup (Pl. 3c). The squat jar – no doubt suggested by gourds such as the mounted examples found at Sutton Hoo – probably first appeared in the sixth century but its heyday is in the seventh (p. 10). The palm-cup, on the other hand, which has numerous parallels on the Continent, seems to have flourished largely in the sixth century, the earliest form being a hemispherical cup with a rounded rim, usually decorated with vertical mould-blown ribbing. The lower ends of these ribs sometimes form cross-designs at the base, the cup seeming to stand on four 'toes'. A variety of mould-blown designs is recorded, suggesting that a number of glasshouses made these cups. Towards 600 this form was joined by a more open shape with folded rim and usually vertical ribbing. Both types survived into the seventh century.

In the seventh-century claw-beaker the thread-trailed neck began to dominate the claw-decorated body, and the resultant imbalance may have tempted the makers to include a further row of claws, although this offered difficulties of placement, difficulties which the maker of the Wickham beaker perhaps tried to avoid by using a top line of projecting bosses in place of a third row of claws. As the beaker itself becomes progressively taller and its sides straighter, the claws themselves become flatter and press closer to the body (Pl. 4b). This tendency continues beyond the pagan Saxon period and the deposition of grave-goods in burials, and can be best

followed in still–pagan Scandinavia (p. 3). The bell-beaker dis-
appears and the cone-beaker, possibly pre-empted by the claw-
beaker in its adoption of a tall, conical form, also fades away. In
their place comes another type of tall, unstable glass – the 'bag-
beaker', with rounded base, decoration of notched vertical strips
and slightly spreading thread-trailed neck (Pl. 5a). Of eight known
examples, five have been found at the 'late' cemetery at Faversham
and only two on the Continent. This distribution raises the presumption that by the seventh century England may have had its
own glass production, perhaps at Faversham itself. A unique
beaker from the Kentish cemetery at Sarre is a curious hybrid of
bag-beaker and claw-beaker, shaped like the former but decorated
with pairs of claws vertically superimposed in panels outlined by
vertical strips like those on the bag-beaker.

The rare bag-beakers are considerably outnumbered by the squat
jars (p. 9), which vary in shape from depressed globular vessels
with narrow, sometimes slightly everted necks to taller and
narrower flask-like forms. Their decoration is equally various,
from plain neck-threading with or without vertical body-threading
to thicker threads worked into mesh designs or laid on in the form
of collars and vertical ribs. Vertical mould-blown ribbing also
occurs, while some jars are left plain. They are difficult to classify,
with nearly a hundred examples occurring in England, whereas
they are rare on the Continent. In England only eleven pieces
turned up outside Kent, whereas the Faversham cemetery alone
produced forty-three specimens, a distribution suggesting that this
type too is English, probably made in Kent itself. A similar picture
is presented by another seventh-century form – the 'pouch-bottle'
(Pl. 5b) – which, in squatter versions, almost overlaps the squat
jar. Examples are decorated in the same range of techniques
and are evidently seventh-century cousins. Their distribution
underlines this affinity, for of fourteen English-found examples
thirteen come from Kent. These seemingly English glasses co-
exist through the seventh century with the palm-cups, which
are now left plain though normally they have a folded rim,
their open hemispherical shape deepening progressively into a
bell-form foreshadowing the funnel-beaker (p. 11).

The evidence of Anglo-Saxon cemeteries is echoed by the far
sparser and more fragmentary finds on settlement sites. These not
only turn up within Saxon-controlled territory but also on the
'Celtic fringe' in Cornwall, Wales, Scotland and Ireland. The concentration of coloured and opaque-white glass fragments in these
places suggests that in some instances they housed workshops

where these attractive, and no doubt costly, materials were worked up into such items as beads and bangles (p. 14).

In the eighth century, settlement sites provide the only evidence for the types of glass used in England. Fortunately, small fragments can often be interpreted by means of parallel finds in pagan north Europe. Thus fragments from a vessel at York revealed an amber-coloured neck on an olive-green body – a two-colour feature regularly found in continental glasses of Carolingian date (751–987). At Dorestadt in Holland, supposedly dating before AD 864, has been found a fragmentary funnel-beaker with a darkish blue rim welded to a pale green body. Two intact Swedish funnel-beakers – one from Ås-Husby in Uppland, the other from Birka (Pl. 5c) on Lake Mälaren – show the same feature.[16] The former has a strong dark green, the latter a dark blue, rim. Both are dated to the ninth century. Another well-preserved beaker or jar from Birka, somewhat resembling the York fragment in profile, has a deep purple rim, the body being almost colourless (Pl. 5d).[17] Accompanying finds suggest an early tenth-century date.

A second type of coloured embellishment characteristic of the Carolingian era involves the use of two-colour twists applied as cordons on an almost colourless glass. At Hamwih, the Anglo-Saxon precursor of Southampton (probably seventh to tenth century), were found the rim of a greenish bell-tumbler decorated with a twist of opaque-white and light blue and the fragments of two squat jars, one with a trail of these colours but with opaque yellow added, and this recurs with a cable of opaque-white on the second jar. The opaque yellow was found again at Hamwih on the rim of a dark green bowl, and also on a greenish bowl-fragment found at Whitby monastery (perhaps eighth to ninth century). These yellow threads appear also in Scandinavian finds (Pl. 6a), as on a green-rimmed beaker found in a ninth-century burial at Vik (Hopperstad) in Norway,[18] and a shallow, yellowish-green bowl from an early eighth-century grave at Valsgärde in Sweden.[19] In England opaque yellow thread-decoration recurs at Portchester and Waltham Abbey.

A number of English fragments – at Whitby monastery, Hamwih and Portchester – reveal a green base-glass shot through with streaks of red, sometimes so numerous that the glass appears predominantly red. This is a common characteristic of Carolingian glass, and fragments have been discovered on the Carolingian glasshouse site at Cordel, near Trier.[20] Some of these derived from pointed funnel-beakers like those found in Sweden, and fragments of these vessels were also excavated at Hamwih. These parallels forcibly suggest that the glass used in late Anglo-Saxon England closely resembled that of contemporary continental Europe, where it was no doubt made.

In one field a clear line can probably be drawn between the pagan and the Christian periods in Anglo-Saxon England – the use of window-glass. In Roman times glass windows were common both in town buildings and country villas, and window-glazing seems to have weathered the crises of the fourth century to survive into the fifth, as at the Great Casterton Villa in Rutland. In the earlier raids, when 'the fire of their rage licked the western ocean with its red tongue', the Saxon invaders seem to have destroyed all before them, and it seems likely that they enjoyed the sound of broken glass. We hear no more of window-glass in England until well into the seventh century. The Venerable Bede records in his *History of the Abbots* that in 675 Benedict Biscop, Abbot of Monkwearmouth, sent to Gaul for glass-makers to embellish his new monastery:

> When the work was approaching completion, he sent emissaries to Gaul who should bring makers of glass, artificers hitherto unknown to the British, to glaze [literally 'to lattice'] the windows of the church and of the galleries and upper rooms [? refectories]. It was done, and they came: nor did they only complete the required work, but familiarised the English too with this type of work henceforth, and taught them – a craft by no means ill-suited to [the making of] lamps . . . or vessels for a great variety of purposes.

It was possibly in consequence of this episode that St Wilfrid, Bishop of York, is said before (?)678 to have fitted St Peter's Church there with window-glass in place of linen cloth or a fretted slab, so that 'the light shone within, yet the birds and rain could not penetrate.' Until recently knowledge of the window-glass of this era derived entirely from such literary texts, but excavations at Monkwearmouth and Jarrow (the sister house) have turned up glass which may well be that of Biscop's Gaulish workers.[21] At both sites it consists of hundreds of quarry fragments tinted greenish- or bluish-colourless, pale blue, olive-green, amber, greenish-blue and streaky red; while the site at Monkwearmouth has yielded a bright emerald-green and a dark cobalt-blue.

All this glass is thin and markedly bubbly by contrast with Roman window-glass. The quarries are normally small, varying from 6.7 cm (2⅝ in.) to 2.8 cm (1⅛ in.) in width, rectangular quarries being frequently divided to produce two right-angled triangles. They were normally 'grozed' on two or more sides –

reduced in size by nibbling with a glazier's slotted tool. This gives the glass edge something of the appearance of a knapped flint. Some of the Durham quarries so formed are of quite elaborate shapes. After shaping, the quarries would be set in 'cames' – lead strips of 'H' sections which gripped the edges of the glass and out-lined the design, being soldered together at points of junction. Examples of such cames were found at both sites. The windows bore no further painted decoration, and were probably of purely formal design. Comparable fragments, dating from the end of the Carolingian period and found at Séry-lès-Mézières in France, have been reconstructed into a reasonably convincing round-headed panel representing a cross pattée with alpha and omega below its arms.[22] Simple designs of this sort probably formed the subject-matter of the Durham windows.

The glass of these windows was made by the cylinder or 'muff' technique as in Roman times. The process is described in the treatise *On Divers Arts* by the monk Theophilus, written in the early twelfth century. Essentially the same practices were presumably followed in the earlier period represented by the Durham glass. Theophilus writes:

> If you want to make sheets of glass, take the iron blowpipe, put its end in a pot full of glass, and when the glass sticks to it turn the pipe in your hand until as much glass as you want agglomerates around it. Take it out at once, put it to your mouth, and blow gently . . . You should also have a smooth, flat stone in front of the window [the gathering-hole], on top of which you should gently strike the glowing glass, so that it hangs down equally on all sides [marvering]. At once blow quickly and repeatedly . . . When you see it hanging down like a long bladder, put the end into the flame and as soon as it melts, (when you blow) a hole will appear. Then take a round piece of wood made for the purpose, and make the hole as wide as the middle (of the cylinder) . . .[23]

The two edges of the cylinder then had to be pinched together, the pipe knocked off from the other end and transferred to this point of contact. The open end was then re-heated and opened up with the wooden instrument, and the cylinder pinched together as before. The pipe was knocked off and the cylinder carried on a stick by a boy to the annealing furnace,

> . . . which should be moderately hot . . . kindle a large fire in the furnace where it is to be spread out and flattened. When the furnace is red-hot take a hot iron, split the glass (muff) along one side and

put it on the hearth of the red-hot furnace. When it begins to soften, take iron tongs and a smooth, flat piece of wood, and opening it up on the side where it is split, spread it out and flatten it with the tongs as you want it. When the glass is completely flat, immediately take it out and put it in the annealing furnace, which should be moderately hot, in such a way that the sheet does not lie down but stands up against the wall.

The buildings at Monkwearmouth and Jarrow were destroyed by Scandinavian raids about 867 and the glass, if not made in the seventh century, cannot be later than the ninth. On the whole it seems more likely to belong to the earlier period, for by 758 the art of making window-glass seems again to have been lost in the north. In that year Cuthbert, Abbot of Wearmouth, again had to send to the Continent – this time to Mainz – asking for the services of glass-makers 'because we are ignorant and useless in that art.' Possibly Cuthbert was unaware of conditions outside the kingdom of Northumbria, just as Benedict Biscop seems to have been unaware of the glass industry which probably existed in Kent in his day (p. 12). At any rate it is certain that window- and vessel-glass were both being made in England in the ninth or tenth century, for fragments of both have been found on a glasshouse site within the precincts of the Saxon abbey at Glastonbury.

That glass was not reserved for the windows of ecclesiastical buildings alone is shown by finds on secular sites at Hamwih and Thetford, and by the discovery of a few thin fragments of window-glass, together with lead cames, on the site of the probably tenth-century Saxon palace at Kingsbury, Old Windsor.

Of vessels of this period only one probable example is known from English finds. This is a green bowl with wrythen mould-blown ribbing, found in Shaftesbury Abbey (Pl. 6b).[24] The abbey was only consecrated in 888, so the glass is unlikely to be of a much earlier date than this. It conforms in its general proportions with a bowl, decorated by angular applied trails, found in the Church of St Pierre at Chartres and dated to the Merovingian period.[25] The shape probably derives from the squat jar of the seventh century, and looks forward to a medieval type of low bowl with thread decoration of which examples have been found in Germany.[26]

One further type of glass-making in Anglo-Saxon England calls for mention – the secondary use of mainly opaque glasses in the making of mosaic canes, beads, bangles, and so on. This industry, which requires a relatively modest installation and furnaces adequate merely to soften glass to the point where it can be worked in a pasty state, is of great antiquity and survives in primitive cultures into modern times. It seems that throughout its history glass manufacture has depended on specialist producers for certain types of glass. Prominent among these were the coloured opaque glasses used for the purposes indicated, as well as in the manufacture of enamels – glasses which melt at relatively low temperatures and can thus be used to decorate metalwork. Evidence comes from various parts of the British Isles to suggest that small-scale industry of this sort was fairly widespread during the Dark Ages. At Dinas Powys in South Glamorgan a considerable quantity of fifth- to sixth-century glass, much of it with opaque-white trailing, was found in a context suggesting that metal and glass were being worked there; and at Garranes, a contemporary Irish site, fragments of glass vessels and rods were found with crucibles and moulds indicating a comparable manufacturing centre. In the same country a *crannog* of eighth- to tenth-century date at Lagore yielded fragments of vessel-glass including one coloured fragment, the presence on the site of moulds for making glass studs suggesting that the glass was the raw material for a secondary melting process.

The excavation of a Viking house at Brough Birsay in Orkney has yielded a find which may throw light on one of the sources of such specialised glasses. There was found 'a rough mosaic cube of opaque pale blue', together with other coloured glasses and bead fragments. Theophilus devotes a chapter of his book to the 'Various Colours of non-translucent Glass'. He says: 'Different kinds of glass, namely, white, black, green, yellow, blue, red and purple, are found in mosaic work in ancient pagan buildings. These are not transparent but are opaque like marble, like little square stones, and enamel work is made from them on gold, silver, and copper.'[27] We may reasonably suppose that the same source was exploited earlier, when mosaic tesserae would have been more readily available.

The most striking and coherent results of such an industry are to be seen at Monkwearmouth. Here were found two mosaic-glass plaques of considerable complexity, one square and the other a truncated triangle.[28] Both are formed of slices of square canes, themselves made up of square and triangular elements to give simple geometric patterns, the colours used being opaque-white, red, yellow and pale green, with translucent blue. It is suggested that such plaques – the rectangular example is 12 mm (7/16 in.) square – were used for the embellishment of book covers, and mosaic plaques used in this way are known from continental examples. There was almost certainly a tradition of this kind of work in the British Isles, as is indicated by the similarity of the mosaic canes in the sixth-century Sutton Hoo treasure[29] to those used to decorate the lost eighth-century Witham bowl and the seventh-century Scunthorpe bowl.

That glass of mosaic character was actually made – or at least adapted for use – at the Northumbrian monastic sites is suggested by the stump of a mosaic rod found at Jarrow and patterned with a saltire cross having opaque red arms and an opaque-white square at their point of junction, the whole on a dark blue translucent ground.[30] This stump, which could only be the raw material for decorative elements of the type already described, was found in a Saxon timber building with a coin of Eanbald II (796–830+). Fragments of slag on the site pointed to its being a monastery workshop. A parallel may perhaps be offered by the fort at Garranes, where the finds included three pieces of *millefiori*, one inserted in the end of a bronze tube, presumably ready for further working.

To these instances of the secondary working of opaque-glasses may be added the bead factory unearthed in recent years in the Viking area of York; a probably seventh- to eighth-century monastic workshop re-using Roman glass at Repton in Derbyshire;[31] and a tenth-century workshop at Lincoln making rings and beads.[32]

CHAPTER 2

Medieval Glass
(c. 1066–1500)

*The emergence from the 'Dark Ages', and potash-lime glass,
17 – Imported colourless glass with coloured thread-decoration,
19 – Coloured glass, 24 – Imported enamelled and gilt glasses,
26 – Green goblets, 28 – Glass-making in England, 29 –
Lamps, urinals, bottles and flasks, 31 – Laboratory glass and
linen-smoothers, 36 – Window-glass, 38.*

The Norman Conquest and the subjugation of Saxon England
coincide with a period which is indeed a dark age in the history of
glass. With the exception of fragments found in a putative
eleventh-century hall at Waltham Abbey,[1] and the Shaftesbury
Abbey bowl of perhaps tenth- to eleventh-century date (p. 14), no
eleventh-century glass vessel is known from England. Moreover,
we have to wait at least a century after the Conquest before identifiable glass vessels occur. In the matter of window-glass we are
little better off. Yet it is intrinsically improbable that there
was a break in glass-making in England lasting for over 200 years.
The late Saxon period was an era of brilliant cultural achievement,
and it is doubtful whether the English of the eleventh century
would have dispensed with glazed windows and glass vessels, even
if it meant re-introducing a lost art from the Continent. There
appear to have been glasshouses at work in Belgium and France in
the eleventh century.[2] Furthermore, it is known that glass-making
was often associated with Benedictine monasteries. The earliest
Venetian glass-maker known by name appears in a deed of 982 con-
veying property to the Benedictine Order,[3] and just a hundred
years later 'Robertus vitrearius' witnessed a deed of gift to the
French abbey of Maillezais.[4] Benedict Biscop, also a Benedictine,
had obtained glass-makers from Gaul (p. 12), and his eleventh-
century Benedictine successors would certainly have been able to

do the same. It can only be assumed that this apparent void in the history of English glass-making is due to the chances of archaeological discovery.

However likely it may be that glass did not cease to be made in the eleventh and twelfth centuries, nothing is identifiable until we get to the late twelfth century, and then it is window- rather than vessel-glass (p. 39). A few pieces survive on the Continent, notably in France, to give us some idea of contemporary vessel-glass. They include long-necked bottles with spherical bodies in thin glass, a form recognisable in an eleventh-century French MS. A second form resembled it but had a slender applied spout, made by the same technique as the claws of the Merovingian claw-beaker (p. 6).[5] A third form was a cup-topped lamp, an example of which was found at Anger in a context apparently of about 1040. This differs little from the lamps current in the thirteenth and fourteenth centuries in England (p. 31).[6]

By about AD 1000 a fundamental change had taken place in the glass-making of northern Europe. Presumably because of increasing difficulties in communication with the Mediterranean area, the glass-makers turned from soda as a fluxing agent to potash derived from the woodlands in which they worked. The main sources were beech and bracken. Theophilus recommends beech for both firing and as a source of ash – an obvious economy. This change had a considerable effect on the durability of the glasses produced, and it is a fact that a great many medieval glasses have simply decayed to a black powder in the damp soil of northern Europe. Just when this change occurred is not established. At Cordel (p. 11) a soda-lime glass was still in use in the ninth century, but the change had almost certainly taken place within the next hundred years, although its incidence was probably not uniform.

With the thirteenth century the picture begins to clear and the archaeological finds become relatively abundant. The first striking feature of this complex of material is that whereas much of it is in the green 'forest' potash glass just alluded to, much is in a fine relatively colourless material, often with applied decoration in coloured glass. Clearly this glass is of a greatly superior quality and it may be presumed that it was the luxury glass of the day. Its occurrence on palace sites, as at King's Langley, or in the remains of houses belonging to rich merchants, as at Southampton and Nottingham, strengthens this presumption.[7] Although the high table in great houses was normally served in precious metals, there is evidence from manuscript illuminations that glasses too were used, at least in France; and what was acceptable in France was certainly acceptable in contemporary England.[8]

The question remains, however, as to where these sophisticated glasses were made. It seems very unlikely that in northern Europe, where the glass-makers had disappeared into the woods to make their mainly green or yellow potash glass, luxury glass of this kind was technically possible. On the other hand, much glass of this type has been discovered on various sites in (mainly southern) Italy.[9] Some of these sites date from the late twelfth to early thirteenth centuries, and since the glasses echo types which are found on the eleventh- to early twelfth-century glasshouse sites at Corinth in the Greek Peloponnese,[10] there may be here a line of development which passes from Corinth to Italy, leading up to the indisputed pre-eminence of Renaissance Venice. This suggestion is buttressed by the fact that many glasses of this period found in England have analogues in glasses excavated on Yugoslav sites of comparable date, often located on ancient trade routes.[11] It seems logical to suppose that both English and Yugoslav imports emanated from common or related centres. We know from documents that later on Southampton merchants imported much glass from Italy, and many of the thirteenth- and fourteenth-century colourless glasses found in England come from Southampton. It is a reasonable assumption that they too came from Italy.[12]

Although therefore not English-made, this glass demands attention as representing the best available in the thirteenth and fourteenth centuries, fit for the tables of the rich and powerful. It no doubt spurred the northern glass-makers to imitate it in their own materials, as we know they did (pp. 20, 28).

Most fragments of this type of glass apparently belonged to drinking-glasses. These vessels are decorated with self-coloured or coloured applied threads and cordons, the latter sometimes notched or waved, and with usually self-coloured 'prunts', often drawn out into a thorn-like projection, or sometimes applied in a snail-like coil. The most usual colour was a light cobalt-blue, but manganese-purple also occurs, and when the blue is applied to a yellow base-glass (p. 24), it appears dark green. The drinking-glasses fall into three main types: a goblet with a tall stem, usually with a central knop or trailed motif (fig. 1); a small cup with a waved 'ogee' profile, standing on a notched applied foot-rim (fig. 3); and two shapes of beaker, one cylindrical with a flared rim (fig. 5), the other barrel-shaped with cup-top (fig. 5).[13]

It was long thought that stemmed drinking-glasses (fig. 1) were an invention of Renaissance Venice, earlier glasses being in the

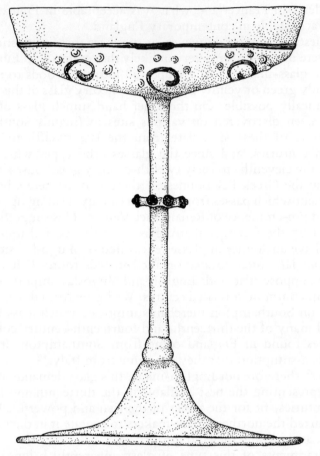

Fig. 1 Goblet of greenish-colourless glass, with self-coloured blobs and threading in blue. Found in High Street, Southampton. Probably Italian; *c.* 1300–50. H. approx. 20 cm (8 in.). Artist's impression.

form of tumblers. There is now plenty to show that this view is wrong. England apart, several fragmentary glasses of fine quality from south Italy document this shape as a product of the twelfth to fourteenth centuries;[14] and numerous copies made in the green northern forest glass demonstrate that stemmed glasses of far more delicate and fragile forms than those of fifteenth- and sixteenth-century Venice were used in the early Middle Ages (fig. 2).[15]

The form itself, with its tall, thin stem, central knop and exaggeratedly large foot, obviously imitates contemporary precious metal goblets, most of which have disappeared into the melting

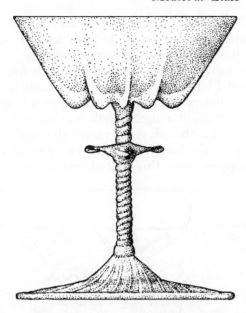

Fig. 2 Goblet of pale
green glass, ribbed and
with pincered knop.
Found in High Street,
Southampton. Northern
European; *c.* 1300–50.
H. approx. 15 cm (6 in.).
Artist's impression.

pot. At least two survive, however, to show the general order of form – the King John Cup belonging to the Corporation of King's Lynn, of the early fourteenth century;[16] and an example in the Museo Poldi-Pezzoli in Milan with the Avignon hallmark of about 1330. French royal inventories of about 1300 refer to stemmed goblets of this type, echoing contemporary Gothic architecture.[17]

Perhaps the most striking example of this form found in England is a fragmentary goblet excavated from a fourteenth-century deposit in Southampton (fig. 1).[18] The bowl was decorated with applied trailed blue threads and colourless prunts, and the knop consisted of a horizontal wheel, each spoke with a blob of blue at its tip. Even more elaborate is a fragmentary goblet from the Bank of England site, now in the Museum of London. This greenish-colourless glass has thin blue spiral threading round the lower part of its spreading bowl, while the basal angle is marked by a self-coloured notched cordon. The stem is decorated with no less than three horizontal annular knops, to the periphery of which are attached four vertical threads, alternately blue and self-coloured, which are pulled out into 'V' loops between the knops and finally attached to the base of the bowl. The foot shows the beginnings of the tall conical 'instep'. A second fragment in the same collection has a vertically ribbed bowl round the base of which runs a notched self-coloured trail. The stem is hollow-blown in one piece with the foot and at mid-height there is a crimped collar of blue glass.

The second drinking-vessel within the blue-threaded family is a cup with an 'S' profile, wider at the top than at the base, which has a notched applied cordon of self-coloured glass as a foot (fig. 3). These little drinking-cups have been found at Faenza with four-teenth-century pottery and Mantua-coined money of Lodovico Gonzaga (1369–82).[19] The decoration usually consists of a hori-zontal trail, below which are angular zigzag trails reminiscent of late Anglo-Saxon glass. Some threads pass under the slightly kicked foot, being overlaid by the foot-ring. Quite exceptionally, four cups found at Southampton have this type of decoration in a

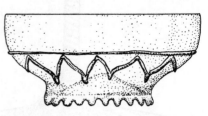

Fig. 3   Cup of colourless glass with applied threading in blue. Probably Italian; fourteenth century. Scale approx. ½. Artist's impression based on Faenza fragments.

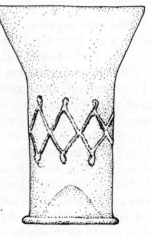

Fig. 4   Beaker of colourless glass with applied blue threading. Found at Winchester. Probably Italian; fourteenth century. Scale approx. ½. Artist's impression.

dark manganese-purple glass. The fact that four of these rare glasses, of late thirteenth- to mid-fourteenth-century date, occurred as a group in a harbour-town strongly suggests that all are imports.[20]

The cylindrical beakers of this family do not run so true to form. A fragmentary example found in Winchester shows a cylindrical lower part and a spreading lip (fig. 4). It is decorated with a criss-cross design of blue threading with the marked angular character already alluded to, the base being edged with a plain self-coloured cordon. At the late thirteenth-century Dominican Friary at Boston,

Lincolnshire, was found a fragmentary beaker of this type decorated with slightly wrythen vertical ribbing. Comparable fragments of late twelfth- to thirteenth-century date have been found in Apulia, and a pale blue beaker found at Corinth (p. 19) was decorated with a self-coloured trail round the foot, a dark blue thread round the lip, and vertical mould-blown ribbing.[21] These glasses seem to follow the general lines of contemporary Islamic beakers.

Fig. 5 Beaker of brownish-colourless glass with self-coloured trail and prunts. Found at King's Langley. Probably Italian; fourteenth century. H. approx. 10 cm (4 in.). Artist's impression.

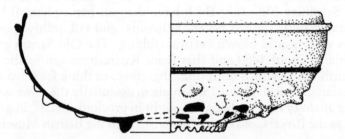

Fig. 6 Bowl of colourless glass with self-coloured and blue prunts and blue threading. Found at the Dominican Friary, Boston, Lincolnshire. Probably Italian; late thirteenth century. D. 17.5 cm (6⅞ in.). After Moorhouse (Charleston, 1972, fig. 9).

The last type of these blue-threaded drinking-glasses is a barrel-shaped beaker with a cup-top, usually defined below by a horizontal trail, sometimes in blue, sometimes self-coloured. The main decoration, however, was a diaper of prunts – usually self-coloured – covering the body. The upper part of a beaker of this type, with blue thread defining the constriction between body and rim, was found at King's Langley in a late thirteenth- to fourteenth-century context; two fragments of a second example had a self-coloured trail and pointed prunts on the body (fig. 5).[22] Similarly prunted fragments have been found in Apulia, and again the prototype may be traced to Corinth, where an eleventh- to twelfth-century example is recorded.[23] A colourless beaker from Log in Slovenia provides yet another example of parallel finds in England and Yugoslavia.[24] This parallelism has direct bearing on the last important English glass of this type – a depressed hemispherical bowl ornamented with blue threading and colourless prunts – found in the Dominican Friary at Boston, in a late thirteenth-century context (fig. 6).[25] Here, as on the Southampton cups, the blue thread-decoration of the body passes underneath the colourless notched foot-rim. The nearest analogue is a bowl of slightly differing shape found at Novo Brdo, in Serbia, in a fourteenth- or early fifteenth-century context. This has a simple blue thread running above the tops of a series of vertical mould-blown ribs, at the base of which is a notched foot-rim.[26]

A distinctive variant of the blue-threaded glasses is found in a series of fragments of markedly yellow, almost fluorescent, metal found at a number of fourteenth-century sites. Dr D. B. Harden has published two goblets which add yet another shape to the fourteenth- and fifteenth-century repertory, one from Knaresborough Castle, Yorkshire, the other from the royal castle at Old Sarum, near Salisbury (fig. 7).[27] Both have deepish hemispherical bowls decorated with applied notched threads, and tall hollow pedestal stems with mould-blown vertical ribbing. The Old Sarum glass is datable to about 1400 and that from Knaresborough to the early fifteenth century. It is tempting, therefore, to think forward to the Venetian glasses of about 1500 made in essentially the same way. A closer analogy may perhaps be sought in precious metals, in goblets such as the Royal Gold Cup of about 1390 in the British Museum. It

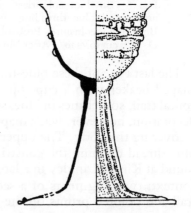

Fig. 7 Fragmentary goblet, yellow glass with (?)blue trailing (appears green). Found at Old Sarum, Wiltshire. Probably Italian; about 1400. H. about 12.5 cm (4⅞ in.). After Harden (1975), fig. 13.

seems possible that this shape may have emerged towards 1400. As has already been pointed out, the blue threads decorating these glasses appear dark green on the yellow base-glass.

A popular type of glass in the High Middle Ages exploited the great colouring power of copper to produce an opaque sealing-wax red material. This was used for whole vessels, as well as for red thread-decoration on near-colourless (usually greenish) glass. Some at least of these pieces may have been made in England, for a crucible containing opaque red glass was found on the Chaleshurst glasshouse site near Chiddingfold, Surrey, and a few red-threaded green fragments have also been found on Wealden glasshouse sites, and were presumably made there.[28] The material, however, was equally familiar in south Italy and at Corinth,[29] so some at least of these vessels may have been imports. A fine jug found at Southampton in a context of about 1300–50 is of pale green glass decorated with a continuous spiral of opaque red threading from base to neck.[30] The superior quality of the green base-glass suggests that this jug is an import. Another jug, however, found at Pevensey Castle in a context of about 1500, seems closer in quality to contemporary English-made glasses, which by this time may be allowed to have improved somewhat in quality. The jug is decorated with red threads drawn into looped patterns which give a pleasing rhythmic effect of thicks and thins.

The solid opaque red vessels appear mainly to have been jugs or flasks, dating from the late thirteenth to probably the late fourteenth century. This glass, with its oblique reference to semi-precious stones such as jasper, has a 'precious' quality which suggests that it was a luxury glass. The character of the sites on which it has been found – Northampton Castle and the houses of undoubtedly wealthy merchants at Nottingham and Southampton – strengthens this supposition.

An exceptional coloured glass may appropriately be mentioned here, namely, a roughly made jug in cobalt-blue glass, found at Penhallam in Cornwall, and dated about 1300–50.[31] Glass-makers have seldom had much difficulty in producing cobalt-blue glass, and it was being manufactured in quantity for church windows at this period, even if it cannot be proved that it was actually produced in England. This jug, apparently the only blue vessel-glass so far known from an English medieval site, may also have been an import.

Other unequivocal imports come from further afield than Italy. A few Near Eastern glasses have been found on Anglo-Saxon sites, but it was probably with the Crusades that Europe became aware of the sophisticated glass produced in Syria during the twelfth to fourteenth centuries. Best known were the enamelled and gilt glasses, of which Damascus and Aleppo were the most renowned centres of production. Europeans indeed associated Damascus with all that was most luxurious in glassware. The expression *façon de Damas* is frequently used of glasses listed in fourteenth-century inventories – as in that of Charles V of France, drawn up in 1379–80, which contained at least ten glasses described in this way and usually mounted in precious metals. King Henry IV of England in 1399 had a 'little pot for theriac *(triacler)* of wrought silver with an Alexandrian glass' and 'another glass *(verre de glass)* painted outside', a probable reference to enamelled and gilt decoration. The epithet 'd'Alisandre' used of Henry IV's *triacler* no doubt related to the port of shipment rather than the place of manufacture. These sparse literary references are buttressed by a number of actual glasses found in England. Most notable is the famous 'Luck of Edenhall', documented in the possession of the Musgrave family of Edenhall, Cumberland, since 1729 at the latest, and probably at Edenhall ever since it was first brought back from the Near East (Pl. 7a). It is of a type attributed to Aleppo about 1240, and the glass is preserved in its fourteenth-century *cuir bouilli* case, evidence of the reverential care accorded to such glasses and reflected in the ritual with which the 'Luck' was traditionally handled in the Musgrave household. The presence in England of this truly royal glassware is further attested by the necks of enamelled and gilt bottles found in the Chapel of the Pyx at Westminster, and on the site of Restormel Castle in Cornwall, the seat (1268–72) of Richard, Earl of Cornwall, son of King John.[32]

Also at Restormel were found fragments of another kind of enamelled glass, usually known as 'Syro-Frankish', a description based on the assumption that it formed an offshoot of the Syrian enamelled glass industry, made under western influence – perhaps even by European craftsmen – in the Christian Kingdom of Jerusalem.[33] This glass is painted predominantly in red, yellow, blue, green and white enamels, a characteristic trick being to paint on both sides of the glass. There is no gilding. The vessels are normally cylindrical beakers with slightly flaring lip, a slight basal kick and a self-coloured thread laid round the angle of the foot. The decoration sometimes includes European armorials, and the beakers are often inscribed with religious formulae (e.g. 'Ave Maria Gratia Plena'), with a cross potent as a mark of punctuation. The distribution of surviving 'Syro-Frankish' glasses may perhaps give a clue to their origin. They are found in Sweden and Denmark in the north, in England and Ireland in the west,[34] Fustat in Egypt in the south, and Caucasia in the east. Examples have been found in Italy[35] and Sicily, but not in Spain. The Italian finds bring to mind another fact. In the Venetian archives have been found references to 'painters of beakers' *(pittori di bicchieri)* at dates between 1280 and 1325.[36] The considerable evidence for Italian exportation of glass into England, already discussed, supports the notion that Italy, and specifically Venice, produced these enamelled glasses. Apart from Restormel, Launceston Castle (also in Cornwall, Pl. 7b), Southampton,[37] Wolvesey Palace at Winchester, Dale Abbey in Derbyshire,[38] and Dublin, have all produced fragments of beakers.

This, however, is not the full count of medieval enamelled glasses found in England. A fragment from Cheapside, now in the Museum of London, is painted on the underside in red, green, blue and black, and in white on the upper surface. It comes from a pale green bowl, and is painted on a green ground with the upper part of a human figure with black hair, red robe, and blue cloak, a red quatrefoil to his left (Pl. 7c). Some linear decoration, now appearing pinkish-brown, may have been the base for gilding.[39] The only known parallel, a fragmentary bowl apparently representing the German Emperor enthroned, was found in or near Basel in Switzerland. Enamelling on both surfaces of the glass seems to link these two exceptional pieces to the 'Syro-Frankish' group, although their form and decoration seem to set them apart. Equally distinctive, and of a kind apparently peculiar to England, are two fragments of almost colourless glass on which have been overlaid thin roundels of blue glass. One, found in Queen Victoria Street, also in the Museum of London, is gilt with a shield of arms between dragon supporters; the other, from Weoley Castle, Warwickshire, found in a fourteenth-century context, is similarly gilt with confronted lions.[40] No parallels with these pieces seem to have turned up on the Continent, but it is nevertheless difficult not to suppose that the English finds are imports.

A further testimony to the ramifications of medieval trade is provided by two tiny fragments of yet another type of gilt and enamelled glass, one excavated at Seacourt, near Oxford, the other from the Augustinian priory at Breedon on the Hill, Leicestershire.[41] Both bear traces of gilding on blue glass, and come from a well-recognised class of cylindrical flasks (and occasionally beakers) found mainly in Greece, Cyprus and south Russia.[42] There seems little doubt that they were made in Byzantine territory in the eleventh and twelfth centuries, the English-found examples being perhaps broken and discarded in the thirteenth century.

Such were the glasses with which the great could indulge themselves during the thirteenth and fourteenth centuries. It is necessary
now to turn to such as could be afforded by humbler folk. First,
however, one category of glasses must be mentioned which seems
to be of equivocal status. Alongside the colourless goblets with
prunts and blue-thread decoration already surveyed (pp. 19–21)
runs another series almost certainly modelled on them, but made
in green glass (fig. 2). This glass does not seem to be so subject to
decay as much of the more mundane green potash glass. Nor can
long-stemmed glasses of this fragility have been intended for the
brutal conditions of life in the homes of the commonalty. They
must have been used in the upper strata of society without being
quite as rare and costly as the colourless glasses. The most striking
example is a large goblet about 20 cm (8 in.) high which was
excavated at Ludgershall Castle, Wiltshire, a fourteenth-century
royal hunting lodge.[43] This find gives some indication of social
status, and its testimony is borne out by illuminations in contemporary French manuscripts, such as one which dates before 1320
showing St Louis giving food and drink to the poor. Tall stemmed
glasses with wide feet and ribbed bowls are to be seen standing on
the table and held by the beneficiaries of the Saint's charity.
Another fourteenth-century miniature shows Juno, Athena and
Venus – exalted company if ever there was – at a table on which
stands a comparable glass.[44] These goblets share many features
with the colourless blue-threaded goblets. Like them, they may be
either two- or three-piece glasses. The Ludgershall goblet has a
solid stem with a vermicular collar about two-thirds up, but a
glass from Nieuwendoorn in Holland has a hollow stem blown in
one piece with the foot,[45] like one of the colourless glasses from
the Bank of England (p. 21). This way of making the stems may
prefigure the pedestal-stems of the late fourteenth-century goblets
from Old Sarum and Knaresborough Castle (p. 24). The goblets of
both stem types, almost without exception, have pronounced
vertical mould-blown ribbing, often drawn out into sharp fins
round the lower part of the bowl; and where the foot is preserved it
is usually very wide. A goblet found at Winchester has a mould-
blown mesh-pattern on its bowl in place of the ribbing. There are
further variants in the embellishment of these monumental glasses.
A Southampton example has a wheel-type central stem-knop with
three spokes (fig. 2), recalling the six-spoke colourless variant
(fig. 1), both glasses coming from the same fourteenth-century
deposit;[46] a London fragment found in a fifteenth-century context
originally had a series of free-hanging rings threaded into eyelets

attached to the lowest part of the bowl.[47] Many of the solid stems are twisted to give a cable effect. This general type of goblet is widespread in northern Europe, being found also in France, Belgium and Holland.[48]

From these impressive table-glasses we descend to vessels for humbler domestic uses. Before considering these in detail, however, we should look at the evidence for glass-making in England itself during the earlier Middle Ages. Although a certain Henry Daniel *vitriarius* (glass-man) in Norfolk is mentioned in the reign of King Stephen (1135–54),[49] the earliest record in an area known later for its glass industry occurs in Surrey. In a deed of not later than 1240 twenty acres of land near Chiddingfold in Surrey were granted to Lawrence Vitrearius (Lawrence the glassman). In late Latin this word certainly denoted a glass-maker, but in medieval Latin the sense seems to have shifted to include the concept of 'glazier', a man who makes and repairs glass windows. Since Chiddingfold was for centuries the heart of the glass industry in the Surrey/Sussex Weald, it seems a little perverse to suppose that Lawrence was anything other than a glass-maker. A glazier would not require an estate of twenty acres, whereas glass-makers often bought woodland for fuel. The earliest certain reference to glass-making in this district dates from 1351, when John Alemayne (John the German) was paid 43s 6d for 'white' glass to be used in the glazing of St George's Chapel, Windsor, while 'to William Holmere for carriage of the said glass from Chiddingfold to London' was paid the sum of 8s. Thereafter numerous fourteenth-century glazing accounts refer to glass obtained in Chiddingfold or the Weald generally. However, although the Weald may be the best documented area of the medieval glass industry, there is evidence from other parts of the country that the manufacture was by no means confined to the south. From 1284 to 1309 at least, the Abbey of Vale Royal carried on the manufacture in Cheshire,[50] and the inevitable involvement of the Church with glass-making is doubtless reflected in the fact that there was a 'glashous' attached to Salisbury Cathedral, although this may have been no more than a glazier's workshop. In 1349, for the glazing of St Stephen's Chapel at Westminster, John de Brampton, an important London glazier, was instructed to buy glass in Shropshire and Staffordshire,[51] and it was certainly made in these parts. In 1380 'John Glasewryth of Staffordshire' is mentioned: in that year he took a lease of half a glasshouse at Kirdford in Sussex and was therefore certainly a glass-maker. In all these counties there is a later history of glass-making, as there is in Lancashire and Yorkshire, and there seems

little doubt that there were glasshouses scattered about in many of
the wooded areas of England. Glass-making was a peripatetic craft,
moving from one place to another in accordance with the avail-
ability of woodland for the supply of fuel. Thus at Bagot's Park in
Staffordshire fifteen glasshouse sites have been uncovered in an area
of approximately 1½ square miles, each furnace being presumably
abandoned either because its situation became uneconomic as the
surrounding woodland was cut and the fuel had to be fetched from
ever further away; or because the furnace itself wore out.[52]

There can be little doubt that in the twelfth to fourteenth centuries the making of window-glass, primarily for church use, was
the mainstay of the glass industry. Compared with window-glass,
vessel-glass was of little account. This comes out well enough in
the pages of the monk Theophilus, writing in the early twelfth
century.[53] After nine chapters devoted to the making of window-
glass (pp. 13–14), he continues:

> When you want to make vessels, prepare the glass in the way
> described above. When you have blown the amount of glass you
> want, do not make a hole in the base . . . but separate it intact from
> the pipe using a flat piece of wood that has been dipped in water.
> Quickly heat the pipe and immediately stick it to the base. Now lift
> up the vessel, heat it in the flame, and with a round piece of wood
> enlarge the hole whence you separated the pipe. Shape its rim and
> enlarge it as much as you like. You will also widen the base round
> the pipe so as to be concave underneath . . .[54]

He then goes on to describe how threads of glass can be taken from
the pot, to be used as handles or to lay a decorative trail: 'Turn it
around close to the flame so that the thread adheres.' In the succeeding chapter on 'Long-necked flasks', he describes how the paraison
is swung over the head to elongate the neck, and this concludes his
remarks on vessel-making. His prescription for making long-
necked flasks may perhaps be reflected in the simple long-necked
bottles seen in early French miniatures (p. 18); and his observations
on the making 'of as many handles as you wish' perhaps refers
to the making of lamps with three or more loop handles for
suspension.

Vessel-glass, in W. A. Thorpe's phrase, was 'the little dinghy
which was towed through the Middle Ages by the great ship of
"stained glass".' Clearly, however, the two were made in the same
glasshouses. On the Blunden's Wood glasshouse site near Hambledon, Surrey, datable to the years about 1330, fragments found on

the spot indicate that both 'crown' window-glass (pp. 38–39) and vessel-glass were being made in the same furnace. In 1380, when John Glasewryth made his contract with John Schurterre's widow at Kirdford, it was stipulated that she should pay him 'for a "sheu" of "brodeglas" 20d and for a hundred of "vessel" 6d for his labour', clear evidence that John was prepared to turn his hand to either.

It may be taken from John Glasewryth's contract that for vessel-glass the unit of measurement was a hundred. This hundred, as with dozens in the pottery industry, was a notional unit, varying in accordance with the nature of the objects made – a larger number of small pieces, or a smaller of large or complicated pieces. What were these home-made glasses of medieval England?

One of the commonest representations of glass in medieval manuscripts is that showing lamps with cup-tops and narrow tapering stems (Pl. 8a), and an intact example found in France has been tentatively dated to the eleventh century.[55] No complete lamp had been found in England until the 1950s when fragments were discovered in Winchester between 1951 and 1955 which could be reconstructed to show the appearance of an intact lamp of probably thirteenth-century date (Pl. 8b). Fragments from Waterperry, near Oxford, allow the partial reconstruction of a lamp with a rim diameter of 13 cm (5⅛ in.) of twelfth- to fourteenth-century date, whereas late medieval fragments from Bayham Abbey, Kent, yield diameters between 9 and 11.5 cm (3½ and 4½ in.). The tell-tale feature of these lamps in excavations is the thick stub-end of their long stem. This invariably has a pontil mark on the squared-off or rounded base, the diameter varying considerably. The stubs have been found on probably fourteenth-century glasshouse sites in the Weald, and a characteristic example was found at Blunden's Wood (p. 30). The shape had a long currency, for a sixteenth-century example in a brighter and more resistant blue-green glass has been found at Northampton;[56] and in Germany the Wise and Foolish Virgins of the fourteenth century hold lamps essentially the same as those represented by Martin Schongauer at the end of the fifteenth.[57]

These lamps were suspended from a harness, usually of three chains attached to a ring into which the lamp was slipped, and held a wick floating in oil (Pl. 8a). The general shape – cup-top and slender stem – goes back to solid-stemmed forms made in the Near East in late Roman and Byzantine times and intended for insertion into holes in horizontal wheel-shaped bronze *polycandela*.[58] The numbers of the tell-tale stubs found on medieval sites (particularly abbeys) suggest that their use was widespread.

A second type of vessel-glass, almost as common, was the urinal. This was not just a *vase de nuit* but an important resource of medieval medicine. Much later, William Vaughan in his *Naturall & Artificial Directions for Health* (1602) recommends: 'In the morning make water in an vrinal: that by looking on it, you may ghesse some what of the state of your body.' The date is immaterial. From carvings and manuscript illuminations of the thirteenth and fourteenth centuries to the graphic arts of the fifteenth, sixteenth and seventeenth centuries, the theme of the doctor holding up his urinal to the light is universal. It was the symbol of the doctor-saints,

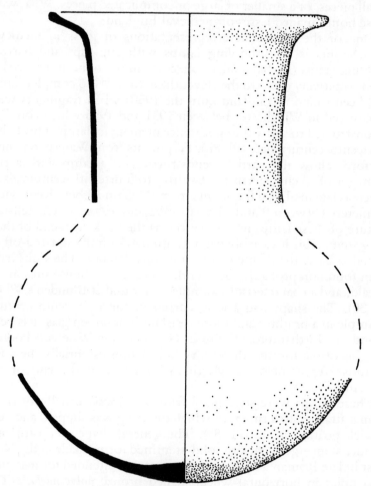

Fig. 8　Urinal, clear green glass with patchy weathering. From Winchester. Fourteenth century. Scale approx. ½.

Cosmas and Damian, and Hendrik Goltzius could represent 'The Physician as God' holding the urinal in his right hand.[59] Being of unstable form, it was kept in a cylindrical basket with a cover and loop handle and hung up when not in use. When a patient visited the doctor he took his basket and its diagnostic contents with him.[60] Edward I (1272–1307) is known to have possessed 'duo urinalia vitrea',[61] and his more prodigal successor Henry VIII had at Westminster 'vii cases of wicker twoo of theym p[ar]telye guilte w[i]th vii brode mouthed Urynalls in theym w[i]th laces of thrid [thread] to eache of theym.'[62]

The urinal took two main forms, with minor variants. One was essentially a spherical bottle with cylindrical neck and wide, horizontal rim; the other a pear-shaped container with sloping sides running right up to the wide lip. Fortunately, reconstructable examples of both types exist in England – the spherical form found in Winchester from the fourteenth century (fig. 8), and the piriform type from London in a deposit of about 1500 (Pl. 8c). The wide rim of the urinal tended to have a slightly up-turned edge. Of the two types, the spherical form seems to have been far commoner in England, as it is in pictorial representations. Its most characteristic feature is the thick convex base, with pontil mark on the outside; with this is often found the wide, up-turned rim. These fragments are of common occurrence, especially in *garderobe* pits, and the reason why so few examples have survived complete is no doubt that, to make uroscopy feasible, the naturally greenish glass had to be blown very thin to make it reasonably colourless. It is a strange fact that these giveaway fragments have apparently not so far been found on English medieval glass-making sites, or have not been recognised. A neck fragment found at Bramber Castle in Sussex, however, seems almost bound to be of local origin. The metal of these glasses, and the way they weather, strongly suggest that they are of English manufacture. As with lamps, it seems that the cylindrical-necked form changed very little from medieval times until almost 1700.[63]

A similar conservatism of form characterises perhaps the most widespread type of green vessel-glass found on English sites – the bottle (fig. 9). Bottle-necks, narrow and wide, with slightly flaring rim, were found on the fourteenth-century Blunden's Wood site, together with wide bases having a shallow kick. Some had spirally wrythen rib-moulding.[64] This picture is standard right through to the seventeenth century. Of fragmentary examples from Writtle, Essex, two have plain necks and a third a spirally ribbed neck.[65] They date from the late fifteenth to early sixteenth century, yet

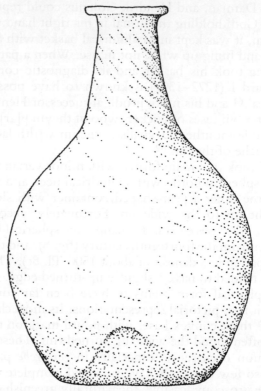

Fig. 9 Bottle of green glass with wrythen mould-blown ribbing. Late medieval or sixteenth century. Artist's impression based on Wealden finds.

differ hardly at all from a bottle with wrythen neck and part of the wall preserved, found in London in a context of about 1600. The shape recurs at Nonsuch Palace, where most of the finds date from the seventeenth century and none, except luxury objects, are likely to antedate 1540. The bottle-necks found on medieval sites vary greatly in height, taper and diameter. If these variations corresponded to different functions, there is as yet no means of knowing what these were. The mould-blown ribbing is sometimes vertical but more often wrythen, sometimes very pronounced but sometimes almost imperceptible. None of these distinctions appears to correspond to any chronological development, and until a greater body of material throws up diagnostic features for dating, it can only be said that at present we can hardly distinguish between a fifteenth- and a seventeenth-century bottle of this kind.[66]

If this bottle, standing some 20.5–27 cm (8–10½ in.) high, may

PLATE 1

a. Beaker with 'cut out' foot, bubbled green glass with self-coloured trail. From Howletts, Kent. Probably fifth century. H. 11.5 cm (4½ in.). B.M.

b. Bell-beaker with knobbed base, bubbled green glass with self-coloured trails. From Faversham, Kent. Probably fifth to early sixth century. H. 9.8 cm (3⅞ in.). Ashmolean Museum, Oxford.

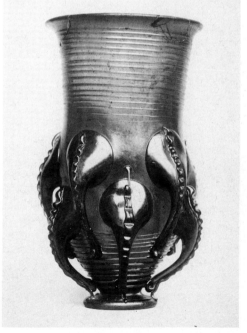

c. Bell-beaker, bubbled green glass with faint mould-blown ribbing. From Faversham, Kent. Probably sixth to seventh century. H. 12.9 cm (5¹⁄₁₆ in.). Ashmolean Museum, Oxford.

d. Claw-beaker, green glass with applied self-coloured threading and hollow-blown 'claws'. From Howletts, Kent. Probably sixth century. H. 16.5 cm (6½ in.). B.M.

PLATE 2

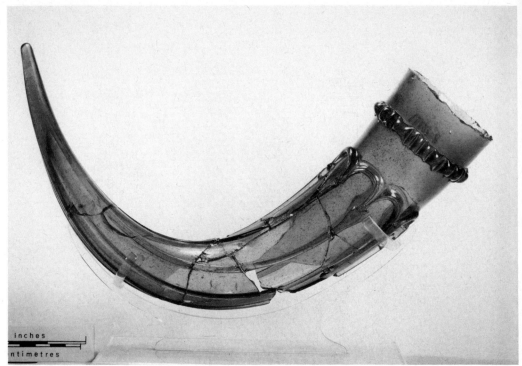

a. Drinking-horn, olive-green glass with applied and tooled decoration. From Rainham, Essex. Probably sixth century. L. 33.6 cm (13¼ in.). B.M.

b. Drawing showing drinking-vessels, not necessarily of glass, from an Anglo-Saxon calendar (Cotton MS Julius A vi). Tenth century. British Library.

PLATE 3

a. Claw-beaker and bottle, of amber and pale green glass respectively, both originally decorated with thread-trails, the former with hollow-blown 'claws'. From Lyminge, Kent. Probably fifth century. H. of beaker 18.5 cm (7¼ in.); of bottle 16.5 cm (6½ in.). Maidstone Museum.

b. Squat jar, bubbly dark blue glass decorated with applied and tooled self-coloured threads. From the Temple Well at Pagans Hill, Somerset. Probably seventh to eighth century. H. 8.65 cm (3⅜ in.).

c. Palm-cup, bubbled green glass with mould-blown ribbing and folded rim. From St Martin's-in-the-Fields, London. Probably sixth to seventh century. H. 8 cm (3⅛ in.). B.M.

PLATE 4

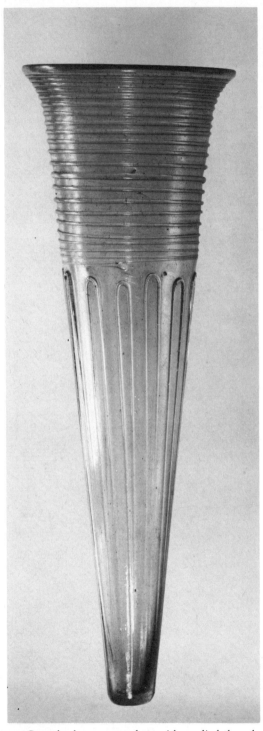

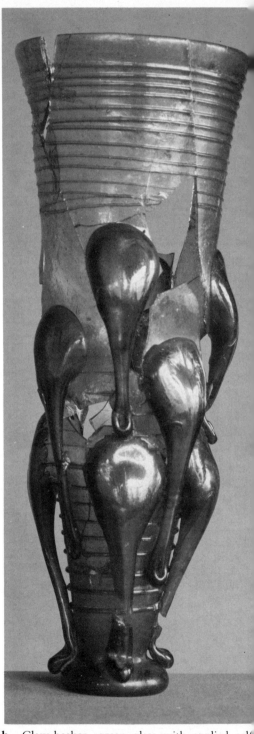

a. Cone-beaker, green glass with applied thread-decoration. From Kempston, Bedfordshire. Probably fifth to early sixth century. H. 26.5 cm (10½ in.). B.M.

b. Claw-beaker, green glass with applied self-coloured threading and hollow-blown 'claws'. From Ashford, Kent. Probably seventh century. H. 25 cm (9¾ in.). V.A.M. (B.M. loan).

PLATE 5

a. Bag-beaker, bubbly green glass with applied self-coloured spiral trail and tooled threads. From Faversham, Kent. Probably English; seventh century. H. 21.7 cm (8⁹/₁₆ in.). B.M.

b. Pouch-bottle, bubbly green glass with applied self-coloured trail and zigzag threads. From Bungay, Suffolk. Probably seventh century. H. 12.7 cm (5 in.). B.M.

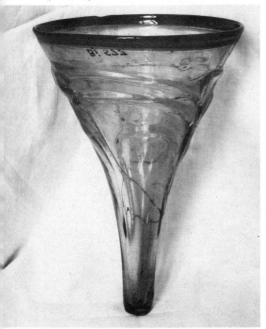

c. Funnel-beaker, greenish glass with self-coloured threads partially incorporated in the body, and dark blue applied rim thread. From Birka (Björkö), Sweden. Probably Rhenish; ninth century. H. 15.3 cm (6 in.). Statens Historiska Museum, Stockholm.

d. Beaker, almost colourless bubbled glass with applied purple rim thread. From Birka (Björkö), Sweden. Probably Rhenish; first half of tenth century. H. 6.1 cm (2½ in.). Statens Historiska Museum, Stockholm.

PLATE 6

a. Beaker, pale green glass with applied dark blue rim thread, yellow trails and applied ribs of white and yellow twists. From Birka (Björkö), Sweden. Probably Rhenish; ninth century. H. 10.2 cm (4 in.). Statens Historiska Museum, Stockholm.

b. Squat jar, green glass with faint wrythen mould-blown ribbing. Allegedly found under the pavement in front of the High Altar of Shaftesbury Abbey. Probably tenth to eleventh century. H. 7.3 cm (2⅞ in.). Library of Winchester Cathedral.

PLATE 7

a. Beaker of bubbled yellowish glass, gilt and painted in enamel colours (the 'Luck of Edenhall'). Syrian (Aleppo); *c.* 1250–65. H. 16 cm (6¼ in.). V.A.M.

b. Beaker of greyish-colourless glass, painted in enamel colours and inscribed [MA]RIA. GRACI[A PLENA]. From Launceston Castle, Cornwall. Perhaps Venetian; late thirteenth century. H. 10.3 cm (4⅛ in.). Duchy of Cornwall. V.A.M.

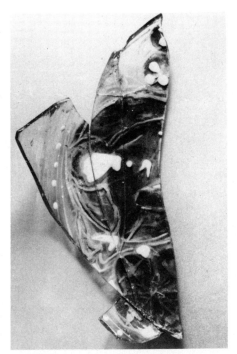

c. Fragmentary bowl, greenish-colourless glass painted in enamel colours. From Cheapside, London. Uncertain origin; perhaps late thirteenth century. D. 12 cm (4¾ in.). Museum of London.

d. Phial, pale green glass. From St Swithin's House, Walbrook, London. Probably English; about 1500. H. 6.5 cm (2½ in.). Museum of London.

PLATE 8

a. 'The Nativity', miniature in a Psalter from Carrow Abbey. English; about 1250. Walters Art Gallery, Baltimore.

b. Lamp, green glass. From a pit near Westgate, Winchester. Probably English; early thirteenth century. H. 17.6 cm (6⅞ in.). Winchester City Museum.

c. Urinal, green glass. From St Swithin's House, Walbrook, London. Probably English; about 1500. H. 22.5 cm (8⅞ in.). Museum of London.

PLATE 9

a. The 'Weoley Cup', *cristallo* with gilt and enamelled decoration, in a silver-gilt mount with London hallmark for 1547–8. Venetian; early sixteenth century. H. 23 cm (9 in.). The Founders' Company.

b. Vase of opaque-white glass *(lattimo)* with enamelled decoration of a king's head within a roundel (? Henry VII) and a device of a portcullis (personal badge of Henry VII). Venetian; about 1500. H. 19.8 cm (7¾ in.). B.M.

Beaker (the 'Fairfax Cup'), aque turquoise glass enamelled colours and gilt, with scenes m the story of Pyramus and isbe. Venetian; late fifteenth to ly sixteenth century. H. 9.2 cm ⅝ in.). V.A.M.

d. Bowl, *cristallo* with gilt and enamelled decoration. Venetian; late fifteenth to early sixteenth century. D. 16 cm (6¼ in.). V.A.M.

PLATE 10

a. 'The Marriage at Cana' by
Hieronymus Bosch (c. 1450–1516)
showing the table set in part with
green glass beakers and low
Roemers, the 'cupboard' with
plate in the background and the
sewer or cup-bearer (with napkin)
standing with his back to the
onlooker. Flemish School; late
fifteenth to early sixteenth
century. Boymans van Beuningen
Museum, Rotterdam.

b. 'Nativity' (detail) *predella* panel, by
Carlo Crivelli (active 1457–93); showing
inghistera and inverted *moiolo*. Venetian
School; late fifteenth century. National
Gallery, London.

c. Tankard (the 'Parr Pot'), colourless glass with
opaque-white *(lattimo)* stripes, the mounts of silver-
gilt and the cover enamelled with the Parr arms,
probably for Sir William Parr. London hallmark for
1546. H. 14 cm (5½ in.). Museum of London.

PLATE 11

a. 'The Pleasures of Taste' (detail), workshop of Jan Brueghel, the Elder (1568–1625). Netherlands, School; c. 1617–18. The picture shows Venetian-style glasses used beside precious metal vessels on the buffet. Indianapolis Museum of Art, Indiana.

b. 'The King and Queen of Bohemia dining', by Bartholomeus van Bassen (1590–1652), the figures attributed to E. van der Velde. Dutch School; dated 1634. The royal couple are shown faced by a noble 'sewer', while the cup-bearer carries a glass for replenishment across to the serving-table beside the buffet. Present owner unknown.

PLATE 12

a. Goblet, the foot replaced in fruit-wood and base metal, the bowl with initials R$_B^I$B in a cartouche, and date 1577. H. 20.3 cm (8 in.). Corning Museum of Glass.

b. Goblet, the bowl with initials 'A T', 'R T', and date 1578, in cartouches. H. 21.6 cm (8½ in.). Fitzwilliam Museum, Cambridge.

c. Saucer-topped goblet, with initials $_{DLP}^{M\ M}$ allegedly for Marthe Mansion de la Pommeraye, a heart transfixed by two arrows, and the date 1578. H. 14 cm (5½ in.). Musée de Cluny, Paris.

d. Goblet, the bowl with initials 'A F' (twice) and date 1580. H. 13 cm (5⅛ in.). V.A.M.

All probably made in the London glasshouse of Giacomo Verzelini, and engraved with the diamond-point by Anthony de Lysle.

PLATE 13

a. Goblet, with 'John . . . Jone' in one cartouche, the Royal Arms of Queen Elizabeth I in another, and D͟I͟E͟R͟ 1581 in a third. H. 21 cm (8¼ in.). V.A.M.

b. Goblet, with panels enclosing heraldic devices of an eagle perched on an infant, and an eagle's leg erased, and smaller cartouches enclosing 'R G' and '1584', round the rim: 'TO.HIS.BROTHER. RICHARD.GRENHAL'. H. 16 cm (6¼ in.). Birmingham City Museum & Art Gallery.

c. Goblet (foot replaced) with 'K Y', a merchant's mark, and the date '1583', in three cartouches, below inscription: 'IN:GOD:IS:AL:MI:TRVST'. H. 22.5 cm (8¾ in.). Corning Museum of Glass.

d. Goblet with trailed thread decoration below cartouches enclosing initials 'R P' and 'M P' and the date '1586', above which: 'GOD.SAVE.QUYNE. ELISABETH'. H. 16.5 cm (6½ in.). V.A.M.

All probably made in the London glasshouse of Giacomo Verzelini, and engraved with the diamond-point by Anthony de Lysle.

PLATE 14

a. Goblet with 'ladder' stem and gilt decoration including inscriptions: 'WENYFRID GEARES' and 'DIEV ET MON DROIT', with date 1590. Probably made in Giacomo Verzelini's glasshouse, and gilt by Anthony de Lysle. H. 19 cm (7½ in.). From the Christian Brothers Collection, The Wine Museum of San Francisco.

b. Goblet, the foot mended with metal straps (the 'Vickers Glass'). Perhaps made in Giacomo Verzelini's glasshouse; about 1580. H. 13.5 cm (5¼ in.). Royal Library, Windsor.

c. Goblet with applied opaque-white threads, engraved with initials 'G S' and date '1586' (twice) within cartouches, above inscription: 'IN:GOD:IS:AL:MI:TRVST'. Probably made in Giacomo Verzelini's glasshouse and engraved with the diamond-point by Anthony de Lysle. H. 14.5 cm (5¾ in.). B.M.

d. Wine-glass with lion-mask stem and diamond-point engraving including inscription: 'BARBARA POTTERS 1602'. Probably made in Sir Jerome Bowes's glasshouse; 1602. H. 20.5 cm (8⅛ in.). V.A.M.

PLATE 15

a. Wine-glass with cigar stem, from Gracechurch Street, London. Probably made at Sir Robert Mansell's Broad Street glasshouse; first half of seventeenth century. H. 21.5 cm (8½ in.). Museum of London.

b. Wine-glass with hollow-blown inverted baluster stem. From Nonsuch Palace. Possibly made at Sir Robert Mansell's Broad Street glasshouse; first half of seventeenth century. H. 15.2 cm (6 in.). Museum of London.

c. Wine-glass with lion-mask stem. From Gracechurch Street, London. Probably made at Sir Robert Mansell's Broad Street glasshouse; first half of seventeenth century. H. 21.6 cm (8½ in.). Museum of London.

d. Wine-glass with coiled wrought stem. English or Netherlandish; mid-seventeenth century. H. 11.7 cm (4⅝ in.). Corning Museum of Glass.

PLATE 16

Portrait of William Style of Langley. English School; dated 1636. The window is glazed above with leaded design and armorial panel, and shuttered below. Present owner unknown.

be taken to be in a sense the standard medieval English bottle there were certainly other types, both larger and smaller. From Tyne-mouth Priory came a relatively short-necked bottle which prob-ably stood nearly 30 cm (12 in.) high, made of glass 3 mm (⅛ in.) thick or more.[67] This massive vessel, unfortunately not datable from its context, was decorated with applied vertical and horizon-tal threading which formed an overall lattice. At one point there is an angular 'elbow', already noticed as characteristic of thirteenth- and fourteenth-century glass (p. 22). A comparable fragment at Winchester came from a context suggesting a fourteenth-century date. At the other extreme, small bottles (which, being compact, have a better chance of survival) seem to have been rare. At Blunden's Wood, however, bottle-necks as small as 1.3 cm (½ in.) in diameter were found,[68] which suggests a small container; and in Germany small flasks, ranging in height from about 5.5 to 7.5 cm (2⅛ to 3 in.) can be dated twelfth to fourteenth century.[69] These tiny phials are drop-shaped, with a simple horizontal out-turned lip, and were evidently made by Theophilus' method of merely elongating the paraison. In Germany such phials have normally survived above ground as reliquaries. The same usage prevailed here in the Middle Ages, and the Kalendar of the Treasury of Exchequer mentions in 1345 'a glass bottle in which is contained the oil of Saint Mary of Sardenaye', while a glass flask containing the blood of St Thomas the Martyr was among the relics of the church at Durham.[70] Three tapering cylindrical bottles containing oil, found embedded in church walls in different parts of the country, have been interpreted as medieval reliquaries;[71] but since bottles of this shape have been found in seventeenth- to eighteenth-century contexts and none in controlled excavations of medieval sites, this tradition has come under suspicion in recent times.[72] One small flask, however, closely resembling one half of an hour-glass, was found 'in a prepared cavity' in the chancel of Anstey Church in Hertfordshire, and was discovered to contain blood.[73] This would seem to have a good claim to be a reliquary, and small flasks of comparable shape found in Germany can be dated to the late fifteenth century.[74] Indeed, this period seems to have seen the development of a number of types of small phial. Most numerous, and probably restricted to the late fifteenth and the sixteenth century, are small bottles with globular body, longish cylindrical neck and spreading lip, found in Germany.[75] One example used as a reliquary has a wax seal dated 1498, while another found in Lübeck accompanied pottery of about 1450–1500.[76] The English equivalent of this, with neck roughly sheared off instead of having an out-turned rim, is represented by a phial (Pl. 7d) found in London in context with the piriform urinal of about 1500 already described (p. 33).[77] Other London finds of the same type come from a context of about 1600.[78] In general it seems that there was a considerable increase in the use and manufacture of glass in England towards 1500.

Of fifteenth-century date too are some surviving pieces of laboratory equipment. We know that glass of this kind was made in the Weald in the sixteenth century and there seems no reason why this should not have been so in the fifteenth century, if not in the fourteenth. One may recall the Canon's Yeoman in Chaucer's *Canterbury Tales*:[79]

> . . . sondry vessels maad of erthe and glas,
> Oure urynales and oure descensories,
> Violes, croslets and sublymatories,
> Cucurbites and alambikes eek.

The alembic (see Pl. 19c) was the most important vessel of the alchemist's laboratory, and by far the most difficult to make. In

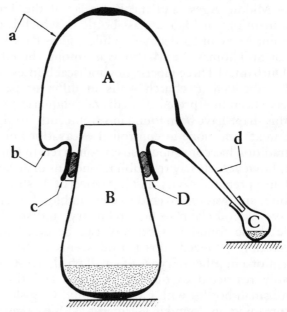

Fig. 10 A typical glass still of the medieval period and later. A. alembic; B. cucurbit; C. receiver; D. lute; a. dome of alembic; b. collecting channel; c. rim of alembic; d. spout. After Moorhouse (1972).

essence it was a deepish hemispherical vessel to be inverted over the top of the container ('cucurbit') of the liquid being distilled, the distillate flowing down the dome and through a tube into a second vessel, the 'receiver' (fig. 10). In order that the liquid should enter the tube, it was necessary to collect it in a channel formed round the base of the alembic dome. The technique of affixing the spout was essentially the same as that used for the claws of the Anglo-Saxon claw-beakers (p. 6). The 'nozzle of (a) posset cup' found on the Crouchland furnace site near Kirdford in Sussex[80] was probably in reality an alembic tube, and a fragmentary alembic found at Bramber Castle, Sussex, was no doubt made in the Weald not far away. More complete examples of alembics have been found on the sites of Selborne Priory, Hampshire (mid-fifteen century) and St John's Priory, Pontefract, Yorkshire (late 15th century).[81] The same sites produced cucurbits, round-based vessels with straight sides tapering upwards (compare Pl. 19b). The taper of the cucurbit and the corresponding slight flare of the alembic collar ensured that these components were relatively easily interchangeable. The cucurbit normally stood in a pottery base filled with sand or the like, which protected it from direct heat while affording it a firm seating. The receiver could be any sort of vessel of the right size, and the Yeoman's 'urynales' and 'violes' may well have answered this purpose. The alembic, with its cucurbit and receiver, was the basic apparatus for distillation, but far more complicated pieces of equipment, with tubes running from one vessel to another, are represented in fifteenth- and sixteenth-century German wood-cuts[82] but are as yet unrecognised in England.

One further utilitarian object was almost certainly made in the English country glasshouses. This was the linen-smoother, or 'sleek-stone' in seventeenth-century parlance, examples of which occur on sixteenth-century glasshouse sites, and on occupation sites much earlier. The sixteenth-century examples are normally mushroom-shaped, the stalk being a handle for applying pressure on the slightly convex head (fig. 11). The modern name of linen-smoother possibly obscures its use for a number of other processes requiring a smoothing action.[83] The medieval calender had no handle, and examples appear on Viking occupation sites both in Scandinavia and the British Isles, reappearing in later medieval contexts in England. Two thirteenth- to fourteenth-century examples were found at the village of Hangleton, Sussex,[84] and no less than eleven were found in strata at Winchester dating from the twelfth to the fourteenth century. They range in diameter from about 6.5 cm (2½ in.) to about 9 cm (3½ in.), and in thickness from

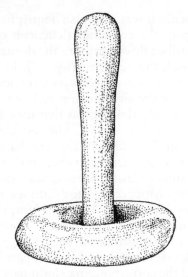

Fig. 11 'Slick stone' or linen-
smoother, green glass. Sixteenth to
seventeenth century. Artist's
impression based on Woodchester
finds.

about 2.5 to 4 cm (1–1½ in.). They normally reveal on the concave
back a tail of glass coiled round into the concavity. Since the Viking
examples tend to be smaller in diameter, the sixteenth-century
pieces larger (about 9 cm or 3½ in.) and the eighteenth-century
examples larger still (as much as 13 cm or 5 in.), it seems reasonable
to see a chronological progression, although development was
probably never uniform. No example of a calender has been found
on an early Wealden site, but the 'plano-convex discs' found on the
glasshouse site in Delamere Forest, Cheshire, probably dating
from the fifteenth century, may have been such 'slick-stones'.[85]

However much the vessel-glass of medieval England may dominate the interest of later generations, it was undoubtedly window-
glass which formed the staple of the glass-maker's craft. As has
been seen, the muff or split-cylinder method of making window-
glass described by Theophilus (pp. 13–14) appears to have been the
favoured technique since late Roman times. By the early fourteenth
century, however, another method had established itself in France.
This was the crown technique, by which a paraison was blown,
transferred to the pontil, then opened out and finally spun so that
centrifugal force expanded the whole paraison into a circular sheet.
The merit of this method was that the glass, being reheated as
necessary, retained its glossy fire polish, whereas the surface of
muff glass tended to be adversely affected by tool marks and by
contact with the surface on which it was flattened. The dis-
advantage of crown was that the circle of glass could not be divided

into straight-sided panes without wastage. In particular, the centre, where the pontil had been attached, was unavoidably thickened, giving an often useless 'bull's eye'. By tradition this technique was discovered by Philippe de Caqueray, who had been authorised in 1330 to found a glasshouse at La Haye in Normandy. This tradition has now been shown to be unfounded.[86] The crown method was in fact practised in the Near East from late Roman times onwards, small circular panes with folded edges being made to be set in plaster, or latterly in lead cames.[87] At what stage the circles were induced to grow in size is uncertain, and it may be in the manipulation of these larger discs that the Norman 'invention' consisted. Lawrence Vitrearius (p.29) and, later on, a certain William le Verir (*Verrier* or glassman), mentioned in 1300, are often said to be of Norman origin, but there seems to be no proof of this, although it is probable enough in itself. However that may be, crown glass seems to have been made in England by the second quarter of the fourteenth century, since much of it was found at Blunden's Wood *c.* 1330.[88] That it may have been cullet makes little practical difference, since it almost certainly demonstrates that this type of glass was being made in the Weald at this time, even if not at the Blunden's Wood site itself. Both crown glass and muff glass were probably used side by side in fourteenth-century windows, depending on the source from which the glass came.[89]

Although the Church was by far the most important customer for window-glass, the glazing of secular buildings was probably commoner in the late twelfth and thirteenth centuries than is commonly recognised.[90] Thus at Ascot Doilly Castle, Oxfordshire, four small pieces of pale green window-glass less than 2 mm thick were found in the fill of the tower, and since the tower was demolished about 1200 the glass must be of this general date.[91] In 1238 glass was inserted into the window of a *garderobe* at the Palace of Westminster 'so that the chamber may not be so draughty as it has been.'[92] Similar records recur throughout the thirteenth century, and it may reasonably be assumed that the custom of glazing windows was gradually spreading down the social scale. It is recorded that in 1441 even a pigeon loft was glazed, and by 1500 there seems to be good evidence that peasant houses occasionally had at least some glass windows.[93] Even in the most prosperous homes, however, the glazed portion of the window usually only occupied a part of the space available, the remainder being filled by a wooden shutter or even a wickerwork panel. Medieval man must frequently have been reminded that a window was primarily an opening for the wind rather than for the light.

Window-making for both ecclesiastical and domestic use was the province of the glazier, and in view of the historical developments sketched above, it is not surprising to discover that a London guild of glaziers is mentioned already in 1328.[94] To this guild belonged John Geddyng who, in 1351, was scouring the Chiddingfold district for glass suitable to glaze St Stephen's, Westminster; as did John Brampton, glazier, who was paid thirty shillings in 1378 for 'white glass of the Weald, bought for making the said windows in the King's chamber [at Woodstock Palace].'[95] John Geddyng was Third Upper Warden of the guild from 1373–81, and John Brampton Third Master during the same period.[96] That glaziers of this eminence, executing royal commissions, should obtain their glass from the Weald speaks for the high quality of window-glass available there.

The glazier's craft was confused with that of the glass-maker on the one hand, and merged with that of the glass-seller on the other, ambiguities which were not finally clarified until the seventeenth century. Strictly speaking, the glazier received his raw glass from the glasshouse and was responsible for forming it into windows – whether for rooms or for smaller spaces such as lanterns. A glazier was often also a painter on glass, a skill which in the earlier Middle Ages involved the simple rendering of internal details and shading by means of a black pigment *(grisaille)*. This had then to be fired in a simple kiln. Towards 1300 sulphide of silver to produce a yellow stain was added to the glass-painter's resources, providing a colour difficult to obtain in 'pot metal'.[97] This pigment was always painted on the reverse of the glass, so that the black painting on the front outlined the yellow wash on the back.

The normal procedure for making a painted glass window was first to work out the whole design for each opening, and then to scale it up on a large table; in the fifteenth century paper was probably introduced for this purpose. The artist relied as far as possible on the leading to outline his design, which was essentially a coloured mosaic with painted internal details. Pieces of the appropriately coloured glass were therefore cut from the sheet by drawing a hot iron across the glass, which cracked along this line. This rough shape was then reduced to size and form by the grozing-iron (pp. 12–13). These pieces were assembled over the cartoon on the table, and the *grisaille* details were painted in following the underlying design. The painting was then fired and the pieces re-assembled on the cartoon, where they were held in position with nails until the 'H'-sectioned lead cames were laid round them and soldered. The completed panel was held in place in the window opening by horizontal iron 'saddle-bars' let into the masonry, and the panel was fastened to these by twists of copper wire soldered to the leading.[98]

Not all glaziers could be artists and many must have restricted themselves to cutting and fixing plain quarries. Until Renaissance times windows were mostly simple square- or diamond-lattices fixed into wooden frames. These were fixed into the window openings, but were regarded as furniture rather than building fixtures.[99] When you moved house, you took your glass windows with you.

One or two refinements of the glazier's trade deserve mention. Ruby glass was made at the furnace by 'flashing' colourless glass with a thin layer of the red, the copper colorant being so powerful that a solid ruby sheet of normal thickness would be virtually opaque. The glaziers learned to abrade this flashing so that the colourless glass was laid bare and could be painted with *grisaille* or yellow-stain if desired, a trick particularly useful in rendering heraldry or details of costume. Flashed blue and other colours were later introduced and used in the same way. Yellow-stain could be employed to produce intermediate colours – for instance, green when used on blue. Lastly, probably towards 1500, the diamond-point was introduced to cut glass, facilitating the accurate shaping of individual pieces of glass and thus minimising the laborious process of grozing.[100] The ground was laid for a great refinement of secular glazing to come.

CHAPTER 3

The Rise of the English Glass Industry: Tudor and Stuart

(c. 1500–1675)

It is a curious fact that we know less about the glass used in England in the first three-quarters of the fifteenth century than we do of that in almost any period before or after. This is a paradoxical phenomenon in an age when a wealthy merchant class was aspiring to a standard of comfortable living unrivalled before its time; and when great strides were being made both in Italy and in Germany in the development of new kinds of glass. It may well be that as far as home-made glass is concerned, the English were content to con- tinue with the types which had served them during the fourteenth century, for we have already seen that several shapes and kinds of glassware seem to vary very little from the later Middle Ages until the seventeenth century. The imported glassware therefore calls first for attention, although its use would have been restricted to the wealthiest members of society. These glasses become relatively common towards 1500 and increase in number as the sixteenth century progresses.

The luxury glass of this period, as earlier, came from Italy, where, by the mid-fifteenth century, Venice had established herself as the single most important centre of glass-making in Europe. This supremacy was founded partly on the Venetian glass-makers' long experience of producing coloured glasses, both opaque and translucent, in the service of their extremely important bead manu-facture; partly, and paradoxically, on their mastery of the technique of decolourising glass to produce a material *(cristallo)* as nearly as possible approximating to the rock-crystal from which it derived its name. Virtually colourless clear glass was already being made in the thirteenth century (pp. 18–19), but for some reason as yet im-perfectly understood, the manufacture of *cristallo* experienced a dramatic upsurge after 1450.[1] This renaissance may have been due in part to the use of pure siliceous pebbles from the Ticino river, and in part to a refinement in the use of manganese as a decolorant. Most probably, however, it was the product of technological inno-vation on several fronts in this dynamic period of Venetian glass-making. *Cristallo* was to ensure the dominance of Venetian glass-making in the ensuing two and a half centuries. Its manu-facture was at first virtually restricted to three families at Murano,[2] the little island near Venice where almost all 'Venetian' glass had been made since 1292. The impact of *cristallo* is seen mainly in two fields: domestic utility glass with simple furnace-worked decor-ation or none at all; and luxury glasses with enamelled and gilt decoration. In the former, pride of place went to the long-necked bottles, usually on a pedestal foot made in one piece with the body, called by the Venetians *'inghistere'* (fig. 12). Associated with the *inghistere* were tumblers *(moioli)* of cylindrical or, more usually, truncated conical shape. These were often plain but sometimes decorated with mould-blown ribbing.[3] Both are frequently seen in fifteenth-century paintings, the *moiolo* often inverted over the mouth of the *inghistera* like a tooth-glass on an old-fashioned wash-hand stand (Pl. 10b). Fragments of both types, often in association and sometimes in remarkable numbers, are found on English sites. Southampton is the single most prolific source, frag-ments of no less than eighteen bottles and twelve beakers having been found in a single garderobe deposit in a house in Upper Bugle Street there.[4] A number of examples have also been found in London. Southampton, however, seems to have been a prime port of entry for Venetian glass, for not only have numerous specimens been excavated there, but the fifteenth-century port records fre-

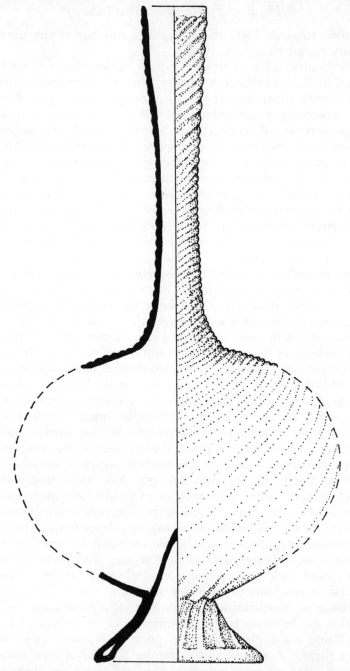

Fig. 12 Flask *(inghistera)*, colourless glass with wrythen mould-blown ribbing. Found at Quilter's Vault, Southampton. Probably Venetian; about 1500. Scale approx. ½. After Platt and Coleman-Smith (Charleston, 1975, no. 1522).

quently mention glass coming from Italy and the Netherlands. The later entries often include the magic word 'crystal' instead of the vaguer term 'glass'.[5]

The *cristallo* glasses of about 1500 were often decorated by the old medieval device of blue trailing, as on a small bowl found at Upper Bugle Street, Southampton, with a blue trail above a calyx of vertical mould-blown ribbing (cf. p. 24).[6] A bowl of exactly this type is represented in a painting of the 'Virgin and Child' by Piero di Cosimo (d. 1521).[7] A more ambitious footed bowl found on the same site has blue side handles as well as blue threading.[8]

Far more important than this medieval survival was the use of enamelled and gilt decoration. Like *cristallo* itself, the technique of enamelling, already practised at Venice in the late thirteenth century (p. 27), appears to have been revivified in the mid-fifteenth.[9] The earliest of the enamelled glasses were probably coloured (translucent blue, manganese-purple and more rarely green, or opaque turquoise) with decorative themes derived from classical mythology or the realm of the grotesque. Some of these themes were also used – presumably later – on *cristallo*. The most striking example with an English provenance is a goblet, mounted in a silver-gilt foot, belonging to the Founders' Company of London (Pl. 9a).[10] This was stated by the donor in about 1640 to have come as booty from Boulogne when it surrendered to Henry VIII in 1546. The mount has the London hallmark for 1547–8, and the tradition seems likely enough. The glass itself, however, must have been made about 1500. It is painted with *putti* riding seahorses and a king similarly mounted, while between each pair of figures is depicted a Renaissance trophy surmounted by a skull. Far more frequent are the enamelled glasses with no more decoration than borders formed of coloured enamel dots laid on gold leaf, itself etched with a point to give imbricated or other formal designs (Pl. 9d). At Southampton two small bowls of the type already mentioned (above), with mould-blown ribbing and trailed threading – one in blue, the other self-coloured – were found at Upper Bugle Street; and another was excavated earlier in Quilter's Vault there, in an early sixteenth-century context.[11] A similar example was found at Henry VIII's Nonsuch Palace, whither it must have been taken in the 1540s, and a fifth has been excavated in Winchester. Less frequently found in this country, but not uncommon in the Near East, is a beaker with an enamelled and gilt border above mould-blown ribbing like that on the bowls. Upper Bugle Street in Southampton provided two examples, and a third without the enamelled decoration.[12] Representations of similar beakers are found in Hugo van der Goes's 'Portinari Altarpiece' of about 1475 and in a miniature by the 'Master of Mary of Burgundy' in the Bodleian Library, Oxford, dated about 1500.[13] Southampton has also furnished two of the rare examples of gilt and enamelled decoration on coloured glass – a fragmentary blue bowl on pedestal foot, and a tiny fragment of a border design on a manganese-purple glass.[14] The inventory of King Henry VIII's glasses, probably made in 1547, includes among more than 600 pieces a number described as 'paynted', such as 'iiii standinge Cuppes of blewe glasse wth covers to theym paynted and guilte', or 'Twoo greate glasses like boles standinge uppon feete of blewe and white [colourless?] partelye guilte'.[15]

One of the most distinctive types of Venetian enamelling was executed on opaque-white glass. Venice was the most important entrepot in the trade between Europe and Asia, and as early as 1442 the Doge Francesco Foscarini had received gifts of Chinese porcelain. It was natural that this miraculous new substance should be imitated, and one of the ways of doing this was by using opaque-white glass, the decoration being partly executed in blue enamel copying the underglaze blue of the originals. This painting *'alla porcellana'* was frequently blended with polychrome enamelling of the types already described.[16] A fragment of this opaque-white *(lattimo)* glass has been found at Southampton, but more important is a two-handled vase enamelled on one side with a king's head and on the other with a portcullis, now in the British Museum (Pl. 9b).[17] The portcullis was a personal device of Henry VII, and the portrait head is very probably Henry's own, copied from the English coinage. A second vase, of the same shape but of green glass, was recorded in 1897 as having a similar crowned head on one side and the royal arms of England on the reverse.[18] Both glasses may have been diplomatic gifts to Henry VII, if not direct commissions of the King. Henry VIII's inventory mentions 'a cruse wth ii covers painted blewe wth A kinge crowned on the side'.[19]

An opaque turquoise was occasionally used as a base for enamelling, and one extant glass of this type has probably been in England almost since the time it was made (Pl. 9c). This is the small beaker known as the 'Fairfax Cup' (Pl. 9c).[20] It is enamelled in polychrome with the Ovidian story of Pyramus and Thisbe, and has its own fitted wooden case bearing the seal of Sir Thomas Belasyse as Lord Fauconberg (1577–1653). The case was in turn enclosed in a wash-leather bag containing a slip of paper inscribed: 'In this bag is the Antient Cup of our Familye putt into this bagg, August the 21, 1649, by me, C. ffairfax'. Sir Thomas Belasyse was himself a

Fairfax through his mother, Ursula, eldest daughter of Sir Thomas Fairfax of Denton; and his grandmother was a Fairfax of Gilling Castle, both in Yorkshire. The glass was evidently a Fairfax family heirloom, and may well have been acquired new in the time of Sir Thomas Belasyse's grandparents.

One type of Venetian glass did not lend itself to enamelling. This was the brown semi-opaque marbled glass called *'calcedonio'* from its resemblance to calcedony or agate. Only one example appears to have been excavated in England – at Baconsthorpe Castle in Norfolk – but Henry VIII's inventory refers several times to 'bottelles or flagons of glasse iasper colloure', 'three bolles of Glasse w^thoute covers of iasper colloure', 'twoo standinge cuppes of glasse wth covers iaspar coloure' etc.[21] Comparable with *calcedonio* in being probably inspired by Roman originals was the Venetian *'millefiori'* (thousand flowers) glass, made by embedding in a colourless or pale blue transparent matrix sections of cane carrying flower-like designs. The canes themselves were simply the composite mosaic rods used in the bead industry, normally formed of concentric layers of red, blue, turquoise and white with a star-like formation in cross section made by forcing the gather into a serrated mould. The sections, owing to their flower-like appearance, were called *'rosette'* (little roses). A Murano inventory of 1496 lists several types of object made *'de rosette'*.[22] A number of pieces have been identified in English collections as belonging to this category, among them a ball 4 cm (1½ in.) in diameter recorded in the nineteenth century as having been 'ploughed up in the Forest of Ormesby, Lincs'.[23] Its form recalls the passage from Marcantonio Sabellico's *De Situ Venetae Urbis (Concerning the Situation of the City of Venice)*, written in 1495: 'But consider to whom did it first occur, to include in a little ball all the sorts of flowers which clothe the meadows in Spring. Yet these things have been under the eyes of all nations as articles of export.' A number of such *millefiori* balls are recorded. One or two fragments found in Southampton and London confirm that *millefiori* vessels too were known in England in the years about 1500.[24]

Millefiori glass was rare and seemingly short-lived. A contemporary technique of almost equal complexity was destined to last through the seventeenth century and to enjoy a very wide diffusion. This consisted of embedding threads or strips of opaque-white glass *(lattimo)* in a crystal matrix to give patterns of vertical parallel bands. This was probably done by picking *lattimo* canes up on a gather of crystal and marvering them until incorporated. The paraison would then be pinched together at the bottom so that all the canes radiated from a single point, the surplus button of glass being cut off. The white might consist of either flat stripes or twists of varying complexity. A paraison with canes twisted in one direction could be blown inside a second with stripes running in the other direction, to produce a mesh-pattern, air bubbles being trapped between the two layers (*'reticello'* or 'little net'). In due course, coloured (usually blue) canes were occasionally mixed in with the *lattimo*.

The first documentary record of this technique occurs in Venice in October 1527, when Philippo and Bernardo Serena received a privilege for their newly discovered method of ornamenting glasses 'with stripes having twists of thread'.[25] Plain *lattimo* stripes possibly preceded twists, and in any case actual use may have antedated the patent application.[26] By 1540 these techniques were well enough established to be mentioned in the technical literature. Vannoccio Biringuccio, in his *Pirotechnia* (or *Arts of Fire*) published in Venice that year, writes: 'Look too at the large things as well as the small, that they make of white or coloured glass and that seem to be woven of osier twigs equally spaced', an apt figure of speech to suggest the effect of these glasses.

Many examples of this glass have been excavated in England, some in contexts suggesting a date before 1550. More precisely documented is a small group of tankards with globular body and cylindrical neck, decorated in this striped technique and mounted in English silver-gilt mounts. Best known is the 'Parr Pot', once in Horace Walpole's collection (Pl. 10c). The mount, hallmarked for 1546, bears in enamels the Parr arms, probably for Sir William, Lord Parr of Horton, uncle of Catherine Parr, last Queen of Henry VIII.[27] A virtually identical 'pot' in the British Museum bears silver-gilt mounts with the London hallmark for 1548–9;[28] and a third example, having coloured bands alternating with twisted *lattimo* canes, has mounts with the same date marks.[29] These glasses, surviving from the 1540s, echo entries in Henry VIII's inventory. The shape was one already established in German stoneware (also found with English mounts), and is probably referred to in the inventory as 'a glasse like a potte'. It has been suggested that these glasses may have been made in London itself (pp. 52–53), but there is so much evidence to show that the Venetians tailored their shapes to suit their customers that it seems more probable that these glasses catered for a special English taste. Examples of the shape are found in tin- and lead-glazed earthenware and in Isnik pottery, all with English silver mounts.[30]

Henry VIII's inventories contain a number of entries which

probably refer to glasses with *lattimo* decoration. Thus in one there are 'A bason and twoo lavers of glasse all of diaper worke'; 'xii bolles of glasse wth one cover to theyme all wrought up wth Diap (i.e. diaper) worke white'; 'xiiii other standinge Cuppes of glasse Diap worke of sondrye fasshons'; 'one glasse wth white work the foote and Cover garnished wth Silver and guilte'; 'one basen white worke nette fashon'; 'one playne potte of glasse wth one handle punte [?] iii rowes blewe and white' (perhaps alternating blue and white stripes) etc. The terms 'diaper' and 'net fashion' suggest that the collection already included *reticello* ('redesello' or little net) glasses, two years before the technique is first mentioned in Muranese documents.[31]

To understand the significance of such Venetian glasses, one has to have some conception of their functions. For this one needs in turn some idea of how meals were served to a 'soverayne' in the late Middle Ages, whether he was King or Lord (Pl. 10a). He normally dined and supped in his Great Chamber with guests of high enough rank to eat there rather than in the Great Hall. Five divisions of the household were involved: the ewery (for ewers and basins, with the appropriate linen); the cellar (for wine); the buttery (for beer); the pantry (for bread, salt and cutlery); and that of the usher, who controlled the proceedings generally. The preliminaries were supervised by subordinate officers, the yeomen. Trestle-tables were erected in the Chamber, and the yeoman usher and the yeomen of the ewery and pantry supervised the laying of the lord's table. Nearby the yeoman of the cellar was arranging his 'cupboard' with an array of plate as grand as the occasion demanded. The projecting ledge of the 'cupboard' was often for the service of beer and wine furnished by the yeomen of the buttery and the cellar respectively The preliminaries thus completed, the yeomen's places were taken by gentlemen – the sewer (or server), who disposed the dishes on the table; the carver; and the cup-bearer, whose duty it was to 'assay' the wine, to pour it and offer the cup to his lord on his knees. A small procession, headed by the chief household officers, then fetched the food from the kitchen, carrying it ceremonially through the Great Hall back to the Great Chamber. Here the sewer arranged the dishes, and the carver cut off 'sayes' ('assays') of the meat, as he had previously of the bread. Only at this point was the lord summoned by his gentleman usher. He washed his hands in a basin proffered by a gentleman on bended knee, and a second dried them on his towel. The lord was then seated and his guests arranged above or below the salt, or at other tables. These procedures varied but the general ceremonial was commonly observed (Pl. 11b).[32]

John Russell's *Boke of Nurture*, apparently written about the mid-fifteenth century, prescribes:

> Son, when thy sovereignes table is drest in thus array,
> kover alle other bordes with Saltes; trenchers & cuppes thereon ye lay;
> than emperialle thy Cuppeborde with Silver & gild fulle gay,
> thy Ewry borde with basons & lauour, watur hoot & cold, eche other
>   to alay.
> loke that ye have napkyns, spones, & cuppis euer y-nowe
> to your soueraynes table, youre honeste for to allowe,
> also that pottes for wyne & ale, be as clene as they mowe;
> be euermore ware of flies & motes, y telle the, for thy prowe.[33]

William Harrison, in his *Description of England* (1586), writes:

> It is a world to see in these our days, wherein gold and silver most
> aboundeth, how that our gentility, as loathing those metals [because
> of the plenty] do now generally choose rather the Venice glasses,
> both for our wine and beer . . . and such is the estimation of this
> stuff that many become rich only with their new trade unto Murana
> . . . from whence the very best are daily to be had . . . And as this is
> seen in the gentility, so in the wealthy communalty the like desire
> of glass is not neglected.

Not everybody agreed with this scale of values, for when Lord Buckhurst had to prepare Sheen Palace for an important visitor in 1568, he had difficulty in satisfying the Queen's officers: 'And where they required plate of me, I told them that I had no plate at all. Such glasse vessell as I had I offred them which they thought to[o] base.'[34] In King Henry VIII's time the precious metals were not available in such profusion, but Venetian glass too was then far rarer. The needs of his household may be seen in the royal glass inventory.[35] On the very first folio there are fourteen basins and sixteen lavers of glass in association, evidently for the ewry. There are nearly 160 cups and 'pots', no doubt for the service of drinks (p. 49); some 35 bottles and flagons, and 200 trenchers and spice plates, some presumably for actual table use, some to adorn the 'cupboard'. On one folio are recorded 'vi Cuppes of Assaye white glasse ptelye guilte'. These bowl-shaped cups are seen in fifteenth-century pictures borne by the lord's cup-bearer, while the yeoman of the cellar fills it with wine for tasting.[36] Venetian glass readily suggested itself for this function, since it had the reputation of breaking when touched by poison. Almost a century later Philip Massinger could still write of crystal glass:

Than hold one drop that's venomous, of itself
It flies in pieces and deludes the traitor.[37]

Sir Thomas Browne, however, took a more sceptical view: 'Though it be said that poison will break a Venice glass, yet have we not met with any of that nature.'[38]

Other accessories of the feast may be identified in isolated entries in the inventory. Thus there is a single item: 'one Pound hollowe Sesterne [?] of glasse ptelie guilte wth the kynges Armes', presumably a large cooler for bottles and glasses.[39] A 'cistern' of this kind is in the Victoria and Albert Museum. Almost the last item in the inventory is 'A greate fountayne of glasse beinge muche broken',[40] no doubt a successor to the medieval table-fountains used at great banquets. In 1453 Philip the Good of Burgundy gave a feast in the Château of Lille, at which 'there was a very beautiful fountain, partly of glass and partly of lead, a quite new kind of work, for there were little bushes, leaves and flowers of glass, of so novel workmanship it was a marvel to behold.'[41] One medieval table-fountain survives,[42] and one or two of sixteenth-century date, all of goldsmith's work; and from them we may get some idea of what the glass fountains may have looked like. A generation later (about 1550–5), expatriate Italian glass-makers at Beauweltz in modern Belgium made for the future Philip II of Spain a table-centre in the form of a bulb with foliage and flowers, growing from a boat-shaped bowl. A drawing of it survives.[43] Its highly wrought decorative elements were not calculated to survive usage for very long. It is not surprising that Henry VIII's table-fountain was 'muche broken'.

The use of glass for table decoration finds a parallel in the substitution of glass for plate on the 'cupboard' or buffet. It is not easy to document this development but when, in 1581, the Prince of Mantua was married, 'there was there, besides most rich sideboards and ordinary glassware, a display of various beakers, decanters, jars, and other most beautiful vessels of Venetian crystal, so that I think all the shops of Murano had met there; and of that there was need, for all the signori invited, after they had drunk, broke the beakers, which they held as a sign of great joyfulness.'[44] Glass vessels in quantity on the buffet are depicted in at least two paintings (Pl. 11a) by Jan Brueghel the Elder (1568–1625) working in collaboration with Hendrik van Balen (1557–1632);[45] and a similar grouping of glasses is to be seen in a 'Bacchanal' by Rubens (1577–1640).[46] The phenomenon had probably been in existence some time before it was noted, whether in words or in paint.

The service of drink required as much ceremony as regulated the service of food (Pl. 11b). Nicholas Breton (1545?–1626) wrote: 'A Trencher must not be laid, nor a Napkin folded out of order, a dish set downe out of order . . . a Glasse filled, nor a Cup uncovered nor delivered out of order.'[47] A glance at any sixteenth- or seventeenth-century picture showing a meal will reveal that very few drinking-vessels stood on the table at one time: the modern practice of having as many glasses as people was quite alien. William Harrison (p. 50) wrote:

> As for drink, it is usually filled in pots, goblets, jugs, bowls of silver in noblemen's houses; also in fine Venice glasses of all forms: all which notwithstanding are seldom set on the table, but each one, as necessity urgeth, calleth for a cup of such drink as him listeth to have, so that, when he has tasted of it, he delivereth the cup again to some one of the standers by, who, making it clean by pouring out the drink that remaineth, restoreth it to the cupboard from whence he fetched the same. By this device . . . some tippling is furthermore cut off.

Lord Fairfax's orders to his servants after the Civil War prescribe:[48]

> ### The Cup-Board
> Let no man fill beere or wine, but the cup-board-keeper, who must make choice of his glasses or cups for the company, and not serve them hand over heade. He must also know which be for beere and which for wine; for it were a foule thing to mix them together.

Not only was the guest not left with a glass, with the attendant risk of 'idle tippling', but often two or more people had to share a glass. At the Field of the Cloth of Gold the French ladies had affected to be shocked by the English ladies who handed flagons and cups round for each to drink from in turn:[49] but in the mid-sixteenth century in France there was often only one glass to a table, so 'A man should wipe his mouth on napkin or table-cloth.'[50] If there was one glass to two guests, 'one should empty every time one drinks so as to leave nothing for his companion', a situation presumably alleviated by the cupboard-keeper.

The supremacy of Venetian glass was challenged by attempts to make glass of similar quality in England itself. In the 1530s a group of Netherlands glass-makers in Southwark obtained naturalisation papers, but it is not known what they made. In September 1549 a group of eight Venetians, whose names are recorded, were summoned by the Council of Ten in Venice to return from London to Murano, which they had left owing to shortage of work. Their contract still had time to run, and when it appeared they might abscond they were committed to the Tower. It seems that they obtained dispensation from Venice and stayed on to complete their contract, probably returning home in 1551, leaving behind Giuseppe Cassilari, who remained in London until 1569 with an Antwerp colleague named Thomaso Cavato.[51]

An interlude of no lasting significance was the sojourn in England of one Cornelius de Lannoy, coming apparently from the Netherlands in about 1564 to give instruction in glass-making and to practise alchemy. Already in 1565 he is described as discontented with the facilities available here.[52] Nothing further is heard of him.

The real beginnings of a crystal glass industry in England date from 1567. In that year Jean Carré, a native of Arras but coming from Antwerp, arrived in London, apparently with the undeclared intention of taking over the English glass industry. The most important branch of this was the manufacture of window-glass, to be dealt with later (p. 71), but he also aimed to introduce the making of Venetian-style drinking-glasses. By July 1567 he appears to have obtained a licence from the Corporation of London to build a furnace.[53] With his partner Pierre Briet, he aimed to obtain the soda *(barilla)* needed to make crystal from an Italian merchant named Giovanni Suigo, known to have sojourned in London until at least 1578.[54] Carré's furnace was probably built in the Hall of the Crutched Friars, the presumed work-place of Edward VI's Italians. It was well established by 1574. It is not known who Carré's first workmen were, but in 1570 a Venetian named Quiobyne Littery arrived from Antwerp, and in 1571 'Joseph, a Venetian and glassmaker' is found in the same house, having recently arrived in London. This simple register entry probably conceals the name of the most important glass-maker to run the London *cristallo* factory – Giacomo Verzelini.[55]

Verzelini was born in Venice in 1522 but came to London from Antwerp, where in 1556 he had married Elizabeth Vanburen, an Antwerp lady of good family. Verzelini was therefore fifty years old when Carré died (1572), and having presumably had some twenty years' experience of glass-making before coming to England, he was well qualified to take over the Crutched Friars, although Peter Campe, Carré's brother-in-law, was formally charged with the responsibility under Carré's will.[56] Verzelini's position, however, was far from secure. As a foreigner

he could not own property, and the licence under which he operated was in Carré's name, not his. Furthermore, he had enemies,
notably among the glass-sellers who controlled the profitable
import trade in Venetian glasses. To strengthen his position he
sought a licence from the Crown, requesting a twenty-one-year
monopoly in the making of crystal drinking-glasses. Despite
protests from the Glaziers' Company that this would mean the
'overthrow of fifty households using only the trade of selling of
glasses, besides the hindrance of the merchant adventurers bringing
trade into this realm', Verzelini obtained his patent on 15 December
1574 (not 1575 as given in the older literature). It granted freedom
to sell wholesale or retail, provided that prices were competitive
with those of foreign makers; prohibition on the manufacture of
Venetian-style glass by others; and prohibition of imports, on
penalty of confiscation and imprisonment. It was made clear
that one reason for the grant was that Verzelini was teaching
his craft to native Englishmen, and would be obliged to continue
doing so.[57]

Verzelini's progress received a severe check in the following
autumn. On Sunday, 4 September 1575, as Holinshed records in
his *Chronicles* (1586): 'About seven of the clock in the morning a
certain glasshouse which sometime has been the crossed friars hall
neere to the tower of London burst out in a terrible fire . . .
whereas the same house a small time before had consumed great
quantitie of wood by making of fine drinking glasses: now itself
having within it neere fortie thousand billets of wood was all
consumed to the stone walls.' This setback no doubt further
emphasised Verzelini's legal vulnerability. He applied for naturalisation, and was granted denization on 26 November 1576.[58] In the
meantime he had set about restoring the glasshouse, adding to it
quarters for his household. He appears to have prospered, for he
later bought property in Kent in and around the manor of Downe.
These purchases no doubt helped to assure him of a reliable source
of fuel.

Verzelini was now well established in the City of London, fam-
iliarly known as 'Mr Jacob', and in 1581 as 'Keeper of the glasshouse'. Verzelini's path was still not entirely clear, however, for in
1579 he had been 'fined' by the confiscation of glasses which he had
sold to a glassman who was not a freeman of the City. The Privy
Council intervened, ordering the Corporation to restore the
glasses. In October Verzelini was again at odds with the City
authorities being forbidden to use his furnace during the winter.[59]
Infringements of his patent must also have caused him concern.

Sebastian Orlandini, a Venetian, who had set himself up at Beckley, near Rye, to make beads and enamels (not covered by the patent) began also to make crystal drinking-glasses. When John Smith, a London glazier, bought an interest in the concern and moved it to Ratcliffe in London, in 1580, Verzelini petitioned the Privy Council for protection. His move succeeded and in February 1581 the Council ordered the furnace to be demolished. Further-more, although Verzelini's patent provided for a ban on imports, considerable numbers of glasses were evidently brought in at various times – quite apart from the freedom of the nobility to furnish themselves with Venetian glass at will. There is only one recorded instance of Verzelini's invoking his rights against illegal importation.

The glasses attributable to Verzelini's glasshouse have been reasonably well identified, not so much by the characteristics of the glasses themselves as by their decoration – paradoxically, the one element not provided in the glasshouse itself. A preliminary list of five glasses established by Wilfred Buckley in 1929[60] has now grown to a dozen, all but one diamond-engraved. This scratching technique had allegedly been 'discovered' (it was known in Roman times) by the Venetian Vincenzo di Angelo dal Gallo, who in 1549 applied for a patent to protect his technique of engraving glass with the diamond-point, which he claimed to have been practising for some fifteen years but which had many copyists. He was granted a concession for ten years[61] but the practice nevertheless continued to spread. It was known to Johann Mathesius, the Joachimsthal pastor, who, in his famous sermon on glass-making, published in 1562, refers to 'Venetian glasses decorated with scrolls scratched on them with the diamond-point'. The earliest known dated diamond-engraved glass, of 1566, was probably made in Austria since it bears the arms of Vienna. It confirms Mathesius' observations on scrollwork, the main decoration consisting of leafy arabesques, the leaves with firm diagonal hatching. These features are fairly con-stant in European engraving before 1600.[62]

The earliest of the putative Verzelini glasses is a goblet, unfor-tunately lacking stem and foot, dated 1577 and decorated with a broad central frieze in which two scrollwork panels alternate with cartouches enclosing the date and the initials R_B^IB (Pl. 12a). Above this is a hunting scene in which hounds pursuing a stag and a unicorn alternate with trees, the foliage rendered in spiral scribbles, the space-filling being otherwise in firm hatching. Bounding the central frieze are thin wave-borders, and below is a further border of linked cross-hatched ovals. These themes recur throughout the

Verzelini *oeuvre*. Second in date (1578) is a large goblet in the Fitzwilliam Museum, Cambridge (Pl. 12b). Its round-funnel bowl resembles that of the previous glass, but it retains its stem of a wide hollow knop mould-blown with soft vertical ribbing above a pedestal-like foot. The hunting frieze recurs with the same scribbled in-filling for the foliage. The firm hatching is here accompanied by groups of curved strokes. The central zone is divided by three cartouches, one enclosing the date and the other two the initials 'A T' and 'R T' intertwined with lovers' knots. The panels between are filled with hatched arabesques and it is noteworthy that no two panels of this type within the Verzelini group appear to be of exactly the same composition. As before, the central zone is bounded by running waves, but the lowest border is a row of vertical hatched petals.[63]

Less easily accommodated in the series is a glass, also dated 1578, in the Cluny Museum, Paris (Pl. 12c). It has a shallow bowl, a stem composed of a wide hollow-blown ribbed knop between pairs of smaller depressed knops, and a rising pedestal foot with narrow folded edge. It has the hunt border similarly rendered, within the limitations imposed by a narrower field, and the arabesque-filled panels alternating with three cartouches. These enclose motifs with French connotations, notably three fleurs-de-lis, for France. The second encloses the date and a heart transfixed with arrows, and the third the initials $\substack{A\\M\,M\\DLP}$, allegedly those of Marthe Mansion de la Pommeraye, wife of Gédéon Picard, a doctor in Poitou – where the glass is first recorded, in 1864.[64] This French intrusion is discussed below (p. 58).

The fourth glass (Pl. 12d) differs in both shape and decoration from those so far discussed, but is anchored firmly in England by the history of its ownership, having been given by Lady Georgiana Smythe to Horace Walpole. It is listed in his *Description of Strawberry Hill* (1774) as: 'A large flattish drinking-glass . . . with the initials of an English lady's name . . . and the date 1580.' Between the wide slope-sided bowl and the tall pedestal foot is a broad, depressed hollow knop with mould-blown ribbing. There is no hunt frieze but merely a border of slanting hatched petals, punctuated with trefoil motifs resembling those below the animals' bellies on the preceding glasses. In the three cartouches are the date and the initials 'A F' intertwined with love knots, repeated twice.

From 1581 dates a goblet so like the 1578 glass at Cambridge that little further description is called for (Pl. 13a). It is inscribed 'John . . . Jone' and $\substack{DIER\\1581}$ in two cartouches, while a third encloses the Royal Arms of Queen Elizabeth. The goblet is said to have come from the West Country, and there are a number of branches of the Dier (Dyer) family to be found in Somerset, including two John Dyers of Wincanton who married ladies named Jane *(sic)* and whose dates are compatible with that on the glass. Fragments of two further goblets of this type have been found in excavations in Southampton, one with the middle digits of a date in the 1580s.[65]

New features distinguish a goblet now in the Corning Museum, New York (Pl. 13c). Instead of the wide ribbed knop we find a mould-blown lion-mask stem, and instead of the hunt frieze a border of spiked cresting above the inscription 'IN.GOD.IS.AL. MI.TRVST', the motto of the Pewterers' Company of London. One of the most elegant glasses in the whole series, it has a slightly more pointed bowl than the 1577, 1578 and 1581 goblets, and the taller stem improves its proportions. Unfortunately the foot has been broken off and the break obscured by pewter strapping. The main decoration comprises three cartouches enclosing respectively the initials 'K Y' with a lover's knot, an elaborate merchant's mark, and the date '1583'. The motto forms a link binding this 'K Y' glass to the 'G S' glass of 1586 (p.158).

A recent discovery is a goblet dated 1584, differing in several respects from the glasses already discussed (Pl. 13b). Its bowl is shorter and wider than those of the 1577, 1578 and 1581 goblets, and its stem is a hollow-blown, ribbed, inverted baluster. The usual decorative scheme is replaced by two large and two small cartouches, the larger panels with the normal framing of curved double lines, the smaller with characteristic late Elizabethan strap-work surrounds, all on the familiar arabesque ground. The large cartouches contain heraldic devices of an eagle perched on a child in swaddling clothes and of an eagle's leg erased, while the small ovals enclose the initials 'R G' with lover's knot, and the date '1584'. Above is inscribed: 'TO.HIS.BROTHER.RICHARD.GRENHAL'. The Richard Greenhall concerned may have belonged to the Greenhalls of Ribchester, near Blackburn in Lancashire; the significance of the emblems remains unexplained.[66]

The stem form of the Grenhall goblet is echoed in a glass (Pl. 13d) which rivals in elegance the 'K Y' glass of 1583. This goblet is decorated with a fine applied trail which has been blown into a ribbed mould to give a most attractive light ripple. On the narrow plain band left at the top the engraver has written the toast 'GOD.SAVE.QUYNE.ELISABETH', above a running plant scroll punctuated by cartouches enclosing the date 1586 and initials 'R P' and 'M P', probably for Roger Puleston, of Emral, Flint (Clwyd) and his wife Maud, daughter of Sir Thomas

Hanmer, who were married in 1556. The year 1586 was not only their thirtieth wedding anniversary but also that in which England rejoiced at the foiling of the Babington Plot, a circumstance probably giving special point to the toast.[67]

From the same year of 1586 dates a goblet (Pl. 14c) which displays further features of the Verzelini repertory. In bowl form much like the hunt-decorated glasses of 1578 and 1581, it is much shorter in the stem and narrower in the foot. It is unique in being decorated with two horizontal applied cordons, each composed of a gilt ribbon between opaque-white threads. There is also gilding at the lip and on the stem, a small rib-moulded depressed knop between mereses. Again the engraver has been restricted by his glass. Between the cordons there is room only for the familiar motto of the Pewterers' Company, 'IN:GOD:IS:AL:MI:TRVST', and above, space only for a narrow zone of arabesques, broken by three cartouches enclosing the initials 'G S' (twice) and the date.[68]

All these glasses, except that in Paris, were found in England and seem to be the products of a single engraver working in England, although perhaps not directly for Verzelini. Later practice suggests that engraving was normally carried out in separate workshops. Fortunately one engraver is known from contemporary records. This was Anthony de Lysle, mentioned in the parish of St Martin le Grand in April 1583 as 'graver in puter and glasse, borne under the obedyence of the French King', who had obtained papers of denization the previous year.[69] He had fallen foul of the Company of Pewterers in 1582–3 by gilding pewter without its consent. Since all the glasses so far reviewed seem homogeneous in style, and since de Lysle is the only contemporary engraver known, it seems likely that he, in fact, engraved the putative Verzelini glasses dated between 1577 and 1586. Furthermore, his French connection perhaps puts the *tazza* glass of 1578 in its proper context. It seems perfectly plausible that de Lysle in England should engrave for an old French friend or customer an English glass on which he deployed a style perhaps first learned in France. Like Verzelini, de Lysle had probably lived in London some years before applying for naturalisation.

De Lysle indeed may also have decorated the last dated glass of the Verzelini era – a goblet of 1590 embellished not with point-engraving but with gilding, a technique with which, as we have seen, de Lysle was familiar (Pl. 14a). The goblet has a deep round-funnel bowl, on a hollow, mould-blown 'ladder' stem – an inverted baluster with vertical panels of transverse rungs – a type frequently found in English excavations but rare on the Continent. The bowl bears the arms of the Vintners' Company and the inscription 'WENYFRID GEARES' above emblems including a fleur-de-lis and an Irish harp, with the date '1590' above a sword. Round the bowl is the inscription 'DIEU ET MON DROIT' and on the foot the Garter motto *Honi soit qui mal y pense*. Formerly belonging to the Dukes of Northumberland, it is referred to in an inventory of the 1770s at Alnwick Castle as: 'A very ancient Glass said to be Queen Elizabeth's, made in 1590.'[70]

This family of glasses is so intimately tied together by style, as well as by their English provenance and connections with London Livery Companies, that it is difficult not to conclude that they emanated from the one English glasshouse legally permitted to supply such glasses in the period covered by the inscribed dates (1577–90). This impression of homogeneity, moreover, is greatly reinforced by the shapes of the glasses themselves. For many of them it is difficult to find any continental parallels. We know nothing of any style specific to Antwerp, from which the English style might be expected to have developed. If, however, Netherlands style were to be judged from the pattern-book of the Italian-manned glasshouse at Beauweltz (*c*. 1550–5), there are few points of similarity, except possibly an early tendency to use a rising pedestal foot. The Beauweltz stems are nearly always mould-blown lion-masks or plain ovoids, never the depressed ribbed knops of the Verzelini glasses.[71] Signs of compliance with continental tastes, however, perhaps show themselves in the lion-mask of the 'K Y' glass (1583), the elegant ribbed inverted balusters of 1584 and 1586, and the tall ribbed 'cigar' stem of an undated *tazza* dish with hunt frieze excavated in the City of London.[72]

There are two further goblets which have traditionally been associated with Verzelini. The first is a plain crystal glass (Pl. 14b) with hemispherical bowl and a stem composed of a central flattened knop below a small solid baluster, its junction with the foot masked by an ancient mend of three metal straps. The shape of its leather case makes it clear that the glass originally had a cover, now lost. With the case is a paper inscribed in an eighteenth-century hand: 'This Glass belong'd to Queen Elizabeth, out of which she drank: it has been in Mr. Vickers's family Time out of Mind. In 1726 I was married to Mr. Vickers.' The goblet, of dark-toned 'metal', has much in common with the Paris glass of 1578 and may quite well be an example of English *façon de Venise*.[73]

Less certain is the origin of a robust goblet of manganese-purple glass, the stem and foot replaced in silver, in the Cecil Higgins Art Gallery, Bedford. The bell-shaped bowl, encircled by three sub-

stantial cordons, seems to have no analogue. The glass is traditionally associated with Bishop Ridley, burned at the stake in Oxford in
1555, the pedigree being traceable back to John Ridley, Vicar of
Preston-next-Faversham (1617–44).[74] The date 1555 rules out
Verzelini and Carré, but admits the possibility that it was made by
Edward VI's Venetians (pp. 52–53). Its shape, simple decoration
and purple colour, however, suggest the robust style of an earlier
period. Nicholas Ridley studied on the Continent before returning
to England and Church preferment, and he may have brought the
glass with him.

Apart from the troubles already referred to, Verzelini was not
left indefinitely in the enjoyment of his patent rights. More than
three years before his patent had run its term, an old and trusted
courtier named Sir Jerome Bowes obtained in February 1592 what
was in effect a reversion of Verzelini's patent, in consideration of
services rendered; but – more practically – also in consideration of
an annual payment of 100 marks (£66 15s 0d) to the Crown, a
stipulation not in Verzelini's patent. Sir Jerome Bowes had been
English Ambassador to Russia and his conduct there lived in
English as well as Russian memory. Pepys records:

> Because some of the noblemen there would go upstairs to the
> Emperor before him, he would not go up till the Emperor had
> ordered those two men to be dragged downstairs, with their heads
> knocking upon every stair till they were killed. And when he was
> come up they demanded his sword of him before he entered the
> room. He told them if they would have his sword they should have
> his boots too. And so caused his boots to be pulled off, and his night-
> gown and nightcap and slippers to be sent for, and made the
> Emperor stay till he could go in his nightdress since he might not go
> as a soldier.[75]

The rights accorded this unorthodox diplomat were to run for
twelve years from the end of Verzelini's patent (December 1595)
and were virtually unchanged, except that Bowes was granted
powers of search to ensure compliance. He was also obliged to
make Venetian glass available to the nobility at reasonable prices,
or suffer them to furnish themselves independently.

Verzelini is stated to have retired in 1592, and Sir Jerome Bowes
appears not to have become active in the glass business until 1596,
as might be expected, though it is not clear what the situation was
between these two dates. Verzelini's sons may have continued at
the Crutched Friars, and they appear even to have challenged the

validity of Bowes's patent. Bowes was declared to have been 'much letted and hindered' by Verzelini's sons, and complained that his 'license and authorities . . . was impugned by the Versalyns.' In this predicament he turned for assistance to two members of the Salters' Company of London, William Turner and William Robson. Turner undertook to rescue the patent and to prolong it beyond the original proposed term of 1607. With Robson he was to assume responsibility for making the glass and take over the crystal monopoly as Bowes's assignee against an annual payment of £500. By 1598 Francis Verzelini was in prison, to be joined later by his brother Jacob. Bowes and his allies were able by open warrants of the Privy Council to stop the import of Venetian glasses, or the building of furnaces to make crystal. They themselves erected a furnace on part of the old Blackfriars monastery, and by 1601 production was sufficient to require greater storage space. Nevertheless, Turner's payments to Bowes seem to have been erratic and in 1605 he was forced (characteristically, at sword-point) to make them weekly rather than yearly. Turner now prudently retired to Yorkshire to manage other interests, leaving Robson in sole charge of the Blackfriars glasshouse. Robson set about securing a new patent to extend Bowes's privileges for a further twenty-one years, with apparent success (5 October 1606). In 1607 a reversion of the patent was granted to Sir Percival Hart – probably heir to the childless and ageing Bowes – and a certain Edward Forsett, the patent to run for twenty-one years from the date of the termination of the 1606 grant.

In 1607 Robson became involved in litigation concerning illegal importations of glass and the validity of his own rights as assignee of Bowes's patent. Although he appears to have prevailed, a certain Edward Salter set up a furnace in 1608 for crystal glass, having obtained a royal grant giving him the exclusive right of 'making of all manner of drinking glasses, and other glasse and glasse workes not prohibited by former letters patent.' With this he probably aimed to penetrate the gaps left in the Bowes patent by its restriction to the 'art of making drinking glasses or other glasses whatsoever like unto such as be most used in the said town of Morano.' He proposed to make cruets, dishes, salts and distilling equipment, but above all beakers and cylindrical beer-glasses, in crystal. With five partners he built a new furnace at Winchester House, Southwark, employing Italian workmen. Robson proceeded to sue Salter, but the workmen asserted that in making cylindrical drinking-glasses he was not working in the Venetian style, although such glasses occasionally were made to commission in Venice for export. Robson riposted that in that case they were covered by the terms of Bowes's patent. Ultimately Salter appears, while not losing his privilege, to have leased his interest to Robson against an annual payment. By 1610 Robson seems to have been in complete control of the crystal industry in London, prospering sufficiently to afford large sums in rent to Bowes and Salter.

In 1611, however, the company of Sir Edward Zouch, Bevis Thelwell, Thomas Mefflyn and Thomas Percival obtained their twenty-one-year privilege to make glass by the use of coal (p. 74), and by September 1612 had begun to venture into the field of crystal manufacture. In 1613 Robson counter-attacked by obtaining open warrants from the Privy Council to enforce his two crystal patents – those of Bowes and Salter – and when Zouch failed to comply by ceasing production, appealed direct to the Privy Council. In October the Council ruled that Zouch and Company should cease making glass in the Venetian metal and style, but that regarding Salter's patent the parties should settle by direct agreement. Zouch, however, circumventing the Council, appealed direct to the King, who ordered that the matter should be re-opened by the Council. Sir Edward Coke, the great upholder and codifier of the Common Law, and at this time Chief Justice of the Court of King's Bench, was charged with the investigation. Coke, on grounds of timber-conservation, found for Zouch, who, to help matters along, offered £1,000 a year to compensate the patentees who would lose by the grant of an exclusive patent to his own company. By this means Coke hoped to 'enforce them to yeald to that reasonable composicon which hath bene offered by setting this just patent affote which overthrowes thother that is so offensive to the common good.' The new patent, issued on 4 March 1614, was sweeping in its provisions, extending the company's privilege to all types of glass whatever, to be made by the use of coal, against the annual payment of £1,000. The patent was to run for twenty-one years, during which time all imports were forbidden. Existing glass patents were revoked and their beneficiaries forbidden to make glass by wood-firing. The patent met with Parliamentary opposition but Robson was finally forced to close his Blackfriars glasshouse in October 1614.

Despite the busy background of the war of patents, very little is known of the crystal glass made during Robson's management of the Bowes patent. The only certainly English-owned glass of the years between 1592 and 1614 is a bell-bowled goblet. This has a tall lion-mask stem, is diamond-engraved with the inscription 'Barbara Potters 1602' and was perhaps a christening glass (Pl. 14d).

In its elongated stem this glass seems to mark a tendency to stem-height which becomes pronounced in succeeding decades.

If the Barbara Potter glass is the only goblet-form so far attributable to the Robson era, there are numerous cylindrical beakers which may have been made under the Salter patent. There were probably two types: a relatively short beaker, usually with milled foot and flaring rim;[76] and a tall, straight-sided glass on a high foot made from a second paraison.[77] The short beaker probably echoed in shape the contemporary silver beaker with projecting gadrooned foot-rim, a feature probably imitated by the milled foot. One of the commonest versions of this beaker found on the Continent also occurs in English finds, notably in Plymouth and London. This has an applied trail laid from the centre of the foot almost to the rim, sometimes a fairly thin thread, sometimes a comparatively broad ribbon. The paraison has then been blown into a vertically ribbed mould dividing the broader ribbon into a series of protrusions resembling table-cut diamonds; or giving the thinner and closer threading a rippled effect.[78] The foot was pushed in to give a low kick, and a turn of thick thread laid round the basal angle and milled, usually with a 'rigaree'. Fragments of ten of these glasses were found in 1940 in Gracechurch Street, London, in a cellar thought to have contained a glass merchant's stock. The cellar was sealed by a layer of burnt material associated with the Great Fire of 1666, but some of the glasses seem to be considerably older, and these beakers may well represent glasses made under Salter's patent.[79] Fragments have also been found at Winchester, Norwich, Canterbury, Ipswich, Northampton and elsewhere.

The second shape of glass decorated with 'chequered spiral trail' is considerably rarer. The body is made as a tall cylinder, the trail starting in the centre of the base, while the foot is normally a plain pedestal with folded edge, made from a second paraison. The body is usually about 4.5 cm (1¾ in.) in diameter, the foot spreading to a maximum of about 10 cm (4 in.). The general shape is well enough known on the Continent in enamelled glass, or in *lattimo*-striped *cristallo*.[80] Marvered-in *lattimo* decoration of this kind is known from English finds, but is usually so well made as to suggest Venetian origin. A second type of tall beer-glass, however, has its decoration of *lattimo* threads standing proud of the surface, both in vertical ribs and in horizontal bands which call to mind the Verzelini 'G S' glass dated 1586. These beakers too are mounted on a tall pedestal foot, but the body tapers towards its base, assuming somewhat the character of a 'flute'. Similar glasses appear in pictures by Hendrick ter Brugghen (1588–1629), notably in his

'Jacob and Laban', dated 1627. Some nine of these flute-like beakers were found in Gracechurch Street,[81] and other London examples are known, suggesting that this was a common glass in the first half of the seventeenth century. At least one glass of this general form, but with only horizontal bands of milled *lattimo*, is known from a British collection with a long family history (Pl. 17d). Cylindrical beer-glasses were also frequent in green glass, and are dealt with below (p. 89).

By this date the making of 'Venice' glasses in England was an accepted phenomenon and probably no irony was intended by the pedlar's cry in a ballad of about 1620: 'Venice Glasses fine were newly made in London to drinke your Beere or Wine come now my Pack's undone speake betime.'

When Sir Robert Mansell assumed full monopoly powers in 1615 (p. 75) he undertook a reorganisation of the glass industry, against bitter opposition from the wood-burning glass-makers. By 1617 he had built a new furnace for crystal drinking-glasses in Broad Street, probably in the old monastic church of the Austin Friars, just as Carré had used the Crutched Friars buildings and Bowes the Blackfriars. Robson's Venetian and Venetian-trained workmen were probably absorbed into Mansell's employ. A certain 'Barnarden', resident in Broad Street in 1618, may even be the 'Barnardine' recorded among Verzelini's team in 1577.[82] As manager, Mansell installed none other than William Robson, who, now reconciled to Mansell, supervised the crystal works until sent to manage the window-houses on Tyneside (p. 76). His place in Broad Street was taken by a young Welshman named James Howell, not long down from Oxford. From Howell's book *Familiar Letters* (*Epistolae Ho-Elianae*, first published 1645–55) we learn valuable details of the Italians at Broad Street – 'those hot Venetians', as he called them in a letter of 1 March 1619. This was written on the eve of a continental journey undertaken partly to organise the supply of *barilla* from Alicante, in Spain, and partly, it seems certain, to recruit skilled personnel. In June, at Middelburg in Holland, he managed to enlist 'Sig. Antonio Miotti . . . one of the ablest and most knowing Men for the guidance of a Glass-Work in Christendom'. Miotti had in fact managed a glasshouse in Middelburg since 1606,[83] so Howell was justified in his hope 'to have done Sir *Robert* good service thereby'. In a report from Venice (30 May 1621) he wrote that he was sending his letter by a cousin of Mazalao (one of the Venetians at Broad Street, a kinsman of Miotti). He refers also to meeting '*Camillo* your *Consaorman*' who 'could he be sure of Entertainment . . . would return to serve you again, and

I believe for less Salary'. The 'Consaorman' (*conciatore* in Italian) was of prime importance in a glasshouse, for he superintended the composition and founding of the batches. Camillo had probably still been working in London when Howell left in early 1619; we do not know whether he ever returned.

The Mazalao (Mazzola) referred to by Howell was probably the Francesco Mazzola recorded in London in August 1621.[84] The Venetian Ambassador described him as 'a man without religion and with all the vices' and blamed him 'for bringing hither almost all the glass workers of Murano'. It was no doubt Francesco who gave Howell the introduction to his cousin at Murano. The Mazzola were an important Muranese glass-making clan, who supplied a number of recruits to the industry elsewhere in Europe, notably in France, where their name was corrupted to Massolay.[85] Prominent among them was Paolo Mazzola, who apparently left Venice for London about 1640 and then wandered via Liège and Maastricht to Rouen and elsewhere in France. His strength lay in making drinking-glasses, particularly those with elaborate stems 'of extraordinary fashions' (p. 70).[86] A number of other Italian glass-makers are recorded in London, some from such famous families as the Seguso or the Barovier, but no more is known of them than their mere presence here.[87] One, however, may be taken to epitomise that restlessness which plagued Mansell throughout. This was Giovanni Maria dall'Acqua (variously spelled), of a famous family whose members included at least two heads of the Glass-makers' Guild in Murano.[88] In 1617 dall'Acqua was suborned to go and work in Scotland, where he appears to have taken part in several short-lived concerns, returning disgusted to London around 1619. History seems to have repeated itself after 1623, when the importation of glass was once again permitted (p. 66). Mansell wrote of himself:

> Thereuppon . . . his workemen and servants were drawne from him and went into Scotland . . . Sr Robert Mansell to settle the Manufacture here was inforced to purchase in the Scotch patent at 250^li per annum. After his men returned out of Scotland they made such ill condiconed glasse as at one tyme he lost 2000^li thereby. By that meanes he was enforced to p(ro)cure a whole new company from Mantua in Italie, for the bettering of the Condicon of his glasse, wch in 15 yeares before he could not effecte by the Venetians.

It is not known whether dall'Acqua was a party to this second migration; but when about 1630 'one Vecon his principall Clarke' (surely a misprint for 'Bacon'?) absconded to France and set up a rival crystal house, dall'Acqua seems to have accompanied him.[89] He was obviously a craftsman of the highest calibre, for his wages were very high, amounting to 38 shillings a week apart from his 'extraordinaries' of between 20s and 40s a week. The word 'extra-ordinaries' suggests that dall'Acqua made his extra income by working bespoke orders 'of extraordinary fashions'.[90]

When 'Vecon' absconded, Mansell complained to the Privy Council that fourteen of his Italians had 'on the suddaine runne away'. The considerable importation of *façon de Venise* glasses from France which ensued impelled the Council to revise the order of February 1623. Thenceforth only importation from Venice itself was permitted.

Even these staff difficulties were not the whole sum of Mansell's troubles in the crystal manufacture. In 1621 Isaac Bungar, his arch-enemy (pp. 73, ff.), persuaded the ship-masters to increase from 14s to 24s a ton the price of Scottish coals, used at Broad Street; and finally to cut off supplies entirely. Lady Mansell, however, acting energetically as her husband's manager in his absence at sea, took the risk of using Newcastle coal, happily with complete success. With this history of interrupted production and fluctuating importation, it is difficult to assess what proportion of the early seventeenth-century *cristallo* glasses found in England are likely to be home produced. Ostensibly there was a total ban on importation from 1615 until 1620, after which, under special conditions, glass might be sent from Scotland. In 1623 importation was freed, to be restricted in 1630 to glasses from Venice alone. In 1626 over 10,000 crystal drinking-glasses were imported; and in 1630 more than 5,000. The nobility might also procure 'cupboards' of drinking-glasses direct from Venice. Thus the Earl of Arundel, one of the Glass Commissioners of 1619, could import six chests at a time when the ban was otherwise being strictly enforced.

Not a single documentary glass survives from Mansell's mon-opoly, and our knowledge derives mainly from archaeology. Sir Robert himself, however, did leave some clues. In a series of self-justifying documents he indicated the downward trend of crystal glass prices since 1615.[91] As he took the date-base back to Verzelini's day, one may plot a series of price changes, thus:

	Sir Verzelini	*J. Bowes*	*1621*	*1624*	*(?)1635 or 1639*	
'Ordinary', large	7s (or 7/4d.)	6s 4d	6s	4s 6d	4s	⎫ per
'Ordinary', small	4s	4s	–	2s 6d	2s 6d	⎭ dozen

The latest document makes it clear that the 'large ordinary' were for beer and the 'small ordinary' were for wine. It has been proposed that these 'ordinary' glasses were of green forest metal, but since Mansell notes that the material used had gone up from £20 to £30 per ton, and this is the recorded price range for imported soda, it appears that, although 'ordinary', these glasses were soda-glasses – especially since the same document later specifically mentions green glasses separately. A similar chart of price changes can be drawn up for 'Cristall'. This Mansell divides into two categories – 'crystal . . . glasses – made by me (which never were before in this Kingdome)'; and 'crystal . . . glasses formerly made and imported from Venice.' The latter were 'now sold by my Merchant', showing that he now controlled the sale of Venetian glasses. The prices per dozen were:

	1621	1624	(?)1635 or 1639
Crystal beer, home-made	18s	15s	9s
Crystal wine, home-made	16s	12s	5s 6d up to 7s for 'extraordinary fashions'
Crystal beer, Venetian	20s to 24s ('without covers')	–	10s to 11s *ditto*
Crystal wine, Venetian	18s	–	7s to 8s

From all this it may be deduced that Mansell was making crystal which he claimed to be of better quality than any formerly made in England – the 'ordinary' soda-glass of Verzelini, Bowes and of his own early patents.

This correlation of charges, and the terminology used, suggest that beer-glasses were larger and wine-glasses smaller, and not that they differed in shape or type. This is borne out thirty-five years later by John Greene's orders for Venetian glass (pp. 104–5). In the drawings accompanying these orders, out of hundreds of dozens of glasses represented, only two dozen are of the beaker form normally regarded as a beer-glass. Among the rest – all stemmed forms – a given pattern may be for beer, claret or sack, or all three. The only distinction appears to be one of size – beer largest, claret middling and sack, roughly the equivalent of sherry, smallest. In Mansell's 1621 and 1624 price schedules there is also a category of 'smallest crystal wine' (presumably the rough equivalent of Greene's sack glasses) at 12s and 10s respectively, or two-thirds of the price of the corresponding beer-glasses. It may have been to such that Lady

Verney alluded in a letter of 1637:[92] 'Chuse me sixe wine glasses; I
have cuch [sic] littell ons and none as my lord uses.' Evidently the
stemmed beer-glass was replacing the beaker-shape in favour. This
is perhaps why the cylindrical beer-glass is not mentioned in
Mansell's schedules.

It is extremely difficult to pin down the varieties of drinking-
glass produced under Mansell. If we turn once more to the
Gracechurch Street 'hoard' (p. 63), it is clear that by far the commonest stem-type is the so-called 'cigar' stem, an elongated
inverted baluster accounting for more than half of the total height
of the glass (Pl. 15a). Fifty-six examples were recorded from the
site, and the type is one of the commonest excavated in London.
The most usual form is separated from the bowl by a small baluster
section joined by a merese to the bowl (Pl. 15a). A possibly earlier
form has the stem surmounted by two mereses somewhat apart.[93]
Two of the later Verzelini glasses, the Greenhall goblet of 1584
(Pl. 13b) and the 'G S' glass of 1586 (Pl. 14c) show similar features,
and excavated London examples come from contexts of about
1590–1620. The cigar stem may reasonably be assumed, therefore,
to date from the late sixteenth to early seventeenth century, a
hypothesis confirmed by the evidence of Jacobean silver wine-
cups.[94]. Examples with exaggeratedly tall stems bear hallmarks for
1603/4, 1606, 1608, 1609/10, 1613, 1616/7, 1618 (four examples),
1623/4, 1627, 1631 (two examples). Some of these silver cups have
bowls chased with lozenge-diaper resembling mould-blown mesh-
patterns on glass. Throughout history glass forms have often been
inspired by silver, but occasionally the reverse has been true; that
this may be one such occasion is suggested by a long-stemmed
wine-cup (hallmarked for 1617) which has three applied 'wings'
exactly as on the stems of 'façon de Venise' glasses. The cigar stems
conform in material well enough with the categories of the price
lists – the 'ordinary' glasses being thicker and brownish, the
'crystal' thinner and greyish-colourless.

The cigar stem is normally joined to the foot by a disc from
which the material has been smoothed upwards over the presumably rough end of the hollow-blown stem. This feature is shared by
other glasses. One type has a shorter inverted baluster stem with
pronounced shoulder. Eleven examples were found at Gracechurch
Street, and many more on other London sites and elsewhere
(Pl. 15b).[95] They too have their silver parallels, in a series of wine-
cups bearing hallmarks of 1635, 1637/8, 1641, 1648 and 1657. A
glass found at Montgomery Castle, near Welshpool, may date
from before 1625,[96] and an occasional Elizabethan silver cup

resembles the Charles I pieces listed above. This stem is probably the basic form of which the cigar stem is the greatly elongated version.

If these stem-types run parallel, so do the hollow-blown stems decorated with festoons and lion-masks (Pl. 15c). They display the same variability of material, presumably Mansell's 'ordinary' and 'crystal'. The taller and heavier 'ordinary' stems seem to be finished off at the base as described above (p. 68), while the finer 'crystal' specimens tend to have a second disc above the merese, forming a capstan element. Nine of the first kind and ten of the second were found on the Gracechurch Street site.[97] It is possible that the 'crystal' glasses are imports. Three stems of the former kind were found at Basing House, destroyed in 1645, but the lion-mask seems to disappear after 1650.[98]

The lion-mask stem was a cliché of *façon de Venise* glass. More specifically English was the so-called 'ladder' stem, on which vertical panels enclosing raised mould-blown bosses gave the impression of a ladder, a rare form on the Continent of Europe. The Winifred Geare goblet of 1590 (Pl. 14a) offers the first identifiable example, a finely plumped-out specimen. A somewhat slimmed-down version occurred at Gracechurch Street,[99] complemented in the Museum of London by a second example, its rather pointed round-funnel bowl remaining almost intact. Comparable examples have been found at Nonsuch Palace and at West Bromwich Manor, Staffordshire, in contexts suggesting a date before 1650. Like the lion-mask stem, the ladder stem apparently did not survive the Civil War. The English-found examples were almost certainly also English-made.

Another contemporary type was the globular knopped stem, often with mould-blown, vertical ribs. Its origins may readily be traced in the ribbed, hollow-blown knops of the Verzelini glasses, themselves Venetian-descended; but whereas Verzelini's ribbed knops were large, those of the Mansell era shrank in size and combined with a tallish capstan-section below and a small inverted baluster above to give a fairly tall stem in the contemporary taste. The knop was to swell again later (pp. 104–5). Gracechurch Street provided four fragments of the plain knop and three of the ribbed,[100] one with a spreading hemispherical bowl rather than the common round-funnel. Further examples of the stem are known from Bristol, Canterbury and elsewhere. The most distinguished, although slightly variant, descendant of this stem is displayed by the 'Royal Oak' goblet of 1663 (Pl. 20c).

Presumably all these relatively simple stem-forms were available at the basic rates quoted in the Mansell lists. The tariff presumed to date from 1635, however, lists crystal wine-glasses at up to 7s per dozen for 'extraordinary fashions'. These are the glasses which only the most skilled masters, normally Venetians, could make – men like Paolo Mazzola and Giovanni dall'Acqua (pp. 65–6). Fortunately, a number of glasses with complicated wrought stems have been excavated in England, notably yet again at Gracechurch Street.[101] These stems seem to take two forms. In one a thick coil of finely ribbed tubing was laid down in a series of superimposed loops, terminating below in a large open ring (Pl. 15d).[102] These glasses have many continental analogues (some to be seen in seventeenth-century still-life paintings) but the ring-terminal, almost universal in England, is relatively uncommon there. An inventory of Marston Hall in 1605 includes: 'It(em) – one great knotted glasse wth a Couer called Charyne Crosse',[103] which may have been of this type. Whereas the English finds seem to rely on colourless glass for the tubular stems, on the Continent these were predominantly coloured.

The second main type of wrought stem exemplified at Gracechurch Street has a vertical coil of glass laid like a bed-spring round a vertical stalk of the same tubing, with the open ring below. This coil is then decorated with pincered 'wings' of blue glass.[104] A London find in the Victoria and Albert Museum shows a round-funnel bowl above the tightly coiled stem. Fragmentary wrought stems occasionally occur singly on English sites, but the twenty-seven examples from Gracechurch Street form by far the biggest group. With these 'extraordinary fashions' the tale of stemmed glasses comes to an end.

Other types of crystal glass are far less certainly of English origin. A few small plates of *cristallo* are known from Waltham Abbey,[105] Nonsuch Palace, Basing House[106] and Exeter, and were possibly the 'trencher plates' of Salter's patent. They range from 15 to 19 cm (6–7½ in.) in diameter, and the archaeological evidence suggests a mid-seventeenth century date. In 1609 among East India Company 'Goods to be brought from England, vendible in India' were 'glass trenchers for sweetmeats' – a likely enough use for these plates.[107] Fragments of small cruets with tall neck reinforced by a thread of glass, rod-handle, curved spout and folded foot have been found on several sites (Bristol, Basing House,[108] Exeter etc.) and may well be Mansell's. The representation of similar cruets in Netherlands still-life paintings of the 1630s and 1640s suggests a date, and the Basing House fragments must antedate 1645. Also found there was a fragment of what was evidently a flat tray with pedestal foot;[109] another fragment occurred at Bristol. The cruets may well have been the successors of those mentioned in Salter's patent, and such cruets standing on low trays are seen in pictures. They often appear in pairs, and were presumably for oil and vinegar. The Marston Hall Inventory of 1605 included '5 Crewett glass'.[110]

As has been hinted, the seventeenth century saw a continuing and intensified struggle to obtain from the Crown patents which would bestow special economic privileges on the holders. It also witnessed a stiffening resistance in Parliament to the whole system of monopolies, regarded as one aspect of the objectionable extension of the royal prerogative under James I and Charles I. There were, however, economic limits within which even the prerogative had to work, and in the glass industry these were the necessity to maintain an acceptable supply, balanced against the growing urgency of conserving the country's timber resources. The crystal side of the glass industry has already been considered, but with apparently only one furnace working in London for most of the period, this was evidently the least important aspect of the industry economically, although its expensive products made it pro rata more profitable. Far more important was window-glass, and to a lesser extent green vessel-glass, both types carried on at this time mainly in woodland glasshouses.

   Jean Carré, whose activities in the crystal industry have already been mentioned (p. 53), on his arrival in England set about obtaining from the Queen a licence to build furnaces for window-glass in the Weald. By July 1567, when he obtained it, he had apparently already established two furnaces in Fernfold Wood, near Alfold, on the Surrey–Sussex border. These he operated as part of a company including his son-in-law Peter Appel; Peter Briet, probably an old business associate; and one Jean Chevalier, chastelain of Fontenoy in Lorraine, who was related to the glass-making family of de Hennezell, and whose function was to enlist workmen for one of the Alfold furnaces. The de Hennezells were experts in the broad-glass (or muff) method of making window-glass. The second furnace at Alfold was devoted to the crown (spun) method (p. 38), to which end members of the Norman family of Bungar(d) were installed by October 1568. Before this the partnership had absorbed a certain Anthony Becku, whose relations with Carré are uncertain in every respect save that they were invariably strained. He had probably been admitted because he too was seeking a window-glass monopoly. Before a monopoly could be granted it had to be established that window-glass was not already manufactured here. The master of a Chiddingfold glasshouse attested that he did not and could not make window-glass, but only vessel-glass. This evidence is not very impressive, however, since vessel-glass was sometimes made in separate glasshouses; and the Norman crown process would hardly have been entirely forgotten, even if the Lorraine method was unknown. Nor does it take any account of other centres, for crown was certainly being made in Staffordshire (p. 78). No doubt the needs of London were given paramount consideration and the Weald was London's natural supplier.

Anyway, the authorities were satisfied, and Becku and Carré received letters patent dated 8 September 1567, granting exclusive rights to make window-glass by either technique. They were required to produce 'enough glass for glassings [windows] as shall suffice . . . within owre said realme' at rates competitive with imports. They had also to compensate the Excise for lost import duties, and to teach Englishmen the art of window-glass making. This last stipulation caused much trouble, for neither the Lorrainers nor the Bungars were obliged by their contracts to divulge their closely guarded secrets. Becku's attempts to enforce compliance caused the de Hennezells to return to the Continent, and the Normans to attack Becku's son-in-law and agent 'with a hot yron having hotte glasse metall apon yt'. The episode finally broke the Carré–Becku partnership. Carré tried to get further Lorrainers for his Alfold furnace, but in May 1572 he died, leaving his interest to his widow. She delegated the management to her son-in-law, Peter Appel, who with Briet, and with Becku's assent, tried in 1576 to obtain a new patent which would prohibit imports and thereby eliminate competition. No such patent appears to have been granted, however, and the old patent was not enforced. 'Green' window-glass making spread to furnaces not controlled by Carré's company, which, hampered by financial and other difficulties, probably ceased effective existence.

While the lapse of Carré's patent eased the monopoly position, the intensified persecution of Protestants on the Continent in the 1570s caused a steady stream of immigrants, including Lorraine glass-makers. A number of window-glass furnaces are known to have been established at this time, notably in Sussex and Hampshire, the registers of the Walloon church in Southampton recording many glass-makers, most of them working at Buckholt, not far away. In the 1580s there was a gradual migration of these men westwards and into the Midlands, a dispersion traceable by the appearance of the glass-making family names – de Hennezell

(Hensey), du Tisac (Tyzack), de Tittery and others – in the registers of many parishes. Staffordshire was an important area for their colonisation, partly because glass had been made there since the Middle Ages and local landowners anxious to put their woodlands to profitable use were familiar with the industry; and partly because the best clay for glass-pots was to be found near Stourbridge. Isolated glasshouses were undoubtedly to be found in widely scattered localities throughout the country. Occasionally a glass-house would be set up on the estate of a magnate building a new house which required extensive glazing.

The largest single concentration of glass furnaces, however, seems still to have been in the Weald, where many of the original glass-making families remained. The reason for this was undoubt-edly its proximity to the London market, for transport was one of the chief costs of the business. One factor was working against the glass-makers – the increasing scarcity and consequent rising cost of fuel, for which they had to compete with the iron-masters. If London prices were low and fuel costs were rising, the glass-makers' profits suffered, and shortly after 1600 one of them made a bid to dominate the market. This was Isaac Bongar, of the Norman family (Bungard) already mentioned, which had moved to Wis-borough Green and prospered. Isaac Bongar invested his wealth in woodland, and was thereby enabled to control fuel supplies to his fellows, many of whom apparently fell under his influence and co-operated with him in cornering the London market. This was achieved by lowering prices and raising quality in the face of threatened competition, and by raising prices and relaxing quality control when the threat passed. Bongar's customers were members of the London Glaziers' Company, which he appears to have domi-nated by allying himself with some of its members – notably a certain Lionel Bennett – and finally by becoming a member of the Company himself. By these methods, which have a modern ring, Bongar amassed a considerable fortune and large estates in Sussex. After 1610, however, he was threatened by a new development.

Allusion has already been made to the growing concern of Government at the shrinkage of England's woodlands. Legislation in 1585 had curtailed the installation of new iron furnaces in the Weald. The same Parliament passed a Bill forbidding any glass-house to be erected within twenty-two miles of London, seven miles of Guildford, or anywhere on the Sussex Downs. Fortu-nately for the glass-makers, the Bill did not receive the royal assent. In this atmosphere it was natural that people should turn their thoughts to alternative sources of fuel. In 1610 the first patent, issued to Sir William Slingsby (who had coal interests in North-umberland), authorised him to 'erect ovens, furnaces, and engines' for a number of industrial processes, including glass-making, using 'sea-coal and pit-coal'. The ambitious scope of this patent was perhaps its undoing, since one type of furnace could not suffice for so many processes. Not surprisingly, therefore, a new patent was issued in the very next year (25 March 1611), against Slingsby's strenuous objections, for glass-making with coal in a furnace of a different design. The process was evidently directed to window-glass manufacture, one of the patentees being Thomas Mefflyn, the King's Glazier. The consortium was headed by Sir Edward Zouch, a wealthy courtier. It included Bevis Thelwell, another man of means who held posts at Court, and 'Dr' Thomas Percival, prob-ably the inventor of the new furnace. They were granted the exclu-sive right to make glass with coal for twenty-one years, against an annual payment of £30. Simon Sturtevant, another man interested in coal processes, in his book *Metallica*, published in May 1612, states that: 'Very lately, by a wind furnace, green glass for windows is made as well by pit coal at Winchester House in Southwark as is done in other places with . . . wood fuel.' This was the glasshouse set up by Edward Salter in 1608 for the manu-facture of crystal (p. 61), and it was probably acquired by Zouch's company for the experimental and initial production phases of their enterprise. Sturtevant's reference to green glass makes it clear that the *cristallo* furnace must have been adapted for its new role, and the mention of a 'wind furnace' suggests that underground air ducts led to a central grill on to which the coals were fed. This type of instal-lation accords with the known characteristics of the later English coal-burning furnace.

Zouch's company met strong opposition from the landed gentry, who anticipated diminished sales of wood, and from the glass-makers themselves, who saw their livelihood threatened. The company's main interest at this stage was apparently in window-glass, and by 1613 it appears to have installed a window-glass-house at Lambeth. With the grant of a second patent dated 4 March 1614 (p. 62) the company's monopoly was extended to cover 'drinking glasses, broad glass and other glasses and glass works'. The draft was annotated: 'Forbids – all others to make glass with wood', and this bureaucratic minute was given full force on 23 May 1615 by a Royal 'Proclamation touching glasses':[111]

. . . to provide that matters of superfluitie do not devoure matters of necessity and defence; understanding that of late yeares the wast of

Wood and Timber hath been exceeding great and intollerable by the
Glasse-houses . . . as it were the lesse evill to reduce the times unto
the ancient manner of drinking in Stone [stoneware], and of Latice-
windowes, then to suffer the losse of such a treasure . . . Therefore
We doe . . . straightly . . . ordaine, that . . . no person . . . shal
melt, make, or cause to be melted or made, any . . . Glasses whatsoever with Timber or Wood, within this Our Kingdome of
England and Dominion of Wales.

This rang the death knell of the woodland glass-makers, and their
natural opposition found its focus in Isaac Bongar, who became the
implacable enemy of the patent. For the time being, however, the
wood-burning furnaces were allowed to continue on sufferance.
Bongar himself appears to have been given concessions to work his
furnaces intermittently until 1618 at least.

In January 1615 the patent was reissued to an expanded company
of nine including the old members. Most important of the new
men was Sir Robert Mansell (1573–1656), already with a distinguished naval career behind him, who was deeply interested in
speculative commercial ventures through the East India Company,
the North-West Passage Company, and particularly the Virginia
Company. The new patent was a re-affirmation of the old in
stronger terms, forbidding wood-firing and the importation of
glass from abroad.

The remaining new members of the expanded company were
speculators and courtiers whose capital helped the company's
finances, and whose influence at Court was a useful asset. Later in
the year they were happy to be bought out by Mansell, along with
the old patentees, against annuities of £200 each. Mansell was now
nominally in sole control of the English glass industry. He was,
however, saddled with an annual payment of £2,800 (£1,800 to his
erstwhile partners, and £1,000 to the Crown in compensation to the
pre-Zouch patentees), together with the outstanding obligations of
the Zouch partnership; and this load of debt, apart from the
naturally heavy expenses incurred in the experimental phase of the
new process, were to be a permanent financial embarrassment to
Mansell, making his total costs uncompetitively high. In addition,
he was forced to fire his London furnaces with expensive Scottish
coal, then considered the only coal suitable for his purpose.

Mansell's first task on the economically all-important window-
glass side of the industry was to establish coal-burning furnaces in
the most favourable locations – near suitable coalfields and accessible to water transport. He tried first in 1615 at Kimmeridge on the

Isle of Purbeck, where the landowner, Sir William Clavell, owned a vein of shale coal previously used in an alum works. This was discovered to be too sulphurous and Mansell turned to Milford Haven, where neither coal nor transport facilities were suitable. At about the time of the Kimmeridge experiment Mansell had also established two furnaces at Wollaton, near Nottingham, to exploit the coal measures on Sir Percival Willoughby's estate. John Squire, a green drinking-glass manufacturer, previously employed at Bishop's Wood, near Eccleshall (pp. 84–5), was charged with constructing the new furnaces, one for window-glass, the other for vessels. He was joined in the summer of 1615 by Jacob Hensey (Hennezel), a broad-glass maker from Bagot's Park, near Abbots Bromley in Staffordshire, who had been arrested in June under the terms of the 'Proclamation touching Glasses' (p. 85). Glass was made in both furnaces until 1617 but had to be carried by the Trent and Ouse to Hull for trans-shipment thence to London. As Mansell said, 'Coles and transportation arose to a greater charge than the business could beare', and the furnaces were quenched. Probably towards the end of 1617 attempts to make glass were started at Newcastle upon Tyne, for the register of All Saints Church there records that on 11 February 1618 'Edward Henzey servant to Sir Robert Mannsfield was buried'.[112] Here Mansell was finally successful. The price of coal was less than half that paid at Wollaton, and water transport already existed in the fleet of colliers sailing regularly to London. The cases of window-glass travelled stuck upright into the coal, and the colliers returning half-empty could carry cullet, mainly off-cuts of the London glaziers.

Throughout this experimental period the supply of window-glass to the London market was inevitably erratic. To pacify the London glaziers Mansell was constrained in April 1616 to allow Bongar and Edward Hensey to work out their materials in the Weald. This enabled him to close down his expensive London production, although he was periodically forced to re-start it to satisfy the glaziers. Production in Newcastle was at first beset with troubles, some of them probably fomented by Bongar. By 1620 Newcastle could be relied upon to supply the London and East Coast markets. For the rest of the country Mansell relied on furnaces licensed to use the coal process, and in 1624 he asserted that there were nine broad-glass furnaces working in England.[113] It seems certain that there were also a number in remoter areas which continued clandestinely to use wood fuel. In 1621 an investigation undertaken at the instance of certain disaffected London glaziers revealed that: 'The Citty of London was founde soe plentifully stored and with soe good, as none of us could truly say that ever wee knewe the Citty better provided than att that very tyme.' Before this, however, Mansell himself had gone to sea in command of a fleet to put down the Barbary pirates. He left his affairs in the hands of his wife (p. 66).

Lady Mansell's resolution was soon put to the test. Bongar, apparently reconciled to Mansell before his departure, gave vent to such 'disgraceful speeches' that Lady Mansell got him imprisoned. On his release, he attempted, as already related, to stop supplies of Scottish coal for the London crystal furnace (p. 66). Although he was frustrated in this, his opportunity came with the Parliament of 1621. The long-standing indignation against monopolies, especially those associated with the Duke of Buckingham, was now coming to a head. Existing patents were referred to the Committee of Grievances, its consideration of the glass patent being urged in two petitions organised by Isaac Bongar for the glassmen. On 16 May Sir Edward Coke, who in 1613 had spoken so persuasively for the patent, now in reporting to the Committee spoke equally forcefully against it, and the House condemned it out of hand. Before the Lords' concurrence could be obtained, however, Parliament was prorogued. Some of the most objectionable patents were abolished by royal proclamation in July, but the Privy Council accepted Lady Mansell's plea that proceedings concerning the glass monopoly should be deferred until Sir Robert's return.

Sir Robert Mansell reappeared in the summer of 1621 to find that little had changed except that glass could now be freely imported from Scotland. Parliament reconvened in November 1621, considered the glass patent in December and moved to urge the King to suppress it – but the King did not concur. In October 1622 Mansell pressed for a resolution of the uncertainty, and a Committee of the Privy Council in February 1623 recommended cancellation of the old patent in favour of a new patent to Mansell alone, forbidding wood-firing and cancelling his payments to the Crown, but permitting the importation of glass. The new patent, issued in May 1623, survived the passing of the Statute of Monopolies in the 1624 Parliament. An exchange of pamphlets with Bongar was followed in 1626 by a lawsuit to test the patent's exemption from the statute. The suit failed, and this was apparently Bongar's final act of overt opposition.

In 1623 the Privy Council had advised that Mansell's patent should not be renewed when it reached its term in 1638. During the 1630s, however, the Crown was in great straits for money, and Mansell treated with Wentworth for an extension of his patent against annual payment of £1,500. The patent was to include glass-making in Ireland, all imports, except those from Scotland and Venice, being forbidden. The additional burden on Mansell's finances forced him again to raise the price of window-glass – by the considerable sum of 2s the case. The consequent complaints of the Glaziers' Company induced the Privy Council to take Mansell to task for the quality as well as the price of his glass, stating that 'by experience in their owne buildings and others in the ordinary use of glass [they] found the same was not so faire, soe cleare nor soe strong in wearing as the same was wont to be.'

The whole framework of Mansell's window-glass enterprise was finally broken in 1640, when the Scottish army invaded Newcastle and the workmen fled. For lack of ships glass already made could not be shipped nor coals got to the glasshouses in London. The final blow fell when, in 1642, Mansell was summoned to attend the Grand Committee of Grievances, and on 30 May was ordered to surrender his patent to the Clerk of the House. The outbreak of the Civil War in August finally destroyed any possibility of reviving the monopoly. Mansell nevertheless reinstalled his furnaces in Newcastle, although he now faced open competition. He died in 1656 and his enterprises passed into other hands.

Our knowledge of the political and legal background to the window-glass industry is unfortunately of little help in building up a picture of its operations and its products. It has been suggested that the making of window-glass had virtually died out in England by 1550, to be revived after 1567 by Jean Carré's French craftsmen (p. 72).[114] This hypothesis seems untenable, for in 1543 Thomas Harvey, glass-maker, paid as rent in Abbots Bromley thirty shillings and 'unam fen(estram)' (one window); and a glasshouse site in nearby Bagot's Park, dating from before 1550, apparently produced predominantly crown window-glass.[115] In the Weald too the mid-sixteenth-century glass-makers at Knightons, near Alfold, seem to have been making crown glass.[116] There was every reason why an existing glass industry should have prospered at this time, marked everywhere by a steady crescendo of building activity. Imported glass was clearly preferred for buildings where cost was no object, but the home-made product would find its outlet at the lower end of the market. In the iconoclastic years after 1550 much stained glass in churches must have been replaced by acres of plain quarries, which hard-pressed parishes were probably glad to acquire from the cheapest source possible.

It is not easy to calculate how many glasshouses worked to meet the demand for window-glass. When Jean Carré established his two furnaces in the Weald, he appeared to anticipate covering the needs of the whole country (or perhaps just of London?). Yet in 1571–2 about as much glass was imported from the Continent as in 1567–8, the year of Carré's arrival.[117] Although admittedly he had recurrent difficulties with his furnaces, it hardly seems that they made a great impact on the situation. By 1614, and probably earlier, there were at least nine window-glass furnaces in the Weald, and Isaac Bongar operated a double furnace.[118] The situation is confused because some masters – but not the Lorrainers – seem to have made both window- and vessel-glass.[119] The Weald concentrated on the London market, but there were numerous other glasshouses dotted about the West Country and the Midlands. Mansell was forced to suppress wood furnaces in Devon and North Wales, and in the more obvious Midland districts of Staffordshire and Worcestershire.[120] The uncertainty is compounded by the fact that archival sources cannot always be correlated with archaeological evidence. In 1624 Mansell wrote that he had 'caused to be erected 9 broad-glass Furnaces in the several and most remote places of the Kingdome from London . . . to the end that all the subiects might be served alike.'[121] By this date he was annually supplying London with some three to four thousand cases from Newcastle alone. The location of his remaining glasshouses is uncertain, as is their capacity, but it seems unlikely that the total output of all Mansell's houses reached 10,000 cases a year (approximately 1,800,000 square feet in area, or 1,000 tons in weight).[122] This certainly represents a very large increase and reflects the dramatically accelerated pace of building under Queen Elizabeth and James I. Not only were new buildings – some of them palatial in scale – springing up apace, but their fenestration made unprecedented demands for glazing. The most famous example is 'Hardwick Hall, more glass than wall', built by the Countess of Shrewsbury (Bess of Hardwick) between 1591 and 1597. The saying neatly sums up the changing ratio between window area and wall space in this era of lavish building. Wollaton and Longleat, and many more, must have required glass on a commensurate scale.

It is remarkable that although there must have been a seller's market, the price of window-glass, after rising sharply in the mid-sixteenth century, remained reasonably steady through Queen Elizabeth's reign, dropping slightly towards 1600 and remaining fairly constant at about 1½d per square foot throughout the monopoly until 1637.[123] This figure could be multiplied by three or four when the window came made up by a glazier, the cost of lead and his time being added. For painted decoration the cost was naturally even higher. Thus, in the early sixteenth century, Sir Thomas Lucas supplied the Bury glazier Robert Beston with Normandy glass, 'he to make of every caas atte lest iiii^{xx}x fete' (90 square feet) and to receive 'for every skochon of armes garnysshed wt. helmettes, targettes, and scriptures [inscriptions], and for every fote of imagery viii$^{d.}$, and for every fote of white glas, dubled, inured [probably 'fired'] and garnyshed wt. flowres, poises [mottoes] wt. luse (?) and colours, ii$^{d.}$.'[124] The 'skochons' of arms no doubt included a heaume with mantling and a motto, and probably the elaborate notched shield normal in Tudor heraldry. Surviving stained glass panels show a costly mosaic of coloured glasses elaborately cut, and occasionally further 'jewelled' by the difficult abrasion technique (p. 41). The necessary details had then to be painted in *grisaille* and yellow-stain, the panels fired, and finally leaded up – making them four times as expensive as the simple painted panes referred to in the last part of Sir Thomas Lucas's commission. Such work must have compensated many a glazier for the loss of ecclesiastical commissions.

In domestic glazing the diamond-quarry became the almost universal mode, sometimes left plain, sometimes painted in *grisaille* and yellow-stain, following a fashion established before 1500. These decorated quarries often alternated with the plain. In 1508 William Duxford, a London glazier, was paid 'for setting up of which Normandy glas, oon rowe of quarells white, the second rowe powdered or inured wt. bromecoddes [broom-pods].'[125] The lozenge-shaped quarry was the easiest unit into which to divide the awkward circular crown sheet – some 76 cm (30 in.) across and much thickened in the centre. When the cylinder method was established the provision of rectangular panels became easier. These could be leaded or, if large enough, secured by wooden glazing-bars, thus ultimately making possible the sash window. In the meantime the rectangular panel was an ideal vehicle for the new technique of enamel painting which had evolved on the Continent, notably in Switzerland during the sixteenth century. By painting his design in enamel colours without a break over the surface of the panel, the artist could avoid cutting out coloured shapes and laboriously leading them together. It became possible to produce polychrome heraldic or decorative panels with one or two firings and minimal leading. Much of this work was done by Dutch or German artists, such as Bernard Dininckhoff, who signed a heraldic panel formerly at Gilling Castle in Yorkshire (1585),[126] or Abraham and Bernard van Linge from Emden, who worked on an ambitious scale during the Laudian revival of stained glass (e.g. panels at Wadham, Lincoln, Queen's and other Oxford colleges; and at Wroxton Abbey near Banbury).[127] English artists also practised glass painting. Baptista Sutton is recorded as having executed a window for St Leonard's, Shoreditch, in 1634,[128] while Richard Butler and Lewis Dolphin painted the chapel window at Hatfield House some time before 1610.[129] The van Linges also painted purely decorative secular quarries, such as those with birds, beasts, fruit, flowers and human figures painted by Abraham for Lydiard Park, Wiltshire, in 1629, or the similar polychrome panels at Gorhambury House (1620–6).[130] These panels, mainly rectangular, but sometimes round-headed, are set in an elaborate pattern of leading. The patterns derive from Walter Gedde's *A Booke of Sundry Draughtes* (1615), published as a guide to glaziers (fig. 13). This book was partly based on current designs, but greatly elaborated them; and such leaded patterns may be found with plain as well as enamelled quarries (Pl. 16; cf. fig. 13).

The windows of this period were not normally made to open, ventilation being sometimes provided by hinged wooden shutters filling the window space above or below (Pl. 16).[131] In the sixteenth century glass windows were not generally regarded as integral with a building, but were moveable chattels. Thus in 1590 a Doncaster alderman bequeathed his house to his widow, but his windows to his son. In 1599, however, Sir Edward Coke ruled that glass fixed to a window frame with nails was an integral part of the fabric.[132] Nevertheless, as late as 1663 Henry Oxinden could write to Katherine Oxinden: 'I think Thou needest not leve above a dozen bords in the hal window, and if soe, they must be taken out before Mr. Holmsden come. There may be new quarries put in their roome for 1ᵈ· a peice. Pray take out the 2 quarries in my studie window of the Lyon and the Foxe.'[133]

If the late-medieval English glass-makers made both window- and vessel-glass in the same furnace, on the Continent there appears to have been greater specialisation. The Lorraine families of Hennezel, Tisac, Tittery and Bisval concentrated on *gros verre* produced by the cylinder-process, while the Bigault, Bonnay, Du Houx, Finances and Massey families specialised on *menu verre*, or small vessel glasses. This distinction was probably imported into England by Carré. Some of the Lorraine makers of *menu verre* stuck to their *métier* when they crossed the Channel – men such as Abraham Bigo (Bigault) at Kimmeridge,[134] or Isaac Du Houx at Denton.[135]

Fig. 13 Design for a leaded casement (cf. Pl. 16), from Walter Gedde's *A Booke of Sundry Draughtes* (1615).

Sir Robert Mansell treated the green vessel-glass industry much as he treated the window-glass industry, devoting to it a furnace in London but otherwise relying on provincial lessees to satisfy local demand using his coal process under licence. Whereas with window-glass he directly controlled production, with the vessel-glass he was apparently content in 1616 to lease his Ratcliffe furnace for £300 per annum to four London glass-dealers led by Thomas Robinson. There was then no effective Glass Sellers' Company, as there was to be later, for although a charter was obtained from Charles I in 1635, the City of London refused to enrol it. This would have given the Company a retail monopoly in glass table-ware, looking-glasses, hour-glasses and all categories other than window- and spectacle-glass, already controlled by the Glaziers' Company and the Company of Spectacle-Makers. Whereas Mansell had in the Glaziers' Company a powerful trade body to deal with, and reason to maintain a tight control on production and marketing, with vessel-glass he apparently kept a slacker rein. Only Abraham Bigo and his patron Sir William Clavell gave him the sort of trouble that he experienced with Isaac Bongar, Clavell persisting in vending the Kimmeridge glasses on the London market, reserved by Mansell to Robinson and his partners.

Our knowledge of the glasses produced in Mansell's furnaces derives largely from finds on glasshouse sites of the wood-burning era. These agree well enough with those made at Denton (p. 86), probably one of the earliest provincial coal-fired furnaces, operated by Isaac Du Houx, and suggest a continuity of style. If of the fifteen furnaces recorded in 1590 one was devoted to crystal and seven or eight to window-glass, then six or seven must have made vessel-glass.

The migration of the French glass-makers may be traced by the familiar names appearing in documents, or by the characteristic glass shapes occurring on glasshouse sites. Occasionally the two coincide. Thus the Lorraine names Tyzack, Hennezel and Du Houx occur together with the Norman name Vaillant in the registers of the Walloon Church at Southampton (1576–9), said to be of the glasshouse at 'bouque havt', or Buckholt in Hampshire, amid the woodlands between Winchester and Salisbury. A glass furnace was excavated there in 1860, and surviving finds suggest that beakers and goblets with pushed-in bases – type-fossils of this phase of glass-making (p. 87) – were common. The presence of window-glass indicates that here too both types were being made in the same glasshouse, Tyzacks and Hennezels perhaps concentrating on window-glass, the Du Houx on vessels.

From Hampshire the lines of this diaspora went generally north-wards and westwards. By 1598 Sir Jerome Bowes was complaining that 'certaine persons that lately have erected howses and furnaces . . . for making of Drinking Glasses, namelie in the countie of Gloucester and one Hoe [Du Houx] a Frenchman hath built a glass house and furnace and doth make greate quantitie of glasses.'[136] This member of the Du Houx clan perhaps worked at Newent in the Forest of Dean, where a likely site exists at May Hill.[137] The local archives, however, record only the names of Abram Tyzack 'son of a frenchman at the Glasshouse' and Jasper Pilney 'a french-man of the Glasshouse' in 1599, and in 1601 of Antony Voydyn 'glassfounder'.[138] Possibly Du Houx established himself elsewhere in the county. There is indeed evidence for the presence of the Du Houx in Bristol 'before the end of the 16th century'.[139] At Newent finds have included the typical pushed-in base-fragments, as well as 'chequered spiral-trail' fragments, tubing and linen-smoothers.[140] There was certainly a glasshouse there before 1621, when Abraham Liscourt represented the West Country glass-makers in opposing Mansell's patent. Experiments with coal burning may even have been tried, Newent being a place where ample wood supplies coin-cided with coal measures.[141] The same may be true of Newnham-on-Severn, where tradition avers that 'the first House in England for Glass worked with stone coal is said to have been erected here . . . by Sir Edward Mansell *(sic)*.'[142] Though wrong in detail, this may contain some truth. Certainly by 1696 there were two bottle houses at Newnham, and a further three at Gloucester, where Tyzacks are mentioned in the seventeenth-century church regis-ters.[143] Most important of all Gloucestershire sites is undoubt-edly the glasshouse in Collier's Wood, Woodchester, between Nailsworth and Stroud. Here furnace remains, with numerous glass fragments, were found in about 1877 and thereafter. The glass resembles in almost all respects that found on contemporary 'Lorrainer' sites elsewhere (pp. 87–91).[144]

Perhaps an outlier of the Gloucestershire sites is that at St Weonard's, between Hereford and Ross-on-Wye. Here exca-vations in 1961 at Glasshouse Farm revealed a rectangular furnace, together with crucibles and fragments of window- and vessel-glass of Lorrainer types.[145]

Better documented are the men who went to Staffordshire. From 1582 onwards Hennezels, Tyzacks and Titterys begin to appear in the church registers of Eccleshall, near Stafford, and in 1931 a well-preserved furnace was found in Bishop's Wood on the Bishop of Lichfield's land.[146] It is probably no coincidence that the incumbent, William Overton, had until 1579 been rector of Balcombe, Sussex, and was therefore familiar with the glass industry.[147] Part of this area was known as Blore (i.e. Blower) Park, and not far away were the probable sites of two more furnaces. The Bishop's Wood structure was a typical four-pot furnace well built of solid stonework, and from its vicinity came window-glass and a number of the characteristic pushed-in beaker bases (p. 87), bottle necks and a handle.[148] In 1585 Edward Hensey is recorded as moving from Bishop's Wood to Blithefield on the Bagot estates, some twenty miles to the west, and in June of that year Ambrose Hensey made an agreement with Richard Bagot; the latter to build a glasshouse in Bagot's Park and to supply fuel, the former to provide his own clay (for pot-making), ash for the batches, etc.[149] Land clearance in Bagot's Park during 1965 revealed at least fifteen furnaces, of which one was excavated in 1966 (p. 78). This site probably antedated 1550 but none of the others could be excavated.[150] We therefore do not know what types of glass Ambrose or Edward Hensey made on the Bagot estates. Edward Hensey finally moved back to Wisborough Green in the Weald, having married Sara Thietry (Tittery) at Eccleshall in 1602, concluding his peripatetic career by returning to work and to die at Oldswinford, near Stourbridge, in 1621.[151] These Henseys were succeeded at Bagot's Park by yet another, Jacob, who moved there after 1607, remaining until 1615, when he was tempted to take up Mansell's employ at Wollaton. There he joined John Squire, a vessel-glass maker who had himself worked in Bishop's Wood until 1612 (below). He was probably the 'Jacob Hensey gent.' mentioned in the Wisborough Green records in 1599, and possibly the Jacob Hensey employed by Mansell at Newcastle upon Tyne in 1619.[152] The careers of these Henseys, mainly centred on Staffordshire, demonstrate their readiness to uproot themselves to follow their calling. Of their glass we unfortunately know nothing.

When the Henseys moved from Bishop's Wood, the Du Houx and the Bigos perhaps moved in from Cheswardine, Shropshire, to replace them.[153] The John Squire at Wollaton in 1615 appears to have worked previously with Abraham Bigo in north Staffordshire[154] and 'John Esq. glassmaker' is certainly recorded in the Eccleshall registers in 1600.[155] All these men were vessel-glass makers, and it may well be they who made the Blore Park glasses.

By 1612 another Lorrainer turns up in Kingswinford, near Stourbridge, in the person of Paul Tysack, possibly the son of John Tysack of Ewhurst, Surrey, and therefore also reared in the Weald.[156] Paul Tysack was essentially a 'broad glass' worker, and little or no vessel-glass of this period has apparently been found in the Stourbridge area.

In Lancashire our earliest record occurs in the Ormskirk parish register: 'A stranger slayne by one .of the glassemen beinge a ffrenchman then working at Bycarstaffe and bur(ied) 10 Dec 1600.' A site discovered at Bickerstaffe Hall farm, near Ormskirk, is probably that of the glasshouse concerned, and the vessel-glass found there was wholly in line with the Lorrainer types (pp. 87 ff.).[157] More important is the site of the Denton glasshouse, south-east of Manchester, almost certainly worked by Isaac Du Houx from at latest 1616, when the birth of his daughter is recorded in the Stockport parish register. By 1618 Du Houx was already a man of some substance and seems to have remained in the district until at least 1636, when the birth of another daughter is recorded. Du Houx appears to have run Denton as Mansell's lessee from 1621, the furnace showing every sign of having been coal-fired, the earliest so far discovered. Its fine-quality glass will be discussed later (pp. 89–91).[158]

A number of other Western sites furnish proof of glass manufacture. Ruyton-Eleven-Towns, near Shrewsbury, has produced (apart from window-glass) the pushed-in bases of beakers, knopped stems, mould-blown fragments and tubing. Comparable fragments were found at another site two miles distant, and a third local site is mentioned in a document dated 1602. Near Congleton, Cheshire, crucible fragments, a pushed-in base, mould-blown fragments and muff window-glass have been found. Lastly, work on the Kenilworth bypass motorway in 1970–1 revealed two probable glasshouse sites, one in Glasshouse Wood and a second nearby.[159]

In the North Riding of Yorkshire two glasshouses have been excavated near Hutton-le-Hole – one at Hutton Common, the other in the Rosedale Valley. Magnetic dating, coins and pottery suggested dates for both in the last quarter of the sixteenth century. The glass found at both sites is very similar, and fits well into the framework of types which it is now time to discuss.[160]

William Harrison in his *Description of England* (1577) wrote: 'The poorest also will have glass if they may; but sith the Venetian is somewhat to deere for them they content themselves with such as are made at home of ferne and burned stone.' The very idea of the lower orders drinking from glass vessels was probably revolutionary at this period, and when in 1615 the use of wood fuel for glass-making was forbidden the proclamation ran: '. . . it were the lesse evill to reduce the times unto the ancient manner of drinking in Stone (i.e. stoneware)' (p. 75). The reason why common green drinking-glasses are not found before the mid-sixteenth century is probably that they did not exist. When 'the poorest' did create a demand for glass drinking-vessels, it was to the Continent that glass-makers turned for models. Harrison refers to 'our wine and our beere', and for the former the stemmed Venetian goblet obviously set the standard; for the latter, the German cylindrical beaker offered a readily available prototype (Pl. 17a). Frequent reference has already been made to the beaker with pushed-in foot, the robust foot being probably the commonest find on any glass-house site of about 1600. It was made by pushing in the convex base of the paraison to form a concave re-entrant within the body of the glass, the double layer thus formed being worked into a pedestal foot of double thickness, the entrapped air keeping the rim-fold hollow (fig. 14).[161] The one-piece manner of working has ancient origins, and was used for making tall, narrow cylindrical drinking-glasses as early as the fourteenth century in Central Europe.[162] The Lorraine glass-makers, whose origins appear to have been in Bohemia, may have inherited this one-piece habit of working, which they practised with a skill in no way inferior to that of the Venetians in their own genre. The tall Bohemian glass seems to have evolved into the shorter *Keulenglas* (club glass) of sixteenth-century Germany, which retains the characteristic slightly inward sloping rim.[163] Sir Hugh Platt, in the *Jewell House of Art and Nature* (1594), specifies for one of his experiments: 'Take a Beer glasse of six or eight inches in height and being of one equal bigness from the bottom to the top', obviously the norm for a cylindrical beer-glass (Pl. 17a). Fortunately, one such glass has been preserved (Pl. 17c). It is of pale green glass, made in the one-piece technique, and stands 18.25 cm (7¼ in.) high, neatly between the limits specified by Platt. A number of other fragmentary beer-glasses found in London show the same incurving mouth.[164] This rim is fairly commonly found on glasshouse sites – Woodchester,[165] Blore Park,[166] and particularly at Hutton and Rosedale.[167] It also occurs at the late Wealden site of Sidney Wood.[168] Wrythen mould-blown ribbing is everywhere the commonest form of decoration.

A second type of beaker with pushed-in base co-existed with the cylindrical glass just described. It has become familiar from numer-ous reconstructions made by Messrs Powells some time before 1923, based on fragments found at Woodchester.[169] Their number tends to suggest that this was the main beaker shape of this period. In fact, the Woodchester fragments could not be assembled to give the complete profile of a single glass. The guess was finally

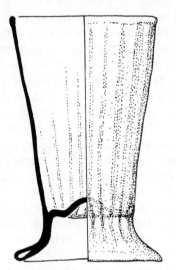

Fig. 14 Beaker, green glass made in one piece and mould-blown with vertical ribbing. From Nonsuch Palace. English; late sixteenth or seventeenth century. Scale approx. ½. Museum of London.

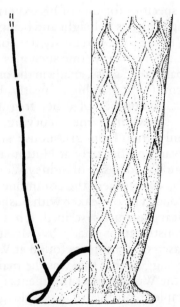

Fig. 15 Beaker, green glass made in one piece and mould-blown with mesh-design. From Hutton, Yorkshire. English; late sixteenth or early seventeenth century. Scale approx. ½. After Crossley and Aberg.

authorised by a virtually intact glass of this shape excavated at the palace of Nonsuch (fig. 14). It too was of vertically ribbed glass, somewhat thicker-waisted than most of Powell's reproductions. Surviving base fragments show that these glasses had many different profiles with feet of varying height. A partially reconstructable beaker at Hutton (fig. 15) showed a wavering profile rising from a base of medium height, suggesting a compromise between the two types. It was decorated with a mould-blown mesh-pattern, and this with dimpling and rib- and flute-moulding (often wrythen) constitutes the commonest ornament on these glasses. The origin of the second beaker type is probably to be sought in France or the Low Countries, where beakers similarly proportioned and decorated are in Belgian collections, often deriving from church treasuries, where they were probably placed as reliquaries. Similar glasses appear in late fifteenth-century Netherlands paintings, and surviving glasses are reasonably dated to before 1550.[170] An example is also to be seen in a mid-sixteenth-century French print showing a glass hawker.[171]

A second main family of more or less cylindrical beaker-glasses is made in a quite different way, aping its betters in crystal glass. The base is slightly kicked, a trail of glass being laid round the basal angle and pressed in the horizontal plane so that the glass will stand flat. In addition the trail was often notched, milled or waved for decoration. Two variant shapes seem to occur, one with a gently flaring rim, the other roughly cylindrical throughout. The first we have already met in crystal glass (p. 63), and the green glass occasionally copies the chequered spiral trail decoration. Examples may be cited from Rosedale,[172] Woodchester,[173] Newent[174] and Denton.[175] The applied notched foot-rim is very common, occurring at Woodchester,[176] St Weonard's,[177] Hutton,[178] Bickerstaffe,[179] and in the Weald at Brookland Farm,[180] Knighton's,[181] etc. An example found at Eccleshall is almost certainly of local manufacture. Not infrequently the foot shows a mould-blown pattern which must have extended overall. At Woodchester certain wall fragments are decorated with raspberry prunts overlying a pair of horizontal applied threads, a type of ornament used on mid-sixteenth-century Venetian-style glass.[182] A raspberry prunt was found at Hutton together with two rosette-like prunts, christened by W. A. Thorpe 'jam tart' motifs, made by nipping out the edge of an applied circular pad.[183] Similar rosettes are known from Blore Park[184] and Rosedale,[185] while Woodchester produced over half a dozen.[186] Comparable motifs occur on German joke-glasses of about 1500.[187]

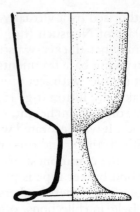

Fig. 16   Goblet, green glass made in one piece. From Hutton, Yorkshire. English; late sixteenth or early seventeenth century. Scale approx. ½ (rim profile reconstructed). After Crossley and Aberg.

Stemmed goblet forms also occur on Lorrainer sites and may equally be regarded as *façon de Venise* glasses in green forest metal. These are executed in the one-piece technique, the pushed-in base being increased in height and narrowed so that sometimes it forms a reasonably tall stem (fig. 16), often with a knop at the top. Such stems are already found in the Weald but are still short, with a depressed globular knop at the top, two examples coming from Sidney Wood at Alfold.[188] At Woodchester[189] and Hutton[190] the goblets lack the knop but are taller, whereas at Denton[191] and Rosedale[192] the Wealden model is followed, with mould-blown ribbing added. These two forms may well have continued side by side into the seventeenth century. They were combined, however, in a number of stems excavated in Oxford and London which are taller, with the knop at the top.[193] Under Mansell the same technique was used in *cristallo* to produce even taller and narrower knopped stems – *tours de force* presumably of English workmen transferring from the green glass to the *cristallo* code.[194] A few examples exist of three-piece goblets clumsily made in green glass with rib-moulded stems.

A notable example of the pedestal-stemmed goblet (Pl. 19d) was included in the Gracechurch Street hoard.[195] It had an apparently cylindrical bowl decorated by four turns of thin threading below which are two thick threads, the lower one dragged down at four points – a decoration of unusual complexity. Fragments of similar glasses at Woodchester[196] suggest for this goblet a date about 1600.

The green drinking-glass was perhaps the main sixteenth-century innovation in the country industry, but there were other new forms too. Among bottles the old Wealden type with roughly hemispherical body and tapering neck, often spirally ribbed, seems to have continued well into the seventeenth century. Their inferior metal suggests that they may have been produced mainly at the more conservative glasshouses. To this essentially medieval flask were added a number of new types. Most interesting, because it emphasised the Lorrainers' continental contacts, is a small flattened bottle with wrythen mould-blown ribbing on a second gather, the top of which is usually visible at the shoulder. The type is known in sixteenth-century Germany,[197] and seems to have been reasonably common in England, intact examples having been found at Oxford (Pl. 18a), Nonsuch Palace and probably also Ipswich. Three examples were found on the *Mary Rose*, which sank in 1545. That it was absorbed into the English repertory seems assured by finds at Woodchester,[198] Blore Park,[199] Rosedale and Hutton.[200]

A further innovation of the later sixteenth century was the hexagonal mould-blown flask (Pl. 18b). Earlier moulds – referred to in glass-makers' wills – were apparently restricted to vertical ribbing, and the new type, which imparted the whole shape to the paraison blown into it, was certainly used in the Weald, where bottle-bases have been found on furnace sites at Sidney Wood, Pickhurst and Brookland Farm;[201] and comparable finds have been made elsewhere, as at Denton,[202] Hutton[203] and Woodchester, where an intact hexagonal bottle came to light (Pl. 18b). The square-section bottles (fig. 17) were probably made to fit in wooden cases with compartments, and neck fragments found at Jamestown in Virginia, a seventeenth-century settlement, have pewter screw-caps ('vices' in the parlance of the time) and were almost certainly from cased sets made for sea travel. In such flasks were transported all sorts of precious liquids unobtainable in the New World – medicaments, toilet preparations and spirits. James Howell, writing to Sir Sackville Trevor in 1625,[204] says, 'I send you my humble thanks for the curious Sea-chest of Glasses you pleas'd to bestow on me.' At this period the word 'glasses' is more likely to refer to bottles than to drinking-glasses, usually specified as such. As to the contents, we find in an inventory of a house at Cockesden in 1610, 'Item, a very fyne seller for wyne, with eight glasses.'[205] Lettice, countess of Leicester, had in her 'Sweete-meate Clossett', in 1634, 'Imprimis, a curious seller for glasses, imbroydred . . .'[206] and an inventory of 1589 mentioned 'thrie glassies to pute rosse [i.e. rose] water in viiid.'[207] At this period case-bottles were fairly small – some 15 cm (6 in.) high – but these dimensions increased, as may be seen in the Dutch genre paintings of the later seventeenth century. Some of these 'squares' have longer necks than others and were probably intended to store liquids on a shelf rather than in a

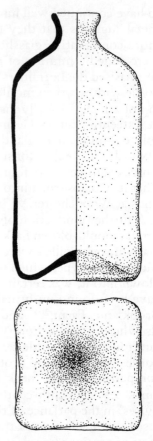

Fig. 17   Case-bottle, green glass blown in
a mould. From Hutton, Yorkshire. English;
late sixteenth or early seventeenth century.
Scale approx. ½ (neck reconstructed).
After Crossley and Aberg.

case (Pl. 17b). A series of four was found at Waltham Abbey in a pit
dating from 1639 or later.[208] It cannot be assumed that all bottles of
these types found in England were of English origin. In 1626 '22
sellers with glass bottles' from Flanders are mentioned in the
Customs records.[209]

These angular bottles have their cylindrical counterparts, and in
this century the cylindrical apothecary's flask, or vial, established
itself and was destined to last well into the nineteenth century (Pl.
18c).[210] At first made of thin green glass, it was translated into
colourless flint glass in the eighteenth century, the two types co-
existing until superseded by the wholly mould-blown medicine
bottles of the mid-nineteenth century. Alongside the 'square' and
the cylindrical vial went the wide-mouthed containers holding
anything from pickles to non-liquid medicaments (fig. 18). Both
cylindrical and rectangular varieties almost certainly derive from

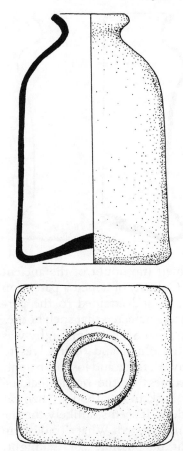

Fig. 18 Square jar, green glass blown in a mould. From Basing House, Hampshire. English; first half of seventeenth century. Scale approx. ½. After Moorhouse (1971).

the pottery *albarello*, sometimes copied exactly, as in a jar from Nonsuch Palace (fig. 19). Narrower cylindrical jars also occur, occasionally lightly ribbed (Pl. 18d), and fragments were found at the Rosedale glasshouse.[211] A Canterbury fragment shows mesh-moulding instead of ribbing. The rectangular wide-mouthed bottle had many continental parallels, such containers being used for drugs, as their labels often reveal. An intact example in sea-green glass (fig. 18) found at Basing House must date from before 1645.[212] Partly to supply the apothecary with his drugs, the manu-facture of distilling equipment (pp. 36–7) naturally continued without abatement throughout the seventeenth century (Pl. 19b, c).

Far more important than the miscellaneous types described was an entirely new kind of bottle made of dark, almost black, thick glass for the storage and transport of beverages – wine, beer and cider (Pl. 19a). This was 'the English bottle'. Its origin has been

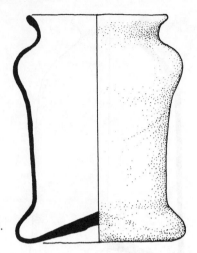

Fig. 19   Drug-jar *(albarello)*, green
glass. From Nonsuch Palace. English;
seventeenth century. Scale approx. ½.
Museum of London.

contested. When, in 1661, John Colnett (no doubt of the ancient
Netherlands glass-making family of Colinet) obtained a patent on
the grounds that he had 'invented . . . and attained to the perfection of making glass bottles', his peers objected that such bottles
had been in public use for thirty years; that Sir Kenelm Digby was
the first inventor and had employed Colnett and themselves to
make them. Colnett offered no effective defence and lost his patent,
which argues for the general correctness of the bottle-makers'
case.[213] Thirty years takes the story back to the 1630s, when Sir
Robert Mansell was firmly in the saddle. It seems unlikely that he
would have left such infringements uncontested. What a tradesman
could not attempt, however, might be possible for a knight.
Furthermore, as a sailor, Sir Robert could not but have approved,
however grudgingly, of Sir Kenelm's victory over the combined
French and Venetian fleets at Scanderoon in 1628. Their relationship was not cordial, however, despite a common dislike of the
Duke of Buckingham. In 1633 Sir Kenelm, on the death of his wife,
had gone into retirement for two years; and it was possibly during
this period that he experimented with the making of stronger kinds
of bottle. He had an enquiring mind and was to become a founder
of the Royal Society, which concerned itself much with glass. He
spent his years of retirement at Gresham College, where the natural
sciences were cultivated, and had as a friend James Howell, who
could have advised him on coal-burning furnaces and put him in
touch with working glass-makers. In some of his recipes, published posthumously as *The Closet of the Eminently Learned Sir
Kenelm Digby opened* (1669), he showed specific interest in the bottl-

ing of fermenting liquids, particularly metheglyn, or mead, for which he shared an enthusiasm with James Howell. He advised readers to 'draw it into Glass-bottles', and recommended that the bottles be stopped 'close with Cork tied in'. The Civil War no doubt obscured the early development of this invention, and it is difficult to trace it much before 1650. Two bottles are known which must have been made before 1651,[214] and in this year 'two doussen glasse bottles of the best Canary Dick Weeden hath' were sent by carrier from Berkhamsted in Hertfordshire to Kent, showing that the bottles were of glass tough enough to withstand such a journey.[215]

From now on it was customary to put on a bottle an applied pad with the owner's mark (Pl. 19a), often with a date, and these welcome indications have made possible a typology of the 'beverage' bottle from 1660 onwards (figs 20, 21). We learn from his *Diary* that in 1663 Pepys 'went to Mr. Rawlinson's and saw some of my new bottles, made with my crest upon them, filled with wine, about five or six dozen.'[216] This was a small number – the contemporary Earl of Bedford ordered the best part of 700 bottles a year for twenty years from 1671 onwards[217] – but it supports the assumption that already wine was being laid down in bottle.

The technique of corking bottles had long since evolved in England. Sir Hugh Platt in his *Delights for Ladies* (1602) had recommended that beer should be bottled when ten or twelve days old, so as to let the ferment settle a little, 'making your corks very fit for the bottles (perhaps of salt-glazed stoneware) and stop them close.' Another author, Gervase Markham, in his *The English Hus-wife* (1615), adds that the corks should be 'tied in with pack-thread'. Pack-thread continued in use for bottling mineral waters until the early nineteenth century, but for bottled ale it tended to be replaced in the eighteenth century by brass wire. Both thread and wire were secured to the string rim, a thread of glass lapped round below the bottle-rim, thus also strengthening the neck against the pressure of the cork. The ultimate development of the corked bottle, with the cork driven home flush, depended on the invention of the corkscrew. The first mention of such an implement, which was called a 'bottle-screw' in the eighteenth century, occurs in 1681 – 'a Steel Worme used for the drawing of *Corks* out of *Bottles*' (N. Grew, *Musaeum Regalis Societatis*).[218] It may reasonably be supposed that the invention antedated by some years its first recorded mention.

The 'English bottle' soon had an enormous international success, since it allowed the storage and maturing of wine in bottle. Being

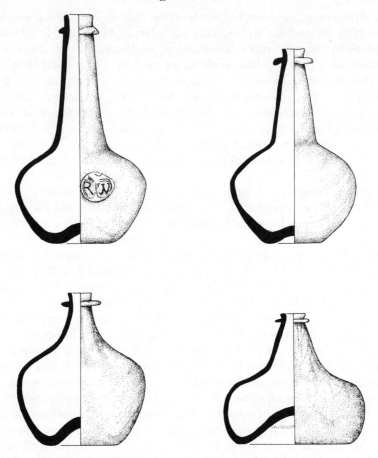

Fig. 20   Type series of dark green bottles showing changes between about
1650 and 1715: (a) before 1652; (b) *c.* 1655–65; (c) *c.* 1675–90; (d) *c.* 1685–1715.
Scale approx. ½. After Hume (1961).

not only robust but almost black, it protected wine from the
destructive effects of light. These qualities naturally recommended
themselves in wine-growing countries, and Savary des Bruslons in
his *Dictionnaire Universel de Commerce* (1723 ed.) comments that the
wicker-covered flask was being supplanted by 'les bouteilles de
gros verre'. Throughout the eighteenth century the French strove
to imitate the English dark bottle and the coal-burning furnace
which made it possible. Alongside the new English crystal glass
(pp. 109, ff.) the dark glass bottle formed the spearhead of the
English penetration of continental markets, making England for
the first time a net exporter of glass.[219]

When Charles II returned to England in 1660 the framework of the glass industry created by Sir Robert Mansell (d. 1656) had been broken. Green glass probably continued to be made throughout the interregnum, but the demand for luxury glass was presumably not so great – 'Many people regarded fine crystal as a relic of royalty . . . Many more confused wine-glasses with drunkenness.'[220] Nevertheless, Cromwell found it worthwhile to tax 'Venice drinking Glasses' at the rate of 4s a dozen, and it may be that the country's requirements were mainly imported.[221] With the Restor-

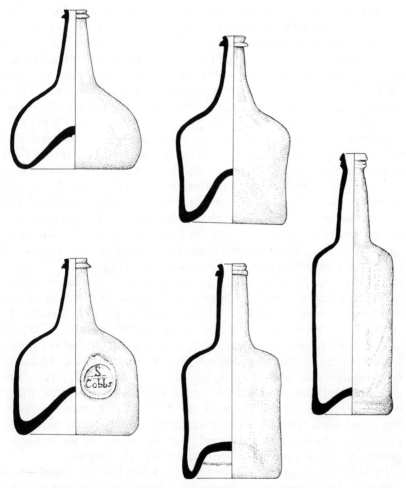

Fig. 21 Type series of dark green bottles showing changes between about 1710 and 1800: (a) *c*. 1710–30; (b) *c*. 1730–45; (c) *c*. 1740–60; (d) *c*. 1750–70; (e) 1770–1800. Scale approx. ¼. After Hume (1961).

ation, however, there was an upsurge of demand for luxuries, not least for those with which the King's companions in exile had become familiar on the Continent. Glass-makers were available to meet the need, but capital was essential and money short. The ideally placed capitalist emerged in the person of George, 2nd Duke of Buckingham (1628–87), probably the richest man in England and intermittently the King's favourite. The age of monopolies, however, was over and the Duke proceeded more circumspectly than Sir Robert Mansell would have been content to do.

Three months after Charles's return on 18 August 1660 he entered into an agreement with one John de la Cam, 'one of the Councellors and Master Doctors Ordinary to the King of Ffrance', to set up a manufacture of 'Christall De roach or Venice Christall' for a period of ten years. The Duke was to provide Rutland House in the Charterhouse Yard as the site of the glasshouse, and pay for building and workmen's wages up to a maximum of £6,000. Furthermore, he would obtain a patent from the King to exclude competitors. De la Cam, for his part, undertook to pay 6 per cent per annum interest on half the capital for three years, and to refund half the initial outlay over the same period; on signature of the agreement he would 'discover unto the said Duke of Buckingham . . . the Art and Mistery of melting of Christall Deroach . . . and all other his Art and Skill therein.'[222] No further details of this glasshouse are known, although it seems extremely likely, in view of the subsequent history of patents for crystal glass, that Buckingham did in fact obtain his privilege. By 1668, however, de la Cam had taken over management of a glasshouse in Nijmegen,[223] and he had almost certainly left the Duke's employ years earlier, probably before the end of 1661. In November of that year a licence was apparently granted to Martin Clifford and Thomas Paulden for the exercise of their 'Arte skill and invention of makeing Christall Glasse' for a term of fourteen years. This was confirmed as a patent a year later.[224] Martin Clifford was a crony of the Duke of Buckingham and helped him in his literary endeavours. It is significant that he became Master of the Charterhouse, where the glasshouse was presumably located, in 1671.[225] He was no doubt Buckingham's front man in this enterprise, Paulden being the practising glass-maker presumably making use of de la Cam's processes. Their nominee status emerges in the sequel.

In 1663 Buckingham applied to the King for a renewal of *his* patent and its extension to cover the manufacture of mirror-plate. The Attorney General reported on 20 July 1663 that there was no objection, and on 4 August the King announced his will and

PLATE 17

a. Satirical print, 'A New Yeare's Guift for Shrews', engraved by Thomas Cecill. English; about 1630. In the bottom right-hand corner the husband drinks from a tall cylindrical beer-glass. B.M.

b. Frontispiece (details) of *The Workes of that famous Chirurgion Ambrose Parey . . .*, London, 1634, engraved by Thomas Cecill. View of an apothecary's shop and distilling equipment. B.M.

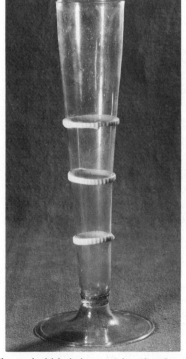

. Beaker, pale green bubbled glass, with ould-blown diaper of dots, and pushed-in ot. From Honey Lane Market, Cheapside, ondon. English (probably London); about 600. H. 18.5 cm (7½ cm). Museum of London.

d. Flute, bubbled brownish-colourless glass with applied and notched horizontal ribbing of opaque-white glass. English (probably London) or Scottish; first half of seventeenth century. H. 26 cm (10¼ in.). Royal Scottish Museum.

PLATE 18

a. Flask, of flattened section, pale green glass with wrythen mould-blown ribbing on a second gather. Allegedly excavated in Oxford. English; late sixteenth or early seventeenth century. H. 11 cm (4⅜ in.). V.A.M.

b. Hexagonal mould-blown bottle, pale green glass. Found on the site of the Woodchester glasshouse, Gloucestershire, and probably made there; about 1600. H. 14 cm (5½ in.). Gloucester City Museum & Art Gallery.

c. Phials, pale green glass. English; probably seventeenth century. H. of tallest 17 cm (6¾ in.). V.A.M.

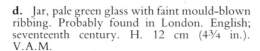

d. Jar, pale green glass with faint mould-blown ribbing. Probably found in London. English; seventeenth century. H. 12 cm (4¾ in.). V.A.M.

PLATE 19

a. Bottle, thick dark green glass, with seal of a king's head (inn name); initials 'R M P' for the owner and his wife, and date 1657. Found at Wellingborough. English; 1657. H. 23 cm (9 in.). Central Museum & Art Gallery, Northampton.

b. Cucurbit, green glass. Found at Chester. English (perhaps Cheshire); probably seventeenth century. H. 28.5 cm (11¼ in.). Grosvenor Museum, Chester.

c. Alembic head, green glass. Found at Eccleshall Castle, Staffs. English (perhaps Staffordshire); probably seventeenth century. H. 13 cm (5⅛ in.). L. of spout 13.5 cm (5⅜ in.). Stafford and Mid-Staffordshire Archaeological Society, Stafford.

d. Goblet, green glass with pushed-in foot and applied decoration. From Gracechurch Street, London. English; about 1600. H. 14 cm (5½ in.). Museum of London.

PLATE 20

a. *Roemer, cristallo* with diamond-point engraving of the four 'Seasons' and inscriptions WᴴE with a wreath, and 'August the 18th, 1663'. Probably English (perhaps the Duke of Buckingham's glasshouse, London or Greenwich); 1663. H. 22.5 cm (8⅞ in.). B.M.

b. The 'Scudamore' (or 'Chesterfield') flute, *cristallo* with diamond-point engraving of the Royal Arms of England, the Scudamore arms, swags of fruit, trees (? apple trees) and 'S' repeated. Probably English (perhaps the Duke of Buckingham's glasshouse, London or Greenwich); mid-seventeenth century. H. 37 cm (14½ in.). Museum of London.

c. The 'Royal Oak' goblet, *cristallo* with diamond-point engraving of the Royal Arms of England, King Charles II in the Boscobel Oak, and portraits of him and his Queen, Catherine of Braganza; the Royal Arms of England and date 1663. Probably English (perhaps the Duke of Buckingham's glasshouse, London or Greenwich); 1663. H. 14.5 cm (5¾ in.). Philadelphia Museum of Art.

d. (?) Sack-glass, *cristallo* with hollow-blown stem of human masks, and diamond-point engraving of bird and vine-scroll, with inscription: 'Sᴰᴹ DRINK AND BE SOBER. 1663'. Probably English (perhaps the Duke of Buckingham's glasshouse, London or Greenwich); 1663. H. 15.4 cm (6⅛ in.). Corning Museum of Glass.

PLATE 21

a. Wine-glass, *cristallo*. Found in Dordrecht. Venetian or Netherlandish; about 1670, but of a type current in contemporary England. H. 11.2 cm (4½ in.). V.A.M.

b. Double-cruet (foot missing), *cristallo*. Found in London. Venetian or English; about 1670. H. 17 cm (6⅝ in.). Museum of London.

c. Beaker, *cristallo*, with mould-blown decoration. Found in Cannon Street, London. Probably English; about 1670. H. 7.4 cm (2⅞ in.). Museum of London.

PLATE 22

a. Posset-pot, clear lead-crystal, with mould-blown decoration and raven's head seal. From Wentworth Woodhouse, Yorkshire. Probably 1677–8. H. 8.5 cm (3⅜ in.). Toledo Museum of Art, Ohio.

b. Posset-pot, clear lead-crystal, with mould-blown decoration and raven's head seal. From Wentworth Woodhouse. Probably 1677–8. H. 8.5 cm (3⅜ in.). Pilkington Glass Museum, St Helen's.

c. Posset-pot, clear lead-crystal, with mould-blown decoration on a second gather, and raven's head seal. Probably 1677–8. H. 7 cm (2¾ in.). Fitzwilliam Museum, Cambridge.

d. Bowl, crizzled lead-crystal, with diamond-point engraving. Crest and (on reverse) coat-of-arms of Butler Buggin, of North Cray, Kent, impaled with those of his wife Winifred Burnett (married 17 July 1676). Probably 1676. H. 9.8 cm (3⅞ in.). V.A.M.

All probably Savoy glasshouse of George Ravenscroft.

PLATE 23

a. Bowl, crizzled lead-crystal, with mould-blown and applied decoration, and raven's head seal. About 1677. D. 24.1 cm (9½ in.). V.A.M.

b. Bowl and stand, crizzled lead-crystal, with mould-blown and applied decoration, and raven's head seal. About 1677. D. of bowl 17.8 cm (7 in.). Fitzwilliam Museum, Cambridge.

c. Bottle, crizzled lead-crystal with mould-blown ribbing NDW and applied decoration, and raven's head seal. About 1677. H. 20.3 cm (8 in.). B.M.

d. *Roemer*, crizzled lead-crystal with mould-blown and applied decoration, and raven's head seal. About 1677. H. 16.5 cm (6½ in.). V.A.M.

All probably Savoy glasshouse of George Ravenscroft.

PLATE 24

a. *Roemer*, clear lead-crystal, with mould-blown, applied and diamond-point engraved decoration, and raven's head seal. Probably engraved to celebrate the visit to Danzig of King John III Sobieski in 1677–8. H. 27.3 cm (10¾ in.). Muzeum Narodowe, Warsaw.

b. *Roemer*, crizzled lead-crystal, with mould-blown ribbing NDW on body, applied decoration, and raven's head seal. About 1677. H. 18.5 cm (7¼ in.). Corning Museum of Glass.

c. Jug, crizzled lead-crystal, with mould-blown and applied decoration, and raven's head seal. About 1677. H. 22.8 cm (9 in.). Cecil Higgins Art Gallery, Bedford.

d. Vase, crizzled blue lead-glass, with mould-blown ribbing NDW on body and applied decoration. About 1676–80. H. 21.5 cm (8½ in.). Toledo Museum of Art, Ohio.

(a)–(c) probably and (d) possibly made in George Ravenscroft's Savoy glasshouse.

PLATE 25

a. Tankard, crizzled lead-crystal with mould-blown decoration, applied silver mount, and raven's head seal. Probably Savoy glasshouse of George Ravenscroft; about 1677. H. 9 cm (3½ in.). V.A.M.

b. Posset-pot, crizzled lead-crystal, with 'S' seal. From Ham House. London; about 1680. H. 8.5 cm (3⅜ in.). Fitzwilliam Museum, Cambridge.

c. *Roemer*, crizzled lead-crystal, with 'S' seal. London; about 1680. H. 19.5 cm (7¾ in.). Barry Richards Collection.

d. Bottle, crizzled purple lead-glass, with mould-blown ribbing NDW on body. London (perhaps Savoy glasshouse of George Ravenscroft); about 1680. H. 16 cm (6¼ in.). V.A.M.

PLATE 26

a. *Left,* sweetmeat with mould-blown ribbing and applied threading; *centre,* tankard with mould-blown ribbing; *right,* posset-pot with mould-blown ribbing and diamond-point decoration. All lead-crystal and about 1680–90. H. of sweetmeat 12 cm (4¾ in.). V.A.M.

b. Three drinking-glasses, lead-crystal with mould-blown ribbing, those to left and right with applied pincered decoration. About 1685–90. H. of right-hand glass 17.2 cm (6¾ in.). V.A.M.

PLATE 27

a. Three goblets, lead-crystal with mould-blown ribbing (NDW on two, which also have applied tooled threading and raspberry prunts). Two have dated coins in the hollow stems: centre, 1680; right, 1684. About 1685–90. H. of centre glass 27.9 cm (11 in.). V.A.M. (*centre* and *right*); Barry Richards Collection (*left*).

b. Two ale-glasses and a small *Roemer*, lead-crystal with mould-blown decoration. About 1690–1700. H. of centre glass 15 cm (5⅞ in.). V.A.M.

PLATE 28

a. Decanter-jug, lead-crystal with mould-blown and applied decoration. About 1685–90. H. 29.2 cm (11½ in.). Ashmolean Museum, Oxford.

b. *Roemer*, lead-crystal with mould-blown ribbing and applied raspberry prunts. Late seventeenth century. H. 24.6 cm (9¾ in.). Merseyside County Museums.

c. *Roemer*-type wine-glass, lead-crystal with mould-blown ribbing and a coin of 1670 in the hollow stem. Late seventeenth century. H. 14 cm (5½ in.). Dr L. H. B. Light.

d. Pocket-flask, lead-crystal with mould-blown ribbing NDW, and applied and tooled decoration. Late seventeenth century. H. 15 cm (5⅞ in.). Ashmolean Museum, Oxford.

PLATE 29

a. Posset-glass and cover. H. 27.5 cm (10⅞ in.). Fitzwilliam Museum, Cambridge.

b. Goblet. H. 26.8 cm (10⁹⁄₁₆ in.). Corning Museum of Glass.

c. Punch-bowl and cover. H. 39.5 cm (15½ in.). Castle Museum & Art Gallery, Nottingham.

d. (?) Posset-glass. H. 16.2 cm (6⅜ in.). Cecil Higgins Art Gallery, Bedford.

All lead-crystal with mould-blown ribbing and applied tooled ornament. Late seventeenth century.

PLATE 30

Goblet and cover, lead-crystal with mould-blown ribbing NDW, and applied tooled ornaments. Late seventeenth century. H. 58.5 cm (23 in.). Museum of London.

PLATE 31

a. *Left,* wine-glass (foot restored in metal), lead-crystal with four-lobed stem and cold-painted decoration; *centre,* wine- or beer-glass, purple lead glass with four-lobed stem and cold-painted inscription: 'God Bless King William and Queen Mary'. About 1690; *right,* tankard, brown glass with applied thread-decoration. Late seventeenth century. H. of centre glass 12 cm (4¾ in.). V.A.M.

b. Tankard, opaque-white glass with applied threading. Late seventeenth century. H. 9 cm (3½ in.). V.A.M.

c. Mug, opaque-white glass with applied threading and silver rim. Late seventeenth century. H. 8.2 cm (3¼ in.). V.A.M.

PLATE 32

a. Three goblets, lead-crystal. *Left,* inverted baluster and bowl inscribed in diamond-point: 'God bless Queen Ann'; *centre,* inscribed in diamond-point: 'Sʳ (or Sᶦ) Simon Boosington'); *right,* hollow bulb enclosing coin of 1690. About 1690–1710. H. of centre glass 38 cm (15 in.). V.A.M.

b. *Left,* dram-glass with acorn-knop, inscribed in diamond-point: 'Take a dram, Old Boy'; *centre,* wine-glass with bowl wheel-engraved with arms of Burton, of Hotham Hall; *right,* cordial- or wine-glass with inverted baluster stem. All lead-glass. *Left* and *right,* about 1700–20; *centre,* about 1720–30. H. of centre glass 18 cm (7 in.). V.A.M.

pleasure that 'upon surrender of a grant made by Vs unto Martin Clifford & Tho. Powlden, Esq[res] of the benefitt of their Invencõn for the making of Cristall Glasse' a grant should be made to Thomas Tils(t)on, a London merchant, 'not only of the sole makeing & venting of the said Cristall glasse, but also of looking Glasse plates of all sorts of glasse w[t]soever', for fourteen years. This was confirmed on 4 September[226] and converted into a patent on 19 October.[227] That Tilson was now Buckingham's nominee is substantiated by a later document of 1676, in which John Bellingham (see below) averred that about 1671 the Duke '(did) informe and assure your said Orator Bellingham that he had a patent from his Ma[tye] that now is granted to him in the name of Thomas Tillison *(sic)* for the sole making the said glasse plates.' It is certainly no coincidence that on 25 July 1664 a proclamation forbidding the importation of glass-plates was published,[228] while on the very same day the articles of incorporation of the Glass Sellers' Company (pp. 103–4) included the clause 'Provision made for saving the rights and privileges of one Thomas Tilson . . . Maker of Christall Glasses who holds Letters Patents *(sic)* of the King.'[229]

The Duke of Buckingham had a factory for mirror-plate in Vauxhall from before 1671, when Bellingham began work as manager there, and it may well have been to this establishment 'lately set up at his expense' that fifty bags of saltpetre were delivered by the Navy Commissioners of Ordnance in 1666.[230] Since in this period the Vauxhall glasshouse was the only one legally making mirror-plates, we may reasonably assume that it was founded not later than 1663, the year of the Buckingham–Tilson patent. When the question of a renewal of the import ban on mirror-plates – apparently lifted in 1668 – was raised again in 1669–70, it was stated that there was 'but one Glas house in England that makes plates for Looking glasses and he has a pattent for it [sic].'[231] Between March 1671 and about April 1674 John Bellingham ran the factory on the Duke's account, as we know from a suit in Chancery which he brought against Buckingham in 1676.[232] Bellingham was a specialist in making mirrors by the blown process, having previously worked in two Dutch glasshouses devoted to this manufacture: at Haarlem in 1666–7 and at Amsterdam *c.* 1669–70.[233]

In June 1674 the Venetian representative in London reported that George Ravenscroft (pp. 109 ff.) 'has maintained here in London for severall months one Pietro Rossetti, a native of Murano, a master manufacturer of mirrors, intending to open a furnace in partnership with him. But fearing the issue he has given this up and Rossetti is now going to France.'[234] It was this man who has been traditionally associated with the Duke of Buckingham at Vauxhall, the dates being variously given as 1670 or 1673.[235] Both Bellingham and Rossetti were essentially experts in the plate-glass business, although Bellingham in Haarlem also had a contract for drinking-glasses, and there is no suggestion in the documents that anything other than plate-glass was made at Vauxhall, which continued in the same line into the eighteenth century. On 19 September 1676 Evelyn visited Lambeth and recorded in his diary: 'We also saw the *Duke of Buckinghams* Glasse worke, where they made huge *Vasas* of mettal as cleare & pondrous & thick as Chrystal, also *Looking-glasses* far larger & better than any that come from *Venice.*' The large vases were undoubtedly the great cylinders of glass used for making plate by the muff process.

The year 1674 seems to have been a bad one for the trade, the Glass Sellers resolving that 'the trade had grown very low and the only way to better and advance the same was to get a prohibition of all wrought looking glasses.' The Venetian representative reported in July that the Duke 'has now sold it (i.e. his furnace for mirrors) to his creditors';[236] and George Ravenscroft is known to have entered into an agreement with Buckingham in 1675, employing a man named Benjamin Baker, who had a long history in the plate-glass industry.[237] This no doubt lies behind Bellingham's com-plaint that 'the said Baker and one Ravenscroft having sett up glasse houses for makeing such sorte of glasse as aforesaid (i.e. plate) did make greate quantities thereof and sold the same to your Orator Bellingham's damage', while the Duke did nothing to enforce his patent. It may have been at this point that the Duke relinquished control of Vauxhall, two years or so before the expiry of his patent due on 19 October 1677.

Since there is no evidence that drinking-glasses were made at Vauxhall, it seems likely that the duke exploited that side of his double patent – after the departure of de la Cam – in a glasshouse at Greenwich. On 10 June 1673 Evelyn again is a witness: 'Thence to the *Italian Glasse-house* at Greenewich, where was Glasse blowne of finer mettal, than that of *Muran* &c.' It is constantly averred in the literature that this glasshouse was founded by the Duke of Buckingham, though without evidence cited, but it seems likely enough and hard fact may underlie the myth.

There are at least three important mid-seventeenth-century glasses which have a serious claim to be of English origin. All are decorated with the diamond-point. Possibly the earliest is the 'Scudamore' flute-glass (Pl. 20b), decorated with the Royal Arms within the Garter ribbon. On the reverse are the arms of Scudamore (gules, three stirrups leathered and buckled or) on a lozenge-shaped escutcheon, normally denoting a maiden lady or widow. Connecting these two armorial devices are swags of fruit and flowers, while the middle section of the flute is occupied by four trees, three having a blighted aspect while the fourth is in full leaf. Below this is the letter 'S' repeated three times, no doubt for Scudamore. There are two possible lines of descent for this glass, but since it was formerly owned by the Earls of Chesterfield and is often called the 'Chesterfield flute', it more probably came down in the family of Sir James Scudamore of Holme Lacey in Hereford-shire, whose daughter Mary married Sir Giles Bridges of Wilton in 1622. Their descendant Catherine, eldest daughter of John Brydges, married Edwin Francis Stanhope in 1753. From them descended the Scudamore–Stanhope line, of which the Earls of Chesterfield were head.[238] The flute is distinctive in shape, with a short stem composed of a ribbed bulb between mereses. It has been suggested that it might be of Netherlands origin, brought in at the Restoration, but in fact the Netherlands glass of this type almost invariably has a hollow-blown inverted baluster for a stem, as may be seen from the large number surviving in Dutch collections, as well as from numerous representations in Dutch paintings, like those by Hendrick ter Brugghen (1588–1629), David Bailly (dated 1651), Jan Steen (dated 1666), and others. It has not been possible to identify a single example with a spherical knop. In England, how-ever, the vertically ribbed knop had been familiar from Verzelini's time, was common during the Mansell period, and is a constantly recurring feature about 1670 (pp. 104–5). The general proportions of the Scudamore flute, moreover, differ from those of the Netherlands flutes, but are seen again in William Dobson's painting, 'Prince Rupert and Col. Murray persuading Col. Russell to rejoin the Royalist cause'.[239] It must be conceded that a very similar glass appears in a painting by Velasquez[240] and both glasses might indeed have been Venetian exports. Certainly glasses resembling the Netherlands flutes were in use in England, for a fragmentary example was found in a house at Waltham Abbey which was prob-ably built about 1640. Certain features of this glass suggest that it too is more likely to be of English make.[241] The same cannot be said of the 'Exeter flute', in the Royal Albert Memorial Museum, Exeter, decorated in diamond-point with a bust-portrait of Charles II above an oak spray springing from a sawn-off tree trunk. It is inscribed below the rim 'God Bless King Charles the Second', a feature which might suggest English origin, were it not that a virtually identical flute shows William Prince of Orange, also with an oak spray, but inscribed 'Vive le Prince d'Orange'.[242] This glass has never been considered English, and it would seem to take the Exeter flute with it to Holland. The latter was perhaps made for a member of Charles II's entourage when he embarked at Scheveningen on 24 May 1660.[243] W. A. Thorpe records that twice in 1665 the Royalist Sir Richard Wynne acquired 'King glasses', perhaps comparable glasses engraved with loyalist sentiments.[244]

That glasses were in fact engraved in England is suggested by the accounts of Sir Francis Throckmorton for 14 February 1656/7, when he paid 6d to see the 'Italian that did cut glasses'.[245] That this might refer to a glazier seems improbable, for a glazier's work was commonplace and hardly worth 6d to see, and was unlikely to be practised by an Italian. The engraving of the Scudamore flute shows no particular Netherlands affinities, and the same is true of two further glasses with strong claims to be English.

The first of these, and the more famous, also records a Royal occasion.[246] It is a goblet of brownish soda-glass with a cylindrical bowl and a stem composed – like that of the Scudamore flute – of a ribbed hollow-blown knop (Pl. 20c). The bowl is diamond-point engraved, the front showing the Royal Arms with the date 1663, the reverse the head of Charles II framed by oak leaves above a tree trunk, symbolising the Boscobel oak, as the inscription 'Royal Oak' makes clear. At the sides are the figures of Charles and his consort, Catherine of Braganza, whom he married in May 1662. This extremely unflattering likeness is identified by the inscription 'Reg[ina]', and the bust-portrait of the King on the other side is scarcely more flattering. The rendering of the two main themes, though skilful, seems to bear no particular resemblance to con- temporary Dutch work.

As for the shape of this glass, its stem finds distinct echoes among the goblets of the Mansell era (p. 69), while the combined features of cylindrical bowl and spherical ribbed knop occur again in the Greene drawings (pp. 104–5). By then, probably 1667, the shape may have become somewhat old-fashioned, for very few were ordered. The two versions differ in detail and if the Greene drawing represents the Venetian norm, the Royal Oak glass is perhaps more likely to be English.

The last of the probably English glasses with diamond-point en- graving is the 'Seasons' *Roemer* in the British Museum (Pl. 20a).[247] Of reasonably colourless glass, it has the true *Roemer* characteristic of a hollow cylindrical stem opening directly into the base of the slightly ovoid bowl, but the normal conical foot is here replaced by a spreading pedestal foot. This rare shape is matched on the Continent by at least two examples.[248] Significantly, a fragmentary and much smaller green glass *Roemer* of this shape has been excavated in London.

The British Museum *Roemer* is engraved with four oval panels enclosing bust-figures of the Seasons, Spring and Summer as females with appropriate attributes, Autumn a young man, and Winter an old man. Round the rim, and diverging to fill the spandrels between the panels, is a trail of fruiting vine; and round the foot runs a stag hunt. On the stem are the initials $w^H\text{E}$ and the inscription: 'August the 18th, 1663'. This arrangement of initials, denoting a man and his wife with their joint surname, is common on contemporary English delftware. There is no means of knowing whether decoration and incriptions are by the same hand. The diamond-point engraving is not up to the best Dutch standards, although the subjects probably come from a suite of Netherlands engravings. The hunt subject on the foot is the common property of the age and recurs later on certainly English glasses. The idiosyncrasy of shape, the English inscription, and the absence of anything specifically Dutch in its engraving suggest an English origin for this glass.

Apart from these famous glasses there are a few pieces of this period which can claim consideration as English. The first is a small brownish-colourless wine-glass with hollow-blown stem of addorsed human masks, inscribed in diamond-point, 'Drink and be Sober 1663', the inscription accompanied by an artlessly drawn bird (Pl. 20d). The mask stem is essentially a pre-Civil War feature and it seems possible that the inscription was added to an older glass. Whether it is a Puritan sentiment or an ironical reflection on the capacity of the bowl, there is no means of knowing.

There are a few glasses with cylindrical or hemispherical bowl and hollow-blown dumb-bell stem which have long been tentatively regarded as English.[249] They have neither English inscription nor pedigree, but they appear to have come to light in England and have no obvious continental characteristics. Their generally compact, short-stemmed forms probably locate them in the mid-seventeenth century, when such proportions were apparently in vogue in much of Europe. The engraving seems to be if anything more Venetian than Dutch in style, and it was perhaps something like this that Sir Francis Throckmorton paid 6d to see in 1656/7.

The Restoration period was marked by one development of great moment. This was the granting on 25 July 1664 of a Royal Charter to the Company of Glass Sellers, enrolled in the Chamber of London on 28 September.[250] As already mentioned (p. 83), there had been an abortive attempt in 1635 to create such a body, to control the sale of vessel-glass as the Glaziers' Company controlled the supply of window-glass. The Glass-Sellers' Charter gave them a governing body consisting of Master, two Wardens and twelve Assistants, empowered to enforce standards, levy fines and other punishments on recalcitrant masters, journeymen and apprentices; and above all to 'search for false and deceitful goods.' Order 16 of its bye-Laws[251] was simply headed 'Against pedlars and hawkers', against whom the Company in its early years maintained a remorseless policy of persecution. In 1692 they expended £38 8s 3d 'Payd in Charge of prosecution of Hawkers' and in 1696 a further £30 – by far the largest sums in the Company's accounts at this time.[252]

Already in 1670 a Court minute[253] 'Ordered that 5 of the Court be authorized to treat with all the white Glassmakers about London and to agree upon what terms and prices they will furnish this Company', with a view to obtaining a prohibition on imported glassware. This move probably mirrors a growing confidence and sense of power and common interest on the Company's part which is apparent from a separate source. This is the series of letters written between October 1667 and November 1672 by the London firm of Michael Measey and John Greene (both Company members) to their supplier of glass in Venice (British Library, Sloane Ms 857).[254] John Greene, son of one Glass Seller and father of another, both of the same name, was Renter Warden 1671–2, Upper Warden 1673, and Master 1679. In 1690 he gave the Company a handsome marquetry collecting box ('The Poor's Box'), still extant. Michael Measey was nominated as an Assistant in the original Charter (25 July 1664) and is mentioned thereafter until at least 1668. Their supplier was Allesio (Alvise) Morelli, member of a Murano glassmaking family wealthy enough to possess three ships devoted to their overseas glass trade.[255]

Greene's nine letters to Morelli are accompanied by more than 400 drawings reproducing the shapes of the glasses commissioned and noting quantities. The letters themselves were full of specifications and admonitions to the supplier, such as 'That all the Drinking Glasses bee verij well made . . . as exactelij as possible maij bee to the formes [i.e. drawings] for fashion.' The drawings are mostly extremely repetitive, reproducing drinking-glasses (the larger sizes for beer, the smaller for wines) with round-funnel or conical bowls, the latter most frequently flat-based (Pl. 21a). These are mounted on short stems composed usually of a spherical knop, sometimes vertically ribbed, or a squat baluster or inverted baluster welded to bowl or foot by mereses or short capstan-like forms in a variety of combinations. Departures from this norm are relatively rare. A few shapes are carefully drawn and sometimes annotated in the accompanying letter – large beakers for beer or French wine (Pl. 21c), and small beakers for brandy (sometimes stacked one inside another in a 'nest'); large covered goblets or bowls with decorative handles and finials, for beer or claret; spouted posset-pots; trick-glasses of two kinds; hollow-stemmed *Roemers* with prunts. Rare forms are the flute, of which two dozen were ordered in January 1672; and ·the beaker with flaring lip already discussed (p. 67), an outmoded form of which a mere two dozen 'thick and strong' were ordered in February 1670. Apart from the drinking-glasses there are vases ('flouer pott glasses') of four main shapes, with decorative side handles; largish 'cruets' resembling the vases but without handles, and two-spouted 'gimmel' cruets for oil and vinegar (Pl. 21b).

In his instructions to the hapless Morelli in August 1668 Greene directed that 'the drinking glasses be made . . . exact according to the patterns both for size fashion and number.' There are no indications of sizes in the manuscript, but careful scrutiny reveals that, in fact, they are drawn to scale – beer-glasses about 16.5 to 17.3 cm (6½–6¾ in.) in height, claret-glasses ('for French wines') about 14.5 cm (5¾ in.); and sack-glasses ('for Spanish wine') about 12.7 to 14 cm (5–5½ in.). The same shapes were used in all these sizes, and bowl-forms were combined with stem-forms in a great variety of simple basic elements. Thus in the order of 28 August 1668 items one to twenty consist entirely of beer-glasses (286 dozen), all with flat-based conical bowls normally trimmed round the basal angle with an applied cordon, plain, milled or waved. The stem-formations – all balusters or spherical knops, plain or ribbed, with various combinations of merese – recur several times, but combined with bowls of varying taper, differing decorative cordon, etc., which sustain the variety. In this order forty dozen glasses are shown as covered. Although there are occasional overlaps the drawings show a remarkable diversity within a coherent style. It is striking that so much weight should have been placed on such slight differences. Similar observations apply to the claret and sack glasses, of which 116 and forty-eight dozen respectively were ordered, the ordinary drinking-glasses thus totalling 5,400 items, apart from tumblers and miscellaneous shapes. Loss from breakage and the use of damp packing material (seaweed) cut down actual deliveries considerably. Writing on 17 September 1669 and referring probably to this very consignment, Greene says, '. . . we desire . . . that speciall care bee taken in the . . . well packing them up, for the last wee Recevied from you . . . manij of the Chests weare verij Ill Conditioned for their was above forety dozen broken and some of the chests had Taken watter which does staijne and rott the Glasses.'

Most of these glasses were doubtless in more or less colourless *cristallo*, and any divergence from this rule was normally clearly stated. The quality of the *cristallo*, however, was always a matter for concern, and Greene frequently treats Morelli to his animadversions on this topic. In the letter just quoted, he writes, 'Directions 1st that the drinking glasses be made of verij cleer whit sound mettall', phraseology which he repeats more or less verbatim on 17 September 1669 and 10 February 1671. On 30 November 1671 he is more explicit:

> [I] onlj give order for these that I now send for and that theij be made . . . of verij good cleer whit sound Mettall; for truelj the last you sent me the Mettall was indifferent good and cleer, but not so sound and strong as theij should have bin made; for therin Lies the exelencj of your Venice glasses that they are generallij stronger than ours made heer . . . Therfor S^r I praij take such care that these be made of verij good sound mettall and thicker and stronger than the last.

By January 1672 a new note is discernible. Significantly, the accompanying list contains a new category of glasses. Alongside the thirty dozen 'beer glasses' and the twenty dozen 'Claret (glasses)', 'to be made of exelent good sound mettall', are six dozen each of 'Thick beer' and 'Thick Claret', the accompanying drawings showing the internal profile of the bowl to emphasise the thickness of the bowl-base. They herald a new concept of glass which places solidity above delicacy.

Cristallo, however, was by no means the only kind of glass imported by John Greene. On the drawings accompanying his letter of 10 February 1670 the flower pots (vases) are annotated '1 doz. Calsedonia/1 doz. Speckd enamel/1 doz. all milke whit'. In the letter of 28 August 1668 '1 doz. speckled enamel'd covered beer glasses' and '1 doz. Clouded calsedonia covered beer glasses' had been specified, and it is clear that 'clouded calsedonia' is the Venetian *calcedonio*, an opaque glass incorporating brownish and greenish colours swirled together (clouded) to imitate the natural chalcedony after which it was named. This type of glass was already known in Italy before 1500 (p. 47), and Antonio Neri gives three recipes in his *Art of Glass* (1612). No certainly seventeenth-century example appears to have been excavated in England, but the material continued to be imported until at least the 1740s.

'Speckd enamel' glass admirably describes the opaque-white glass ('enamel') decorated with incorporated blobs and dots of coloured glass – usually blue and red, but occasionally also manganese-purple and yellow – which was fashionable in seventeenth-century Europe.

The drawing sent with Greene's letter dated 10 February 1670 mentions vases 'all milke whit', an obvious reference to the opaque-white glass called in Venice *lattimo*, and made at Murano since the fifteenth century at latest (p. 46). The drawings accompanying Greene's letter of May 1671 include two sketches of vases ('Floure-potts'), one with a cap-cover and perhaps to be identified as a tea-caddy, both inscribed: 'These must be made in your Milk whit glass and Strong.' These opaque glasses were a speciality of certain of the Murano workshops (notably the Miotti glasshouse 'Al Gesù').[256]

Apart from glass vessels, there were large orders for mirror-plates and for strings of beads. It is abundantly clear from these documents that Measey and Greene knew exactly what they wanted, and intended to get it.

When in 1669 members of the Glass-Sellers' Company tried to obtain a prohibition on the import of Venetian mirror-plates (p. 99),[257] they met bitter opposition from the rest of the looking-glass trade – the grinders, polishers, foilers and frame-makers – who readily foresaw what price-fixing under a monopoly would do for their trade. They made play of the fact that home production was insufficient to supply demand – a demand increased by the growing fashion for plate-glass in coach windows. There seems to be no evidence that a prohibition was effected, and John Greene certainly continued throughout to obtain his plates from Venice – until 1673. The petition to obtain a prohibition on imported mirrors was linked with a similar proposal affecting drinking-glasses:

> Concerning prohibiting Venice Drinken glasses every owne that in them knoows the Great difference there is betuene venice glasses and the best made in England yet if the Parliam^t: and ze gentrij of the nation can be satisfyed with English glasses, There is none of ye shopp keepers will oppose it However it will be a Losse to the King in his Customes and a prejudice to the marchants in their returns from those parts.[258]

This reluctant assent from the 'shopp keepers' (i.e. the Glass-Sellers' Company) reveals a conviction that at least adequate supplies, in quantity and quality, would be forthcoming from the English glasshouses. The document is dated December 1670. On 15 November the Company had ordered, 'That 5 of the Court be authorized to treat with all the white glassmakers about London and to agree upon what terms and prices they will furnish this Company . . . in order to obtaining a Prohibition . . . of all sorts of foreign drinking glasses.'[259] On 24 November the Court Minutes record: 'Upon Report made as to foreign drinking glasses It is agreed that the Company do endeavour to obtain a prohibition.'[260] The parallel with the actions of the mirror-makers is precise. Again, however, there is no evidence that a prohibition was ever obtained.

Up to January 1672 John Greene was still ordering his glasses from Morelli. It does appear that in practice the glass merchants turned progressively to domestic suppliers for drinking-glasses; and that these were busy experimenting to improve their metal in the direction of solidity, clarity, brightness and freedom from colour, the qualities which John Greene had constantly demanded. As early as May 1671 he had written, '. . . it will not be mij Interest to send to Venice for neither drinking Glasses nor Lookeing Glasses, for we make now verij Good Drinking Glasses in England and better Lookeing Glasses than anij that comes from Venice.' Girolamo Alberti, Venetian Secretary in England, who in January 1673 had written home: '. . . they cannot . . . get the clearness and strength of venetian crystal', was a year later forced to say, 'They already made crystal glass here in perfection.' In June 1674 he was writing: 'The glass trade also might revive though it now suffers from the extreme beauty of the English drinking glasses. They are very white and thick, in imitation of rock crystal, but very far from real perfection though they strike the eye and surpass those of Venice. In spite of this they are soft, fragile and extremely dear.'[261] With this we are on the threshold of the new era, when the English glass industry was to achieve a pre-eminence which it enjoyed for the next 150 years at least.

CHAPTER 4

The Dominance of Lead-Crystal
(c. 1675–1825)

John Houghton, the economist who produced his series of *Letters for the Improvement of Commerce and Trade* between 1681 and 1703, wrote in his one hundred and ninety-eighth letter, dated 15 May 1696, 'I remember the time when the Duke of Buckingham first encouraged glass plates and Mr. Ravenscroft first made the flint glasses.'[1] Houghton's testimony, given so near the time of the events recorded, and coming from one so interested in economic developments, must be taken very seriously; and indeed there is little occasion to question it. The role of George Ravenscroft, therefore, calls for close scrutiny.

First for the man himself. W. A. Thorpe, in his *History of English and Irish Glass* (1929), identified him as George Ravenscroft of Hawarden in Flintshire (now Clwyd), scion of the Ravenscrofts of Bretton, born in 1618 and deceased in 1681.[2] More recent investigations,[3] however, have suggested that he was almost certainly a

member of the cadet Barnet branch of the family, second son of
James Ravenscroft (d. 1680), who inherited estates at Alconbury in
Huntingdon, and Barnet in Hertfordshire; and others in Essex and
Monmouthshire, apart from a London house in Fetter Lane. A
lawyer like his father, Thomas Ravenscroft, founder of the family's
fortunes, James was also a merchant 'beyond the Seas'. Although
he had been a J.P. for Huntingdon, Oliver Cromwell's own county
and strongly pro-Parliament, James was a Roman Catholic and
stood well with Charles II after the Restoration. His son George
(1632–83) was sent to the English College at Douai in 1643, leaving
in May 1651 to return to England. He evidently engaged in the
Venetian trade, for in 1666 Charles II himself wrote to the Doge of
Venice on behalf of George Ravenscroft and his father, requesting
repayments from the Venetian State Bank of money of which the
Ravenscrofts considered they had been defrauded. This letter
makes clear that 'during his residence in Venice' George had acted
as his father's agent. Girolamo Alberti, Venetian Secretary in
London, referred in 1674 to 'the Englishman Ravenscroft, the one
who resided at Venice for many years where he traded and brought
home a considerable capital.'[4] In the same letter Alberti records that
'George Ravenscroft has received twenty cases (that is, of un-
polished Venetian mirror-plates, illegally imported) by the ship
Success.' He is recorded elsewhere in 1671 as part-owner of a former
Venetian ship, the *Hopewell*,[5] and it is known that his brothers John
and Francis were merchants in Venice. He was apparently engaged
in the trade of currants from the Levant (in which Venice played an
important part) and in 1679–82 was involved in a dispute over
'poynt laces', a Venetian speciality.

Here then was a London merchant deeply involved in the
Venetian trade and having a specific interest in glass. Furthermore, he had a brother, Francis, who is known to have made glass
in the Savoy, the main site of George Ravenscroft's glass-making
activity (see below). There can be little doubt that this is the
George Ravenscroft who is to be credited with the introduction
of 'flint glass' manufacture.

A document of 1677 states that Ravenscroft 'in 1673 built and set
on work a Glass House in the Savoy',[6] and this may have been one
of the 'two new furnaces lately opened for very fine large crystal'
mentioned by Alberti in a dispatch dated 15 September 1673.[7] In
late February or March 1674 Ravenscroft petitioned the King for a
patent for the making of a 'sort of crystalline glass resembling rock
crystal' and this petition was amplified in a minute by the Attorney
General dated 9 March, 'that the glass is of a finer sort and made of

other ingredients than any other glasshouses in England have used, and that the invention may be of considerable public advantage as the glasses thereby made equalize, if not excel, those imported from Venice and France.'[8] The patent was granted for a term of seven years on 16 May 1674,[9] but already on 27 April Ravenscroft had concluded an agreement with the Glass Sellers that they would 'take and buy the said Glasses of Ravenscroft, and . . . Ravenscroft covenanted that he would not at any time during a term of three years keep any more than one furnace with two chairs . . . at work at any one time unless the said Glass Sellers . . . require that more glasses should be made, and it is further agreed that Ravenscroft may in that case set up a Glass House at Henley on Thames with one furnace, two chairs . . .' This indenture was incorporated in another dated 5 September 1674, and it was probably then that the concession regarding a second glasshouse at Henley-on-Thames was made, as the change of tense in the agreement suggests ('it is further agreed').[10] In June Alberti records that 'one Vicenzo, sur-name unknown, has come to London and intends to work there in the furnace of the Englishman Ravenscroft.'[4] This man was prob-ably Vincenzo Pompeio, a Muranese, who later, in 1677, obtained a concession to make crystal glass and mirrors at Antwerp 'd'après des procédés particuliers'.[11] When Ravenscroft did set up his second furnace at Henley-on-Thames (p. 112), his right-hand man there was not a Muranese, but a certain 'Seignior da Costa a Montferratees',[12] that is, of the Duchy of Montferrat, in which was situated the glass-making centre of Altare. Other members of the Da Costa family are known, also identified as Altarists. A certain Baptista da Costa, 'Herr von Barremont', who was associated in a glasshouse in Nijmegen after 1665 may have been the same man as Ravenscroft's employee.[13]

On 13 October 1674 ten members of the Glass-Sellers' Company wrote to Ravenscroft requesting that Samuel Moore 'now Clerke' should 'have the bespeaking of all Glasses made at Henly on Thames; for that Mr. Moore better knowes what is fitter to be made for the Trade both as to ffashion and size, than any other there.'[14] This was a reminder that Ravenscroft was not regarded as being completely conversant with the trade. Nearly a year later, on 18 September 1675, the Company authorised Ravenscroft to sell abroad, within six months, £400 worth of his 'flint glasses made before the first of August last'.[15] There may perhaps be a hint here of the imperfections in the Ravenscroft metal which were to come into the open during the year following.

In 1676 Dr Robert Plot FRS published his book *The Natural*

History of Oxfordshire. In his chapter on Arts he gives an account of
the Henley-on-Thames glasshouse which is vital for understanding
the development of Ravenscroft's glass:

> To which may be added the invention of making glasses of *stones or
> other materials* at Henley-on-Thames *lately brought into England* by
> Seignior da Costa a Montferratees and carried on by one Mr.
> Ravenscroft who has a patent for the sole making of them; and lately
> by one Mr. Bishop. *The materials they used formerly were the blackest
> flints calcined* and a white Christalline sand adding to each pound of
> these, as it was found by the solution of their whole mixture by the
> ingenious Dr. Ludwell Fellow of Wadham College, about two
> ounces of Nitre, Tartar and Borax. But the glasses made of these
> being subject to that unpardonable fault called *crizelling caused by the
> two (sic) great quantities of the Salts in the mixture*, which either by the
> adventitious Niter of the Air from without or warm liquors put in
> them would be either increased or dissolved; and thereby induce a
> Scabrities or dull roughness irrecoverably clouding the transparency
> of the glass; they have chosen since to make their glasses of a great
> sort of white pebbles which as I am informed they have from the
> river Po in Italy; to which adding the afore-mentioned salts but
> *abating in the proportions* they now make a sort of pebble glass which
> are hard durable and whiter than any from Venice and will not
> Crizel, but under the severest trials whatever, to be known from the
> former by a Seal set purposely on them.
>
> And yet I guess that the difference in respect of Crizeling, between
> the present glass and the former lies not so much in the calx, the
> pebbles being Pyrites (none but such I presume being fit for vitrifi-
> cation) as well as flints; but rather *wholly in the abatement of the salts*,
> for there are *some of the flint glasses strictly so called whereof I have one by
> me* that has endured all trials as well as these last. But if it be found
> otherwise that white pebbles are really fitter for their turns than
> black Flints, I think they have little need to fetch them from Italy
> there being enough in England of the same kind, not only to supply
> this but perhaps foreign nations.[16]

There are several points to be noted about this passage. First,
da Costa and not Ravenscroft is credited with the original innovation of making glass of 'stones and other materials'. Secondly,
although the developments discussed must have occurred before
1676, there is no clear time scale, but only two stages of development – first the use of calcined flints, then of 'pebbles'. Thirdly,
although it has been assumed that Plot actually visited Ravenscroft
at Henley, and claimed in his work that 'there (is) . . . nothing here
mentioned, but what either the author has seen himself, or has

received unquestionable testimony for it', the tone of the passage does not convey the impression of an actual visit. It may be that Dr Ludwell was Plot's informant.[17]

Whatever the chronology of these events, the problem of crizzling was subsequently overcome. On 3 June 1676 the *London Gazette* published an advertisement:

> Wee under written doe certify and attest that the defect of the flint glasses (which were formerly observed to crissel and decay) hath been redressed severall months agoe and the glasses since made have all proved durable and lasting as any glasses whatsoever. Moreover that the usual tryalls wherewith the essay of glasses are made have bene often reiterated on these new flint glasses with entire success and easy to be done againe by any body, which proofs the former glass would not undergoe, besides ye distinction of sound discernible by any person whatsoever.[18]

The advertisement was signed by Samuel Moore, and by Hawley Bishopp, the man mentioned by Dr Plot. It was repeated virtually unchanged on 3 July and again on 5 October and 2 and 8 November 1676. In the last three there was the significant addition 'and for further assurance a Seal or Mark hath lately been set on them for distinguishing them from the former fabric and shall be continued'[19] – a feature mentioned by Dr Plot. The character of the seal is not specified, but there are a few extant glasses with a plain, small, button-like seal which may date from this phase. In fact, sealed glasses had been referred to as early as 27 March 1676 in a bill for glass supplied to the Earl of Bedford by the London Glass Seller Thomas Apthorpe: '12: new fflintt wine Glasses mrd £0:16:0'. The use of the abbreviation 'mrd' on other comparable bills leaves little doubt that it stands for 'marked'.[20] There is, of course, no guarantee that the seal was Ravenscroft's, for the idea of authenticating glasses with seals was clearly in the air. The need to make the seal unequivocal is reflected in subsequent documents. On 29 May 1677 Ravenscroft signed a new agreement with the Glass Sellers,[21] rehearsing *inter alia* that he had 'brought the work to better perfection' and stipulating that 'a Raven's head shall be made or set in all glasses to distinguish the same from all others.' The raven's head seal is mentioned later in the same year in *London Gazette* advertisements of 25 October and 1 and 19 November.[22]

All the glasses marked with the raven's head seal which have been tested contain lead in varying proportions. Lead-glass is the classic material of the succeeding period, and it is known from an advertisement of 1700 that litharge (protoxide of lead) was then regularly used by English glass-makers. Clearly, therefore, at some juncture Ravenscroft began to add oxide of lead to his batches.[23] But when did this occur? The mixture described by Dr Plot contains no lead, and would have produced a borosilicate glass with an impracticably high melting point. Whether this formula was correctly reported or not, it is clear that the resultant glass was subject to 'crizzling', a defect which produces an internal network of glistening lines and a gradual breakdown of the surface – Dr Plot's 'Scabrities or dull roughness'. Crizzling is caused by instability in the glass, usually due at this period to the habit of boiling the fluxing alkali repeatedly in an effort to purify it. This resulted in a reduction of the calcium content. Calcium is a glass stabiliser, and without a stabiliser the alkali is leached out of glass by atmospheric action, leaving the silica network exposed and weakened. Plot probably recognised this mechanism even if he did not understand it, and refused to believe that the defect was due to the nature of the silica (calcined flints and pure sand); or that it would be remedied by changing from flints to river pebbles (*cuogoli*, the normal source of silica in Venice) rather than by modifying the alkali ('the salts'). Actual examination of sealed Ravenscroft glasses, however, does reveal that the silica used was exceptionally pure; and the main effort of glass-makers in this period – as John Greene's correspondence testifies – was directed towards producing a robust, clear and colourless glass, as near as possible to rock-crystal. This ideal was recognised in John de la Cam's phrase 'Mistery of Melting Cristall de roach'; and in Ravenscroft's own patent for 'a Perticuler sort of Christaline Glasse resembling Rock Christall'.

Flint was recognised quite early as an acceptable substitute for the Venetian *cuogoli*, and in a patent application of 1663 the petitioners claimed to 'have found out a way never yet before discovered, of extracting out of Flints all Sorts of lookeing glasses . . . and all manner of Christall glasses.'[24] Merrett in his *Art of Glass* (1662) had mentioned this source of silica, and the Royal Society had directed its attention to the question. Robert Hooke, one of the Fellows especially interested in glass, records a visit with Sir Christopher Wren to a new glasshouse on 29 July 1673, during which he 'saw calcind flints as white as flower'.[25] July 1673 is the date given for the start of Ravenscroft's activities at the Savoy, and it is difficult not to see a connection. About this time the normal 'English crystal' is replaced in trade descriptions, first (April 1674) by 'fine flint Christalline glasses' and then (from November 1675 onwards) by simply 'flint glasses'.[26] This is the expression used in the Glass-Sellers' letter to Ravenscroft dated 18 September 1675.[27] Ravenscroft's patent, dated 16 May 1674, bears the marginal annotation 'Flint and Pebble Glass', and we may reasonably detect in this the essential nature of his 'invention' at this date. When later he added lead oxide to his batch, the process began by which 'flint glass' gradually came to be synonymous with lead-glass.

It has been surmised that the presence of the lead ingredient was concealed from Dr Plot, or his informant Dr Ludwell. It must be remembered, however, that crizzling takes some time to reveal itself. Many of the sealed glasses (presumably not earlier than mid-1677) are crizzled in varying degrees, yet must have seemed in perfect condition when they emerged from the lehr. The defect must have developed thereafter, notwithstanding the seal. Thus the apparent cure recorded by Dr Plot may not have been lasting. It is certainly difficult not to see the Company's permission to sell abroad (18 September 1675; see p. 111) as a measure to get rid of tainted stock. The Glass Sellers' 'Certificate of Improvement' no doubt confirms the use of lead by this date, 3 June 1676 – its mention of 'distinction of sound discernible by any person whatsoever' picks on the resonance of lead-glass, a criterion used ever since. Analysis of two raven-sealed glasses, presumably dating from after May 1677, reveals a lead content of $12\frac{1}{2}$ to $14\frac{1}{2}$ per cent and of 27 per cent respectively, presumably indicating that there was a progressive build-up of the lead content. The former of these fragments was crizzled, although marked; the other suffers from a dulled surface owing to burial, but is not crizzled. This piece comes from Nonsuch Palace, the terminal date for which is 1682. An attempt to plot the probable development of Ravenscroft's formula has been made by Dr D. C. Watts[28] with the interesting suggestion that latterly, because of the increasing admixture of lead oxide, the potassium derived from tartar fell to an undesirably low level and was replaced by purified potash. Similarly, the expensive borax could be replaced by potash, thus producing essentially the lead-potash 'flint glass' characteristic of the eighteenth century. Since there are no positively identifiable Ravenscroft glasses from the period before the use of the seal, there seems to be insufficient evidence to warrant a conclusion as to when lead was first added to the batch. The idea of using lead had been incorporated in chapter XCIII of A. Neri's *L'Arte Vetraria* (Florence, 1612), which was accessible to English readers in Merrett's translation (1662). Calcined pebbles and tartar, two of the ingredients used at Henley, also appear in this formula, intended primarily for the manufacture of enamels.

In a further agreement with Ravenscroft (29 May 1677)[21] the Glass Sellers stipulated that he should not keep more than one furnace with three chairs, a compromise between the original one furnace with two chairs (the Savoy glasshouse) and the two furnaces (Savoy and Henley-on-Thames) with two chairs apiece, of the September 1674 agreement. The 1677 agreement gives us a welcome insight into the types of glass produced by Ravenscroft, in the form of a tariff, as follows:

Beer glasses ribbed and plain	7 oz	1s 6d
Clarrett wine glasses of the same	5 oz	1s 0d
Sacke glasses of the same	4 oz	10d
Castors of the same	3 oz	8d
Brandy glasses of the same	2 oz	6d
Beer glasses nipt diamond waies	8 oz	1s 8d
Clarrett glasses of the same	5½ oz	1s 3d
Sacke glasses of the same	4 oz	1s 0d
'Purlee' glasses . . . to be priced at the same rates as foregoing.		
Diamond Crewitts of a pint, ribbed and plain with stoppers to them	9 oz	2s 0d
¾ pint Crewitts of the same sort with stoppers to them	7 oz	1s 6d
½ pint crewitts of the same sort with stoppers to them	5 oz	1s 0d
Quart ribbed bottles	16 oz	3s 0d
Pint bottles of the same	10 oz	2s 0d
½ pint bottles of the same	8 oz	1s 6d
¼ pint bottles of the same	5 oz	1s 0d
Quart bottles all over nipt diamond waies	16 oz	4s 0d
Pint bottles of the same sort	10 oz	2s 6d
½ pint bottles of the same sort	7 oz	1s 6d
Quarterne bottles of the same sort	6 oz	1s 3d

All and every of the said sorts of bottles to have stoppers fitted to them and given in to the rates aforesaid, and also handles if required. . . . All covers for drinking or 'sullibub' glasses ribbed and plain shall be delivered at 3s per lb, diamond or purled all over at 4s per lb, and extraordinary work or ornament at 5s per lb and all purled glasses bottles crewitts . . . to be at the same rates as if they were diamond.

These categories correspond to some extent with surviving glasses bearing the raven's head seal. Some types, however, are not represented by existing sealed glasses, and some of the sealed pieces have no corresponding item in the list.[29] Of the drinking-glasses which head the list a good many stems have survived, all exem-

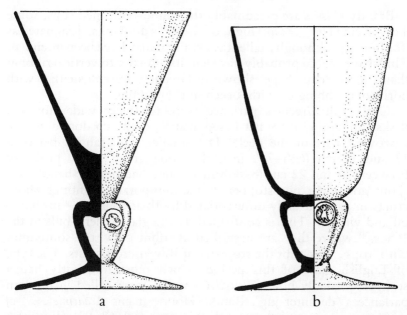

a   b

Fig. 22   Two wine- or beer-glasses with raven's head seal: (a) from Fenchurch
Street, (b) from Aldersgate, London (Savoy Glasshouse of George Ravens-
croft); about 1676–80. Scale approx. ½ (rims reconstructed). Museum of
London.

plifying the four-lobed inverted baluster already seen emerging in
the later Greene drawings (p. 106). As in the drawings, so in the
surviving fragments, two types of bowl are represented – the
straight funnel and the round-based funnel, the former with the
solid base indicated in some of Greene's drawings. A fragmentary
wine-glass with quatrefoil stem and an indecipherable seal, found
at Jamestown, Virginia, is decorated with vertical mould-blown
ribbing corresponding to the 'ribbed' variety specified in the list.
The foot is missing but the glass appears to have stood about 12 cm
(4¾ in.) high. This is even smaller than Greene's sack glass (for
Spanish wine), but the foot may have risen more steeply than
allowed for. It is noteworthy that in all the sealed Ravenscroft
stemmed glasses the bowl seems to merge directly into the stem
without an intervening merese.

There seems to be no means of knowing the exact significance of
the term 'castor'. Casters in silver were usually containers for
sugar, pepper etc. with a pierced top, but the shape seems not to
have come in before the Restoration. No contemporary glasses of
this shape are recorded, and a castor may have been some kind of
sprinkler.

Brandy glasses are presumably the round–bottomed cups, some 4 to 4.5 cm (1½–1¾ in.) high, of Greene's drawings, designated as 'for brandij'; although a taller beaker form may have been intended. This shape would probably have lent itself better to vertical ribbing than the low cup-shape, shown in Greene's drawings either with horizontal ribbing or with 'beech nut' moulding.

'Cruets' in Greene's parlance were relatively wide-mouthed flasks either on a foot or flat-based, usually with a cordon round the narrowest part of the neck. The smaller sizes ranged between 17 and 19 cm (6¾–7½ in.), the 'long cruets' were probably between 20 and 22 cm (8–8¾ in.). They had neither handle nor spout and were not stoppered. Contemporary paintings show cruets in pairs, usually differentiated by their contents – probably oil and vinegar. This is confirmed by the glass-sellers' bills of the 1680s,[30] where they are described as 'fflint crewitts', sometimes with 'tops', no doubt the stoppers of Ravenscroft's lists. The type of English glass of this period which most frequently had a stopper – usually hollow-blown – is the form called in modern parlance a 'decanter-jug'. Randle Holme in his *Academie . . . of Armory . . .*, compiled at much this time (*c.* 1663–82), illustrates under the heading of 'cruet' a piriform jug on a foot, with handle and pouring-lip, not altogether unlike the decanter-jug.[31] He adds that 'every countrey hath its owne forme and shape', and many of the decanter-jugs of this period identified as English may in fact be of continental origin, despite a proportion of lead in their composition. All the surviving decanter-jugs which retain their stoppers seem to be decorated with vertical mould-blown ribbing, above which there is sometimes a decorative chain-circuit; the handle is plain, usually with a thumb-piece; there is a collar round the base of the neck; and the hollow-blown stopper has a gadrooned top to match the body ribbing. They stand over 28 cm (11 in.) high and would certainly hold a full pint. All are of uncrizzled lead-glass and the metal alone would suggest a date about 1685 (Pl. 28a). None of them bears a seal, and until a sealed Ravenscroft example comes to light it would be premature to suppose that his stoppered 'crewitts' have been positively identified.

A unique Ravenscroft sealed bottle does exist (Pl. 23c). It bears the raven's head seal below the string rim on the neck, is flattened in section, and stands on an applied crimped foot. The vertical mould-blown ribbing has been nipped together with the *pucellas* into a mesh-pattern – the 'nipt diamond waies' of the list (frequently abbreviated to NDW). The bottle accommodates 0.9 of a pint and weighs 11 oz, and is therefore fairly identified as one of the 'Pint bottles of the same sort [i.e. NDW] 10 oz . . . 2s 6d' (this being the wholesale price between the supplier and the Company).

The note at the end of the schedule refers to covers for 'sullibub glasses ribbed and plain', and by a curious quirk of chance more of these syllabubs have survived intact than of any other form, both ribbed (Pl. 22a, b) and plain examples being represented – the latter, however, with a short calyx of gadrooning round the base (Pl. 22c). Ironically, none of the covers appears to have survived.

Posset-pots were used for consuming a beverage which was essentially milk curdled with wine or beer and spiced to taste, posset being the warm, and syllabub the cold variety. The spout was so situated that the liquor could be sucked out at the bottom while the more solid part above could be tackled with a spoon. The shape is represented in the Greene drawings with an order dated 28 August 1668 for six dozen uncovered and two dozen covered. Unfortunately the pots are not named in the relevant letter. *The Closet of the Eminently Learned Sir Kenelm Digby, Knt. Opened*, published posthumously in 1669, records:

> My Lady *Middlesex* makes Syllabubs for little Glasses with spouts, thus. Take three pints of sweet Cream, one of quick white wine [or Rhenish] and a good wine glassful [better the ¼ of a pint] of Sack: mingle with them about three quarters of a pound of fine Sugar in Powder. Beat all these together with a whisk, till all appeareth converted into froth. Then pour it into your little Syllabub-glasses, and let them stand all night. The next day the Curd will be thick and firm above, and the drink clear under it.

By this date the vessel, if not in glass, was long-established, for in the play *Sir G. Goosecappe* (1606) mention is made of 'Posset-Cuppes carv'd with libberds faces and Lyons heads with spouts in their mouths, to let out the posset ale' – these were clearly in silver. In some recipes an inordinate number of eggs was included, with various spices, and the quantities indicated suggest that a number of glasses would be required at one time. This is confirmed by the fact that three out of the six surviving sealed Ravenscroft examples came from a single source – Wentworth Woodhouse, seat of the Marquises of Rockingham.[32] Among the glasses supplied to the Earls of Bedford between 1682 and 1690 were '4 fflint sulubub Glasses' (June 1682): '7 fflint sulibub Glases' (June 1687); and '6 fflint sulibub Glases' (June 1690).[33] The dates suggest a summer drink. The price per piece was 1s 2d in 1682, and only 10d in 1690.

Not all the shapes in the Ravenscroft list can be identified in existing objects, but the opposite is also true. There survive raven-sealed glasses of four different types not mentioned in the price list at all.[34] First come bowls of two different sorts: one with 'S' profile, gadrooned base and spreading folded lip (Pl. 23a); the other with concave profile and folded rim, decorated with mould-blown ribbing and a milled cordon round the base (Pl. 23b). The former type stands on its own base-ring, the latter on a wide dish with folded rim and radiating ribbing to match the bowl. The former type came in at least three sizes – 28.2 cm (11⅛ in.), 24 cm (9½ in.), 22.3 (8¾ in.) in diameter respectively; the latter in at least two – 24 cm (9½ in.) and 19 cm (7½ in.). What these bowls were used for is uncertain. The bills for glass supplied to the Earl of Bedford, however, contain an entry on 23 January 1687/8 for '2: fflint Cream bassons' for 2s 6d and another on 3 July 1678 for '2: fflint fruiett dishes' for 4s.[35] The former may well have been bowls of the ribbed variety with stand, the latter the larger bowl-type, in which fruit would certainly have looked well.

Second comes the *Roemer*, the goblet of German origin with ovoid bowl and hollow cylindrical stem, normally made of green glass. At least three models are represented among the surviving Ravenscroft glasses: one with vertically ribbed bowl, stem and foot (Pl. 23d); another with bowl NDW and ribbed foot (Pl. 24b); and a third with plain bowl with basal gadrooning, and plain folded foot (Pl. 24a). All have raspberry prunts on the stem, among which lurks the raven's head seal. The glasses differ from the German two-piece, open-based model in that bowl, stem and foot are made separately, the bowl therefore isolated from the hollow stem. Greene had ordered four dozen of such glasses (February 1671), designating them 'r̄hnish [Rhenish] wine glasses'. He had ordered six dozen of the same form, but without foot, in September 1669, numbers which suggest slight demand. The shape was certainly popular by the two decades before 1700. The sealed *Roemers* also vary considerably in size – from 16.5 cm (6½ in.) through 18.3 cm (7¼ in.) to 27.3 cm (10¾ in.), this last a glass commemorating the visit of King John III Sobieski to Danzig some time between August 1677 and February 1678 (Pl. 24a). It is particularly import-ant for the dating of Ravenscroft glass because it is uncrizzled and shows that by this date the Savoy (or Henley) metal occasionally achieved the perfection which Ravenscroft sought.

One sealed, helmet-shaped jug survives to represent a form com-mon enough in European silver and tin-glazed earthenware, and found also in French glass. It stands some 23 cm (9 in.) high (Pl. 24c), and is matched by a taller unsealed model of 26.7 cm (10½ in.), otherwise identical in all respects. Both jugs are crizzled, and the larger is probably the earlier, antedating the introduction of the seal.

Last comes a small globular jug (9 cm (3½ in.) high) with cylindrical neck, loop handle with seal on the lower terminal, and deep gadrooning round the base (Pl. 25a). Previously identified as the ribbed beer-glass of the price list, it is in fact related in shape to a whole family of mugs made in lead- and tin-glazed earthenware, in salt-glazed stoneware, and in imported Fukien porcelain. A late seventeenth century advertisement refers to this form as a 'jug', but contemporary documents do not reveal its function. No doubt it served the purposes of miscellaneous tippling.

This repertory, all certainly attributable to Ravenscroft's furnaces, gives a fixed point in our understanding of English glass forms about 1675–80. To it may be related a further range of contemporary types (pp. 128–9).

On 30 August 1678, in a letter addressed to the Clerk of the Glass Sellers' Company, Ravenscroft gave six months' notice, as his contract entitled him to do, of his intention to terminate it.[36] On this reckoning, Ravenscroft would have ceased production at the Savoy in late February 1679. In August 1678, however, his patent still had almost three years to run – until 16 May 1681. There has been much speculation as to his motives in withdrawing from an apparently lucrative business; and as to what actually happened after February 1679. An earlier view that increasing years and possible ill health discouraged him is weakened by the more recent discovery that he was at this point only forty-six years old. An alternative hypothesis has been advanced that Ravenscroft, a Roman Catholic, found it prudent to lie low during the Popish Plot disturbances.[37] Indeed, on 28 October 1678, the Earl of Manchester was sent to Charles II to request that 'Mr. Ravenscroft, a glass-man at the Savoy may be secured'. There is an ambiguity here, for a lease on the Savoy had been taken out on 20 August 1676 in the name of Francis, George Ravenscroft's younger brother. Whichever brother it was, a subsequent tradition had it that one of the family had been 'seiz'd upon the Score of the Popish Plot'. October 1678 marked the very climax of the agitations arising from Titus Oates's revelations. Parliament resolved on 1 November that 'there hath been and still is a damnable and hellish plot, contrived and carried on by popish recusants, for the assassinating and murdering the King.' In such an atmosphere it may well be imagined that Roman Catholic glass-makers found it prudent to make themselves scarce.

No more is heard directly of George and Francis Ravenscroft as glass-makers. On 22 February 1682, however, thirteen influential members of the Glass Sellers' Company concluded an agreement with Hawley Bishopp 'of the parish of Saint Mary le Savoy'.[38] The indenture rehearsed that some of the partners had become joint tenants for twenty-one years (from Christmas 1681) of the premises 'called the Masters Lodgings within the Hospital of the Savoy, late in the occupation of George Ravenscroft, gent.' The premises were intended 'by all the parties for the setting up a Glasshouse or Blowing House therein . . .', and each had agreed to lay out £50 'in the art or mistery of Christaline or flint glass making' under Bishopp's supervision, the profits to be equally divided between the shareholders. This was a different form of agreement from Ravenscroft's, who had been obliged to offer all his output to the Glass Sellers corporately.

Hawley Bishopp was mentioned by Dr Plot as having 'lately' carried on the making of 'Glasses of Stones, and some other materials'. With Samuel Moore he had signed the attestation of 3 June 1676 that the fault of 'crizzling' had been overcome; and a month later was co-signatory of the 'Certificate about Flint and Christalline Glasses'. When in August of that year Francis Ravenscroft signed the Savoy lease, this covered 'all that part which Hawley Bishopp had previously occupied.' It seems therefore possible that Bishopp had in fact run the Savoy glasshouse while George Ravenscroft worked at Henley. From Ravenscroft's agreement of 29 May 1677 it emerges that he ran one glasshouse only, since it stipulated that he should not 'keep more than one furnace with three chairs' – as opposed to the two furnaces, with two chairs each, of his earlier agreement. That the one glasshouse was that in the Savoy is confirmed by the advertisements of October and November 1677 referring to 'such as shall buy any [i.e. glasses] marked with the Raven's Head, either from the Glass House situate in the Savoy on the River side, or from Shop-keepers who shall aver to have had them from the said Glass House.'[39] In all his known activities to this date Hawley Bishopp had been associated with Ravenscroft, and in 1682 he was 'of the parish of St. Mary le Savoy'. It is difficult to believe that when he took charge of the Savoy glasshouse in 1682 he was not continuing the manufacture of 'flint glass', after the expiry of Ravenscroft's patent in May 1681.

Bishopp's relations with the Glass Sellers were not uniformly cordial. A memorandum of 3 June 1685[40] complained that whereas most glasshouses sold glasses at eighteen to the dozen, Bishopp only supplied the partners with fifteen to the dozen, and he was instructed thenceforth to deliver sixteen to the dozen. He was also informed that John Newarke had been appointed clerk at the Savoy, just as Samuel Moore had been set to supervise Ravenscroft's output. On 28 April 1688 a further source of annoyance was revealed. From a communication to 'Mr. Bishop, Mr. Racket, Mr. Digby, and Mr. Phine(a)s Bowles'[41] it appears that these glass-makers had complained to the Glass Sellers of the latter's purchase of glasses made outside London, threatening not to sell their own glasses to those engaging in this trade. The Glass Sellers riposted by saying that they too deplored the trade in 'country' glasses, but that it was insignificant, and 'nothing would more conduce to cement the whole trade to you' than that the London glasshouses should refuse to sell glass to the hawkers, the deadly enemies of the settled glass-sellers. This is the last mention of Hawley Bishopp. Presumably he died or declined business some time after 1688.

If Hawley Bishopp almost certainly made glass-of-lead, there is more doubt about the other glass-makers mentioned in the 1688 document. On 1 April 1678 the Glass-Sellers, perhaps forewarned of Ravenscroft's intention to terminate his contract (August 1678), concluded an agreement[42] with Michael Rackett and with John Bowles and his partner William Lillington, that they 'shall have ready sufficient stocks of White and Green glass wares for the service of the said Glass Sellers.'

Michael Rackett is described as 'Master of a Glasshouse . . . for making white and green glasses in the Minories without Aldgate'. This glasshouse on the south side of Goodman's Yard, Whitechapel, had been owned by Mansell's partner, Bevis Thelwall, as early as 1641, and between 1657 and 1663 had been the subject of a dispute between Richard Batson and a man named Lewin. An Edmund Lewin, recorded there as a bottle-maker in 1677, had by 1678 been succeeded by Michael Rackett. Rackett is mentioned in a document of 1691, but in 1699 the glasshouse was advertised to be let. An advertisement of 6 July 1699 shows that 'Drinking Glasses' were produced; and by this date such glasses were certainly of lead-crystal. In 1678, however, Rackett's 'White glass' is likely to have been a leadless crystal: only after the expiry of Ravenscroft's patent in 1681 could he have gone over to lead-glass.[43]

Similar considerations apply to the second of the firms mentioned in the Glass Sellers' agreement of 1 April 1678. This was the partnership of John Bowles and William Lillington, 'Masters of another Glasshouse . . . for making white and green glasses in Southwark.' John Bowles came of a rich Lincolnshire family with property in Kent and Suffolk. His father, Charles Bowles, had held high office under the Commonwealth, and his brother, Phineas, was a Secretary for the Navy. John Bowles was a merchant as well as a glass manufacturer. In 1665 he was engaged in the Levant trade and in glass manufacture, his main interest being the production of plate-glass. He gained control of the Vauxhall works, once the Duke of Buckingham's, and before 1684 had acquired four other glasshouses on the south bank, making window-glass and bottles as well as crystal glass. By 1678 he controlled the Stony Street glass-house in Southwark and since, in 1717, part of this site was known as 'the Flint Glass House', it may be assumed that it was here that Bowles and Lillington produced the 'White glass' demanded by their contract. As with Rackett, it seems unlikely that they were making lead-glass before 1681. Bowles was one of the Commissioners for managing the duties on glasswares in 1695; this is the latest mention of him but the Bowles concerns prospered greatly in the eighteenth century.[44]

Apart from these three 'white glass' houses established before 1680, a further three were set up before 1690 and one in the 1690s. On 16 April 1683 the *London Gazette* published an advertisement: 'His Majesty being well satisfied of the Knowledge and Skill of Henry Holden, Esq. in the Compounding and mixing of Mettle, without any noxious Ingredients, for the making of all sorts of Glasses, has been pleased to cause him to be sworn his Servant in Ordinary, with leave to put his Imperial Arms on all such Glasses as shall be made by his orders . . . the said Mr. Holden is now making his Glasses at his Glass-House in the Savoy.' This must have been in some other part of the Savoy complex, away from Hawley Bishopp's furnace. Henry Holden was a glass-maker of an older generation and had, with John Colenet, obtained a patent for making 'glass bottles, vessels for distillation, etc.' as early as September 1662. It seems clear from the reference to 'noxious Ingredients' that Holden, at least in 1683, was not making lead-glass.[45]

On 11 September 1684 the *London Gazette* carried the advertisement:[46] 'The Flint Glass-House in Salisbury Court in Fleet-Street which hath been sometime discontinued, is now again put at Work by several Undertakers; Where all Persons may be furnished with very Good and Choice Glasses at reasonable Rates.' The phrase 'Flint Glass-House' suggests that Salisbury Court made lead-glass, or at least pretended to do so.

Two months later, on 4 December 1684, the same periodical advertised:[47] 'At his Royal Highness's Glass-house near the Hermitage Stairs in Wapping, are to be exposed to Sale all manner of Flint Glasses, and likewise all sorts of Ordinary and Green, with all other Curiosities that can be made of Glass, all the Glasses being marked with a Lion and Coronet to prevent Counterfeits.' This glasshouse is identified as having stood in Red Maid Lane, now Redmead Lane, in Wapping.[48] The association with the Duke of York probably ended when he ascended the throne as James II in 1685, and must in any case have ceased in 1689. It would appear to have made lead-glass ('Flint Glasses').

Lastly, on 27 February 1693, the *London Gazette* advertised:[49] 'To be sold all sorts of the best and finest Drinking-Glasses, and curious Glasses for Ornament . . . by Francis Jackson and John Straw, Glass-Makers, at their Warehouse in Worcester-Court . . . or at their Glass-House near the Faulkon in Southwark, and at Lynn in Norfolk.' Francis Jackson seems to have come of a glass-making family and was probably the father of Jonathan Jackson, owner of a glasshouse near St Saviours, Southwark, in 1720.[50] Of John Straw nothing is known. It may be assumed that the glasses they made in 1693 were 'flint glass'.

What can be said of the glasses which may be associated with this period? First comes a group of three crizzled pieces all bearing a small seal stamped 'S'. This was originally associated with the Salisbury Court glasshouse,[51] but this concern was not established until 1684, and by about 1680 the crizzling defect should have been generally eliminated; and the counter-proposition has been advanced[52] that 'S' might stand for 'Savoy', partly because the three surviving glasses were closely similar in form to glasses with the raven's head seal, and might therefore have been made at the Savoy glasshouse when Henley was producing the 'raven glasses'. The three pieces are a large *Roemer* (Pl. 25c) almost identical with the Ravenscroft example in the Victoria and Albert Museum (Pl. 23d); a four-lobed wine-glass stem in the same museum; and a posset-pot in the Fitzwilliam Museum, Cambridge (Pl. 25b). All are of lead-glass – which rules out Henry Holden. I have suggested elsewhere that in view of the Glass Sellers' contract with Bowles and Lillington, the 'S' might stand for 'Southwark'.[53] In 1678, however, this would have been in breach of Ravenscroft's patent. On the whole, it seems most likely that 'S' refers to the Savoy glasshouse, perhaps being used at the period when Ravenscróft was at Henley and Hawley Bishopp probably running the Savoy. A seal was first mentioned in October 1676 and the raven's head seal first in Ravenscroft's agreement with the Glass Sellers of 29 May 1677. It is significant that in this document occurs the first mention of Ravenscroft's restriction to one furnace with three chairs. This must refer to the Savoy, where there was apparently continuity of glass-making from 1673 until after Ravenscroft's retirement. Ravenscroft presumably abandoned Henley at this point, and if he had used the raven seal there, transferred its use to the Savoy. The hypothesis of an 'S' seal used in 1676–7 is also consistent with the fact that the glasses concerned are both lead-glasses and crizzled. This would hardly be the case after 1680, although it has to be borne in mind that some English glassmen were still producing unstable lead-glasses at least as late as 1683. A little gadrooned tankard with unmistakable crizzling is known which bears a silver mount inscribed: 'Bought on $\overset{e}{y}$ Thames Janu: $\overset{e}{y}$ 17 $168\frac{3}{4}$'. Progress in the technological arts did not then proceed in a smooth, unbroken, upward curve. Success in one glasshouse did not necessarily imply success in others. Nevertheless, in this debate the pros and cons are finely balanced. A single new discovery could transform our understanding of the problems.

Of the products of the other glasshouses there is less to say. Of the King's 'Imperial Arms' on Henry Holden's glasses, or the 'Lion and Coronet' allegedly used at the Duke of York's glasshouse, there is no trace on surviving objects. Seals of various kinds on glasses have been recorded, however, and one (on a four-lobed stem in the Northampton Museum) has been seen as representing a female figure shooting with a bow, and interpreted as 'Bow(les)' and 'Lilli(ngton)', an interpretation more ingenious than convincing.[54] The Northampton stem is allegedly of a non-lead glass. A sealed posset-pot with basal gadrooning in the British Museum, very close in shape to the Ravenscroft model, but made of a non-lead material, has also been thought to bear the same device. Lastly, a hollow-blown inverted baluster stem excavated in Nottingham bears a seal stamped 'Z' (or 'N').[55] This has so far not been identified, but might conceivably stand for 'Nottingham(shire)', for Houghton's list of glasshouses (1696) shows two flint glasshouses at or near Awsworth, not far from Nottingham itself.[56]

Few of the surviving sealed glasses are free from the taint of crizzling, apart from half a dozen Ravenscroft pieces. It may be surmised that it took some years after 1681 for the knowledge of the lead additive and the accompanying technology to spread to other London glasshouses, and thence to the provinces. By 1696, the date of Houghton's *Letters*, the term 'flint glass' – originally reserved to a *non-lead* glass using calcined flints as a source of silica – had been transferred to lead-glass, then in fact made with white sand, as Houghton says ('Our glass men for making the best flint glass use instead of powdered flints a very white sand such as we strow on writing.'). This process was presumably gradual, as glassmen added greater proportions of lead oxide to their batches. By 1685, however, lead-glass of good quality, free from crizzling, was probably being made by most progressive glasshouses, in London at least. This tends to be borne out by surviving glasses which are obvious successors to the Ravenscroft glasses. Of such are the ribbed bowl once in the Kirkby Mason Collection,[57] exactly similar to the sealed Ravenscroft bowl in the Barry Richards Collection (cf. Pl. 23a), and not very much larger (30.2 cm or 117/8 in. in diameter). This is an obvious candidate for attribution to Hawley Bishopp, working at the Savoy about 1685. A further bowl in the Mason Collection[58] was decorated with a chain-circuit of two threads pinched together, in place of the plain thread on the Ravenscroft model. Although this may be the 'purlee' decoration mentioned in the Ravenscroft list, it is not found on any sealed glass and seems to represent a slightly later fashion.

A second piece similarly attributable to Hawley Bishopp is the small globular tankard formerly in the H. Helliwell Collection (Pl. 26a, centre).[59] This has all the features of the Ravenscroft mug (Pl. 25a) except the seal, although the handle is thinner and rather differently made, and the base is finished with an applied trail.

A direct line of descent may also be deduced for the English type of *Roemer* with bowl and stem made separately. Ravenscroft's model may be seen to undergo some change even within his own *oeuvre*, the later and larger Danzig glass being appreciably thinner in the stem relative to its bowl diameter. This trend continues into the immediate post-Ravenscroft period, and is well illustrated in a 24.7 cm (93/4 in.) example from the William Roscoe Collection now in the Merseyside County Museum (Pl. 28b). Numerous further examples with gadrooned bowl and prunted stem, both large and small, survive. An early example in non-lead glass has an illegible seal on the plain hollow stem,[60] and is evidently by one of Ravenscroft's contemporaries or old-fashioned successors, such as Henry Holden. On the smaller sizes of *Roemer* the stem in due course becomes solid and follows the changing fashions of the day (pp. 143 ff.).

For Ravenscroft's helmet-jug and flattened bottle there seem to be no immediate successors, but his drinking-glasses, our concept of which can only be derived from reconstructions (p. 117), had issue in a series of glasses with funnel or round-funnel bowls stuck directly on to stems of inverted-baluster profile. These show by four vertical creases that they were produced by smoothing off the four-lobed stems of the earlier period (cf. Pl. 31a, left and centre).

These glasses survive mainly from excavations, but are by no means rare. The two types of bowl, however, are also found on a stem where a depressed hollow quatrefoil is set atop a plain capstan; or on an inverted baluster, often with wider knop above it, decorated with external wrythen ribbing (cf. Pl. 26b, centre). Stems of all these types occur in a metal containing more than 30 per cent lead;[61] and thus fit by a natural progression into the post-Ravenscroft period – say, 1685–95.

The wrythen ribbed stem with knop above was also much used with a small gadrooned bowl, sometimes with chain-circuit (Pl. 26a, left), which seems to imitate on a smaller scale the large post-Ravenscroft stemless bowls already mentioned (p. 127). These stemmed glasses, probably for sweetmeats, have their counterparts as dessert-glasses in a small gadrooned bowl without foot, or a vertically ribbed bowl with flaring sides.[62] As early as 1658 Sir Theodore Mayerne had recommended glass bowls for serving creams and Robert May, in his book *The Accomplisht Cook* (London, 1678), prescribed, 'Serve jelly . . . run into little round glasses four or five in a dish.' Contemporary instructions for preparing desserts refer to china dishes, which certainly had no more than a low foot-rim, as mentioned in François Massialot's *Nouvelles Instructions pour les Confitures* (1692) translated into English as *The Court and Country Cook* (1702). At a later date this 'dish' would have been replaced by a footed salver, and examples do survive from this period, gadrooned and plain;[62] a bill of 1682 refers to '1: fflint salver', costing 1s 6d.[63] An unequivocal jelly-glass, formed as a funnel with out-turned lip and a calyx of heavy gadrooning above the low pedestal foot, has been excavated in London and attributed to this period[64] – the forerunner of a richly diversified eighteenth-century series (p. 170). When James II as Duke of York was entertained by the city of Edinburgh 'a dozen jelly glasses' were missing after the party.

Closely akin to the jelly-glass was the posset- or syllabub-glass, which now tended to lose its purely cylindrical form (p. 119) and to assume the funnel shape of the jelly, but with sucking-spout and ear-shaped side handles;[65] alternatively, the body might be slightly waisted, to give an inverted bell shape. Side by side with these individual glasses go far larger spouted receptacles,[66] which suggest that posset-drinking might have been communal – much in the manner of a loving-cup, and only slightly more unhygienic. These broader, squatter vessels correspond closely with the 'possett pott or wassell bowl' illustrated by Randle Holme (p. 118),[67] the term 'wassell' well suggesting its convivial use. There is a good deal of ambiguity surrounding the expressions 'posset', 'syllabub' and 'caudle', all drinks prepared in much the same way. Robert May, in *The Accomplisht Cook* (1685 edition), in a recipe 'to make a Posset', prescribes, 'pour it as high as you can hold the skillet, let it spatter in the bason to make it froth', a method continued in the eighteenth century for the making of 'whip syllabubs'. In a second recipe, however ('To make a Posset otherways'), the instructions run, 'put it in a fine clean scowred bason, or posset pot.' The quantities are in either recipe so large ('Take the yolks of twenty eggs . . .') that the concoction could only have been accommodated in one very large posset-pot, or a number of smaller ones. A 'whip syllabub', in which the alcoholic mixture below was to be covered by a foamy milky mixture above, could be made 'under the cow', thus: 'Put a bottle of strong beer and a pint of cyder into a punch bowl, grate in a small nutmeg, and sweeten it to your taste; Then milk as much milk from the cow as will make a strong froth, and the ale look clear, let it stand an hour, then strew over it a few currants, well washed, picked and plumped before the fire, then send it to table' (1724). In the only picture in which this procedure appears to be recorded, that by Charles Phillips (1708–47) of 'Russell and Revitt Families' at Chequers, the vessel used is a two-handled silver cup of a type often referred to as a 'caudle' or 'posset' cup. Of this type one authority has commented:[68] 'It is, of course, pretty certain that the vessels in question are those which are referred to in wills and inventories by the names given above, but we have so far discovered no means of appropriating the correct name to each object, and it may even be doubted whether our ancestors had very definite views on their proper nomenclature.' This sentiment may be heartily echoed in the case of glass. A large two-handled cup (often covered) has occasionally been identified as a posset-pot – quite possibly correctly – even though spoutless. In silver, these two-handled cups often echo the squat bell-shape of the spouted glasses; and the silver cup with straight sides having a calyx of ornament round the base and an applied band above, closely matches the glasses with gadrooned base and applied decoration (Pl. 29a).

The same ornamental formulae were used on drinking-glasses. Their evolution can usefully be followed in the series of stately cylinder-bowled goblets with coins in the hollow knops of their stems (Pl. 27a). Dated coins permit the fixing of a *terminus post quem* (only), with a bias in favour of supposing that the coin was near-contemporary unless obviously commemorative. The earliest example within this category seems to give the lie to this presumption, the coin bearing the date 1661, but the glass being of a heavy lead-metal – unlikely to ante-date 1680.[69] The round-based bucket bowl is decorated with NDW gadrooning and an applied chain-circuit, the central hollow knop of the stem decorated with raspberry prunts and mounted on a hollow inverted baluster. The inverted baluster is a strong indicator that this glass was not made much before 1690, a diagnosis confirmed by the existence of similar stems on goblets containing coins of 1703, 1706, 1711 and 1713 respectively.[70] The 1706 glass has a round-funnel bowl with diamond-moulding and vertical gadrooning closely resembling the bowls of the group we are examining. The second earliest coin found in one of these goblets is dated 1684 (Pl. 27a, right). It has the almost cylindrical round-based bowl of the others in the group, decorated with NDW gadrooning and a chain-circuit; the stem, on the other hand, consists merely of the bulb containing the coin, separated from bowl and folded foot by a series of indeterminate discs. Akin to this is a goblet once in the A. Waugh Collection. The bowl is virtually identical, but the stem has a small knop above and a small baluster below the hollow bulb, which encloses a James II shilling dated 1686.[71] Last comes a goblet in the British Museum with identical bowl-form, its stem composed of a short hollow inverted baluster below the knop enclosing a coin dated 1687, both elements being decorated with raspberry prunts.[72] The unmistakable family affinity of these three glasses tends to validate the supposition that the coins were inserted when relatively new, and that the glasses were probably made about 1685–90. The recital above of comparable glasses dating from the early years of the eighteenth century should provide a warning against too confident dating by any one criterion. All the features of a glass need to be scrutinised, and even then the possibilities of error are considerable. This applies equally to the eighteenth century.

Similar features may be picked up in a small group of goblets, again with cylindrical bowls, which stand on triple-knopped stems. One of these has in the uppermost knop a groat of 1680 (Pl. 27a, centre), and the group is most probably co-eval with that just described. The 1680 goblet is closely matched by an example in the British Museum,[73] both having a central knop decorated with wrythen ribbing, quatrefoil knops and bowl left plain except for gadrooning. These monumental glasses perhaps represent the work of another glasshouse where a more austere taste prevailed. They are the English manifestation of a fashion also ruling in the Netherlands, where multiple stems of quatrefoil knops support bowls often wheel-engraved above the gadrooning.

The heavy gadrooning and applied tooled ornament of the earlier group of goblets is echoed in a series of elaborate posset-pots, punch-bowls, pocket-bottles and decanter-jugs (Pls. 28, 29). These fretful ornaments have justly been seen as an expression of Baroque taste and a residue in England of the Venetian style, itself one aspect of the Baroque. Venetian workmen and their descendants probably remained within the English industry, and their talents may have been at the disposal of more than one glasshouse on a freelance footing. In the 1684 advertisement of the Duke of York's glass-house (p. 128) occurs the phrase 'all other Curiosities that can be made of Glass', while Jackson and Straw in 1693 advertised 'curious Glasses for Ornament'. It may be surmised that these houses among others produced elaborately tooled glasses such as those illustrated in Pls. 27–30. They are the later counterparts of those glasses with 'extraordinary work or ornament' of Ravenscroft's list, costing 25 per cent more per lb. than the plain or simply mould-blown glasses. Very little of this elaborate work from the 1670s seems to have been identified, but the tradition was probably unbroken, re-emerging in the 1680s with many features unchanged from the pre-lead era: double-looped handles with notched trails; open crown finials (Pl. 29a, c); openwork stems supporting the bowl on four notched straps (Pl. 29b); figure-of-eight and other stems made of twisted cables with notched frills (Pl. 30), and matching cover finials; and bird finials. Impressive though they may be, it is readily apparent, when they are compared with their continental counterparts in soda-metal, that lead-glass did not really lend itself to this kind of manipulation. This phase of English glass-making may be regarded as the last fling of Venetian style in England, even though the Beadle's staff of the Glass Sellers' Company, presented by Robert Croshaw in 1702, shows as the central feature of the Company's arms a goblet with figure-of-eight stem. That so many examples survived is no doubt due to the fact that they were treasured in their day. It is perhaps significant that a number of them have been preserved in continental collections. By the last decade of the seventeenth century, native English taste was inclining in a different direction. Before considering the develop-ment of English flint glasses in the eighteenth century, we should look back to the small group of coloured and other fancy glasses attributable to the last quarter of the seventeenth century.

It will be recollected that glasses ordered by John Greene in 1671 (p. 107) included vases of two shapes 'of your Milk Whit glass and strong'. From 1662 onwards the recipes for making this porcelain-like glass had been available in Christopher Merrett's *The Art of*

Glass. Theoretical recipes are one thing; successful glasshouse practice another. There is no positive evidence of English 'enamel' glass
before 1700, but a few surviving vessels are likely, by reason of
their shapes, to be English and of late seventeenth-century date.
The echoes of porcelain are sustained here, for the shapes in question – a globular mug with cylindrical neck (Pl. 31b), and a tapering
cylindrical tankard (Pl. 31c) – are also found in Fukien *blanc de
Chine*.[74] The porcelain was certainly made to English order, for the
shapes are not native Chinese, whereas they are found in contemporary English salt-glazed stoneware. The horizontal fluting on both
types of stoneware tankard is imitated by fine threading on the glass.
These mugs, moreover, regularly have a scalloped silver band round
the rim, precisely as on the stoneware prototypes. This manufacture probably continued uninterrupted into the eighteenth century.

In coloured glass at least three varieties are known, and none can
have offered any difficulty to the late seventeenth-century glass-
maker. Cobalt-blue is mentioned by Merrett in 1662, who knew
that the colorant came from Germany. The colour is exemplified in
the famous 'Savoy vase' in the Toledo Museum, Ohio (Pl. 24d). Of
a fine sapphire-blue crizzled lead-glass, the vase has NDW decoration on the body, a flaring neck with a frilled collar, and ear-
shaped handles running from rim to shoulder – a perfect repertory
of 'Anglo-Venetian' ornament. Only conjecture justifies the attribution of this piece to the Savoy glasshouse.[75]

Manganese-purple was equally well known in the late seventeenth century, as it possibly had been in the sixteenth (pp. 59–60).
Christopher Merrett recommended the oxide from the Mendip
lead mines, rather than the manganese of Piedmont preferred by
Neri. Three purple lead-glass bottles survive which have a strong
claim to be English-made, two of them in the Victoria and Albert
Museum (Pl. 25d) and the Ashmolean Museum, Oxford.[76] All
have vertically ribbed necks with string-rims below the lip, and
NDW decoration on a second gather covering the body. Two are
crizzled. The lead content is modest, and the possibility cannot be
excluded that they were made in the Netherlands, where bottles of
this general form were favoured. Their basic resemblance in workmanship to the sealed Ravenscroft flask in the British Museum
(Pl. 23c) argues strongly for their Englishness. There is a purple
globular mug in the British Museum and a small wine-glass in the
Victoria and Albert Museum (Pl. 31a, centre), inscribed in unfired
colours 'God bless King William and Queen Mary' (i.e. not earlier
than 1689); its stem betrays the smoothed away quatrefoil cross
section characteristic of the time (p. 127).

In addition to these traditional glass-makers' colours, there is increasing evidence that a gingery-brown metal, presumably based on iron, was favoured by the English glassmen of this era. A considerable number of fragmentary pieces of this colour have come to light in excavations during recent years, normally decorated with marvered-in opaque-white threading. These objects usually take the form of small flasks, and mugs or jugs with globular body and funnel-neck.[77] The Victoria and Albert Museum possesses a small handled mug of the common shape with globular body and cylindrical neck in this material (Pl. 31a, right).

As early as 1682 a distinction was being made between 'thin flint' and 'thick flint' glass, no doubt as the proportion of lead increased. By the middle of 1685 at the latest this terminology had changed to 'single flint' and 'double flint'.[78] It has been suggested that these terms referred to single and double gathers, but it seems as likely that they implied only lighter and heavier glasses. As the metal got heavier the old styles of working probably seemed increasingly inappropriate, although vestiges of them survived well into the eighteenth century. Their relative fussiness seems to have recommended them more for decorative glasses – dessert-glasses, candlesticks, covered jars and the like. For the drinking-glass, the main vehicle of changing fashion, a new order of form develops. Bowl and foot remain mostly plain – the latter normally with a deep fold round its edge, for strength as much as looks – while the decorative focus becomes the stem. Starting from the ball-shaped knop, the true baluster and the inverted baluster – familiar in Greene's drawings twenty years earlier – the glassmen gradually developed fresh forms which would have been wholly inappropriate in soda-glass but which are brilliantly successful in glass-of-lead, with its high refractive index to catch the light, and contrasting dark shadows. These effects were achieved more at the chair than by blowing. Only the bowl and foot were blown, the normally solid stem being built up from the elements mentioned above. The telling bubbles and columns of air were produced mainly by pricking the bowl or the knop and then trapping the air, rather than by blowing in the Venetian manner. The beauty of such glasses derives from the quality of the material and the harmonious proportions of bowl, stem and foot. It may be compared with the beauty of Venetian glass at that moment of poise in the mid-sixteenth century when harmony and proportion were elevated above decorative effects.

Although a general current of development is discernible in these glasses of the 'baluster' period, a firm chronological framework is difficult to establish. If the simple elements mentioned above are taken first, a starting point may perhaps be fixed in a noble goblet, 23 cm (9 inches) high, in the Victoria and Albert Museum (Pl. 32a, right). It has a slightly flaring round-based funnel-bowl, the main stem element being a spherical knop enclosing a sixpence of 1690, separated by a wide merese from a short capstan. Here the knop has been perfectly integrated into the design, a perfection sometimes denied to other glasses where the coin-bearing knop interferes with the overall design. Of this kind are a 17.7 cm (7-in.) goblet in the Fitzwilliam Museum, Cambridge, the bowl decorated with diamond-point engraving and the stem also enclosing a sixpence of 1690;[79] and a 23-cm (9-in.) example of almost identical proportions in the Pilkington Glass Museum, the stem enclosing coins of 1677 and 1682.[80] None of these goblets is of solid build, and the London glass shows a notably light touch. None would seem to qualify for the appellation 'double flint'. This character, and the seventeenth-century style of the engraving on the Cambridge glass, suggest a date not long after those on the coins. A comparable glass once in the G. F. Berney Collection cannot be earlier than 1715, the date on a shilling in its hollow knop.[81] This glass, however, has a domed foot, a feature common in the early eighteenth century, and its rather solid build confirms this later dating. The same may be said of a number of other glasses with Charles II coins in their stems. It has indeed been suggested that these coins in eighteenth-century glasses indicate Jacobite sympathies. These circumstances demonstrate that a number of factors have to be considered where coins give only the *terminus post quem*. Chronology can only be very approximate.

Dated engraving can provide a *terminus ante*, and this criterion too can be applied to the glasses within the narrow range of stem-forms under scrutiny. Thus a handsome goblet in the Victoria and Albert Museum, with solid based funnel-bowl and thick inverted baluster, is inscribed in diamond-point 'God bless Queen Ann', yielding a date between 1702 and 1714, with a strong presumption in favour of the Coronation year of 1702 (Pl. 32a, left). A closely similar glass once in the P. M. Woolley Collection has a Charles II twopenny piece in the upper part of the stem, which is shaped almost as a wide angular knop but with a smaller knop appearing above the foot.[82] This more complex form would suggest if anything a later date, and the glass might qualify as one of the presumed Jacobite propaganda glasses anticipating the Queen's death in 1714. The inverted baluster combined with a small knop at the base of the stem does occur on glasses dated earlier than this by their engraving. A 20-cm (8-in.) goblet with round-funnel bowl formerly in the Dunstan Collection is wheel-engraved with arms and a Dutch inscription including the date $17\frac{3}{5}05$,[83] while a comparable glass in the Grant Francis Collection with slightly more attenuated baluster and domed foot is engraved with the Royal Arms as used before the Union with Scotland in 1707.[84] These two examples demonstrate that these basic types were being made within the first decade of the eighteenth century; further examples show that they continued in use throughout the first quarter.[85]

Some idea of the glasses in use about 1710 is provided by Zacharias Conrad von Uffenbach, who was in London in that year. Early in November he went to Clare Market to visit the 'Blue Bell'

in order to see the Scotchman break glasses by shouting. He . . . has a very strong voice and sings a good bass. When we had eaten he sent for various fine stemmed glasses and picked out those that gave forth a clear tone. He tests them by striking his finger against them . . . He seized the stemmed glasses below by the foot, held them athwart his mouth, and shouted at them from the knop and foot progressively upwards. He repeated this several times until suddenly, with a fairly loud crack, the glass broke apart into a number of pieces . . . Most of them broke off obliquely at the thick knop, which was all the more remarkable in that it was fully a thumb thick, and the glasses were of thick strong crystal-glass, such as is here called 'double flint'.[86]

In due course the simple knops and baluster elements already discussed were transformed into a number of distinctive variants and combined together in apparently endless permutations. It is not possible here to go into all the details of their forms and combinations, but fig. 23 gives a survey of the various elements, and Pls. 32–3 a series of the glasses which exemplify them. These developed forms of 'baluster' may probably be dated somewhat later than the types already discussed, although here too a precise chronology is unattainable. It is, however, possible to deduce from their engraving the dates of some of these glasses with more developed stem variations. Thus a goblet in the Rhode Island School of Design is wheel-engraved with the Prince of Wales's feathers on one side and the monogram 'GP' on the other.[87] This most probably commemorates the elevation of the future George II as Prince of Wales in 1715, a political act of special contemporary significance. The symmetrical stem is composed of a small knop between a true and an inverted baluster on a domed foot, a rela-

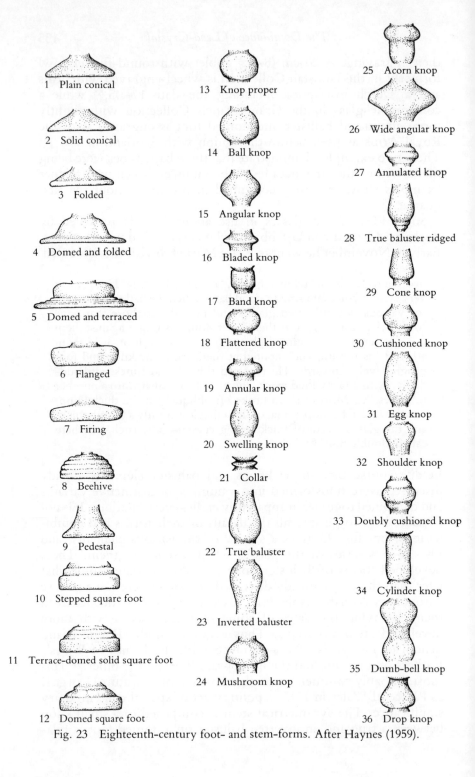

1 Plain conical
2 Solid conical
3 Folded
4 Domed and folded
5 Domed and terraced
6 Flanged
7 Firing
8 Beehive
9 Pedestal
10 Stepped square foot
11 Terrace-domed solid square foot
12 Domed square foot

13 Knop proper
14 Ball knop
15 Angular knop
16 Bladed knop
17 Band knop
18 Flattened knop
19 Annular knop
20 Swelling knop
21 Collar
22 True baluster
23 Inverted baluster
24 Mushroom knop

25 Acorn knop
26 Wide angular knop
27 Annulated knop
28 True baluster ridged
29 Cone knop
30 Cushioned knop
31 Egg knop
32 Shoulder knop
33 Doubly cushioned knop
34 Cylinder knop
35 Dumb-bell knop
36 Drop knop

Fig. 23 Eighteenth-century foot- and stem-forms. After Haynes (1959).

tively complicated arrangement of the simple old elements. A fine example of the wide angular knop occurs on a glass of 17.7 cm (7 in.) with a diamond-point inscription dated 1717, formerly in the Kirkby Mason Collection,[88] while a mammoth ceremonial goblet, almost 38 cm (15 in.) high and previously in the Henry Brown Collection, has the same stem slightly differently proportioned, with diamond-point scribblings including the date 1720.[89] Both stems have a pronounced internal air bubble. The annulated knop, with solid inverted baluster below, occurs on a round-funnel glass inscribed in diamond-point 'To ye pious Memory of Queen Anne', by a calligraphic engraver who dated a number of glasses in the 1720s.[90] The same artist inscribed a small but fat cordial-glass in the Victoria and Albert Museum with his characteristic scrollwork and calligraphy: 'Take a dram old boy' (Pl. 32b, left). The solid-based bowl rests on an acorn knop of classic clarity and simplicity. Also attributable to the same engraver is a goblet, formerly in the Sir J. S. Risley Collection, with a stem composed of a mushroom knop above and a small spherical knob below.[91] These instances suggest that most of the varieties of the baluster glass were established by the 1720s and had probably evolved in the decade after 1710. That glasses like this, large and ponderous, were in current use is demonstrated by a painting of Sir Thomas Sebright and his friends smoking and drinking round a table in 1720 (Pl. 34a). The drink is apparently served in stoneware jugs, although one decanter can just be discerned; and there is little pretence of elegance about this caucus of homespun squires. The robust nature of the glasses was no doubt a recommendation when the drinking began to go deep.

Further significant details are revealed by a group portrait (Pl. 35b) showing Sir Thomas Samwell and his friends sitting round a circular table on which two ordinary bottles are making the round, while a standing guest on the left holds a wickered flask, presumably of Florence wine. The painter has been confidently identified as Philippe Mercier (1689–1760) and the picture tentatively dated *c.* 1730–50, a date substantiated by the shape of the bottles. It is therefore somewhat surprising to see in use glasses with solid inverted baluster stems having a small knop at the base. Presumably an existing set of glasses was maintained in use for ceremonial occasions. And a set it indubitably is, five individual funnel-bowled glasses being reasonably clearly visible. In front of the central figure with his chaplet of vine leaves – almost certainly Sir Thomas Samwell himself – stands a glass several sizes larger than the rest, but otherwise closely resembling them. What does this picture signify? There must be some special reason why the central figure holds this larger goblet, and it is hard to resist the conclusion that it is a toasting-glass which went the round of the table, while at the same time each crony had his own individual glass. The primitive stages of this ritual may probably be traced later in Scotland, where distance from London combined with relative poverty to ensure the perpetuation of old-fashioned customs. It is recorded of eighteenth-century Scotland that 'To serve for the family, there was in many a household only one glass or tankard, which was handed on to the next person in succession as each finished his draft.'[92] Adam Petrie, in his *Rules of Good Deportment* (1720), prescribed: 'Be sure to wipe your mouth before you drink, and when you drink hold in your breath until you have done, which is certainly very loathsome to the company',[93] an injunction which has its counterparts in the fifteenth century elsewhere in Europe. As the glass circled the company it was made the occasion of proposing toasts, a custom which drew down the wrath of contemporary moralists, such as Peter Brown, Bishop of Cork and Rosse, who in 1716 published a *Discourse of Drinking Healths wherein the great Evil of this prevailing custom is shown, etc.* John Philips in his poem *The Splendid Shilling* (1705) took a different view:

> Happy the man, who void of cares and strife,
> In silken, or in leathern purse retains
> A splendid shilling: he . . .
> . . . with his friends, when nightly mists arise,
> To Juniper's-Magpye, or Town-Hall repairs:
> Where, mindful of the nymph, whose wanton eye
> Transfixed his soul, and kindled amorous flames,
> Chloe, or Phillis; he each circling glass
> Wisheth her health, and joy, and equal love.

The lengths to which this process could go is again pointed up from Scottish sources. H. G. Graham records of a later period:[94] 'When the table was cleared of viands, and the glasses once more were set on the shining mahogany, each person proposed the health of every other person present severally and thus if there were ten guests there were ninety healths drunk . . . There were also rounds of toasts, each gentleman naming an absent lady, each lady an absent gentleman. Next followed "sentiments" . . . Each person was called on in turn to propose a wish called a "sentiment" – it might be some crisp sentence, a poetic phrase, a jovial proverb, or, as generally a fatuous moral reflection.' The elements of a similar ritual may be detected in England too. Captain Peter Drake, a gentlemanly Irish desperado of the Marlborough wars, records in his *Memoirs* for 1702:[95] 'Dinner being at an end, and the glass circling briskly, we became very merry.' In 1714[96] he says, 'We drank pretty briskly about, and began to be merry. Toasts went about, mine was called for; I toasted Mrs. Jolly.' Here perhaps there was only a circling bottle, a situation commented on in the *Statistical Account of Scotland*, which recorded that whereas in 1748 in Banff a company might drink twelve bottles from one glass, in 1798 they drank one bottle from twelve glasses.[97] That Captain Drake was accustomed to this style of drinking too is evident from his *Memoirs*. Some time in 1710–12[98] he had an encounter with Lord Mohun, a cantankerous duelling peer. On this occasion things went amicably: 'As soon as supper was over, glasses and a bottle of Burgundy with a flask of Champaign was laid on the table . . . My lord loved bumpers, and ply'd me pretty hard with the same . . . and we sat to it the rest of the night, drinking all the loyal toasts then in vogue.' The evidence as to what these toasts may have been is carried on them by some of the surviving glasses themselves, notably the 'Amen' glasses current in Scotland in the mid-eighteenth century. Apart from the verses of the Jacobite Anthem engraved on them with the diamond-point – 'God Save the King' (i.e. the Old Pretender); 'God Save the Prince of Wales' (i.e. Prince Charles Edward); 'God Save the Church' and 'God bless the subjects all' – they were often also inscribed with toasts such as 'Prosperity to the family of Traquair' or 'A Bumper . . . To the Prosperity of the Family of Lochiell', etc.[99] When, therefore, we find a glass inscribed (or better, scratched) with the diamond-point 'The Duke of Comberld. (Cumberland). Prosperity to Holkham and Wroxham. Prosperity to The English Copper Company', etc. and when it is realised that this goblet is 37.8 cm (14⅞ in.) high,[100] we are taken straight back to Sir Thomas Samwell and his friends.

The same phenomenon may be observed in a contemporary satirical engraving showing a group of clergy and churchwardens seated round a table eating away the parish funds (Pl. 35a). The rector sits at the head holding a goblet larger than the rest at the table. On it is inscribed, 'Prosperity to the Church'. No set of English glasses including a large goblet and a series of smaller glasses *en suite* appears to have been preserved, but one series is known from Norway, the component glasses wheel-engraved with a series of toasts such as 'May trade flourish and Navigation prosper!'[101] It has been stated that these large goblets were called 'constable' glasses, perhaps on account of their commanding size – a theory which gains some support from the distych,

> For a larger, I'll soon change my cup;
> To the brim fill the Constable up.[102]

A 38-cm (15-in.) goblet at Levens Hall, seat of the Bagot family in
Cumbria, is inscribed 'Levens High Constable' and was traditionally used for the toast 'Luck to Levens whilst t'Kent flows' – the
Kent being the local river. The Scottish writer H. W. Thompson
records that 'the largest saving glass (i.e. for toasting the ladies)
held more than a quart.'[103] Although the late Bernard Hughes
asserted that toasting glasses 'were charged with liquor, the con-
stables standing unused upon the table except on special ceremonial
occasions',[104] these monumental glasses evidently did circle the
table, as had been customary in continental Europe since the
Middle Ages. There such glasses were normally covered. In
England goblets with covers were rarer, but a fair number survives
(Pl. 32a). In 1738, at a ceremonial dinner in Bath, the Prince of
Wales pledged delegates from Bristol in 'a very large glass full of
Wine covered'.[105]

The concept of a glass-service, in the sense of a set of glasses of
different shapes and sizes for different types of drink, but held
together *en suite* by uniform decoration, seems to have been established in continental Europe well before the middle of the
eighteenth century.[106] It seems not to have gained general acceptance in England until later, probably not much before 1780. This
was perhaps because wheel-engraving and enamelling, the two
main techniques by which uniformity of decoration could be imposed, were less cultivated here than in the Germanic countries.
Nor was the idea favoured by the mode of serving drinks current
until well into the eighteenth century. The seventeenth-century
custom of serving drinks from a buffet as called for seems only to
have been modified in the eighteenth century by the formalising of
post-prandial drinking. After the dessert the cloth was drawn,
revealing the polished mahogany table below. François de la
Rochefoucauld, who stayed with the Duke of Grafton at Euston in
1784, may be our witness:[107]

> After the removal of the cloth, the table is covered with all kinds of
> wine, for even gentlemen of modest means always keep a large stock
> of good wine. On the middle of the table there is a small quantity of
> fruit, a few biscuits [to stimulate thirst] and some butter.
>
>   At this point the servants disappear. The ladies drink a glass or
> two of wine and at the end of half an hour all go out together. It is
> then that real enjoyment begins – there is not an Englishman who is
> not supremely happy at this particular moment. One proceeds to

drink – sometimes in an alarming measure. Everyone has to drink in his turn, for the bottles make a continuous circuit of the table and the host takes note that everyone is drinking in his turn. After this has gone on for some time . . . a fresh stimulus is supplied by the drinking of 'toasts'.

Port was the main drink circulated on these occasions, as de la Rochefoucauld makes clear elsewhere.

English after-dinner drinking is amply recorded, but the actual procedures at the dinner table are less easy to document. Formal service from a buffet probably began to go out of fashion in the second quarter of the eighteenth century. In the first decade it was normal practice in a great house to have a formal built-in buffet elaborately embellished and fitted with marble basins supplied with running water for washing glasses. The Duke of Devonshire installed an elaborate fitment at Chatsworth in 1704, and the Duke of Chandos had two at Cannons,[108] perhaps referred to by Pope in Epistle IV of the *Moral Essays* (1735):

> But hark! the chiming Clocks to dinner call;
> A hundred footsteps scrape the Marble Hall:
> The rich Buffet well-colour'd Serpents grace,
> And gaping Tritons spew to wash your face.
> Is this a dinner? This a Genial room?
> No, 'tis a Temple, and a Hecatomb.
> A solemn Sacrifice, perform'd in state,
> You drink by measure, and to minutes eat.
> So quick retires each flying course, you'd swear
> Sancho's dread Doctor and his Wand were there.
> Between each Act the trembling salvers ring,
> From soup to sweet-wine, and God bless the King.

Pope's satire of the mid-1730s is faithfully mirrored in Marcellus Laroon's picture of 1725 in the Royal Collection, showing a page carrying a salver of wine-glasses away from the buffet, on which a whole series of goblets is ranged. In the background a waiter appears to be serving glasses from another salver.[109] Only the relative informality and disorder of this picture contrast with Pope's lines, which evoke vividly the stiffness of a ceremonial in which drinking is regimented by courses, culminating in 'sweet-wine' and the royal toast.

If the baluster-glass in England had at its best an incomparable monumentality and a harmony of form, it could also easily lapse into a heavy slovenliness where the lavish use of material seemed an end in itself. A later continental critic, Bosc d'Antic, described English glass as 'beaucoup trop lourd'. Nevertheless, English crystal was the cynosure of continental makers, and all efforts were bent to emulating it. By the time Bosc d'Antic wrote in 1760,[110] English glass had in fact undergone a metamorphosis from its character in the earlier eighteenth century, when glasses were sold by the pound. Too much emphasis has perhaps been laid on the effects of the glass tax imposed in 1745.[111] This Act, which became effective in 1746, taxed glass by the weight of the metal in the pot. There was, therefore, a natural inclination on the manufacturer's part to save on his metal, and a consequent tendency for the value of a glass to shift from its weight to its workmanship. This shift, however, merely accelerated a tendency already perceptible in glass-making, as in the other arts. The formalised architectonic values of the Baroque were towards 1750 giving way before the lighter and more purely decorative spirit of the Rococo. In glass this movement showed itself in an attenuation of the monumental baluster stem, in more graceful inflexions of bowl-form, and in the cultivation of all sorts of decorative techniques.

These natural shifts of style, common to the arts in general, were given impetus in England by the influence of German glass-making. Just as in England glass-makers had groped their way after 1675 towards a concept of glass as a ponderous material resembling natural crystal, so too had those of Central Europe – notably Bohemia, where wheel-engraving of glass had been established before 1600. This new technique of glass decoration called for solid and colour-free glass, a material developed – probably by about 1650 – by adding lime to the potash-fluxed glass current in Bohemia. This crystal glass was perfected by 1680 at latest, and was followed by an explosive expansion of glass-engraving and glass-cutting in Bohemia. The art was gradually diffused throughout the Germanic countries and German/Bohemian glass now swept Europe, forcing even the Venetians into somewhat ineffective imitation. Its dominance was accentuated by political events. In 1713 the Treaty of Utrecht transferred the Spanish Netherlands to the Austrian Empire, and thus opened up the Low Countries to the uninhibited export of German/Bohemian glass. Already before this, however, its influence had been felt in England. As early as 1688 the itinerant glass-dealer and decorator Georg Franz Kreybich, from Steinschönau in Bohemia, had visited London and admired the English crystal glass, recording that 'they made more beautiful glass than what we imported, except that ours was engraved and painted' (i.e. enamelled).[112] The first intimation in English sources of the arrival of German glass occurs in 1709 in the *London Gazette* on 1 October: 'There is lately brought over a great parcel of very fine German Cut and Carved Glasses viz.: Jellies, Wine and Water Tumblers, Beer and Wine Glasses with Covers, and divers other sorts. The like hath not been exposed to public sale before.' The sequel appears in the same periodical on 18 October: 'Whereas the sale of German Cut Glasses at Stationer's Hall on the 13th Instant was interrupted by the great disturbance there made by some Glass Sellers of London whereby the auction could not be carried on. The same goods shall be sold in as small parcels as any one desires at very cheap rates.'[113] The glasses presumably sold, and this sort of gradual penetration no doubt sharply accelerated when a German King ascended the British throne in 1714.

The influence of a Court, however much disliked, has usually proved irresistible in the end, and a number of German features seem to have modified English glass style at this time. Perhaps chief among them was the 'pedestal' stem (p. 145), but important modifications affected the bowl of the wine-glass. To supplement the straight-sided funnel and round-funnel bowls came a number of forms which diversified and softened this rigid formula. Notable among them were the bell-bowl, sometimes exhibiting merely a slight waisting of a tallish bowl; the ogee; and the thistle. On the whole, these German-derived modifications lent a touch of elegance to a glass style which was slimming down after the baluster age, the stem gaining in height at the expense of the bowl and its own thickness, and now compiled mainly of slender balusters and inverted balusters, small globular and flattened knops which often enclosed air bubbles, and sections of straight stem, in varied combinations. One cannot say where balusters stop and these 'balustroids' or light balusters begin, but the trend is unmistakable and may be taken to begin about 1715. In a well-known portrait by Kneller, ascribed to the year 1721, two noble members of the Kit Cat Club are shown holding smallish funnel-bowled glasses with slim baluster stems having small knops above and below.[114] The stems are not yet particularly tall, but the glasses are perceptibly lighter than a full-blooded baluster. It is not to be supposed, however, that the balusters did not in a measure overlap with these lighter glasses. When in 1755 the young Newcastle glass-blower William Brown travelled to Norway to help establish English glass-making methods there, he evidently took with him some styles which would have looked remarkably old-fashioned in London. In the Nøstetangen pattern-book of 1763 one shape called

'Bruns model' ('Brown's pattern') is no more than a goblet with an acorn knop above a small basal knop, such as in England would normally be dated to about 1710–15.[115] It is hardly to be wondered at that the light balusters attributable to Newcastle continue well on into the 1760s, if not later. The conservatism of these Newcastle glasses is illustrated by the fact that a shape used in 1730 by the Dutchman Frans Greenwood for his diamond-point engraving[116] appears virtually unchanged as the vehicle for the Beilbys' enamelling in the 1760s.[117] A closely similar goblet engraved by Greenwood in 1747[118] has an exact parallel in another engraved by J. Van den Blyk in 1776:[119] although the glass might not have been brand new, it is unlikely to have been thirty years old.

Throughout the long evolution of the balusters and light balusters there was a parallel tradition which continued virtually unchanged, because change was hardly possible. This involved the 'drawn-stem' glasses, where the stem was drawn out from the metal of the bowl, sometimes with an enclosed tear formed by pricking the base of it (Pl. 36f). This two-piece vessel had its origins in Venice, where a tall thin-stemmed version was current. This was the soda-glass prototype of the slender English lead-metal toasting-glass of the eighteenth century, apt for those special and dramatic toasts where the glass was snapped between the fingers or dashed against the wall. The English drawn-stem existed in the seventeenth century, for a short-stemmed 'firing-glass' made by this technique and formerly in the Sir J. S. Risley Collection was engraved 'Success to Wil^m. & Mary' (1689–1694).[120] This glass had the typical thick foot made for hammering on the table when responding to toasts at corporate gatherings. The drawn-stem glass existed in numberless varieties – thick or thin stem, plain or folded foot, wide or narrow bowl, with or without a tear – offering almost no means of dating. A wine-glass inscribed 'Charles and Mary Scriven 1709' (formerly C. Kirkby Mason Collection)[121] and a goblet in the Fitzwilliam Museum, Cambridge, with engraving celebrating the Peace of Utrecht in 1713[122] differ very little from a glass once in the W. H. Lister Collection dated 1741, or another celebrating Dean Swift after his death in 1745, previously in the Bles Collection.[123] Occasionally a drawn stem was superimposed on a light inverted baluster (Pl. 36e), or later on an air-twist stem, to make a composite (three-piece) glass conforming in general proportions to the Kit Cat series.

The method of making the drawn-stem glass tended to impose on the craftsman a funnel-bowl of concave, or at most straight-sided, profile. If a relatively cheap glass with round-funnel or bell-bowl were required, a plain columnar stem could be used (Pl. 37b, d). In the second quarter of the century these plain three-piece glasses were sometimes quite elaborately wheel-engraved; and thereafter the cut-stem wine-glass was essentially a plain-stem glass modified by facet- or flute-cutting, whether restricted to the stem or on occasion spreading right over bowl and foot (Pl. 50c). After 1750, when adventitious decoration of some sort tended to be used on every glass of any pretension, the undecorated plain-stem glass probably descended in the social scale, to be used in kitchens and taverns. Here it probably partly replaced the short heavy dram-glasses depicted in scenes of communal drinking by Hogarth and others earlier in the century. The effects of the Excise of 1745 would have fallen most heavily in this sphere, the need for a robust glass being balanced against a cost inflated by the lavish use of metal. The risks of breakage, amply documented by Hogarth, made the plain-stem glass a suitable vehicle for election toasts, as exemplified in the simply engraved glasses made for Sir Francis Knollys in the 1761 Reading election,[124] or for Joseph Taylor at Ashburton in 1739.[125]

About 1710 a further stem-type joined the balusters and baluster derivatives, the drawn and the plain stems. This was the pedestal (or 'shouldered') stem, often wrongly called in England the 'Silesian' stem (Pl. 37a, c, e). Although it certainly derived from the Germanic lands, its origin is much more likely to be found in Thuringia or Hesse, where the so-called 'pseudo-faceted baluster' took the place of the truly faceted (wheel-cut) inverted balusters of Bohemia-Silesia. This pseudo-faceted stem was made by blowing or pressing a gather of glass into a four-, six- or eight-sided mould, the polygonal piece being then tapered in the working to give a wide top and a slender base. In Thuringian practice this stem often had between it and the bowl a knop formed in the same mould, a feature which sometimes (but rarely) recurs in English glasses. Although this type of moulded stem seems to be deeply entrenched in Germany, it seems to occur almost as early in England – assuming that the four-sided pedestal stems inscribed 'God Save King George' (or variants) are accepted as marking the accession of George I in 1714 (Pl. 37e).[126] With their somewhat uncouth lettering they have more the feeling of Coronation souvenirs than of elegant adjuncts to a gentleman's table. Many of them may have gone in the breaking of glasses at the Loyal Toast on such a momentous occasion. A fragment of one has been found in the Thames.[127] It has been asserted that pedestal stems in themselves denoted Hanoverian loyalties – a dubious theory – but later on these angled, usually octagonal or hexagonal, stems sometimes had moulded crowns on the shoulder. These were more commonly replaced by stars (Pl. 37a, c), a detail also found on the comparable German glasses. That the four-sided and the polygonal stems over-lapped in date appears from a glass in the Fitzwilliam Museum, Cambridge, the octagonal stem having stars on the shoulder, while a knop above is taken from a (?)1714 mould inscribed 'God Bless King Georg' (sic).[128] The English glasses are often of high quality, but the pedestal stem seemingly did not have a long vogue in drinking-glasses. It passed readily down the scale to feature on dessert-glasses such as sweetmeats (Pl. 43c) and salvers, or on candlesticks (Pl. 43d) and tapersticks.

All these types of wrought stems were destined to be overtaken in importance by the twist stems which dominate the second and third quarters of the century. The earliest was the air-twist, which probably occurred first among the drawn-stem glasses, where the 'tear' in the base of the bowl had been a constant feature. This was pricked with a blunt tool into the mass of glass at the bowl-base, trapped, and pulled out with the stem itself into a tapering form. It was a simple step to increase the number of air pockets – as was already being done with bubbles in the small knops on light-baluster glasses – and then to twist the resultant threads of air to form a spiral (Pl. 38d). W. A. Thorpe has pointed out that the technique was probably practised as a curiosity quite early in the eighteenth century, citing a (?) calender in the British Museum with an air-twist in the shaft, and a silver mount dated 1716.[129] Dated or datable air-twist drinking-glasses, however, are rare before 1750, and it is impossible to establish a date for their introduction. The expression 'new fashioned glasses' begins to occur fairly frequently in advertisements of the late 1730s, and may refer to air-twist glasses, although the phrase is vague.[130] Only when the epithet 'worm'd' appears, first in an American newspaper in 1746[131] and then, in 1747, on a bill rendered by a London glassman,[132] can one be sure that air-twist glasses are being referred to. A phenomenon normally finds its way into print only some time after it has occurred, and some air-twist glasses are decorated with wheel-engraved ornament of a type datable to the 1730s or even earlier.[133] It seems likely that the air-twist technique was well established in this decade. A glass dated 1737 is recorded.[134]

An air-twist stem drawn out of the base of a bowl, giving a two-piece glass, risks mishap; a three-piece glass permits the stem to be prepared in advance, with enhanced chances of success. Both methods had their teething troubles. In the two-piece glass the twist was frequently irregular at the top, and occasionally petered out below. In the three-piece glass there was often difficulty in keeping the air-threads even (Pl. 38c). By the middle of the century these difficulties seem to have been mainly overcome. There are a number of glasses of the 1750s on which the air-twists are perfectly formed, despite one or more knop-like swellings in the stem (Pl. 38a, centre, and b). This applies to the many glasses with wheel-engraving of Jacobite content – notably those with direct reference to Prince Charles Edward, the Young Pretender – presumably made at the time of the 1745 rising or following the battle of Culloden (Pl. 38b, c). The double-knopped air-twist spiral, well executed, forms one of the handsomest stems made in eighteenth-century England.

In the third quarter of the century a number of variants of the plain spiral air-twist was elaborated, sometimes with a gauze-like corkscrew of fine lines (Pl. 38a, right), sometimes with a double-series air-twist in which one spiral is enclosed within another (Pl. 38a, left). This effect was probably produced by a pronged tool with some prongs grouped in the centre, others on the circumference.[135] The lump of glass pierced by these prongs was then extended and twisted to produce the complex design. The long rod was then divided into suitable lengths for making the stems of a whole set of glasses. The bowl and foot could be varied as desired. A band or crimped collar might add a further touch to the stem (Pl. 38d); and occasionally an air-twist section was combined with elements from the light-baluster repertory to produce a composite stem. What may be regarded as an inferior variant of the air-twist stem, lacking the brilliance of the enclosed air-columns, was the 'incised' twist stem, which was finely rib-moulded and twisted (Pl. 37f).

The heyday of the air-twist glass probably lay within the five years on either side of 1750, and it was soon overtaken in popularity by the opaque-white twist. This was made by a technique which went back to sixteenth-century Venice and which no doubt lingered on, mostly unused, in the glassman's repertoire. That it lay ready to hand is shown by a small seal (or pipe-stopper?) in the Northampton Museum (Pl. 39a). The shank includes a pair of twisted opaque-white tapes, and the head encloses a coin of 1701, suggesting a relatively early date on a par with the air-twist 'calender' of 1716 already mentioned. Both are undoubtedly 'friggers', small objects of curiosity made outside the routine production and often displaying unusual techniques for their own sake.

Opaque-twist stems were made by ranging canes of opaque-white glass round a heat-resistant mould and picking them up on a gather of crystal glass which was then marvered and pulled out while being twisted.[136] Starting as a plain multiple spiral or pair of corkscrews, the opaque-twist was developed to a high pitch of complexity, one column of threads sometimes enclosing a second or even occasionally a third. Such 'three-series' stems are relatively rare. Since the stems had to be produced separately, the opaque-twist glasses are always of three-piece construction. The earliest recorded specimen bore the date 1747,[137] and although phrases such as 'Glasses from the newest patterns now in England', appearing in the early 1750s, may relate to these glasses,[138] the earliest unequivocal reference seems to occur in an advertisement of Jonas Phillips' Glass Warehouse in Norwich (*Norwich Mercury*, 12 February 1757):[139] 'The Goods are entirely new, and of the neatest Patterns now made in England, either cut, flower'd, enamel'd, moulded, worm'd or plain.' Further Phillips advertisements suggest that 'enamel'd' is contemporary parlance and here refers to the opaque-white in the stem and not to enamel painting on the bowl. From the advertisements it appears that his stock was brought in, most probably from London.

About the date of this advertisement, the most coherent identifiable series of opaque-twist wine-glasses was being made in Bristol (Pl. 39c, left). These record some of the privateers known to have been based on Bristol during the Seven Years' War (1756–63). The glasses are more likely to have been made and engraved near the earlier date, when the ships were being commissioned.[140] They are mostly homogeneous in style, with slightly waisted bucket-bowls and opaque-twist stems of various designs, the bowls wheel-engraved with representations of the ships, the inscriptions sometimes in diamond-point. Bristol is known to have been a centre for making enamel glass (p. 187), and offshoots at Chepstow (1764) and Warrington (about 1767), started by Bristolians, are also recorded as making 'enamel' glass.[141] That opaque-twist stems were actually made in Bristol appears from the *Diary* of Silas Neville, who recorded in August 1768:[142] 'After dinner saw the different operations in making a wine-glass and beer ditto and putting the white in the stem; the workman gave us a specimen of the white metal.' In 1769 the New Glasshouses at Sunderland were making 'white enamel',[143] and when James Keith and William Brown migrated from Tyneside to Norway in 1755 (p. 143), they took with them the new art of making opaque-twist stems. The actual making of opaque-white glass offered no great problems at this time, and for those who had not mastered the art the material was available in rod or cake-form from those who had. In the Midlands, Grazebrook and Denham are recorded as making 'smooth enamel glass', probably at Audnam, near Stourbridge,[144] the local glassmen's ability to make twist stems being demonstrated by an anonymous account of a visit to Stourbridge in 1776:[145]

> I was really astonished to see with what facility a process was conducted, that always appeared to me so extremely mysterious . . . particularly the introducing of those beautiful spiral threads of a different colour, so nicely spun within the neck of a wine glass, which appear so inexplicable, is performed, even by children. One of these glasses I desired to be made me as elegant as possible which was done almost as soon as asked for . . . I put the glass into my pocket . . . but the first stile I came to, demolished it for ever.

The making of opaque-twist glasses was probably practised in all the main English centres.

It has been suggested that the opaque-twist stem was a consequence of the Excise Act of 1745, which did not tax enamel. Since the enamel can only have represented a fraction of the weight of a glass, whereas the complex technique must have added appreciably to its cost, changing fashion probably had more than economics to do with the popularity of the opaque-twist stem. The economic argument may gain some weight from the fact that the opaque-twist appears to have gone out at much the same time as a fresh Excise Act (1777) levied 18s 8d on every hundredweight of enamel glass, while doubling the duty on flint glass.[146]

Like the air-twists, the opaque-twist glasses may be differentiated by the shape of bowl or foot, a domed or folded foot occasionally occurring, although this is rare. Not infrequently the bowl is moulded, in vertical (Pl. 40a, c) or slightly wrythen flutes, mesh-pattern, and occasionally with a stylised plant scroll. A pattern of faint horizontal ridges has often been associated with East Anglia, glasses on which they occur being called 'Lynn' glasses, although no connection with King's Lynn has been established. The glasshouse there seems to have closed down before 1750.[147]

The principle of twist-decorating stems was extended to include numerous permutations.[148] Sometimes air-twists and opaque-twists combined to give a 'mixed twist'; opaque-twists were intermingled with a variety of coloured threads – opaque red, yellow ('canary') and brownish-purple; and translucent red, green and blue, etc. – in a seemingly inexhaustible series (Pl. 40f). These are rare in varying degrees, and even rarer is the stem combining opaque-, air- and colour-twists.

All the glasses so far discussed were apt to be decorated by engraving. Diamond-point engraving, firmly established in the seventeenth century, lasted well into the eighteenth. This work is normally anonymous, but one engraver, decorating a 23-cm (9-in.) goblet with a bust of Queen Anne surmounted by two angels holding a crown, signed the foot 'Felix Foster Fecit 1718'.[149] Nothing appears otherwise to be known about Felix Foster. One or two further glasses dedicated to Queen Anne are of considerable elaboration, and may have been the work of professionals. A distinguished series of calligraphic glasses has already been referred to (p. 137). After the 1720s diamond-point engraving tends to be the work of amateurs, although the calligrapher of the Scottish 'Amen' glasses, however simple-minded his art, could reasonably claim to be a professional.[150] Probably of an opposite political persuasion, and certainly of far greater competence, was George Chapman, who signed three glasses between 1755 and 1761. The earliest bears the toast 'The Glorious Memory of K^g Willm' against a ground of formalised plant forms and insects, while the second (dated 1756) is beautifully and more naturalistically engraved with bouquets of flowers and dedicated 'to the memory of Oliver Cromwell' (Pl. 36f). The last and most accomplished is inscribed 'The Glorious Memory' and has fine figural as well as floral subjects.[151] Two of the three glasses originated in Ireland, and George Chapman was presumably an Irish Protestant. The eighteenth-century *littérateur* was apt to carry a diamond-pencil in his (or her) pocket and commit his thoughts to convenient window-panes. The point could equally be turned on a drinking-glass, and there are innumerable miscellaneous inscriptions on glasses recording names, gifts, toasts and a variety of special occasions.

Far more significant was wheel-engraving, an art demanding a long apprenticeship, strict discipline and fixed installations. The glass is cut by putting it to a copper wheel mounted on a horizontal shaft and motivated by a foot-treadle, the actual cutting being done by an abrasive, such as corundum, in a greasy medium applied periodically to the wheel. The size and shape of the cut is dictated by the diameter and profile of the wheel, and the engraver has a rack full of different wheels, changing them in the hollow chuck of the spindle as the work demands. The engraving is built up of these hollow cuts, which can be left matt or polished using progressively finer abrasives.[152]

The beginnings of wheel-engraving in England are obscure. In 1699 a man named Alexander Nichols, 'glass engraver', is recorded at the sign of the Star in Nightingale Lane, Wapping.[153] Glass engraver might merely imply diamond-point work. The well-known Nuremberg engraver Anton Wilhelm Mäuerl (1672–1737) was in England between 1699 and 1710, making paper cut-outs, but he is not specifically mentioned as engraving glass.[154] As early as 1688 the peripatetic Bohemian merchant and engraver George Franz Kreybich had visited London (p. 142). He may have practised his art in England, since on his journeys he often travelled with a portable engraving apparatus. English glasses exist with wheel-engraved decoration datable to the years about 1700. In the Bles Collection was a firing-glass inscribed 'SUCCESS TO Wᵐ & MARY' (1689–94);[155] and in the Grant Francis Collection a goblet engraved with the Royal Arms as borne by Queen Anne between 1702 and 1707.[156] The craftsmen who did this work may have been Bohemian or German, for at a later date a number of German names occur in the written record, particularly in the context of cutting. In the earlier period – before, say, 1725 – these men were probably to be found in the grinding shops of the mirror-makers, their names obscured by their subordination to men like John Gumley or Giles Grendey, who kept shop, issued advertisements, and were generally in the public eye.[157] A number of early eighteenth-century mirrors have borders and slips covering the junction of the main plates which are both cut into abstract shapes in low relief and wheel-engraved with a variety of motifs. Best documented are the mirrors supplied in 1711 to the Earl of Winchelsea and Nottingham by Thomas Howcraft and Richard Robinson of the India Cabinet in Long Acre, London.[158] A large arched three-panel overmantel mirror (Pl. 47a) has two vertical slips in the form of pilasters covering the joins between the central and the two side plates. These slips are cut in bas-relief, and the surfaces engraved with monogram initials below coronets, above which wreaths of flowers and leaves appear to encircle the pilasters, all rendered in wheel-engraving. The main borders of the mirror are formed by acanthus-like leaves cut in a broad bas-relief, each springing from a single circular 'printie', all these being typical cutter's motifs; between them wheel-engraved birds perch on flowering stems – characteristic themes in German engraving, destined to recur on the drinking-glasses of about 1725–40.

A second mirror supplied at the same time has similar borders but a lunette in the cresting engraved with the coronet and crest of the Earls of Nottingham.[159] Correspondence concerning this commission is recorded. One of the mirrors cost £82 1s 6d, a great sum at that time, the bill including 'sholoping [scalloping] ye end glasses and cutting ye scroops – £3; a coat of arms £6 10s 0d; 23 feet of glass borders 6 inches wide £9 4s 0d.' The suppliers offered to reduce the cost if the glass slips were not 'wraught with flourishing' – presumably a reference to the engraving. It will be observed that the engraving of a coat of arms cost twice as much as the cutting work. A number of contemporary mirrors show the broad engraving style which would nowadays be called 'intaglio', but which in eighteenth-century parlance was called 'underhand cutting' from the method of working. Other mirrors show wheel-engraved elements of varying complexity, the most elaborate being a glass – more an ornament than a true looking-glass – having a central plate engraved with a rhymed version of the Lord's Prayer, within an elaborate draped framework supported by cherubim and two kneeling figures. This is framed within a broad border decorated in both underhand cutting and wheel-engraving. The border has clearly been adapted, and may have come from another, contemporary, mirror. The central panel is signed 'J.C. compost delineavt et Sculp. 1728'.[160] It is not known who 'J.C.' was, but it may be noted that there was a looking-glass maker named John Caddey working between 1724 and 1727 at The Cabinet in King Street at the corner of Guildhall Yard.[161]

The *Daily Journal* for 30 August 1735 contains the following advertisement: 'The Glass Sellers Arms. Where are to be had the best Double Flint Glass, Diamond-Cut and Plain, with several curiosities engraved on Glass.' The advertisement was inserted by one Benjamin Payne, who on 12 June had advertised in the *London Evening Post*: '. . . the Arms of all the Royal Family finely engraved on glasses. By Benjamin Payne'.[162] Benjamin Payne had been apprenticed in 1725 to Glisson Maydwell, who became Master of the Glass Sellers' Company in 1739.[163] The firm of George Maydwell (probably Glisson's brother) and Co. specialised in cut glass, and later advertised 'Engraving on Glasses of ev'ry kind in the Newest Taste' (Pl. 46). Benjamin Payne had his training in an establishment which was doubtless in the van of the movement towards cutting and engraving. By a curious coincidence, 1735 also produced the first overt reference to glass-engraving in Ireland. The *Dublin Evening Post* of February 1735 advertised:[164]

Whereas several gentlemen and ladies whose curiosity led them to have their arms, crests, words, letters or figures carved on their glassware, and as several have had cause to complain of the extravagant prices, these are therefore to advertise the public that Joseph Martin living in Fleet Street, Dublin, opposite the Golden Ball, is the only person that was employed by the managers of the glasshouse in Fleet Street in carving said wares, and that there is no other person in the kingdom that does profess to do the like work. He therefore having broken off with the said gentlemen does propose to deal more candidly with those as are pleased to employ him by working at such moderate rates as none hereafter may have reason to complain.

By chance, a glass exists bearing the roughly engraved inscription, 'Lord Arch Bishop of Dublin 1715'.[165] The quality of both glass and engraving suggests a local origin, so Martin may have had a predecessor in Dublin. There was in London between 1714 and 1726 a substantial glass-grinder named John Martin. If it is accepted that some of the earliest engravers worked for the mirror-grinders, Joseph Martin may well have been a younger relative of John Martin striking out on his own.[166] The Dublin glass industry certainly drew its inspiration from London.

At this date the commonest engraved themes evidently comprised heraldic devices or inscriptions, although the ambiguous word 'figures' in Joseph Martin's advertisement admits a doubt. In London at least, work of a purely decorative kind must have been in progress. On a number of glasses of about 1720 occur ornamental borders which are obviously derived from the *Laub und Bandelwerk* of the late seventeenth-century German engravers (Pl. 32b, centre). In this style leafy scrollwork is combined with angular and curved strapwork in symmetrical compositions, providing a framework often enlivened with flowers and small birds. This style derives ultimately from the engraved pattern-books for decorative artists compiled, mainly in Nuremberg and Augsburg, by such designers as Paul Decker. Since many wheel-engravers hailed from Germany, bringing a German style, the earliest of the formal borders on English glasses are likely to be the work of immigrants (cf. Pl. 50a). The designs soon loosened up and became less formal, the engravers perhaps losing some of their technical edge in a less competitive milieu, and an English taste for freedom and informal naturalism gradually asserting itself (Pl. 50d, f). Since elements of the baroque borders, with their little figures of birds, also occur on the early mirrors, this strengthens the assumption that the German engravers may have started work in mirror-grinding shops.

Whereas on the Continent the engravers slid imperceptibly from symmetrical baroque into asymmetrical rococo, in England the baroque borders gave way to an easy naturalism, the main inspiration of which came from the garden, but also included figural themes (Pl. 48f), The term 'flowered Glasses' first occurs in the *Daily Advertiser* for 21 December 1742.[167] The advertisement was inserted by Jerome Johnson, of the Entire Glass Shop at the corner of St Martin's Lane, and this man continued to advertise until 1761 at least, by which date he had moved to the Cockpit White Flint Glasshouse in Southwark, with a sales outlet at the Star in Bow Street, Covent Garden. In January 1752 he calls himself 'the Maker and Glass Engraver', but it is questionable whether he was actually a practising craftsman, although he consistently refers to himself as 'the real workman' and 'the first inventor'. Wheel-engraving really was done in his shop, however, as is shown by an advertisement of 9 November 1756 in the *London Evening Post*: 'Jerom Johnson, at the Entire Glass Shop, &c., is determined to sell off all, and retire . . . The whole Stock in Trade consists of various Cut Glasses and others . . . Also working tools, Lapidary Benches, Scalloper's Mills, Glass Flowerers' and Engraving Tools.'[168]

Although many other large glass-dealers certainly also kept glass-engravers in their workshops, they probably commissioned work from independent craftsmen too. An American visitor to London in 1776 'walkt . . . to the Engravers in the green yard, Pepper alley, near London bridge . . . The flowers, figures and letters (all of which I saw wrot) are performed by little copper blocks moistened with oyl, on wheels, and executed with great ease and surprised (sic) celerity.'[169] In a survey of English engraved glass a number of artists with recognisable styles can be distinguished, and in a recent study of engraved Jacobite glasses, where the sample is a large one, no less than eight different hands have been identified.[170] We do not know in what centres these engravers worked. In due course the technique of engraving spread to most glass-working centres.

The question of the differentiation of glasses in accordance with the drinks served in them has already been touched on for the seventeenth century (pp. 67–8, 104–5). Then the distinction apparently depended on capacity alone – the greatest for beer, the next size for French wine, the smallest for Spanish wine. In the eighteenth century this rule appears to have been partially modified by the adoption of certain *shapes* for certain types of drinks, perhaps most strikingly in the case of the ale-glass. Towards 1700 this appears to have become fossilised as a tallish tapering glass, usually on a short stem, the bowl normally decorated by mould-blown ribbing which ran over into the short stem (Pl. 27b, right). This two-piece glass is usually called a 'short ale' and occasionally the bowl set directly on the foot produces a 'dwarf ale'. The capacity is standard at about 100 cc (3–4 fluid oz.), an indication of the strength of beer (with hops) and ale (without) at this time. The tall, narrow bowl – usually without ribbing – could be mounted on a baluster or other stem to make a three-piece glass; and later in the eighteenth century these ale-glasses might be engraved with a spray of hops and ears of barley indicating their content.[171] This form ran on well into the nineteenth century. Weaker brews, such as 'small beer', were almost certainly drunk from tankards made of glass (Pl. 42c), silver, or other materials. Of glass tankards there is no lack. They fall into roughly two types – a bell-bowl on a low foot, and a flat-based straight-sided vessel either cylindrical or tapering from base to rim. Both have an ear-shaped side handle, and may be decorated with varieties of mould-blown ribbing or mesh-pattern, usually confined to a zone round the base. The bell-shaped tankard frequently has a coin enclosed between foot and body, but this approximate means of dating disappointingly reveals merely that the type was very long-lived indeed.

It is not clear why the narrow-bowled ale-glass evolved as it did, but a hint may be taken from the parallel development of the champagne-glass. Champagne seems not to have reached England before the Restoration in 1660, but thereafter was popularised by such French expatriates as St Evremond and the Comte de Grammont. At this time the *méthode champenoise* which produces today's sparkling pale champagne was undeveloped, and the amber and red still champagnes of Sillery and other centres were appreciated throughout the eighteenth century. Nevertheless, champagne was regarded as an essentially effervescent wine, even though often no more than *pétillant*. As early as 1663 Samuel Butler in *Hudibras* referred to 'brisk Champaign', and by 1676 Sir George Etheredge could call the wine 'sparkling Champaign', epithets which recur in eighteenth-century literature.[172] That this champagne was drunk in flute-like glasses can be demonstrated from various sources. On 2 February 1773 Colebron Hancock, a glass-seller in Cockspur Street, London, supplied the historian Edmund Gibbon with '1 doz. of Champain Flutes 8s'. And when William Ferguson came into the estate of Raith in 1781, Johann Zoffany represented him celebrating among his friends with four tall cylindrical-bowled glasses standing on the table, and one of the company holding his thumb over the bottle.[173] There is no reason to suppose that this momentous episode was being commemorated in beer. Champagne was probably always the most costly wine available in the eighteenth century, and thus appropriate to a great occasion. In 1703 the Methuen Treaty had imposed a tax of £55 a tun on French wines – as opposed to £7 a tun on port'[174] – and the contemporary anti-French sentiment is reflected in Swift's lines:

> Be sometimes to your country true,
> Have once the public good in view;
> Bravely despise Champagne at Court,
> And chose (sic) to dine at home with Port.   *On the Irish Club*[175]

Even among French wines champagne topped the bill, and at Vauxhall Gardens in 1762 it cost 8s a bottle, whereas Burgundy cost 6s and claret 5s.[176]

The champagne-flute was often a vehicle for engraved (Pl. 40e), enamelled or gilt decoration, the vine and grapes motif often emphasising its use for wine rather than ale. Even where there is no decoration the superior quality of a glass, in its metal or its making, may raise the presumption that it is used for champagne rather than for ale (Pl. 40c). Stem-forms varied with the changing fashions which affected other wine-glasses. Occasionally the base of the bowl was decorated with mould-blown fluting. It is sometimes maintained that certain glasses with hemispherical bowls were used for drinking champagne – forerunners of the nineteenth-century champagne-glass. There seems to be no factual support for this idea, and these glasses were almost certainly sweetmeats (p. 171).

Flute-glasses do not seem to have been exclusive to effervescent drinks. The earliest reference, much quoted, is in Lovelace's line, 'Elles of beer, Flutes of Canary',[177] and this convention appears to have lasted on into the eighteenth century. A bill rendered in 1753 by the London glass-seller Thomas Betts includes, '3 Pl(ain) Spanish Flutes'.[178] There may have been inflections of shape or differences of size separating the sack-flute from the champagne-flute. It is possible that the smaller flute usually called a ratafia is in fact a Spanish flute (Pl. 40a). This would accord with the differentiation by capacity familiar since the seventeenth century.

Another drink for which the flute was appropriate was cider, and examples are preserved with engraving representing sprays of fruiting apple, with or without a codling moth; or the words 'No Excise', often accompanied by a barrel. This inscription refers to Walpole's Excise Bill of 1733, or to the Excise of 1763. Sometimes the word 'CYDER' makes the purpose of the glass explicit. These motifs also recur on bucket- or ogee-bowl glasses (Pl. 39d, right), and a distinctive identity was apparently never established for the cider-glass.[179] The name does not even appear in English lists, and occurs only once in Irish advertisements.[180] Since cider was sometimes passed off as champagne, it is appropriate that it should have been drunk from flute-glasses.

E. B. Haynes gave the capacity of an eighteenth century wine-glass as 57 to 85 cc (2 to 3 fl. oz),[181] but a little elementary experimentation shows that it can go as low as 42 cc (1½ fl. oz). An advertisement of 1748, however, refers to 'Wine, Gill and Half-pint Wine and Water Glasses'.[182] A gill is a quarter of a pint, or 142 cc (5 fl. oz), and presumably the name means what it says – a glass to accommodate wine mixed with water, and therefore 2½ to three times the capacity of an ordinary wine-glass. In March 1784 Lord Napier is reported as 'chatting till near 12 – he had a sandwich and wine and water'.[183] It would be tempting to suppose that this type of glass might be the same as the 'goblet' which seems to appear for the first time in the glass-sellers' lists in 1775 in an advertisement by C. Haedy. In 1777, however, the same vendor advertised in the *Bath Chronicle* 'all sorts of drinking glasses . . . and goblets, wine and water glasses',[184] which would seem to rule out the equation: 'goblet = wine and water glass'. In the first half of the nineteenth century, however, references occur to 'three-to-pint' and 'half-pint Goblets', phrases which suggest glasses of the size of the quarter- to half-pint 'wine and water glasses'.[185] If differences existed in the eighteenth century, they must have been very slight. There is apparently no evidence to link these names with any particular shape.

A further complication is the use of the word 'rummer', originally a corruption of the German 'Roemer', and first used in the glass-sellers' lists in 1772 (1770 in Ireland).[186] The original Roemer was a glass, usually green, for drinking 'Rhenish' wine (p. 120). G. Bernard Hughes records that Gayton in his *Pleasure Notes* (1654) ordered 'a lusty rummer of Rhenish'; while Dryden in 1673 wrote, 'then Rhenish rummers walk the round'.[187] Merrett (1662), however, speaks of 'the Romer for Rhenish wine, for Sack, Claret, Beer, plain moulded coloured in whole or in part',[188] a description not altogether clear, but certainly implying that the glass was not restricted to Rhenish alone. In 1732 'Squire Hoare' bought of the glass-seller Glisson Maydwell '12 Wine Glasses 4 Beer 2 Rummers'.[189] Altogether the word seems to have lived right through the eighteenth century until taken up in the glass-sellers' lists in 1770, although its connotation at different dates is uncertain. The old Roemer shape can be traced through the eighteenth century in unbroken succession from Ravenscroft's form (Pl. 23d), the late seventeenth-century version usually having gadrooning round the bowl but retaining the prunted hollow stem (Pl. 28b). Later the stem solidified and followed the general trends of stem evolution in ordinary wine-glasses, the bowl tending to shed the moulded gadrooning. While many of these eighteenth-century Roemers were colourless, others showed an awareness of their German ancestry and were made in green flint glass, through which an air-twist or even an opaque-white twist can sometimes be glimpsed. This conscious reversion to green seems to suggest that these glasses were still intended for Rhenish wines. Their relative rarity perhaps reflects the subordinate place occupied by German wines in contemporary drinking habits. Thus during 1720 to 1739 the Barbers' Company consumed 'Rhenish' to a value of £31 10s 8d, as compared with £948 5s 3d expended on 'Red and White Port'. Lest this be thought a reflection of bourgeois drinking habits only, the Earl of Bristol in the same period spent £15 13s 0d on Rhenish and Moselle wine, but £241 19s 6d on claret and £65 0s 6d on port.[190]

When we come to the 1770s the picture changes. One may look back from the vantage point of the nineteenth century, when rummers regularly appear in glass lists, and surmise that the rummer of the late eighteenth century was probably a capacious glass mounted on a short stem (Pl. 42d). The bowl might be ovoid, a round funnel, or a bucket. An example of the first kind, mounted on a rudimentary stem with a flattened knop on top, once in the Risley Collection, had a bowl wheel-engraved with fruiting vine and the legend: 'Rebecca Creedey, Born April 23rd, 1766'.[191] This inscription is unlikely to be retrospective, and the conical foot of this glass confirms the eighteenth-century impression. G. B. Hughes quotes a writer of 1782 describing a visitor to a wayside inn; he 'ordered in a bottle of the best port the beggarly place could produce and tossed it off in an ecstasy of two rummers',[192] which neatly demonstrates that the glass was roughly of half-pint capacity or more, and that it was used for other drinks than hock. Indeed the rummer probably lent itself well to the consumption of spirits diluted with water, a waxing fashion after 1750. It took its cue from the grog of the Navy – watered-down rum. This association may have contributed to the usage of the word 'rummer', subtly perverting its original derivation from the white wine Roemer. Many of the miscellaneous ovoid-bowled glasses seen in late eighteenth-century satirical graphics may represent the goblets, rummers and 'wine and water' glasses used for diluted drinks of various kinds. A good example may be seen in David Allan's picture 'The Cathcart

Family', painted at Schaw Park, near Alloa, in 1784–5 to commemorate the first cricket match played north of the Tweed. On a table beside a silver ewer (for water ?) stands an ovoid-bowl rummer ready to refresh the sportsmen.

One type of glass which receives little attention in the glass literature is the tumbler (Pls. 42a, 43a), yet it was probably one of the most used glasses in eighteenth-century England – even if mainly among the lower orders. The footman John Macdonald in his *Memoirs* (1763) records of a generous officer, 'Of every bottle of wine he sent me a tumbler-glass full'.[193] Joseph Highmore's picture 'Mr Oldham and his Friends', probably painted in the 1740s, represents four respectable middle-class men gathered round a rather small punch-bowl. One holds a wine-glass, but the central figure sits at ease with his pipe in his left hand and a tumbler carelessly tilted in his right.[194] John Greene about 1670 (p. 105) had used the word 'tumbler' of a vertical-sided glass as wide as it was tall – the larger sizes for beer and wine, and the smaller for brandy. The word recurs intermittently from the late seventeenth century until it appears fairly regularly in the glass-sellers' lists from the 1740s onwards. The slightly tapering shape was by this time established. A technical treatise called *The Elaboratory laid open* (1758) describes with scientific precision 'the common glasses, made, in form of a section of a cone, for drinking water'. They varied in size, and Jonas Phillips of Norwich advertised in the *Norwich Mercury* of 5 August 1758, 'Pint, Half and Quarter Pint Tumblers'.[195] The half-pint size is probably the commonest. The use of tumblers – at least to judge by engraved examples – increased towards 1800, and Hartshorne reproduces from the Sitwell records at Renishaw bills of the 1790s recording large purchases – '2 doz. ½ Pint Tumbrs cut Bottms 16s' on 6 June 1791 followed by numerous further orders up to 1798, giving a total of six dozen half-pint and a dozen quarter-pint tumblers in eight years.[196] It is certainly true that in the British transatlantic colonies tumblers were used in great numbers, the bases of hundreds turning up on excavated sites in Canada and the USA.

Tumblers were decorated in a number of ways – mould-blown, enamelled (pp. 192–3) or gilt. Hughes quoted *The British Journal* for 1773, referring to 'new fashion'd tumblers neatly burned with gold flowers'.[197] They were also wheel-cut, many of the glasses mentioned in the numerous Haedy advertisements between 1766 and 1781 presumably being decorated in this way, since the Haedys were essentially glass-cutters (p. 195).[198] The 'cut Bottoms' of the Renishaw tumblers must have been executed in a cutting shop, whether the phrase implies a smooth cut base or a zone of vertical flutes round it. Tumblers with overall cut decoration are known, one even engraved with the name of the man who made it – James Jagger – and the date 1776.[199] Wheel-engraving, however, was by far the commonest mode (Pl. 42a), and Hughes records a reference to 'Flower'd pint, half and quarter pint tumblers' in the *Weekly Mercury* for April 1771.[200] Apart from the flowers, all sorts of themes, many of them commemorative, were used on these glasses – derived from sport, trade, politics, freemasonry, the army, and particularly the navy. Towards the end of the century the exploits of the navy recur repeatedly, commemorating the victories of Keppel, Rodney, Howe, Duncan, St Vincent and Nelson. It is perhaps relevant that the navy's grog lent itself to drinking from a tumbler, as the tumbler itself did to life on board ship.

At the other extreme was the 'cordial-glass', deliberately small in capacity as its content was strong. A great many drinks sailed under the colours of 'cordials', including gin, the poor man's tipple from 1713 onwards. Usually the word implies a strong concoction, often based on brandy and flavoured with various kinds of fruits, flowers, herbs and spices, with exotic names to match. In 1703 angelica, baum (balm), clary (a pot herb of the sage family), caraway, citron peel, juniper, lemon peel, mint, orange peel, rosemary and wormwood cordials were available commercially at 2s per pint.[201] Their general style may be judged from the recipe 'To make Carraway Brandy' in E. Smith's *The Compleat Housewife* (1753): 'Steep an ounce of carraway-seeds and six ounces of sugar in a quart of brandy for nine days, and clear it off; it is a good cordial.' Small wonder that in Mrs Centlivre's play *The Busy-Body*, Sir Jealous should say to his daughter, ''Tis your ratafia, persico, cinnamon, citron and spirit of clary cause such swimming in the brain that carries many a guinea full tide to the doctor.'[202] Viewed from the opposite end of the telescope, however, these cordials could also be regarded as medicinal. When the young Marquis of Tavistock lay on his death-bed in 1767, 'they offer'd him a cordial, which he refused, saying, "I know I am dying, and 'tis to no purpose to take anything."'[203] The same journalist, Lady Mary Coke, records in 1770 that at Stowe 'we supped in the Grotto . . . but the night shou'd have been a little warmer . . . Mr Walpole thought it rather too cold, and having some apprehension of the consequence, desired when we came back to the House a glass of Cherry Brandy by way of prevention.'[204] E. Smith's recipe for Cherry Brandy prescribed six pounds of cherries, black and red, with a quart of raspberries and mixed spices to four quarts of brandy, and her chapter on 'All Sorts of Cordial Waters', in which this recipe occurs, constantly refers to their revivifying properties. Of 'The Lady Hewet's Water' she writes, 'There never was a better cordial in cases of the greatest illness, two or three spoonfuls almost revive from death.' Three dessert spoonfuls approximately fill a modern liqueur-glass.

The cordial was regarded as an accessory of the tea table. *The Female Spectator* in 1744 (cited by G. B. Hughes)[205] records, 'Tea . . . when taken in excess occasions a dejection of spirits and flatulency, which lays the drinker of it under a kind of necessity of having recourse to more animating liquors . . . None . . . nowadays pretend to entertain with the one without the other, and the bottle and the cordial-glass are as sure an appendix to the tea table as the slop basin. Brandy, rum and other spirituous liquors are become a usual accompaniment to tea.' The tea table was the preserve of the ladies, and it was Lady Mary Wortley-Montagu who wrote, 'I am still of opinion that it is extremely silly to submit to ill-fortune. One should pluck up a spirit, and live upon cordials when one can have no other nourishment.'[206]

Unfortunately, there is little enough evidence to clinch the identification of the cordial-glass. Neither 'cordial-glass' nor 'ratafia-glass' apparently occurs in the glass lists put out in contemporary advertisements. A list of 1772,[207] however, refers to 'all kinds of Wine and Liquor [glasses]', and 'liquor' here may well have the modern sense of liqueur. In a Bohemian pattern-book of *c.* 1800, of three glasses of diminishing size but of the same shape and decoration, two are for wine, while the smallest is for 'liquer'.[208] Common sense would suggest that a strong drink would be served in a small glass, and a number of eighteenth-century stemmed glasses answer this description. One set, now unfortunately dispersed, comprised glasses with diminutive bowls standing together with a small stoppered decanter on a tray, all in cut and gilt green glass.[209]

Glasses with exceptionally small bowls were doubtless for these strong beverages, but there seems to be no hard-and-fast line between cordial-glasses and wine-glasses, which come in varying bowl sizes. Very often small bowls rest on tall stems, producing proportions quite different from those of 'normal' wine-glasses, although these glasses follow the bowl and stem formations of wine-glasses in their succeeding phases. The tall, narrow 'ratafia-glasses' have already been discussed (p. 156). All these glasses are prone to have mould-blown designs on the lower part of the bowl.

The counterpart of the high-class cordial-glass is the dram of tavern and gin shop – the short-stemmed, robust-footed, conical-bowled glass of Hogarth's pictures. The main considerations here were capacity and strength to resist hard usage. The word 'dram' does not occur in the glass lists, but it lived in the language, and is inscribed on a glass which must itself have been a 'dram' (Pl. 32b, left). The rougher glasses which succeeded this were intended not only for gin, but for the other cheap spirits which began to flood the dram shops after 1713: 'Hollands', another kind of corn-based gin; rum from the West Indies, based on molasses and made palatable after 1736, when, because of bonding, the rum matured in cask; arrack from the East Indies, based on cane sugar flavoured with spices; and brandy, penally taxed and frequently obtained through the smugglers' black market.[210] The disastrous effects of 'dramming' are highlighted in Hogarth's print 'Gin Lane' (1751).

A glass which aspired to a comparable durability was the 'firing-glass' (Pl. 39b, centre). The essential requirement was that the glass should stand up to pounding on the table, to simulate the discharge of musketry. There was indeed a tradition of accompanying toasts with gun fire. Thus Dyott records in his *Diary* a dinner attended by the Prince of Wales, later George IV: 'The Prince took the chair himself . . . We had a very good dinner and he sent wine of his own, the very best Claret I ever tasted. We had the Grenadiers drawn up in front of the mess-room windows to fire a volley in honour of the toasts.'[211] The custom seems to have been an old one. The *Proceedings* of London Sessions for 1733 record an exceptional binge of two sea cooks arriving from New England:

> This Cook took a great liking to me, and says he, 'Let's take some Cartridges of Powder, and make Wildfire to run about the Streets, for the Glory of God, that we are come safe to old England;' and so I came by this Powder . . . And as for the Pistol this Cook was an Hannoverian, and a loyal Soul he was to his Majesty, and so he gave me this Pistol, and we drank our Sovereign Lord King George's Health, and at every glass we fired off a Pistol in honour of the Royal Family.[212]

Firing-glasses tend to occur in sets, evidently for convivial drinking in clubs, messes, and especially masonic gatherings. The foot was normally a solid disc up to half an inch in thickness, but there are other varieties – the flanged foot, giving almost the same impression of solidity, and thick 'overstrung' feet with radiating ribbing on both surfaces. After about 1775 versions of the then fashionable square solid plinth-foot lent themselves admirably to

PLATE 33

Four baluster goblets, lead-glass. About 1690–1710. H. of tallest piece 23 cm (9 in.). *Left*, Bristol Art Gallery; remainder, private collections.

Three baluster goblets, lead-glass, with coins in stems: *left*, 1711; *centre*, 1739; *right*, 1701. H. *left*, 22.2 cm (8¾ in.); *centre*, 21.9 cm (8⅝ in.); *right*, 17.8 cm (7 in.). V.A.M.

PLATE 34

a. Painting by Benjamin Ferrers of 'Sir Thomas Saunders Sebright, Bt., Sir John Bland, Bt. and Two other Gentlemen Smoking and Drinking', dated 1720.

b. Painting by Marcellus Laroon (1679–1772), 'Officer and Lady at Supper'; *c.* 1735. Mr and Mrs Paul Mellon Collection.

PLATE 35

a. Print by an unidentified engraver. At the left is inscribed: 'The Bill of the Churchwardens of the Parish of St. – for the year 17– . . .'; on the back wall: 'Our Church Wardens spend yᵉ Silver & gives us yᵉ farthing'. On the goblet is written the toast 'Prosperity to the Church'. Collection unknown.

b. Painting by Philip Mercier, 'Sir Thomas Samwell and Friends', about 1733. Beaverbrook Art Gallery, Fredericton, New Brunswick.

PLATE 36

a. Wine-glass with bell-bowl and annulated knop. About 1720–30. H. 16 cm (6¼ in.). Private Collection.

b. Mammoth goblet with bell-bowl and two flattened knops. Probably Newcastle upon Tyne, mid-eighteenth century. H. 34.5 cm (13½ in.). Private Collection.

c. Wine-glass with spreading conical bowl and baluster stem. About 1720–30. H. 18 cm (7 in.). Private Collection.

d. Wine-glass with slightly waisted conical bowl and cylinder knop. About 1710–20. H. 17.3 cm (6¾ in.). Fitzwilliam Museum, Cambridge.

e. Wine-glass, drawn stem on inverted baluster, with domed foot. About 1725. H. 17.5 cm (6⅞ in.). V.A.M.

f. Wine-glass with drawn stem, diamond-point engraving signed by George Chapman. Inscribed: 'To the Memory of Oliver Cromwell' and dated 1756. H. 25 cm (9⅞ in.). V.A.M.

PLATE 37

a. Wine-glass with bell-bowl, on shouldered stem. About 1720–30. H. 15 cm (5⅞ in.). Fitzwilliam Museum, Cambridge.

b. Goblet, with plain stem, wheel-engraved 'Wilkes and Liberty No. 45'. About 1769. H. 19 cm (7½ in.). Fitzwilliam Museum, Cambridge.

c. Wine-glass with conical bowl, on shouldered stem. About 1720–30. H. 14.8 cm (5¾ in.). Fitzwilliam Museum, Cambridge.

d. Wine- or cordial-glass, plain stem, domed foot and wheel-engraved rose-spray, with inscription 'HEALTH TO ALL OUR FAST FRIENDS'. About 1745. H. 17.5 cm (6⅞ in.). V.A.M.

e. Wine- or cordial-glass, four-sided pedestal stem with moulded inscription 'God Save King George', and thistle-bowl diamond-point engraved 'R SAYER OF BRAINTREE'. Dated 1717 on foot. H. 13 cm (5⅛ in.). Museum of London.

f. Wine-glass, waisted bowl and 'incised twist' stem. Inscribed in diamond-point: 'Mrs. Edwardes 1755 Augsᵗ ye 4th' on the bowl, and 'Mr. Vowl' on the foot. About 1750. H. 17.5 cm (6⅞ in.). V.A.M.

PLATE 38

a. Three wine-glasses with various air-twist stems, that on the *right* with wheel-engraved bowl and domed foot. Mid-eighteenth century. H. of *centre* glass 17.2 cm (6¾ in.). Private Collections.

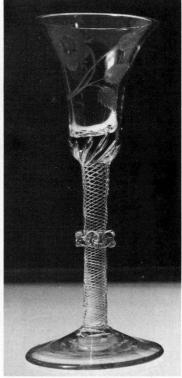

b. Wine-glass, tapering bucket-bowl, air-twist stem above diminishing rings, the bowl wheel-engraved with rose-spray. About 1750. H. 16.5 cm (6½ in.). Fitzwilliam Museum, Cambridge.

c. Wine-glass, double-knopped air-twist stem, the bowl wheel-engraved with bust-portrait of Prince Charles Edward. About 1750. H. 18.8 cm (7⅜ in.). V.A.M.

d. Wine-glass, drawn air-twist stem with applied crimped collar, the bowl wheel-engraved with rose-spray. About 1750. H. 17.6 cm (6⅞ in.). Fitzwilliam Museum, Cambridge.

PLATE 39

a. 'Seal' (? pipe-stopper), the hollow bulb enclosing a William III penny dated 1701, the stem with opaque-white corkscrew. Probably early eighteenth century. H. 9 cm (3½ in.). Central Museum, Northampton.

b. *Left* Sweetmeat with opaque-twist stem, domed foot and notched rim. About 1760–70. H. 14.6 cm (5¾ in.). V.A.M.
Centre Firing-glass with opaque-twist stem, terraced foot, and conical bowl wheel-engraved 'St. Thos. Lodge Arbroath'. About 1760–70. H. 10 cm (4 in.). V.A.M.
Right Wine-glass with opaque-twist stem, the threads continuing into the bowl. Third quarter of eighteenth century. H. 16 cm (6¼ in.). V.A.M.

c. *Left* Wine-glass with bucket-bowl and opaque-twist stem, the bowl wheel-engraved with a ship, above which the diamond-point inscription: 'Success to the EAGLE FRIGATE, John Knill Commander'. Probably Bristol. About 1756–60. H. 16.5 cm (6½ in.).
Right Goblet with ogee-bowl and opaque-twist stem, the bowl wheel-engraved with Britannia and ships, and inscription 'SUCCESS TO THE BRITISH FLEET 1759'. H. 19.7 cm (7⅞ in.). V.A.M.

d. *Left* Goblet with bucket-bowl and opaque-twist stem, the bowl wheel-engraved with rose-sprays and inscribed in diamond-point: 'MS July 25ᵗʰᵉ 1760'. H. 18 cm (7⅛ in.). V.A.M.
Right Cider-glass with bucket-bowl and opaque-twist stem, the bowl wheel-engraved with an apple tree and barrels, and inscription: 'NO EXCISE'. About 1765. H. 17.5 cm (6⅞ in.). V.A.M.

PLATE 40

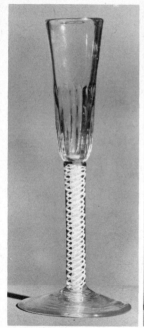

a. 'Ratafia glass', cylindrical bowl with mould-blown ribbing, and opaque-twist stem. About 1765. H. 18.5 cm (7¼ in.). Private Collection.

b. *Left* Wine-glass with ogee-bowl and opaque-twist stem, the bowl wheel-engraved with portrait and inscription: 'LONG LIVE GEORGE PRINCE OF WALES 1759'. H. 15 cm (6 in.). V.A.M. *Centre, Right* Decanter and wine-glass, both wheel-engraved with inscription: 'LOWTHER AND UPTON HUZZA' (Westmorland Parliamentary Election of 1761). H. of decanter 30.5 cm (12 in.). V.A.M.

c. Champagne- or ale-flute, cylindrical ribbed bowl and opaque-twist stem. About 1760–70. H. 19.7 cm (7¾ in.). Private Collection.

d. Wine- or cordial-glass with cut bowl and opaque-twist stem. About 1760. H. 16 cm (6¼ in.). V.A.M.

e. Ale- or champagne-flute, with opaque-twist stem, the bowl wheel-engraved with sprays of flowers framing diamond-point inscription: 'A. Slocombe Pound 1769'. H. 28.2 cm (11⅛ in.). Fitzwilliam Museum, Cambridge.

f. Wine-glass with colour-twist stem (blue and green). About 1770. H. 15.2 cm (6 in.). V.A.M.

PLATE 41

a. Wine-glass, enamelled in colours with the arms of Paton by a member of the Beilby family, probably William. Newcastle upon Tyne; about 1765. H. 18.5 cm (7¼ in.). Museum of London.

b. Goblet, enamelled in colours with the Royal Arms, signed by William Beilby. Newcastle upon Tyne; probably 1762. H. approx. 22 cm (8¾ in.). Cinzano Glass Collection.

c. Beer decanter, enamelled in white by a member of the Beilby family, probably William. Newcastle upon Tyne; about 1765. H. 26.8 cm (10½ in.). Fitzwilliam Museum, Cambridge.

d. Sweetmeat-glass with pedestal stem, the bowl enamelled in white by a member of the Beilby family. Newcastle upon Tyne; about 1765. H. 16.5 cm (6½ in.). Sir Hugh Dawson Collection.

e. Bowl enamelled in white by a member of the Beilby family, probably William; signed 'Beilby Invt. & pinx!' Newcastle upon Tyne; dated 1765. D. 25 cm (9⅞ in.). V.A.M.

f. Two wine-glasses, with opaque-twist stems, the bowls enamelled in white by a member of the Beilby family, perhaps William. Newcastle upon Tyne; about 1765. H. 14.5 and 13.5 cm (5¾ and 5¼ in.). Sir Hugh Dawson Collection.

PLATE 42

a. Tumbler, wheel-engraved with a drinking scene. Mid-eighteenth century. Formerly Bles Collection. V.A.M.

b. Bowl, cut and wheel-engraved with a hunting scene and date 1766. D. 13.5 cm (5¼ in.). V.A.M.

c. Tankard, the base with mould-blown ribbing NDW, the body wheel-engraved and inscribed 'TYZACK Glass Maker'. Probably Newcastle upon Tyne; second half of eighteenth century. H. 15.2 cm (6 in.). V.A.M.

d. Rummer with cut foot, the bowl cut and wheel-engraved with sprays of flowers, and inscription 'MAY GOD BLESS THE HON^BLE MRS HARTOPP' (daughter of Lord Carbury, eloped with her tutor and married, April 1782). H. 15 cm (6 in.). Major J. F. G. Terry Collection.

a. Ale-glass and tumbler, with wrythen mould-blown ribbing. Late seventeenth or early eighteenth century. H. of tumbler 8.2 cm (3¼ in.). Formerly Miss K. Worsley Collection.

b. Jelly-glass with mould-blown ribbing. First half of eighteenth century. H. 11.5 cm (4½ in.). V.A.M.

c. Sweetmeat-glass with pedestal stem and arched rim-decoration. Mid-eighteenth century. H. 20.5 cm (8¹/₁₆ in.). Fitzwilliam Museum, Cambridge.

d. Pair of candlesticks with repeated inverted pedestal stems. Mid-eighteenth century. H. 19.4 cm (7⅝ in.). Corning Museum of Glass.

PLATE 44

a. Pair of covered cups, blue wheel-cut glass with silver-gilt mounts by Thomas Heming (active 1745–1781/2). London hallmarks for 1752–3. Probably London; about 1750–2. H. with cover 32 cm (12⅝ in.). Toledo Museum of Art, Ohio.

b. Finger-bowl/wine-glass cooler, blue glass with gilt decoration. Signed: 'I. Jacobs Bristol'. Bristol, Isaac Jacobs's Temple Street glasshouse or 'Nonsuch Glass Manufactory'; about 1800–10. H. 10 cm (3⅞ in.). V.A.M.

c. Spirit - decanter, blue glass with gilt decoration. Probably London, decorated in the workshop of James Giles; about 1765–70. H. 18 cm (7 in.). V.A.M.

d. Tumbler or water-glass, blue glass with gilt decoration. Probably London, decorated in the workshop of James Giles; about 1765–70. H. 11 cm (4¼ in.). Private Collection.

PLATE 45

b. Tea-caddies ('GREEN' and 'BOHEA'), opaque-white glass painted in enamel colours, with caps of painted enamel on copper and gilt metal. Probably South Staffordshire; about 1755–60. H. 14 cm (5½ in.). Sir Hugh Dawson Collection.

a. Beaker-vase, opaque-white glass painted in enamel colours. Probably South Staffordshire; about 1755–60. H. 23 cm (9 in.). V.A.M.

c. Three smelling- or scent-flasks, opaque-white glass with gilt decoration. Probably London, decorated in the workshop of James Giles; about 1770–5. H. of outside pieces 7.5 cm (3 in.). Sir Hugh Dawson Collection.

d. Vase and cover (not *en suite*), opaque-white glass painted in enamel colours. Origin uncertain; decorated by the painter 'PP' or 'PF'; about 1765. H. with cover 20.5 cm (8 in.). B.M.

PLATE 46

Trade card of Maydwell and Windle, at the King's Arms 'Against Norfolk Street' in the Strand, engraved by Robert Clee. Third quarter of eighteenth century. Private Collection.

PLATE 47

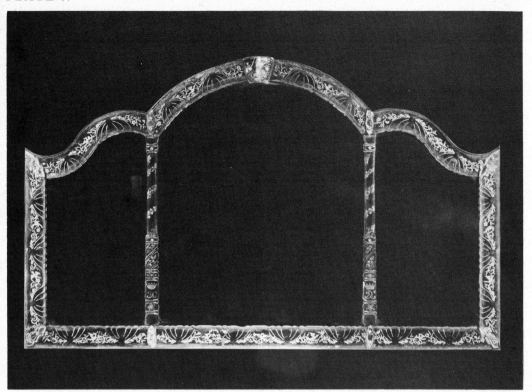

a. Three-panel overmantel mirror with wheel-cut and wheel-engraved decoration. Made in London by Thomas Howcraft and Richard Robinson in 1711 for Burley-on-the-Hill, Rutland. The pilasters bear the coronet and initials of the owner, the Earl of Winchilsea and Nottingham.

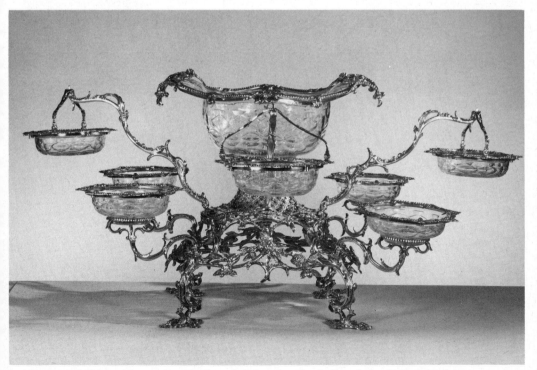

b. *Epergne* of silver with cut glass bowls and dishes. London hallmark for 1763–4. V.A.M.

PLATE 48

a. Cruet, cut glass with silver mounts by Paul de Lamerie. London hallmark for 1725–6. L. of frame 18 cm (7 in.). Ashmolean Museum, Oxford.

b. Decanter and stopper, cut glass. Second quarter of eighteenth century. H. 26 cm (10¼ in.). V.A.M.

c. Cruets, cut glass with silver mounts. *Left* about 1750; *right* hallmarked for 1795. H. of left-hand piece 16 cm (6½ in.). V.A.M.

d. Sweetmeat, cut glass. About 1760–5. H. 16.5 cm (6½ in.). Corning Museum of Glass.

e. Sweetmeat, cut glass with 'corner'd brim', on pedestal stem. About 1730. H. 18.5 cm (7¼ in.). Christ Church, Oxford.

f. Goblet, cut and engraved glass. About 1765. H. 25 cm (9¾ in.). Corning Museum of Glass.

the firing-glass. Trumpet-bowls naturally occurred with drawn stems and occasionally air-twist stems, but the ogee-bowl is also found, often on a short opaque-twist stem. The bowls were frequently engraved, and occasionally enamelled, with toasts and with masonic and other esoteric emblems. These glasses apparently do not occur in the glass lists, perhaps because the more elaborate types, with particular emblems, had to be specially commissioned, while the cheaper sort would appear under 'Articles too tedious for an Advertisement'. 'Engrav'd Free Mason glasses', however, are mentioned in an American advertisement of 1761, and 'Right Free-Masons' in 1769.[213]

Two or three other types of glass devoted to ceremonious drinking call for brief mention. Some wine-glasses have deliberately thickened bowls, evidently to reduce their capacity while maintaining the appearance of fair drinking. These have reasonably been identified as toast-master's glasses, since the Master of Ceremonies needed to stay on his feet when others were falling under the table. On the occasion recorded in Dyott's *Diary*, cited above, twenty-three bumpers were called for, after which the writer 'recommended it to the Society to stand up on our chairs with three times three . . . I think it was the most laughable sight I ever beheld to see our Governor, our General, and the Commodore all so drunk they could scarce stand on the floor, hoisted up on their chairs each a bumper in his hand; and the three times three cheers was what they were afraid to attempt for fear of falling.' The twenty men at table consumed sixty-three bottles of wine.

The toasting-glass on the other hand has been identified as one with an unusually tall and slender stem, apt for snapping between the fingers. The notion doubtless derives from the seventeenth-century custom of smashing the glasses after a particularly solemn toast. Henry Teonge in his *Diary* (1675–9) records, ' . . . every health that we drank every man broke the glass he drank in; so that before night we had destroyed a whole chest of pure Venice glasses.'[214] It is less easy to document the custom in the eighteenth century, although in some causes a comparable disregard for material no doubt prevailed. The more expensive varieties of thin-stemmed glasses – the fine air-twist and enamel-twist wines – are unlikely to have been sacrificed in this way. Their mere survival argues against the likelihood. Cheaper drawn-stem glasses would have made just as satisfactory a noise. The term 'toasting-glass' does not occur in the contemporary trade literature.

A necessary precondition of drinking was to get the drink from the cellar to the table. At one time this was done by a bottle or a special 'serving bottle' in pottery or glass. With the progressive refinement of manners a more elegant receptacle was called for – the decanter.[215] A decanter is normally a vessel (it can be a person) which transfers liquid from one receptacle to another by tilting it. In the seventeenth century it could be a jug, but in the eighteenth century the word settled into the meaning of a flask-like container, normally of colourless glass, used to bring wine or beer from bottle or cask to table. Not unnaturally, in its early forms it tended to follow the evolution of the contemporary green bottle, from the earliest long-necked 'shaft and globe' (Pl. 19a) to the short-necked and squat-bodied 'dumpy' of the years about 1700 (Pl. 56a). Until about 1740 it was apt to have a side handle (see below). When towards 1750 the green bottle began to assume a near-cylindrical shape to facilitate binning, the decanter mimicked it with a sloping shoulder and straight sides, in one variant widening from shoulder to base (Pl. 41c), in the other tapering downwards roughly in the form of the 'flower-pot' bottle favoured on the Continent (Pl. 50e). These two types dominate the third quarter of the eighteenth century. Before they were firmly established, however, the shaft-and-globe decanter remained popular (cf. Pl. 49d) and is the usual vehicle for mid-century Jacobite engraving. It seems also to have been used, without stopper, as a water carafe (or 'craft', 'croft', 'carrost', etc.). More or less contemporaneous with this shape was the mould-blown, vertical-sided flint-glass bottle of square, polygonal or cross form on plan, sometimes with a high kick and often with the string-rim of the green bottle, destined to disappear from the decanter as otiose before 1750. These moulded forms sometimes had pouring lips, sometimes handles, but seldom stoppers. The grinding-in of stoppers, known since before 1700 for special purposes (e.g. in case-bottles containing spirits or perfumes), became current during the second quarter of the eighteenth century, first with a globular stopper, often enclosing air-bubbles (Pl. 41c), and latterly with a pointed 'spire' stopper, which is found with some shaft-and-globe decanters, and which later lent itself well to cutting (Pl. 49d). Occasional vertical-sided, polygonal decanters were cut like the contemporary cruet-bottles (p. 176) and were no doubt the 'diamond-cut . . . Decanters' advertised by Jerome Johnson in 1742;[216] their version of the spire-stopper – perhaps the earliest – exactly echoes on plan the form of the decanter itself (Pl. 48b).

The shouldered decanters of the third quarter of the century were usually blown fairly thin, and tended to be wheel-engraved (Pl. 40b) – occasionally gilt or enamelled (Pl. 41c) – a specialised form being the 'label decanter', on which the name of the wine was engraved in a cartouche which imitated the earlier silver 'bottle-ticket' originally hung on a chain round a bottle or decanter (Pl. 41c). They are first mentioned in an advertisement by Jonas Phillips in the *Norwich Mercury* for 26 December 1755: 'new-fashioned decanters with inscriptions engraven on them, Port, Claret, Mountain, etc. etc., decorated with vine leaves, grapes, etc.'[217] The contemporary lists also refer to cut decanters (Pl. 49d), and plenty of examples survive, made of thicker glass than their engraved counter-parts. The stopper was usually a faceted spire, or a flat circular disc with lunar cuts round the edge or more elaborate cut motifs overall.

Towards 1770 the shouldered decanter takes a new inflection, the shoulder becoming a smooth curved transition between a gently tapering body and a slender neck. The flat stopper assumes an inverted pear shape, and the body of the bottle may be wheel-engraved or lightly cut. Another Phillips advertisement (*Norwich Mercury*, 13 February 1768)[218] refers to 'the newest fashioned Decanters', perhaps indicating this tapered form. Finally the wide, flat base becomes narrower and the decanter wall curves inwards at its base to give a generally barrel-shaped body. On 21 December 1775 Christopher Haedy, the famous cutter and dealer, advertised in the *Bath Chronicle*[219] 'curious barrel-shaped decanters cut on an entire new pattern', the new scheme of decoration being perhaps broad flutes on the neck or round the base, or sometimes running from top to bottom and broken only by thin horizontal cuts. The same epithet, 'barrel-shaped', is also applied to the later and some-what broader decanter with neck-rings which came to be typical of the Irish factories, properly called the 'Prussian' decanter (cf. Pl. 52d). The characteristic stopper here was a 'target', circular with recessed centre, sometimes cut but more frequently made by the glass-pincher with his tongs, producing a raised rim figured with radial lines in relief. In these later phases the neck of the decanter, which had previously terminated abruptly in a flat rim, began to be turned outwards, ultimately becoming a flat and quite wide disc. This was frequently echoed in a horizontal domed 'mushroom' stopper (Pl. 52d), sometimes cut, sometimes moulded.

The taper- and barrel-forms (the latter short-necked) also appear in smaller versions destined to hold spirits. They are frequently made in coloured glass with gold labels, the initial letter of the con-tents inscribed on the stopper. These may be pear-shaped with the taper-form; or the mushroom or a ball finial in the case of the barrel-shape. Spirit-decanters were often made of square cross-section, with short neck and pouring lip, frequently in coloured glass, but also in cut flint-glass.

A whole separate world of glass was devoted to the requirements of the dessert. In this period, except on very grand occasions, the average dinner or supper appears to have comprised two complicated courses followed by a dessert. The rule of thumb was that the dessert should consist of as many dishes as the previous course. The word 'dessert' itself derives from 'desservir' – to clear the table – and normally the cloth was drawn at this point, sometimes revealing a second clean cloth below. Sometimes the elaborate centrepiece, essentially decorative in character, was left undisturbed from the previous courses. This conformed with the general concept of the dessert as an essentially decorative course, intended to delight the eye as much as to tickle the palate. W. King, in his *Cookery* . . . (1708), makes this explicit: ' 'Tis the dessert that graces all the feast.' There were many components in a mid-eighteenth-century dessert, and glass was not necessarily the dominant element. Elaborate layouts resembling a miniature garden, with *parterres*, balustrades and even fountains running with water – or more interesting liquids – furnished the commonest form of dessert for grand occasions; and against this background figures in porcelain, wax or sugar might be arranged in mythological or allegorical compositions. On the continent of Europe the garden furniture and the figures were occasionally all of glass, but apparently not in England. [220] Here on the whole the schemes were less elaborate, and when grand occasions called for more splendid desserts (as with the Parnassus arranged by Lord Talbot for the Coronation dinner of George III), the components tended to be made in confectioners' materials. Real or artificial flowers were much in evidence, and cookery books gave instructions for making them out of sugar confections. The layout was often arranged on mirror-plate to enhance the brilliance of the effect: 'Cottages rose in sugar, and temples in barley-sugar; pigmy Neptunes in cars of cockle-shells triumphed over oceans of looking-glass, or seas of silver tissue', wrote Horace Walpole in 1753. [221] However, there were no hard-and-fast rules.

Hannah Glasse, in *The Complete Confectioner* (Dublin, 1762) writes: 'Giving directions for a grand desert would be needless, for those persons who give such grand deserts, either keep a proper person, or have them of a confectioner, who not only has everything wanted, but every ornament to adorn it with . . . though every young lady ought to know both how to make all kinds of confectionery and dress out a desert.' Her observations are borne out by an advertisement of John Bridge of Johnson's Court, Charing Cross in the *Daily Advertiser* for 23 December 1753: 'Good

Hartshorn Jellies, at 2s a Dozen: 6s a Dozen to be left for Glasses, which will be returned when the Glasses are brought home'; and later in the century George Gascoigne of Bear Lane, Leeds, on his trade card offered 'Deserts for Entertainments'.

Nevertheless, books on cookery and household management gave numerous hints to those wishing to make up their own relatively simple desserts at home. Charles Carter, in *The Compleat City and Country Cook* (1730), gives the plan of a 'Desart' on an oval table with seven dishes corresponding to those of the previous courses. Down the main axis are three dishes, the grandest – 'A Pyramid of Sweetmeats' – in the centre, with 'Jelleys and Sullabubs' above and below it. On one side of this central axis is a dish of 'Lemon Cream and Biskett' and another of 'Peeches', whereas on the other side of the line is a dish of 'Nectrines and Apricocks' and another of 'Pistachioe Cream and Biskett'. The dishes of fruit and those of creams with biscuits are set diagonally to each other, so that any guest was within reasonable reach of any type of dish. A much larger 'Grand Desert' has nine large, and fourteen small, dishes crowding the table top. Down the middle axis again are three dishes – 'A Grand Pyramid of Dry'ed Sweetmeats in Porcelain' in the centre, and above and below it 'A Pyramid of Fruit of sorts [assorted] in Porcelain'. Round the central pyramid is a group of six dishes (or perhaps salvers), four of them for 'Jelly of sorts', and the two largest, on the main cross-axis, for 'Sweetmeats in Glasses'. Each of the circles representing these dishes has smaller circles ranged round the periphery – six on the jelly-stands and eight on the sweetmeat-stands. These almost certainly represent jelly- and sweetmeat-glasses respectively. We may turn from this to an all-glass arrangement given in Hannah Glasse's *Complete Confectioner*. This is shown as a plan, but with the components indicated in words:

Ice cream, different colours.

Whip'd *f*yllabubs.

Clear jellies

Lemon cream
in gla*ff*es.

In the middle a
high pyramid
of one *f*alver

Nonpareils.	above another, the bottom one large, the next ſmaller, the top one leſs; theſe ſalvers are to be fill'd with all kinds of wet and dry ſweet-meats	Golden pippins.
Bloomage ſtuck with almonds.	in glaſs, baſkets or little plates, colour'd jellies, creams, &c. biſcuits, criſp'd almonds and	Bloomage ſtuck with almonds.
Poſtalia nuts.	little knicknacks, and bottles of flowers prettily intermix'd, the little top ſalver must have a large preſerv'd Fruit in it.	Almonds and raiſins.
Lemon cream in glasses		Clear jellies in glaſſes.

Whip'd ſyllabubs.

Ice cream, different colours.

The 'pyramid' is clearly shown in the trade card of Maydwell and Windle (Pl. 46). Here the three-tier system is evident, although the top element is a 'sweetmeat glass'. In the eighteenth century the term probably had a wider connotation, this particular form being more often referred to as a 'top glass' or 'orange glass', since the crown of the whole was often an orange, preserved or fresh.[222] Hannah Glasse writes: 'The little top salver must have a large preserv'd Fruit in it', and an Irish advertisement of 1752 refers to 'pine- [pineapple] and orange-glasses'.[223] A fruit so used may be seen in Joseph Highmore's picture, 'Lady Davers ill-treats Pamela', in the National Gallery of Victoria, Melbourne, probably painted in 1745.[224] This is no grand dessert, but a simple domestic arrangement. A single glass salver holds half a dozen jelly-glasses and, in the centre, a larger glass contains a single fruit. Pyramids, however, might well comprise three salvers as well as an orange-glass. An advertisement of 1772 mentions 'Glass Salvers or Waiters chiefly from 9 to 13 inch to be sold in pyramids or singly, with Orange or Top Glasses.'[225] The large salvers would form only the bottom two tiers of a pyramid, and considerably smaller examples are known which would have assumed the top position. This advertisement also makes it clear that these salvers could alternatively be used as trays for handing round glasses of wine, as we learn independently from pictures. Lady Grisell Baillie, a Scottish lady with a keen provincial eye for London fashion, records in 1727 a dinner for ten at which dessert was served on three-tier pyramids, the lowest salvers holding glasses of dry sweetmeats; the second tier holding four fruit jellies, wet sweetmeats with covers and 'betwixt them high glasses'; the third tier having glasses of white comfits round 'a tall scalloped glass' (Pl. 48e).[226] There was every sort of variation (Pls. 39b, 43c). A shipment from Newcastle to Hamburg in 1746 included 'Pyramid, 4 salvers, 12 lb. at 2s., 1 top branch [probably a lighting fixture] 4s., 5 do. Sweetmeats 8d. 33 Jellies, etc. 4d.'[227] This was no doubt a complete dessert kit.

In a pyramid the wide lowest salver usually stood on a short stem or pedestal foot to give stability, while those above had longer stems to accommodate the jelly- and sweetmeat-glasses ranged round them. These stem-forms followed the fashions in wine-glasses, although air- and enamel-twists are unusual, no doubt because they were mainly masked from sight. Pedestal stems, by contrast, are the commonest of all (Pl. 43c), continuing long after they had disappeared from wine-glasses. They are characterised by a multiple collar strengthening the junction of stem and foot, the latter being normally domed and with underfolded rim. These 'Silesian' stems, though sometimes sharp and well made, were often shapeless and slovenly, perhaps foreshadowing the end of this form. When cutting became the almost universal mode of decorating glass, the underside and foot of the salver began to be treated in this way. Some were made with a revolving top, in the manner of a 'lazy Susan'. These were probably not used for pyramids, but as independent standing dishes to hold jellies and sweetmeats, being possibly the 'middle stands' of contemporary notices.[228] An Irish advertisement of 1772 lists 'cut flowered and plain salvers; jelly and sweetmeat glasses,'[229] and as early as 1755 Jonas Phillips in Norwich announcing his new stock, included 'Glass Salvers of all kinds, Sillabub, Jelly and Sweetmeat Glasses, cut and plain.'[230]

As for the glasses that went on these salvers, their number was legion. Jelly-glasses seem consistently to have been trumpet-shaped (Pl. 43b), with rudimentary stem or no stem at all. They were used for all kinds of wet sweetmeats which required eating with a spoon, as Highmore's picture shows. To jellies and creams the cookery books devote innumerable recipes. Much attention is given to appearance. Elizabeth Smith's recipe for 'Ribbon Jelly' prescribes: 'Then run the jelly into little high glasses; run every colour as thick as your finger; one colour must be thorough cold before you put another on . . . you must colour red with cochineal, green with spinach, yellow with saffron, blue with syrup of violets, white with thick cream, and sometimes the jelly by itself.'[231] One specialised type was the 'whip syllabub', first cousin of the 'syllabub under the cow'. 'Take a quart of cream . . . a pint of sack, and the juice of two lemons; sweeten it to your palate . . . and with a whisk whip it; as the froth rises, take it off with a spoon, and lay it in your syllabub-glasses' – previously partially filled with sweetened wine.[232] These whip-syllabub glasses must be the cup-topped jelly-glasses so obviously adapted to this end, although Highmore's picture shows that ordinary jellies too could be used with a generous top-hamper of whipped cream.

More difficult to interpret are the small side-handled cups which the nineteenth century called 'custards'. This term does not occur in the eighteenth-century lists, and it seems possible that these were 'orgeat' or 'lemonade' glasses. Orgeat was a drink based on barley water flavoured with sweet almonds, and Mrs Raffald, in *The Experienced English House Keeper* (1805 edition, pp. 307–8), after two recipes for 'Ozyat', says 'Send it up in ozyat glasses with handles.' The Sitwell bills at Renishaw include an item '16 handled Lemonade Glasses',[233] and the 1774 Sale *Catalogue* of James Giles (p. 190) included two lots of 'lemonade cups'.[234] A small green-handled cup is known with Giles gilding, and may well be a lemonade cup, while a list of about 1770 at Alnwick Castle includes '18 orangeat glasses with handles'. 'Orangeat' here presumably means orangeade, but may just be a corruption of 'orgeat'. Handled cups for lemonade are illustrated in late eighteenth-century Bohemian glass lists. These glasses too presumably belonged to the dessert service.

Other wet sweetmeats were served up in dishes, and many of the miscellaneous surviving glass dishes – mainly with cut decoration – were presumably dedicated to this purpose. Thus in 1725 Nat Berry bought in Bristol '2 doz. glass saucers for holding sweet-meats.'[235] Jonas Phillips of Norwich in an advertisement of 1755 mentions 'Glass Shells of all sizes for sweetmeats',[236] and cut dishes of this general rococo character survive, often with a leaf-like profile. Many of these forms would serve equally well for dry sweetmeats, such as nuts, 'comfits', candied 'chips' of fruit peel and biscuits. Many of the so-called 'bonnet salts' with double-ogee profile were probably glasses for dry or wet sweetmeats.

Most important in this hierarchy was the 'top glass' itself. Often mistaken for a champagne-glass, it tended to have a hemispherical bowl. As with the salvers, pedestal stems are common, often on a domed and folded foot (Pl. 43c). Unlike the salvers, however, the top glasses were open to decoration of many kinds. Whereas the examples with baluster and balustroid stems usually have plain bowls, those with pedestal stems frequently have mould-blown ornamentation – plain ribbing (often in a panelled version echoing the stem), mesh-patterns, and dimpling. Occasionally these glasses have covers which repeat the decoration of bowl and foot.[237] Where they do not, the rim has occasionally been elaborately decorated with applied arches joined by raspberry prunts (Pl. 43c);[238] or later, on smaller sweetmeats, the rim is sheared into square lappets (Pl. 39b, left), the foot is pincered with radial ribs, and the stem is often an opaque twist. Above all the sweetmeat-glass lent itself to cutting (pp. 172, 177).

Last among the decorative features of the pyramid were Mrs Glasse's 'bottles of flowers prettily intermix'd' which may be seen in Maydwell and Windle's trade card (Pl. 46) – somewhat fancifully represented. All surviving specimens appear to be made from an inverted hollow-blown pedestal stem set directly on a disc-foot, presumably to consort with top-glasses and salvers which themselves had pedestal stems. Other types may yet be identified.

A variant of the pyramid was a tall *épergne* standing on a broad foot and supporting at the top an integral sweetmeat- or orange-glass, while from the central stem branched small curved arms on which hung little sweetmeat baskets with over-arching handles. In the cut-glass period they mimicked chandeliers and had long arms, curved and notched in the prevailing taste, and fastened to the central stem by metal collars (Pl. 49b). The possibilities of variation were limitless, and many variants survive, vulnerable as they are to breakage. An authentic impression of such an *épergne* is to be found in William Parker's trade-card, in the British Museum.[239] The first known mention appears in an advertisement of the London glass-cutter and dealer Christopher Haedy in the *Bath and Bristol Chronicle* for 30 November 1769. This adds to a long list of cut-glasses advertised in 1768 the item 'Laperne' (l'épergne).[240] This suggests an innovation of 1769. In the *Dublin Journal* for 25 July 1772 an advertisement included 'epergnes and epergne saucers'.[241]

Dessert-glasses lent themselves particularly well to cut decoration, and top-glasses were among the earliest to be cut, for a good reason (Pl. 48d, e). The easiest part of a glass to cut is the rim, and the dessert-glass had the advantage over the drinking-glass, which could not be so treated. Secondly, the essence of the dessert was decorative effect, and cutting could be used on all its glass components to give an overall brilliance impossible with drinking-glasses. This is probably why one of the earliest references to a *set* of glasses is an advertisement in a Norwich paper in 1754, offering 'a set of cut and flowered Glass for a desert'.[242]

The glasses of a dessert required a high level of lighting to bring out their sparkle. When, in 1748, Sir Charles Hanbury Williams, British Ambassador to the Court of Saxony, was given a huge service of Meissen porcelain for a table of thirty covers, it included '8 branch candlesticks' and '24 single candlesticks'.[243] It has already been noticed (p. 169) that a dessert ensemble sent from Newcastle to Hamburg in 1746 included a 'top branch', and some idea of how this might have looked comes from T. Hall's *The Queen's Royal Cookery*, published in 1709. This shows a four-tier pyramid apparently with candle-holders branching out at each level, and what appears to be a four-armed 'branch candlestick' at the top.[244] On 10 September 1788 *The Times* carried a significant advertisement of a London sale, to include 'a Dessert Set of Cut Glass with lustres and Epargnes'.[245] Glass for lighting is treated more fully below (pp. 180–5).

Sweetmeats and fruit make for sticky fingers, and with the dessert there appeared accessories which caused much social debate. These were the finger-bowls, usually referred to in the eighteenth century as 'water glasses'. They were used to dabble the fingers, but by some also to rinse the mouth. François de la Rochefoucauld, staying at Euston with the Duke of Grafton in 1784, describes their use: 'After the sweets, you are given water in small bowls of very clean glass in order to rinse out your mouth – a custom which strikes me as extremely unfortunate. The more fashionable folk do not rinse out their mouths, but that seems to me even worse; for, if you use the water to wash your hands, it becomes dirty and quite disgusting.'[246] Both these aspects are commented on by English writers. Smollett in his *Travels* (1766) remarks: 'I know of no custom more beastly than that of using water-glasses, in which polite company spirt, and squirt, and spue the filthy scourings of their gums.'[247] Twiss, on the other hand, in his *Tour in Ireland* (1776), is struck by the habit of rinsing the fingers: 'The filthy custom of using water-glasses after meals is as common as in England: no well-bred persons touch their victuals with their fingers, and such ablutions ought to be unnecessary.'[248] From Smollett it would appear that the water-glass could conveniently be drunk from, and W. A. Thorpe quotes *Philosophical Transactions* for 1779 (Vol. LXXIII, 305) for the phrase 'a common tumbler or water-glass'. *The Daily Advertiser* for 16 May 1744 contains an advertisement for 'Wine, Beer and Water Glasses',[249] which seems to put the water-glass firmly in the category of drinking-glasses. Christopher Haedy, however, lists in *The Bath Chronicle* for 20 November 1766: 'Cut and flowered Wine, Water, Ale, Jelly, Sillabub and Wash-hand Glasses; Tumblers . . .'[250] suggesting that Water-glasses, Wash-hand glasses and Tumblers were separate types. We may surmise that water-glasses were for drinking water, tumblers were truncated conical glasses for various drinks (pp. 159–160), and wash-hand glasses what were later called 'finger-bowls'. 'Wash-hand glasses' are also referred to as 'wash-hand cups', suggesting a low wide vessel, and the beaker-like 'water-glass' was probably replaced in due course by the cup-like 'wash-hand glass', although no doubt the transition was gradual. A Norwich advertisement of August 1758 refers to 'a great variety of Water Glasses',[251] and surviving small globular bowls with slightly everted wide mouths and standing on their own 'plates', datable to *c.* 1750–60, should probably be identified as water-glasses. Apparently the last reference to water-glasses in the glass-sellers' lists occurs in *Faulkner's Dublin Journal* for 9 December 1773[252] although the expression may have continued in common parlance (see above). In 1777 the word 'washers' appears in one of Christopher Haedy's advertisements, 'Wash-hand Glasses' having dropped out of his notices in 1773.[253] By 1779 the term 'finger-glasses' has appeared (in *The Liverpool Advertiser*),[254] to be joined later by 'finger-cups' and 'finger-basins', and in Victorian times by 'finger-bowls', with their connotation of delicate dabbling.

Considering the purposes for which they were used, it is hardly surprising that water-glasses were made in opaque-white, and later in gilt blue, glass (Pl. 44b, d). Sophie von la Roche, in London in 1786, commented, 'The blue glass bowls used for rinsing hands and mouth in at the end are quite delightful.'[255] Blue bowls with gilt key-fret borders, and the plates on which they must have stood, signed 'I. Jacobs, Bristol', survive in a number of collections (Pl. 44b). Isaac Jacobs succeeded to his father's business on his death in 1796, and in 1806 advertised as 'Glass Manufacturer to His Majesty' mentioning 'burnished Gold upon Royal purple colored Glass' in a dessert-service supplied for the King and Queen.[256]

Coloured finger-glasses and the habits associated with them, lasted
well into the nineteenth century. *Miss Leslie's House Book*, published in Philadelphia in 1840, refers to 'FINGER GLASSES – These are
generally blue or green, and are filled with water and set round the
table, just before the cloth is removed . . . The disgusting European
custom of taking a mouthful or two of the water, and, after washing the mouth, spitting it back again into the finger-glass, has not
become fashionable in America.'

   Towards 1800 a distinction appears to have been made between a
finger-glass and a 'wine-glass cooler'. G. Bernard Hughes quotes an
advertisement of 1800 which includes 'Glass finger-cups and wine-
glass-coolers',[257] and in 1801 the Liverpool glassman Gregory
Knight advertised 'Finger Glasses and Wine Coolers'. Hughes
avers that individual wine-glass coolers appeared at the Coronation
banquet of George III and Queen Charlotte, but does not quote his
source.[258] The French artist Chardin had, in 1759, painted a wine-
glass bowl-down in a cylindrical vessel, so a similar practice in
England in 1761 would not be surprising. The vessel seems not to
have acquired a separate name unless by chance it is the 'washer'
mentioned in 1777 (p. 173). It is perhaps no coincidence that the
term 'wine-glass cooler' appears just about the same time as the
object itself becomes unequivocally identifiable – a bowl with two
lips in which the stem of a glass could rest. These appear in Isaac
Jacobs' signed gilt blue glass (Pl. 44b), which fixes their date
between 1796 and about 1820. Hughes illustrates a Henry Alken
print of 1824 in which a wine-glass can clearly be seen inverted in
what appears to be an ordinary finger-glass without lips.[259] Hughes
again cites an early nineteenth-century instruction: 'Hock and champagne glasses are to be placed in the cooler, two wineglasses upon
the table.'[260] The cooling of these glasses for white wine is perfectly logical, and perhaps accounts for the *two* lips on these bowls.

The earliest published reference to cut glass in England appears in
The Weekly Journal for 4 April 1719:[261] 'John Akerman, that lived at
the corner of Birchin Lane . . . has taken a place in the West Walk of
the Royal Exchange, Cornhill, and there continues to sell (amongst
other things) fine cut and plain Flint Glasses.' This was supplemented by a second notice on 27 October 1719:[262] 'John Akerman,
at the Rose and Crown, Cornhill, continues to sell all sorts of tea,
chinaware, plain and diamond-cut flint glasses, white stoneware,
etc.' 'Continues to sell' implies that he had been dealing in
'diamond-cut flint glasses' for some time. Akerman might, from
this second notice, have been taken to be a 'Chinaman', dealing

primarily in porcelain and tea, had he not been known as a prominent member of the Glass-Sellers' Company, holding office as Renter Warden in 1740, Master in 1741 and Upper Warden in 1748.[263] When in 1746 he changed his address to Fenchurch Street, the fact was advertised as far afield as Bath, Oxford and Northampton.[264] His enterprise was one of four firms of glass-cutters mentioned in the *London Directory* of 1755, and it may be traced under various names until about 1785. It is clear, therefore, that he played a leading, if not a dominant, role in the development of English glass-cutting.

Akerman (Ackermann) could well be German, and a glass-cutter would come naturally enough from Germany, where his art was indigenous. The name, however, seems to have been fairly widespread in Europe, including England; nor is it certain that Akerman himself was a glass-cutter. Francis Buckley surmised that Akerman had employed the father of Christopher Haedy, the well-known glass-cutter and glass-seller, who advertised himself as the 'German who was the first that brought the art of Cutting and Engraving Glass from Germany'.[265] There is no factual evidence for this suggestion, and in view of the probable role played by the mirror-grinders in the development of wheel-cutting and engraving (p. 151), it seems more likely that we have to deal with a gradual growth rather than a sudden introduction, whatever Haedy may have thought. A pointer to this may be the phrase 'diamond-cut' in John Akerman's advertisements. Francis Buckley preferred to regard this as describing a diamond-shaped cut motif, perhaps later extended as a generic term to cover other cognate designs. He spoils his own case, however, by quoting John Greene's import of 'diamond-cut' mirrors about 1670.[266] We know of no mirrors of this date with diamond-shaped facets, and from later parlance we may deduce that 'diamond-cut' was the equivalent of 'bevelled'. In 1678 one John Roberts obtained a patent 'for his invention of grinding, polishing and diamonding glass plates for looking glasses, etc., by the motion of water and wheels.'[267] Other comparable patents followed. The 'diamonding' of John Roberts's patent is given a gloss by *The Plate Glass Book* (1764):[268] 'It is not usual, of late, to *Diamond-cut* the Edges of Glasses put into *French* frames', where 'Diamond-cut' clearly means 'bevel'. The tables in this work show 'Grinding', 'Polishing', and 'Silvering' as adding 6d each to the cost of the smallest plate, whereas '*Diamond*-Cutting' only adds 4d. This bevelling is said to have been executed by the same techniques as the grinding, but the shaping of an edge into a complex series of curves and angles could only have been done by a grinding-wheel.

If 'diamond-cut' meant 'bevelled', its application to much of the earliest cut glass becomes immediately understandable. Cut glass itself is very seldom explicitly dated, and we need circumstantial evidence. This is sometimes provided by hallmarked silver used in conjunction with glass, notably the stands and mounts for glass cruet-bottles. However, considerable caution is needed, since the glass bottles and caps have often been interchanged. A series of such stands bears the mark of the famous silversmith Paul de Lamerie, with London hallmarks between 1722 and 1734. They consistently house cut-glass bottles (Pl. 48a), often with elaborate silver mounts.[269] The glasses were blown into a square mould with truncated corners, and the eight vertical faces trimmed on the wheel, much as the mirror-bevels were 'diamond-cut'. The tapering necks are necessarily circular in section, and to effect the transition from octagon to circle a variety of flat bridging facets were cut before the long vertical neck-flutes begin. These are interrupted by pronounced horizontal steps sometimes cut into a series of slightly hollowed facets, probably produced by a gently convex wheel (Pl. 48a). These look forward to a further development of interlocking hollow facets. The diamond-cut style can be seen in its purest form in the tall bottles – basically square on plan, with bevelled angles – put up by fours and sixes in shagreen cases, either for spirits or toilet waters. They have short necks and bubble-filled spherical stoppers which have been faceted into horizontal series of small flat squares or hexagons. Oblong tea-bottles, diamond-cut to the shoulder, have short collar-necks and similar bubbled spherical stoppers,[270] which recur (uncut) on some early shaft-and-globe decanters (p. 164). Similar polygonal shapes occur in bottles and decanters at this date, and two rare cut examples are known which echo on a larger scale the general design of the cruet-bottles, but with long, overlapping, hollow-cut hexagonal facets on the neck (Pl. 48b). The stopper is the prototype of the 'spire' but square in section with the angles bevelled.[271] The date of these pieces can hardly be later than 1740 and might be as early as 1725.

'Two round Glass Sconces scollopt' (scalloped) are mentioned in *The Spectator* for 3 June 1712, and we may suppose that the decorative edge-cutting suggested by this term was already being practised by this date. Scalloped plates are quite frequently seen in early looking-glasses; and in 1722 a glass-grinder named Daniel Robinson is referred to as a 'scoloper' (*Evening Post*, 10 March).[272] In *A General Description of all Trades* (London, 1747) we read under the heading 'Glass Sellers':

These are a Set of Shopkeepers, and some of them very large Dealers whose only Business is to sell all Sorts of White Flint-glass . . . though here and there one are Masters also of the Art of *scolloping Glass*, which is now greatly in Vogue . . . But those to whom this Title did originally belong were the *Looking-Glass-Makers*, a Branch the Cabinet-shops have now much got into. However, there still remain some who follow *Looking-glass-making* only.'

This indicates how mixed these trades had become, and how easily 'scolloping' might be transferred from one branch to another.

The main effects of 'scolloping' are probably to be seen on dessert-glasses, for its natural field was edge-cutting (p. 172). As early as 1722 Lady Grisell Baillie (p. 169) recorded of a dessert at a grand dinner party: 'Jelly 6 glass, 3 of biskits hipd [heaped] as high between two glasses, a high scaloped glass in the middle'[273] (i.e. pairs of jellies alternating with dishes of biscuits round a scalloped sweetmeat-glass). Five years later, at Lord Mountjoy's, the centre of the table had 'a scolloped glass cornered brims' while both ends had 'the same cornered brim'd glasses as in the middle'.[274] There were similar glasses at the sides – a proliferation of cut glasses compared with 1722. A class of sweetmeats with rims cut into pronounced triangular projections (Pl. 48e) may reasonably be equated with Lady Grisell Baillie's 'cornered brim'd' glasses.[275] They are often mounted on pedestal stems, unsuitable for cutting, but the bowls are cut into a series of flat triangular facets in horizontal rows corresponding roughly to the steps on the cruet-bottles. The triangles of one register marry up with the inverted triangles of the row below to make a series of overlapping diamonds. These cuts derive from the art of the diamond-cutter, while the rim-work is in the sphere of the scalloper. Probably by this date the two functions were united. By this time too the functional implications of the term 'diamond-cut' had probably become merged with the concept of the forms cut by this technique, consisting so often of diamonds, whether flat, hollow or in relief.

Much has been made of the effect on the development of glass-cutting of the 1745/6 Excise. H. J. Powell and Francis Buckley maintained that it helped the development of glass-cutting, but W. A. Thorpe held that it retarded it. In fact, a small calculation serves to show that it probably made little difference. Two cut wine-glasses of *c*.1750–60 chosen for investigation weighed about 178 g (6.3 oz) and 218 g (7.7 oz) respectively, and would therefore – allowing for loss through cutting – work out at about two or two and a half to the pound. The Excise worked out at a penny per pound of materials made up, adding about ½d or less to the cost of these glasses. In 1753 Thomas Betts was selling air-twist wine-glasses for 7d each; in 1757 he sold twist-stem wines for 6d each and 'clarets' (probably slightly larger) for 7d each, but 'cut wines' for 2s each.[276] In 1767 Maydwell and Windle sold wines of two sizes for 6d each, but in 1781 Jonathan Collet supplied 'wines cut and engraved' for 1s 6d each.[277] It seems from these figures that the cost of cutting was about twice the cost of the glass itself, and that ½d tax would make very little difference to the cutter. The development of glass cutting, therefore, probably proceeded virtually unaffected by the Excise.

Cut glass was for the wealthy, and cutting was more exploited on dessert-glasses and tablewares than on drinking-glasses, which offered less space for its deployment. The stem and base of the bowl are the main fields for decoration, which really permit only vertical fluting or diamond-faceting (Pl. 50a, c). Rarely is a bowl cut all over and the foot panelled and scalloped (Pl. 48f). More interesting work was done on tankards (Pl. 49c), tea-caddies, sweetmeats, decanters (Pls. 49d; 50e) and cruets. Once again the cruet-bottles repay study. Before the mid-century the old two-compartment stand for glass cruets (Pl. 48a) began to give way to the 'Warwick' frame combining three silver sifters with cut-glass bottles for oil and vinegar. The rings in these frames being normally circular, the bottles change from square to polygonal and thence to circular on plan (Pl. 48c), a form which encourages motifs other than the earlier vertical bevelling. On the neck the old style of faceting continues, but on the body zigzag arcaded patterns may be combined with paired lunate 'sliced' cuts producing horizontal eye-motifs (Pl. 49c, d); or lenticular cuts may be arranged in a diaper to produce fields of diamonds, perhaps the forerunners of the relief diamonds which dominate cutting after the rococo period. Similar motifs may be seen on larger objects such as the bowl and dishes of a grand silver *épergne* in the Victoria and Albert Museum, bearing the London hallmark for 1763–4 (Pl. 47b). They also appear on the larger glasses shown on Maydwell and Windle's trade card (Pl. 46), datable between 1751 and 1762. Here too the low-relief diamond, often cross-cut, is in evidence. The third quarter of the eighteenth century marks the apogee of English glass-cutting, and the rich style of about 1760 becomes even more elaborate towards 1775.

About this time an opposite tendency makes itself apparent, based on the low-relief diamond accompanied by fluting. The beginnings of this style already appear in a pair of bowls, once in

Mrs W. D. Dickson's Collection, with silver rims bearing the London hallmark for 1771–2[278]. They have a broad band of large relief-diamonds between vertical fluting below and a zone of rectangular facets above. By the 1780s this formula had been adapted to serve the elegant simplicity of the Adam style (Pl. 49a), and may well be seen among the cruet-bottles of about 1780–1800, 'elongated in form (Pl. 48c) and cut in long vertical flutes interrupted by bands of low-relief diamonds or narrow horizontal prismatic cuts. About 1800 this austere style was gradually enriched with scalloped rims, spirally cut fluting and horizontal rows of more emphatic prismatic cuts (Pl. 52a). Throughout this period the relief-diamonds tend to grow smaller but deeper, and the stage is set for the moment when cut-decoration enveloped the whole vessel in a carapace of a single design – relief-diamonds or their cognate horizontal deep-cut prisms. This stage had been reached by 1805 on an oval tea-caddy in the Victoria and Albert Museum, cut overall with a diaper of small relief-diamonds and dated by its silver mount. This style of cutting (Pl. 52c), carrying the first intimations of mechanised monotony, may well have been encouraged, if not induced, by the introduction of cutting-wheels powered first by water and later by steam. 'Rich' effects, previously attained by a great expenditure of time and care on the old hand-turned wheels (Pl. 46), could now be achieved by mechanical means in great cutting-shops where men sat at rows of wheels powered from a single source. As early as 1775 Jonathan Collet, of the Glass Warehouse in Cockspur Street, was making enquiries of Matthew Boulton concerning 'a Machine for Cutting Glass'. According to tradition a steam-driven plant for glass-cutting was introduced in 1790 at James Dovey's works at Wollaston Mill on the Stour, near Dudley, and a firm in Bristol was using steam-power by 1810. In 1807 William Wilson, of 40 Blackfriars Road, was advertising his 'Steam Mills for Cut Glass' and steam engines for this purpose were probably in current use in London some time before this.[279]

The overall designs described could be diversified by division into alternating panels of, for example, relief-diamonds and vertical grooving. An exceptionally well-documented jug and two glasses, made in 1809, are ornamented almost entirely with horizontal prismatic cutting (Pl. 53a). These sharp-edged motifs were cut with the mitred wheel, an angled edge replacing the flat surface used for the earlier fluting. It is probably about this time that iron wheels were introduced for the first cuts, followed by a Yorkshire stone wheel for smoothing, and willow wood for polishing. Traditionally 'John Dovey of Brettell Lane was the first to use wrought iron mills for cutting glass', and introduced 'the double mitre and double-hollow stones'[280] – instruments ideally adapted to the cutting of multiple repeated prismatic flutes and diamonds. The diamond motif, which earlier had occasionally been cross-cut, now began to be diversified by cross-hatching (Pl. 52d), producing fields of 'strawberry diamonds', 'hobnails', and so on.

It should never be forgotten that the successive styles of cutting overlapped considerably, and co-existed for many years, according to the conservatism or otherwise of the cutter and his customer.

One of the fields in which cutting found fullest expression was in glassware for lighting. It was early realised that the light-refractive quality of English glass ideally suited it for candle-light – for aesthetic if not for practical reasons, a guttering candle-end constituting a distinct hazard. The first unquestionably English candlesticks seem to be those which have direct affinities with the baluster glasses of the years about 1700. They follow the balusters and light balusters in stem-design, allowing for the fact that the candlestick was normally a taller form, although an occasional squat shape probably reflects the influence of metalwork. To compensate for the higher stem the candlestick tended to have a wide and heavy foot, often domed (Pl. 43d), and frequently ribbed, usually in concentric circles or 'terraced'. Normally the candle-socket was a plain cylinder, sometimes with a strengthened rim and sometimes with an everted lip. There was often no grease-pan to catch the drips of wax or tallow, but occasionally one was built in below the candle-holder, as on seventeenth-century metal and ceramic candlesticks. This no doubt indicates an early date. Somewhat later, as with silver candlesticks, cylindrical slip-in 'save-alls', with grease-pan forming a projecting up-turned rim, were introduced to save drips and to protect the candle-holder itself from direct contact with the candle.[281]

The design of the candlestick followed that of the wine-glass, *mutatis mutandis*, into the era of twist stems, although these last are relatively rare, as with salvers and sweetmeats – no doubt because the 'Silesian' stem was found suitable for all (Pl. 43d). On glass candlesticks it provides a very close approximation to the shouldered stem on silver candlesticks with elaborately moulded feet fashionable about 1740.[282] Some of the earliest cutting on candlesticks is to be found on these pedestal-stem examples – normally a cautious scalloping of the foot, sometimes accompanied by unadventurous facet-cutting of the dome. It must soon have been realised that here was the cutter's most rewarding field, for if the wrought candlestick had caught the light well, its cut counterpart dispersed it with rainbow brilliance.[283] Not for nothing do contemporary advertisements refer to 'fire lustres'.[284] The earliest of these to mention candlesticks is Jerome Johnson's of 21 December 1742: 'At the entire Glass Shop, the corner of St. Martin's Lane . . . Diamond-cut and scalloped Candlesticks.'[285] The wording suggests that both stem and foot (and no doubt candleholder too) were being cut. By the mid-century, according to taste, the candlestick might be cut all over, from the rim of the grease-pan to the edge of the foot, and the third quarter of the century witnessed the greatest complexity of this decoration (Pl. 50b). It found maximum scope in the foot with its domed centre and scalloped edge. The dome permitted a display of the richest motifs, including the relief-diamond and the 'eye' motif. Smaller 'tapersticks' appear to have been used at the tea-table, and are probably the 'Tea . . . candlesticks' referred to in an advertisement of 1766.[286] They were no doubt also used as accessories of the writing-table. An advertisement of 1772 refers to 'cut candlesticks and Tapers'.[287]

Despite their individual brilliance, it would require a great many candlesticks to light a large room adequately, and eighteenth century interiors must often have been gloomy indeed. In 1772 Queen Charlotte's dressing room 'being very large and hung with crimson damask, was very dark, there being only four candles.'[288] Only on special occasions was this level of lighting enhanced, as when in 1769 Lady Cowper 'had an assembly in my great room, with above five dozen wax lights in the room.'[289] In 1739 the cost of wax candles was about 1d each,[290] and Lady Cowper would have spent 5s on lighting. When Sir Robert Walpole entertained the Duke of Lorraine at Houghton in 1731, however, the lighting of two rooms cost him £15 a night.[291] When illumination on this scale was required, the chandeliers of the house would be used. This was often an exceptional measure and when George III visited the Duchess of Portland in 1779, 'Her Grace had the house lighted up in a most magnificent manner; the chandelier in the great hall was not lighted up before for *twenty years*.'[292]

It was presumably not long before the idea of a multi-armed candle-holder was adopted. The earliest appear to be two four-armed holders, one at the Corning Museum, the other in the Victoria and Albert Museum. These have solid arms with candleholder and drip-pan welded on, springing from a central pad of glass between teared knops above and below, the upper one with a complicated finial. This structure fits by a solid peg into a cylindrical socket, itself resembling a candle-holder (and perhaps so used), mounted on a short knopped stem. These candelabra may be dated about 1725 by reference to wine-glass stem-forms, and about this date solid glass candle-arms were fitted to wall mirrors in place of the normal brass arms, being socketed into brass holders. Glass 'sconces' of this character were supplied to John Mellor of Erddig, near Wrexham, between 1724 and 1726 by the cabinet-maker James Moore, a partner of John Gumley.[293] Gumley, in particular, was deeply committed to the looking-glass industry, and it is probable that at this date upholsterers, mirror-makers and sconce-makers were closely connected and in some instances were the same people. Significantly, the word 'chandelier' in a glass context first occurs in an advertisement of John Gumley's in 1714: it offers 'Looking Glasses, Coach Glasses and Glass Schandeliers'.[294] Such 'upholders' would certainly have collaborated with the tradesmen who, in due course, began to supply chandeliers, the hanging counterparts of the multi-armed candelabra. These were undoubtedly modelled at first on brass chandeliers with their sweeping 'S' shaped arms, and the earliest glass chandeliers had arms of this form made in one piece like the candelabrum arms.[295] These were socketed into a brass plate housed in a bowl-shaped glass component which was threaded on the vertical iron rod holding the whole assemblage together. The bowl was normally silvered inside to conceal these working details. The rest of the stem was formed of hollow ball-shaped, conical and flattened members threaded on in sequence and terminating below in a pear-shaped pendant. From an early date – probably 1730 at latest – these components were cut, mainly with overall vertical flutes or flat diamonds, the arms remaining plain. Occasionally the stem-parts were mould-blown with mesh-patterns, presumably imitating the cut diamonds, and the grease-pans with concentric rings.[296]

About this time grease-pans began to be made separately with a central hole to be slipped over the candle-holder, which was integral with the arm. The grease-pans lent themselves readily to edge-cutting, and were the first arm components to be cut. In due course the arms themselves were cut, first in long shallow facets, subsequently in notching of ever-increasing complexity executed on an arm reduced by cutting to a hexagonal section. About mid-century the pans are star-cut; single pendants and upright ornaments such as stars, crescents and obelisks adorn the arms; and cut canopies appear with scalloped rims which are further embellished with pendants. This stage in chandelier development is illustrated in Maydwell and Windle's trade card (Pl. 46) which submits several variations to their clients' taste, including a four-armed table candelabrum.

The full force of rococo elaboration is now loosed upon the glass chandelier (Pl. 51). The 'S' shaped arms are supplemented by snake-like, double-curved arms with which they alternate and which raise the candle-holders to a higher level. With two tiers of arms this gives candles at four levels and changes the general shape of the chandelier.[297] The canopies grow more fantastic and assume a Chinese air with their dangling pendants. The cutting becomes richer, and above all the whole structure is increasingly hung with brilliant-cut drops, not singly now but in strings and clusters. As early as 1756 Jerome Johnson advertised, 'Lustres, High polish'd Branches, Brilliant Drops to hang on the Lustres'.[298] These were perhaps single drops, but by 1775 Christopher Haedy was selling 'Girandoles [candelabra], on the most elegant plan, ornamented with festoons of entire paste.'[299]

The best and most accessible chandeliers of this era are those in the Assembly Rooms at Bath.[300] They were installed in 1771 by two different makers, Jonathan Collet, the presumed successor of Thomas Betts (d. 1767, p. 178), and William Parker, perhaps the most important London glass-cutter of his time, with premises at 69 Fleet Street. Only one of Collet's Bath chandeliers survives. This is an enormous 48-light structure with candles on four levels and the arms profusely notched; the stem-globes are ornamented with cross-cut, low-relief diamonds, and the bottom pendant with deep herring-bone cutting. This magnificent lustre of notably dark glass contrasts forcibly with the remaining chandeliers, which are assured as William Parker's work not only by documents but by the inscription 'PARKER FLEET STREET LONDON' engraved round the bowl of one of them. Parker's lustres are quite different in feeling. Although almost as large, with forty lights apiece, they have a vertical emphasis underlined by the appearance on the stem of urn-shaped members replacing the globes which characterise rococo chandeliers generally, and Collet's in particular. These urns are cut mainly in perpendicular flutes which re-emphasise the vertical feeling of the design. Although the arms themselves are double-curved and closely notched, and would be fully at home on a rococo chandelier, the bowls from which they radiate are lightly cut with low relief diamonds and 'S' shaped flutes. The plainer cutting and the urn shapes clearly herald the neoclassicism to come. The slightly bare look of the Parker chandeliers was perhaps originally modified by a more lavish use of pendants.

William Parker continued as the most important supplier of lustres until almost 1800, his status emphasised by appointment as Glass Manufacturer to the Prince of Wales, for whose palatial establishment at Carlton House he supplied an important series of chandeliers in the 1780s.[301] Bills show that between 1783 and 1786 Samuel Parker (a partner with his father from 1784) was paid the very large sum of £2,421. Unfortunately, although most of the Carlton House chandeliers were later moved to Buckingham Palace, they were probably much altered and are now mostly unidentifiable. Contemporary documented chandeliers, however, show a number of changes. The arms were now truncated short of the grease-pan and fitted with a brass mount into which screwed a glass candle-nozzle with swelling body and horizontal rim turned up at the edge and cut into a Vandyke border. The pan rested on the top of the arm and was cut into a number of points drilled for the suspension of the drops. Sometimes purely decorative arms carried small canopies surmounted by obelisks – a feature also found at Bath. The urns on the stem now tended to be cut with the zone of relief-diamonds above vertical fluting characteristic of cut-glass about 1790 (p. 179). Contrasting with the neoclassical austerity of urns and obelisks, however, festoons of pear-shaped drops begin to appear, suspended between the points of a canopy or between the drip-pans of adjacent arms; and strings of drops terminating in a larger circular pendant hang down from arm-ends. Although echoing the festoons of neoclassical ornament, these swags convey an impression of richness foreign to the more austere side of neoclassicism. Vertical strings of drops might also run from the top canopy to the points of the decorative obelisks, a portent of things to come. These drops were faceted and polished with consummate care and rivalled the work of lapidaries. The precision-made metalwork of this phase plays a major role in the construction of the chandelier, and is destined to become increasingly important.

Towards 1800 chandelier arms, while maintaining their hexagonal section, ceased to be notched. When in 1804 Sir Roger Newdegate of Arbury approached Perry and Parker, the successor firm of Wm. Parker & Co., asking for a chandelier to match those supplied in 1788, they replied advising plain arms since these 'have succeeded those cut with hollows, and are more generally approved.'[302] About this time too the vertical strings of drops, increasingly draped from top to bottom of the chandelier began to obscure the shaft, the vase-forms progressively degenerating in shape and decoration. This tent-like effect was complemented by a basket of pendent strings below the level of the arms, the old canopies disappearing. The arms likewise lost in importance, and the bowl from which they sprang was displaced by an ormolu hoop as the main structural element. To this were affixed short arms, often of metal, to hold the candles, and to it descended the tent of carefully graded drops. Often the basket was replaced by descending concentric circles of icicle drops. Icicles hung down from the grease-pans, and concentric tubes of vertically hanging drops might obscure the upper part of the tent. The lapidary's drops and the ormolu-maker's frame had now virtually obliterated the glass-maker's art.[303]

Table or overmantel candelabra throughout this half-century followed the chandelier in all essentials except shape. About 1775 the square foot came into fashion, and about the same time plinths in Wedgwood's jasperware, Derby porcelain, Blue John, or blue or opaque-white gilt glass, tended to replace the earlier flint-glass bases. Occasionally in the 1780s strings of lemon-coloured drops were used.[304]

Flint glass flourished by virtue of its light-refracting properties. Quite different properties of glass concerned other sectors of glass manufacture. It has already been shewn (p. 132) that towards 1700 opaque-white glass was being made in shapes mimicking those of Chinese *blanc de Chine* porcelain. Although there are few examples attributable to the early years of the eighteenth century, it is unlikely that production ceased in this period. There does seem to have been a technological change, however, for by mid-century the traditional opacifier, tin oxide, had been replaced by arsenic.[305] This change had taken place in Venice before 1741,[306] and it may be no coincidence that glass of this type is first mentioned in England in 1743, when the Countess of Hertford wrote to her son: 'They have made a great improvement in Southwark upon the manufacture of glass, and brought it so nearly to resemble old white china, that when it is placed upon a cabinet at a convenient distance it would not easily be distinguished by an indifferent judge.'[307] Robert Dossie, in his *Handmaid to the Arts* (first edition 1758), refers to an enamel made by the use of arsenic 'in a considerable manufactory near London'; and later states that it 'has not only been manufactured into a variety of different kinds of vessels, but, being very white and fusible with a moderate heat, has been much used as a white ground for enamel in dial-plates, snuff boxes . . .' Elsewhere in the book he writes: 'The white glass made at Mr. Bowles's glass-house in Southwark is frequently used for the grounds of enamel dial-plates and other painted works. It is a glass rendered of an opaque whiteness by the admixture of a large proportion of arsenic.' The juxtaposition of these passages would suggest that it was to glass from the Bowles glasshouse that the Countess of Hertford referred, and that it was a lead-arsenate glass. Dossie's reference to 'painted works' is of some interest, for although it probably alludes to painted enamel on copper (as made in the Midlands and possibly at Battersea), it may alternatively refer to opaque-white glass painted in enamel colours. Certainly such glass in vessel form was being enamelled well before Dossie's second edition of 1764.

On 24 September 1755 Holte Bridgeman, of Aston in the county of Warwick, glass-maker, and John Wood of Birmingham, toy-maker, petitioned for a patent, claiming to have

> invented and brought to perfection the art of performing that sort of painting called enamelling (that is, laying on pigments composed by vitrification and affixing them by fusion on their intended ground) and this in all colours, and whether they be called enamel or glass colours (that is, whether the colouring materials embodied with the vitrified matter do render the same opaque or only stained and semi-transparent) upon all sorts of vessels or utensils of enamel ware . . . these vessels or utensils having been formed by blowing after the manner of the glass houses in England, which art . . . produces vessels and utensils capable of all the same uses as when unenam-elled and adds thereto all the colours and those as beautiful and durable as any on the best porcelain. That the materials used therein are all or most of them produced or manufactured in England, and the said enamel ware being manufactured in a glass house is subject to the excise duty upon glass, and pays the highest duty, that of the best flint glass.[308]

The fate of this petition is unknown, but it is perhaps no co-incidence that the earliest known English enamelled opaque-white glass is a scent flask (or smelling bottle) in the Cecil Higgins Art Gallery, Bedford, inscribed 'Sarah Nelson' and dated 1756. Bridge-man appears to have been a glass-maker of genuine ability in this field, for he went on to serve as technician in the glasshouse at Namur, in Belgium, where he was paid 6 pistoles in 1761 for 'having taught us several compositions in the English manner.' When he left Namur he apparently left behind him a book of recipes, together with samples of his glasses, including opaque-white and a number of colours.[309]

Between 1755 and 1760, however, the knowledge of how to make opaque-white glass was clearly already diffused in the Midlands. A list of glass-makers working in or near Stourbridge in 1760 includes 'Grazebrook and Denham', making 'smooth enamel glass';[310] and a Michael 'Grasebrook' supplied 'enamel' to John

Baddeley, a potter of Shelton in Staffordshire, in 1760 and probably also in 1758.[311] That glass was being enamel-painted in this general area a few years later is suggested by the diary of Lady Shelburne, who was in Birmingham in 1766:[312] 'As soon as breakfast was over we went to see the making of buckles, papier maché boxes, and the melting, painting and stamping of glass.' Since Birmingham and South Staffordshire formed the main centre producing English painted enamels on copper, it is not surprising that opaque-white glass too should have been decorated there. The similarity of the 'composition' glass to porcelain was remarked on by the Countess of Hertford, and is made explicit by an advertisement in *Faulkner's Dublin Journal* (January 1752): 'At the Round Glass House on George's Hill, near Mary's Lane, Dublin . . . jars and bakers [beakers] for mock china.'[313] These components of a chimney garniture – three or five ovoid covered vases (Pl. 45d) alternating with two or four slender waisted beakers (Pl. 45a) – are among the commonest objects made in enamel glass. Their inspiration by porcelain is self-evident.

London and the Midlands have already been mentioned as centres of production of enamel glass, and allusion has been made earlier to the Tyneside and Humberside area (p. 148), and to Bristol *(ibid.)*, where it was used for enamel-twist stems. Bristol has always been particularly associated with enamelled opaque-white glass, but although there is no doubt that it was produced there, Bristol's prominence in this context is due more to historical accident than to technological pre-eminence, because of its association with a man named Michael Edkins.[314] Edkins undeniably decorated both opaque-white and blue glass from various Bristol makers, for his ledger survives to prove that he obtained such glass from Little and Longman (1762–7) and their successors Longman and Vigor (1767–73) and Vigor and Stevens (1773–88); Williams Dunbar and Co. (1765) and Lazarus Jacobs (1763, and 1785–8). Careful study of this ledger, however, reveals that he cannot have done very elaborate work on this glass, such as family tradition ascribed to him. Furthermore, some of the glass attributed to him by his grandson may be dated to about 1755–60, before he set up as a freelance decorator. His work is probably to be found in fairly simple decoration on glass – perhaps even in cold colours – and particularly in gilding on blue glass. The slight decoration on some Jacobs pieces (Pl. 44b) is consonant with the sort of prices noted in Edkins's ledger (p. 209). Once this false connection is broken, surviving enamelled opaque-white glasses can be logically arranged in stylistic groups.

Some of the pieces originally associated with Michael Edkins (mainly tea-caddies, vases and candlesticks) were painted in beautiful clear colours with distinctive sprays of flowers, appropriately nicknamed by the late W. A. Thorpe 'swirled flowers' (Pl. 45b). The caddies bore in addition the name of the tea within a rhythmically painted rococo cartouche, and below this a goldfinch perched on a branch. A striking feature of the whole group is that many of them are fitted with caps, save-alls, etc. in painted enamel on copper, often mounted in 'engine-turned' gilt metal. Both enamels and metalwork of this kind were South Midlands specialities, and one style of painting on the enamels closely resembles the 'swirled flowers' of the opaque-white glass. It is not impossible that these pieces were, in fact, decorated and put together in the Birmingham factory of the toy-maker John Wood.

A second group of glasses was probably associated with Edkins because of their affinity in subject matter with porcelain of a kind once attributed to the early Bristol porcelain works, but nowadays considered more likely to be of Worcester manufacture (Pl. 45a). In any case, the artist of the porcelain seems not be the same as the painter of the glass, despite the similarity of subjects. A style of painting closer to that on the glass is seen on enamelled Staffordshire salt-glazed stoneware, and the clear bright colours are markedly similar. It would seem more likely that this whole school of enamel-painting flourished in the Midlands, where Worcester porcelain, salt-glazed stoneware and opaque-white glass were all being made, rather than in Bristol. The painting of *chinoiseries* on this and allied groups of opaque-white glass may be said to surpass much similar decoration on porcelain (Pl. 45a).

A second, less successful, group of glasses is formed round an object which is both 'signed' with initials and dated 1764.[315] Unfortunately, it is unclear whether the initials are 'P.P.' or 'P.F.', and no painter with either has been identified. The object is a water cup, painted with two peacocks, one perched on masonry; on the reverse is a pair of parrots, somewhat insecurely perched on a tree. Both subjects are rendered on a sort of island, of masonry on one side, and on the other a patch of ground from which grow distinctive leaves and flowers also found on other pieces. At the side of the bowl is a rose spray with a fat bud, details recurring on other pieces – notably baluster-shaped jars of a distinctive shape drawn in to a narrow neck above, and usually covered (Pl. 45d); and a series of cruet-bottles. The flower painting of this group, which normally includes the fat-budded rose, the curious half-shaded leaves, and a honeysuckle which occurs very frequently on the cruet-bottles, distinguishes it sharply from the Staffordshire family of pieces. The shapes too are different, suggesting a different origin. Occasionally the cruet-bottles have the condiment name written in Dutch, and a beaker in the Victoria and Albert Museum is painted with a ship and the inscription: 'Success to an Honest True Blue', features which suggest a centre on the eastern seaboard, possibly Tyneside. It has already been mentioned (p. 148) that in 1769 J. Hopton of the New Glass Houses, Sunderland, advertised 'white enamel' for sale; and, as will be seen (p. 191), Newcastle was certainly a centre for glass-enamelling. London, of course, is another contestant, but the wares seem naïve for metropolitan taste, and the opaque-white glass of Southwark was probably by this date being differently decorated (pp. 190–1).

The opaque-white glass vessels so far discussed were mainly for table use (cruets, water cups, candlesticks, etc.) or room decoration ('jars and beakers' and smaller 'flower bottles'). Much of it, however, was made for the 'toyman' in the form of scent- and smelling-bottles, to be mounted in gold and often put up in shagreen or filigree cases with other toilet requisites. These little flasks, which even more often occur in blue (or more rarely green or purple) glass, are usually rectangular in profile and flat, with slightly rounded shoulder (Pl. 45c). The short neck is roughly threaded to take the screw-on gold cap, and inside this is a tiny stopper with a flattened head. There are also smaller flasks of square section, oval and round covered boxes, and flasks and patch-boxes of lyre shape. Before they went to the enameller or gilder, most were sent to the cutter to be faceted overall with slightly hollowed diamonds. These *objets de vertu* often have marked affinities with similar pieces in painted enamel on copper, and this, taken in conjunction with the fact that glass-cutting and the making of 'toys' were firmly established in Birmingham, has suggested that they may have been of Midlands origin.[316] In 1772 the glass-cutter Isaac Hawker advertised in *The Birmingham Gazette* that he had 'laid in a fresh assortment of cut and plain glass, and a great variety of smelling bottles': and in 1788 he advertised 'All sorts of smelling bottles, cut, mounted in gold, silver, etc.' Nevertheless, the probability that these little toilet accessories were mostly made in London seems somewhat stronger. The enamels which they most resemble are atypical for the Midlands, and there is a reasonable chance that they were made by one of the enamellers undoubtedly working in London.[317] Certainly they seem to demonstrate a continuity with similar objects dating from about 1765 and later which can reasonably be attributed to London (p. 191). The decoration of the scent-bottles is sometimes enamelled and gilt, sometimes gilt only, and the subjects include notably flowers and leaves tied in nosegays, birds in landscape, and *chinoiserie* and pastoral figures. They appear to date from about 1760–70.[318]

Mortimer's Directory (London, 1763) contains an entry: 'James Giles, China and Enamel Painter, Berwick Street, Soho. This ingenious Artist copies patterns of any china with the utmost exactness, both with respect to the design and the colours . . . He likewise copies any Painting in Enamel. He has brought the Enamel Colours to great perfection.'[319] James Giles has long been known as an outside decorator who obtained porcelain in the white – predominantly from Worcester – and decorated it in enamel colours. The wording in *Mortimer's Directory* seems curious if he painted solely *in* enamel *on* china, and since 'enamel' in the eighteenth century could be synonymous with opaque-white glass, it has long seemed possible that Giles decorated that material too. Proof, however, awaited the discovery in 1966 of a Christie sale catalogue 'of the ELEGANT PORCELAINE of English and Foreign Manufacture, part of the STOCK in TRADE of Mr. James Giles, CHINAMAN and ENAMELLER, Quitting that Business; CONSISTING OF Many superb and select Articles of . . . Porcelaine . . . together with an Assortment of cut and gilt Glass; which will be sold by Auction . . . Monday, March 21, 1774, and the four following days.' Lot 75 on the third day consisted of 'two large beakers cut in flutes, painted work, with Tuscan and Grecian figures from Hamilton, 2 less ditto and 1 essence bottle ditto £5.0.0.' This description exactly fits two existing beakers, the gilt decoration of which has been closely copied from D'Hancarville's book on the Hamilton Collection, *Antiquités Etrusques, Grecques et Romaines Tirées du Cabinet de M. Hamilton* (1st edition Naples, 1766–7). This might mean no more than that Giles sold these items by way of trade as a 'Chinaman'. Lot 23 of the second day's Sale, however, consisted of 'a set of cruits in stags heads, patera, festoons, etc. £4.4.0', and examples of these too are known. The importance of this item lies in the fact that pieces of Worcester porcelain are known with the same decoration, quite different both in the gold used and in style from normal factory-decorated Worcester porcelain. These pieces may well have featured in Lot 43 on the fourth day: 'a compleat set of tea china elegantly painted in gold with stags heads, pateras, festoons and husks.' The conjunction of opaque-white glass and Worcester seems decisive.[320]

From the decorations already mentioned it is possible to extend the family of Giles-decorated glass and to form an idea of what his production might have been like before 1774. Clues are provided by what the sale catalogue called 'mosaic' ornaments – paterae, diaper ornaments, husk-, scroll- and other formal border-motifs – and by certain stylistic idiosyncrasies, such as slender trees rendered with strange projections on either side of the trunk, heart-shaped leaves, pebbles strewn in the foreground (Pl. 45c, left), or curious buildings perched on bridges. These gilt motifs are found on blue and other coloured transparent glasses as well as on opaque-white, and among the objects involved are many scent- or smelling-bottles, shuttle-shaped as well as rectangular (Pl. 45c, left and right). An important document is a toilet set containing two gilt blue toilet water bottles made for Sir Watkin Williams-Wynn, who is known from Giles's ledger to have been one of his customers. This set has London hallmarks for 1768–9 on the silver components, and the bottles show some of the familiar mosaic designs, together with a typical rendering of flowers and leaves. On other faces of the bottles are exotic birds amid slender feathery trees, accompanied by the lanceolate leaves and the pebbles already referred to. These important pieces enable us to form an impression of the Giles style about 1765–70 (Pl. 44c), and thus to forge a link with the small faceted flasks of about 1760–5 (p. 180). Apart from the types of glass already named, the Giles workshop decorated opaque-white, blue or green decanters and wine-glasses, spirit decanters (Pl. 44c) and glasses, and large tumblers (Pl. 44d). Sometimes ordinary flint-glass is found with gilt decoration evidently from the same source – with vine-trails, hop-and-barley motifs, or the bucranium ('stag's head') and patera design already mentioned. It is not to be supposed that Giles himself necessarily did this work, but most seems to be attributable to a single artist who concentrated mainly on painting glass.[321]

If Giles only occasionally resorted to the decoration of colourless glass, another atelier – this time in Newcastle upon Tyne – seems to have cultivated it almost exclusively. Thomas Bewick, the famous wood-engraver, records in his *Memoir* of his life, written between 1822 and 1828:

Being now nearly fourteen years of age . . . it was thought time to set me off to business . . . The same year – 1767 – during the summer, William Beilby and his brother Ralph took a ride to Bywell, to see . . . Mrs. Simons, who was my godmother . . . [They] set off that same afternoon to Cherryburn to visit us, and to drink tea. When the Newcastle visitors had given an account of their paintings, enamellings, drawings, and engravings, with which I felt much pleased, I

was asked which of them I should like to be bound to; and, liking the
look and deportment of Ralph the best, I gave the preference to him
. . . I soon afterwards went to R. Beilby upon trial.

Ralph Beilby was the fourth son of William Beilby, senior, who,
according to Bewick, had 'followed the business of a goldsmith and
jeweller in Durham . . . His eldest son, Richard, had served his
apprenticeship to a die-sinker, or seal-engraver, in Birmingham.
His second son, William, had learned enamelling and painting in
the same place. The former of these had taught my master seal-
cutting, and the latter taught his brother Thomas and sister Mary
enamelling.' Bewick also records that Ralph Beilby 'had also
assisted his brother and sister in their constant employment of
enamel painting upon glass.' There were, therefore, four potential
enamellers on glass in the family, but it seems unlikely that Ralph
(b. 1743) spent much time on enamelling, for he was a busy engraver who, in Bewick's words 'refused nothing, coarse or fine
. . . This readiness brought him in an overflow of work.' It may
well be that he helped his brothers with lettering and heraldry, in
which he seems to have been expert. The younger brother,
Thomas (b. 1747), had by 1769 at latest moved away to Leeds as a
drawing master, and it was clearly William (b. 1740) who was the
leading spirit in the enamelling enterprise, naturally enough in
view of the fact that he had been apprenticed in 1755 to a Birmingham drawing master and enameller named John Haseldine. There
are a number of glasses signed 'Beilby', but only one or two which
unmistakably carry the initial 'W'; but some are signed 'Beilby
Jnr.', presumably pointing to William Beilby during his father's
lifetime (he died in 1765). The position of Mary is unclear. Born in
1749, she suffered a 'paralytic stroke' about 1774. Efforts have been
made to differentiate Mary's work from William's, with inconclu-
sive results; but she almost certainly played a subordinate role in the
enterprise. William himself had other preoccupations, for in 1767
he announced his intention of setting up a drawing school in
Newcastle. He presumably continued as a drawing master, like his
brother Thomas, until 1778, when he advertised in the *Newcastle
Journal* thanking his patrons and projecting an exhibition of his
pupils' work. In 1779 he appears to have left Newcastle for good,
setting up in London once more as a drawing master.

On the basis of signed glasses, an acceptable corpus of William
Beilby's enamelled work can be assembled. It begins with some
stately enamel-twist goblets painted with the Royal Arms and the
Prince of Wales's feathers, presumably celebrating the birth in 1762

of the future George IV. These are painted in full heraldic colour, with mantling executed mainly in white enamel with purplish shadowing, and delicately painted sprays and pendants of flowers and leaves in white (Pl. 41b). This white enamel, often with a slightly pinkish or bluish tone, is characteristic, being used alone for all sort of subjects: rustic pastimes (Pl. 41f); architectural fantasies including classical ruins, *chinoiserie* pavilions and Gothic ruins; baskets of fruit; beehives; exotic birds, and so on (Pl. 41d, e). The white was used also for the standard vine-scroll and hop-and-barley motifs (Pl. 41c) and is sometimes accompanied by a pleasing turquoise. The armorials for wealthy customers were painted in full colour, as were the delightful mock coats of arms (Pl. 41a); and a few polychrome country scenes appear within the feathery white rococo scrollwork and flowers and leaves. The considerable number of William Beilby's surviving drawings on paper confirms this range of subject matter as being well within his compass.[322]

The strong affinities between enamel painting on copper and on opaque-white glass made it natural that the latter should borrow yet another technical process from the former. This was transfer printing, probably used in the Midlands enamel industry by the middle of the century, and thereafter developed in the ceramic industry. By this process a paper pull from an engraved plate was 'transferred' to the surface of the object to be decorated, the plate being inked either with a medium incorporating the appropriate metallic pigment, or with a viscous substance on to which the powdered pigment could be blown. The object was then lightly fired. The first intimation of the use of this process on glass comes from a petition for a patent by John Brooks, an immigrant Irish engraver and printer, dated 25 January 1754. This ran in part, 'Showeth that your petitioner has found out and discovered the art of printing on Enamel, Glass, China and other Ware History Portraits Landskips Foliages Coats of Arms Cyphers Letters Decorations and other Devices.' The petition was addressed from York House, seat of the short-lived Battersea enamel factory, where Brooks had probably introduced the printing process and where prints of fine quality were produced. In 1751 Brooks had submitted another petition, this time for 'printing, impressing, and reversing upon enamel and china from engraved, etched and mezzotinto plates.' This petition was addressed from Birmingham, where Brooks specialised in ornamenting japanned 'waiters' (trays) with transfer prints, probably stoved on at low temperatures. Birmingham, as has already been said, was an important centre for enamel production, and there is an eye-witness account of printing

used on enamels there in 1766 (p. 187).[323] It seems reasonable to
suppose that transfer printing on enamels was practised there very
early, and if on enamel, why not on 'enamel' in the sense of
opaque-white glass? One of the earliest known pieces of printed
glass has a subject also found on commercial enamels of Midlands
character. Such glasses, however, are extremely rare, and the later
history of glass printing seems to centre on Liverpool, and particularly on the career of a certain Henry Baker. This man was referred
to in 1756 as 'of Liverpool, Enameller'. In May of that year he is
mentioned in *Williamson's Liverpool Advertiser* as an 'Enameller'.
Baker was apparently transfer printing on pottery in Liverpool in
1763, and in that year and 1764 apparently printed wares for the
Shelton potter John Baddeley. By 1770 he appears to have moved
into Staffordshire, but by 1781 he was back again in Liverpool,
being mentioned in *Gore's Directory* as an enameller living at
32 Mersey Street and practising glass painting. In 1781 he
petitioned for, and obtained, a patent for 'a new method of ornamenting glass by a composition of colours or materials imprinted
or made upon the glass, by means of copper or other plates and
wooden blocks or cutts', the specification showing that he understood the processes of printing and compounding enamel colours;
and a note in the Liverpool Public Library records that 'Harry
Baker . . . produced [by a patent process] subjects after the style of
Bartolozzi, in colours, the complete picture was made by means of
three sheets of glass, each with a print of the subject, two of these
had sections printed in different colours, the whole when assembled gave the lights and shades of the completed picture. They
are signed "H. Baker F. [fecit] Leverpool" (sic)'. Two glass pictures
of this character, representing the 'Comic Muse' and the 'Tragic
Muse', survived until 1907, and were fortunately photographed.
The 'Comic Muse' was copied from a Bartolozzi stipple engraving
of 1775, and both were signed 'H. Baker, F. Leverpoole' (sic). A
number of references to printed glass in Liverpool during the 1780s
probably relate to window-glass, but a few surviving black-printed
opaque-white glasses, mainly tumblers, are decorated with subjects otherwise found only on Liverpool creamwares. One is dated
1788. These eighteenth-century glasses showed the way for the
use on glass of a technique which revolutionised decoration in the
contemporary pottery industry.[324]

The history of window-glass manufacture in England during the
eighteenth century was one of steady evolution rather than of any
spectacular innovation. The two techniques, muff producing rec-

tangular sheets and crown producing circular panes, co-existed in separate glasshouses. Newcastle was the main centre for 'broad' glass, of which the *Encyclopaedia Britannica* (1797) says, 'It is of an ash-colour, and much subject to specks, streaks and other blemishes; and besides is frequently warped.' Crown, with its brilliant unbroken fire polish, was much preferred for the best work. The restrictions imposed by the crown shape, however, made it difficult to get many panes from it, and it was consequently expensive. *The Universal Pocket Companion* (London, 1741) quotes the following rates for glaziers' work:

	£	s	d
Crown Glass in Sashes measured nett per Foot	0	0	11
Ditto in Lead, per Foot superficial	0	0	8
Newcastle Glass in Sashes, per Foot superficial	0	0	6
Ditto in Lead, „ „ „	0	0	5

Since the actual glazier's work cost about 1½d to 3d per foot (i.e. square foot) the difference in prime cost of the two types can be readily estimated. These prices fluctuated in accordance with circumstances – for example, the demand for coal in London, on which depended the transport costs of Newcastle glass. In 1746 the Norwich glaziers promulgated the following rates in the *Norwich Mercury* for 5 April:[325]

London Crown, in sashes or lead	1s 6d a foot
Castle [i.e. Newcastle] Crown in sashes or lead	1s 3d a foot

which may be compared with those of 1741. In 1757 the *Newcastle Journal* (12 March)[326] records, 'William Featherstone, glazier, puts in Crown Glass at 11d per foot and Common [i.e. Broad] Glass at 5d per foot.' By then both types of glass were being made in Newcastle. The best crown, as the tariffs suggest, was made in London. The *Encyclopaedia Britannica* (1797) refers to 'Ratcliff crown glass, which is the best and clearest . . . the other kind, or Lambeth crown glass, is of a darker colour than the former, and more inclining to green.' The Cock Hill glasshouse at Ratcliff was the property of the Bowles family, and the *Leeds Mercury* for 5 May 1741[327] advertised, 'The best Crown Glass from Mr. Bold's [sic] Glasshouse in London or the best Crown Glass from Mr. Cookson's Glasshouse in Newcastle . . . Sash glass is 6d to 8d a foot . . . two of the best window glasshouses in England.'

Even earlier in the century plate glass had occasionally been used for windows as well as for mirrors and coach-glasses. As early as

1698 Celia Fiennes had recorded of the King's Dressing Room at Windsor, 'The windows of all the rooms are large sashes as big as a good looking-glass and are all diamond-cut round the edges.'[328] Glazing of this kind still remains at Hampton Court and Blenheim.

Plate-glass was made in the seventeenth century by blowing large crystal cylinders and opening them up (p. 100). Some time before 1687, however, a method of making plate by casting had been evolved in France, the molten glass being poured on to huge metal tables and smoothed off.[329] This process made possible plates of far larger dimensions.[330] There are indications that the method was taken up in England shortly afterwards (1691), but the initiative came to nothing, and was only revived in 1773 with the formation of the British Cast Plate Glass Manufacturers' Company, having its factory at Ravenhead, near St Helen's.[331] Evidence given before a Parliamentary Committee at this time suggests that imported French cast plates might attain a maximum length of 299 cm (118 in.) and width of 172 cm (68 in.), whereas the largest available English blown plate was only 208 by 122 cm (82 by 48 in.). Ravenhead, the largest industrial installation of the age, began production in 1776, and a mirror at Osterley Park, measuring 244 by 152 cm (96 by 60 in.), is said to have been the first plate made there.[332] This increase in the size of looking-glasses contributed greatly to lightening interiors, an effect accentuated by candle-light.

CHAPTER 5

Tradition and Innovation: The Nineteenth Century

The nineteenth century, which at its outset saw English glass dominant in the world, was destined to witness a variety of developments in glass-making probably without parallel since Roman times. In the meantime, English lead-crystal was universally regarded as the finest glass material extant, and cutting as the ideal mode of decoration for it – an apparently unchallengeable combination. The English glass-cutters had not only created a tradition backed by a skilled and stable workforce, but had developed styles of their own. To these advantages were added the seductive benefits of steam power. In reality, by tending to favour mitre-cutting, the use of steam may have proved prejudicial, for excessive mitre-cutting easily became monotonous (Pl. 52c), sowing the seeds of its own destruction. Meanwhile, every change was rung on relief-diamonds, 'strawberry' diamonds (Pl. 52d), hobnail cutting (in which each relief square or lozenge was cross-cut with a star) (Pl. 54b), horizontal prisms (Pl. 53a), and 'fan' rim-cutting. Additional motifs were parallel edge-cuts round the base of a glass, whether cut vertically or diagonally as 'blazes'; every variety of flat or slightly hollow flute (Pl. 52a); and relief 'pillar' flutes, sometimes used alone, sometimes in combination with other vertical motifs. The 'S' shaped flutes already noticed on the Bath chandeliers (p. 183) also continued into this period and were joined by other curved motifs. The innumerable permutations and combinations of these motifs produced a style of bewildering richness, within which the skilled cutter was able to ring the changes as his ability and fancy permitted. This richness can be seen not only in the surviving glasses but in the drawings of Samuel Miller, foreman-cutter at Waterford about 1830; or those of John Fitzgibbon, who worked for the Cork Glass Company (before 1818). These styles were common to the whole British industry. One group of Miller's drawings indeed is headed 'English, Irish and Scotch patterns', while Fitzgibbon's items include 'London Sugars'.[1]

One of the most elaborate services of the period was made in 1824 at the Wear Flint Glass Co. of Deptford, Sunderland.[2] Commissioned for the 3rd Marquess of Londonderry, whose arms are engraved on most of its components, it is decorated with almost every motif in the 'Regency' repertory – fields of raised diamonds, 'hobnails', and 'strawberry' rectangles; round-notched and serrated rim-cutting with 'fans'; cross-hatching within raised curved leaf-shapes; horizontal prismatic cuts; base-cutting of intersecting edge-cuts and radiating flutes in varying combinations. The far from homogeneous result suggests ambition rather than taste. To the same phase, but showing stylistic coherence without loss of ambition, is a series of glasses with the continental feature of projecting flanges, inviting notched and sometimes swirled cutting, to be matched on decanters by diagonal leaf-shaped shoulder panels in relief (Pl. 52b). A set of decanters and wine-glasses decorated in this manner bears the Prince of Wales's feathers, and was presumably made before 1820.[3] Such glasses have commonly been attributed to Apsley Pellatt, and some are decorated by a process which Pellatt patented in 1831 (p. 200).[4]

At this time Birmingham was establishing itself as a glass-cutting centre in rivalry with London, especially in those lines where glass was combined with metal, as on lamps, *épergnes*, cruets, and so on. In 1818 the local *Directory*[5] records sixteen firms, of which ten dignified themselves as 'manufacturers', implying a considerable output. An index of Birmingham's rise is given by the firm trading in 1818 as Mary Rollason & Son, selling ceramics, glass and lamps, which later became 'Thomas Rollason, Manufacturer of Cut Glass to the Royal Family', with extensive showrooms in Steelhouse Lane. Birmingham may well have led the reaction against the excesses of the Regency style. About 1820 the Paris Conservatoire des Arts et Métiers acquired a few representative pieces of English cut glass, among them a decanter (Pl. 53c), a jug and wine-glasses obtained from Birmingham. The jug and decanter, although decorated with horizontal prismatic neck cutting, had otherwise only light vertical cuts on the body. The decanter, instead of having the Regency barrel shape, was cylindrical, a form especially adapted to vertical fluting. Both shape and simple vertical decoration are foreshadowed in John Fitzgibbon's designs, but the early emergence of this style in Birmingham is documented by the *Pottery Gazette* for March 1883, recalling the development of the vertical 'broad flute' style by a cutter named Morgan, working for F. & C. Osler.[6] The 'broad flute' style is a development of the flat fluting exemplified in the Birmingham glasses acquired by the Paris Conservatoire. It was now extended to the whole surface of a (usually cylindrical) vessel. The *rationale* of this system is expounded by Apsley Pellatt in his *Explanatory Catalogue . . . illustrative of the Manufacture of Flint Glass*, prepared for the Great Exhibition of 1851:

> The object . . . in cutting glass is to present such a surface to the rays of light that . . . they may be broken or refracted, so that 'the play of light' . . . is always on the surface. To effect this it is necessary that . . . the indentations upon the surface, or the projections left by them, be such as to form angles. In the cutting called diamond or prism cutting, this object is at once obtained; the same effect is produced by fluting or flat cutting, because wherever two flat cuts meet, an angle is produced, forming with the line of the interior an imperfect prism; the broader the flat cuts, the more acute the angle, and consequently the greater the refraction of light, and as these cuts are made upon a circular surface, the broader the flats the more expensive
>
> [because more time and more glass had to be sacrificed].

Pellatt exemplified this rule in his own practice, for his illustrated price list, which was published in the late 1830s, presents a paradigm of the broad flute style, his 'fancy shape' decanters with eight flutes costing 16s to 18s, but with six flutes 21s to 24s each.[7] In 1832 John Gold, master cutter at the Aetna Glass Works of G. J. Green, Birmingham, patented a machine for broad flute cutting, both he and Morgan being mentioned in connection with this style in further articles in the *Pottery Gazette* in 1884 and 1889.[8]

A natural extension of the fashion for vertical cut motifs drew on another early Victorian source of stylistic inspiration – Gothic architecture. The cylindrical decanter, now the favoured shape, was frequently divided into vertical arch-topped panels, often forming fields of mitre cutting (Pl. 55d). Similar arched motifs on open shapes had fans between their points – an easy adaptation of a Regency device to convey an allusion to Gothic vaulting.

In 1845 the notorious Glass Excise was repealed. Although its effect on cut glass was probably never as great as sometimes represented, there was now no restriction on the thickness of glass used; a factor which perhaps encouraged the latent Regency style to reassert itself. By the time of the Great Exhibition in 1851, thick blanks had tempted the cutters into a complexity and depth of overall cutting that destroyed the surface unity, and sometimes even the shape, of a glass. It was these 'prickly monstrosities' (Bernard Rackham's phrase) that discredited cutting and appeared to justify Ruskin's intemperate outburst: '. . . *all cut glass* is barbarous, for the cutting conceals its ductility and confuses it with crystal.' (*Stones of Venice*, 1853.) Besotted by his prejudices in favour of Venetian glass, he forgot that glass has its solid and sculptural, as well as its malleable, aspects; and that it was not for nothing that it was often called crystal. The overworked cutting of the mid-century, however, deserved the reaction which Ruskin's strictures rationalised. The immediate effect was to popularise engraving at the expense of cutting, a development which could derive no logical support from Ruskin's views. It harmonised well with a development in glass shapes towards smoothly curving forms unbroken by horizontal ridges. The growing popularity of engraving was echoed in the use of bright edge-cutting on matt areas, a technique mentioned as a decoration for lampshades by Apsley Pellatt in *Curiosities of Glass Making* (1849).[9] The matt areas often assumed leaf-forms outlined and veined by means of polished cuts, analogous to the later 'intaglio engraving'. Pellatt emphasises the difficulty of executing 'curvilinear designs' on the large cutter's wheel, and the style perhaps succeeded best in formalised all-over designs renouncing any attempt at naturalism.

Often allied with cut decoration were one or two techniques restricted to the embellishment of crystal glass. One of these was rather misleadingly entitled 'Crystallo Engraving' by Apsley Pellatt, who obtained a patent for it in 1831. It had nothing to do with engraving, but consisted of taking an impression of the desired motif on a pad composed of Tripoli powder, plaster and brick dust. This was fixed into a recess of the mould into which the vessel was blown, producing a bright intaglio impression which simulated wheel-engraving (Pl. 53d).[10] An analogous effect was created by a more famous decorative technique pioneered by Pellatt in England. This was his 'cameo encrustation', patented in 1819 under the name of 'Crystallo-Ceramie' (Pl. 53b), which he continued to exploit until the mid–century.[11] A white cameo, made of china clay and 'super-silicate of potash', was prepared by shaping it in a mould and slightly firing it. The cameo could either be inserted into a sleeve of crystal glass which was then collapsed by suction, or could be applied to the surface of a glass and covered by a film of crystal carefully smoothed down to eliminate bubbles. These cameos were used in a wide variety of useful wares such as scent-flasks and spirit-decanters, but were found particularly suitable for small essentially decorative objects such as door handles and paper-weights. The process was not original, but improved on foreign prototypes – a good example of the international character of glass-making in this era. It was later taken up by other glass-makers, notably by Allen & Moore, of Great Hampton Row, Birmingham (1844–56), and by John Ford of the Holyrood glassworks, Edinburgh.[12] Similarly Pellatt's crystallo-engraving was imitated, probably by mould-blowing, to produce heads, etc. on crystal vessels, often supplemented by cutting.[13]

The mid-century eclipse of cut glass did not result in the loss of skills necessary for a revival. When the pendulum swung back in the late 1870s, there were still men available to cut the even more elaborate patterns of the 'Brilliant style' practised in both England and America in the 1880s and 1890s (Pl. 55c). This was mainly built round the elaborate star patterns apparently originating in Bohemian Biedermeier glasses, formed by a network of inter-secting lines. These stars undoubtedly developed from the twelve-point 'Brunswick' star, where each point is joined by an edge-cut to the fifth point in either direction. In due course stars of sixteen, twenty-four and even thirty-two points evolved. Analogous to these, and often alternating with them in overall designs, were webs of intersecting radiating lines crossing at common points and leaving blank polygonal islands to be cross-cut in their turn. These designs, based on simple geometrical formulae, were bewildering to the eye and depended for success on great accuracy. They were certainly open to all the objections advanced by Ruskin and were anathema to the adherents of the Arts and Crafts Movement (p. 223). To more unsophisticated minds they symbolised a rich and luxurious mode of life. The style has persisted even into modern times, although its heyday was over by 1914.

The earlier history of wheel-engraving in England has already been sketched (pp. 150–4). Towards 1800 formal engraving on glass was reduced to a few simple border patterns, wreaths, swags of husks, and so on. The neoclassical taste seems not to have been very sympathetic to glass-engraving, and its English practitioners appear to have concentrated mainly on commemorative work. Numerous glasses, particularly tumblers, extol the naval victories of the French wars with accompanying anchors, depictions of ships, Britannia, and bust-portraits of admirals. Merchant ships were also commemorated, usually on rummers or tumblers, with toasts like 'Success to the David'. The army also claimed its meed of glory with regimental badges, portraits of commanders, and so forth. Trade, farming, coaching and sport are all celebrated, and many personal events such as marriages and births.[14] In all these, inscriptions played a central role. It cannot be claimed that the engraving was of a very high standard, especially by comparison with the exquisite contemporary work practised on the continent of Europe. Paradoxically, it is now that we begin to learn something of the identity of glass-engravers, and even occasionally to find signed or otherwise attributable glasses.[15] Thus the Corporation of Wigan appropriately owns a tumbler with flute-cut base and inscription: 'Prosperation [sic] to the Corporation' and 'A Gift to the worthy Corporation of Wigan from John Unsworth, Cut and Engrav'd Glass Manufacturer to His Majesty and His Royal Highness the Prince of Wales, Manchester'. John Unsworth was elected a burgess of Wigan in 1800, and this glass doubtless records the occasion. Unsworth's trade card also survives and confirms his royal appointments, while giving his address as 'St. Anne's Square, Manchester'. No earlier positively attributable glass appears to have survived, but one class of rummers and tumblers may be ascribed to the pottery- and glass-decorating firm of William Absolon, Junior (1751–1815), of Yarmouth, established as early as 1785. His trade card shows him as having 'a Manufactory for Enamelling & Gilding his Goods, with Coats of Arms, Crests, Cyphers, Borders, or any other Device', and records 'NB Glass Cut or Engraved to pattern on Short Notice'. His engraver's work is to be seen on a homogeneous series of rummers and barrel-shaped tumblers with views of St Nicholas Church, Yarmouth; the arms of that city; or a series of ploughs, coaches, gigs and other horse-drawn vehicles closely corresponding with those enamelled by Absolon on cream-coloured earthenware. His glasses were almost certainly imported from London.

Some evidence survives to throw light on the work of the early nineteenth-century Tyneside glass-engravers. In the Nelson Museum at Monmouth is a jug quite elaborately decorated with figures

of Fame, Britannia, etc. symbolising Nelson's victories (Pl. 54a).
It is signed on the base 'John Williams Engraver, Newcastle', and
this man is to be found in Newcastle *Directories* as 'Glass engraver'
between 1824 and 1847. A straight-sided rummer engraved with a
view of Newcastle Bridge is signed 'R. Young', of whom nothing
seems otherwise recorded; and another in the Laing Art Gallery,
Newcastle, is engraved with Neptune and seahorses, and is signed
'T. Hudson'. Thomas Hudson was probably the son of Robert
Hudson, recorded as a glass-engraver in the 1787 Newcastle
Directory, and was himself listed as 'glass cutter' as late as 1853. In
Sunderland a number of engravers are known by name, and more
than one of the Haddock family probably worked on the numerous
rummers engraved with a view of Sunderland Bridge. Opened in
1796, this continued to be celebrated on local pottery and glass long
after the event. A Thomas Haddock, born in 1797, died in 1866;
and Robert Haddock appears in local *Directories* between 1827 and
1853.[16] Robert Greener, another local engraver, executed the
Lambton coats of arms on a large cut service made for Lambton
Castle, probably about 1823. Other Wearside engravers were
Robert Pyle, active between 1834 and 1847, and Thomas Bulmer.[17]
No glasses attributable to them appear to be recorded, but they
may well have executed some of the Sunderland Bridge rummers.

  Wheel-engraving had been established in the Stourbridge district
since 1769 at the latest, when the *Newcastle Chronicle* advertised for
the apprehension of an 'apprentice to the glass-engraving business'
who had absconded from a local firm.[18] Nevertheless, no
eighteenth-century engraved glass can confidently be ascribed to
Stourbridge. A commemorative armorial tumbler dated 1817,
however, is inscribed 'made by Mr. John Parrish of Wordsley'. The
Parrish family are recorded earlier as glass-cutters at Wordsley, but
it is uncertain whether John Parrish was the engraver, or his
employer.[19] We are on firmer ground with William Herbert,
recorded as working for Thomas Hawkes of Dudley.[20] A large
rummer engraved with a stage-coach above a frieze of hops is
signed 'W. Herbert Eng. Dudley'. The coach owner's name yields
a date about 1835, and in this year Hawkes are recorded as producing an important presentation 'plateau' engraved and (acid-) etched
by William Herbert. Parts of an elaborate cut and engraved service
also survive, the claret-jugs engraved with coaching and hunting
scenes, two of which are signed 'W. Herbert' with the dates 1828
and 1833 (Pl. 54b). A rummer in a private collection skilfully
engraved with a glasshouse scene is signed 'Eng. by A. Conne',
no doubt the Augustin Conne recorded as exhibiting at the 1851

Exhibition. Conne and his father, Nicholas, are recorded in London *Directories* between 1823–4 and 1854.[21] Near Stourbridge there was apparently an important engraving shop run by members of the Wood family at Brettell Lane, and Thomas Wood was an exhibitor in 1851. Two bottles attributable to this family and datable to the 1840s show rather simple-minded designs of plants, figures of birds and human beings, engraved through a thin ruby stain.[22] Other names are known, such as John Bourne at Dudley (1828–9),[23] and T. Illidge & Son at nearby Birmingham (*Wrightson's Triennial Directory*, 1818), but their work remains unidentified.

London probably remained an important centre of glass decoration.[24] A certain John Pye is recorded in Robson's *Directory* of 1833 as a glass-engraver at 11 Redlion Court, Fleet Street, and this man was probably associated with Perry and Parker, chandelier specialists, as early as 1819. Family papers record that he was a Freeman of the City, and a jug signed by Pye is competently engraved with the City arms. A mirror panel signed 'Pye' and engraved with a sailing ship is also known. John Pye had a son of the same name, born in 1822, who followed his father's profession, and a number of whose glasses remain in the family. These are decorated with the formal ornamental themes often found on Apsley Pellatt's glasses; it seems likely enough that this Londoner worked for a London employer. Other unknown engravers of comparable competence were doubtless employed by firms who issued trade cards or advertisements earlier in the century, such as W. G. Cave of 157 Fenchurch Street, or T. Illidge of 6 Bartholomew Close who also had a branch in Birmingham (see above).

Despite a reasonable level of competence, these home-produced engravers were outclassed by their continental contemporaries, particularly the Bohemians – men such as Dominik Biemann, of Prague and Franzensbad, with his exquisite finish and psychological insight into human portraiture; or Franz Anton Pelikan, of Meistersdorf, master of complex scenes involving human and animal figures; or Pelikan's fellow-citizen August Böhm, who showed a similar talent for crowded scenes. The growing wealth of Victorian England was a constant lure to these outstanding Bohemian wheel-engravers, and August Böhm himself was in the van of the immigrants. He had apparently left his home town already in the 1840s, and his work made a deep impact on English glass-makers. Apsley Pellatt, in *Curiosities of Glassmaking* (1849), refers to:

The art of engraving . . . so successfully pursued by the Bohemians.

Their excellent arabesque borders, animals and landscapes, are executed in quantities, with surprising rapidity, and at a low rate of wages; from ten to fifteen shillings a-week being in Bohemia a fair remuneration even for a tolerably artistic engraver, who would earn fifty shillings a-week if working in London . . . The most elaborate and splendidly executed artistic specimen of engraving, is now at the Falcon Glass Works, and is the work of a German artist, who devoted several years to its accurate details.'

This goblet, signed by Böhm 'of Meistersdorf in Bohemia' and dated 1840, is deeply engraved with the multi-figural scene of the battle of Granicus, after Lebrun. It was taken to Stourbridge in the second half of the century and still survives there. It was an object of admiration and despair to the local engravers, and plaster casts of it were treasured in Bohemia itself.[25]

Böhm's followers included some of the best talents in Bohemia, and they were dispersed throughout the United Kingdom.[26] Many naturally ended up in the Midlands, notably Frederick E. Kny and William Fritsche, who worked for Thomas Webb and Sons at Stourbridge, and later Joseph Keller, who worked in Birmingham and about 1885 produced *A Collection of Patterns for the Use of Glass Decorators*. However, they are also found in London, in Scotland and in Ireland, where Franz Tieze worked from 1865 for the Pugh Glass Works in Dublin. In London Paul Oppitz (1827–94), from Haida, executed commissions in his own studio for Copeland's, amongst others (Pl. 54c); and Franz Eisert, from Meistersdorf,[27] worked at different addresses from the 1860s onwards. The greatest concentration of these emigré artists, however, was in Scotland. In Edinburgh Ignaz Hauptmann (1818–87) is recorded about 1837, and Emanuel Lerche, who came from Austria about 1853, was employed by him. Lerche was one of the best engravers to popularise the fern motif which enjoyed universal favour from the 1860s for some twenty years. It flourished in another prominent Edinburgh workshop founded by a Bohemian, J. H. B. Millar – possibly Hermann Müller of Meistersdorf[28] – who migrated to Edinburgh towards 1860 and set up a workshop staffed by his compatriots. By 1866 Millar was employing some thirty engravers on work of all kinds – human and animal figures, birds and flowers (including ferns) – ambitious enough to be included in international exhibitions. Work was apparently done for Messrs. Millar & Co., glass dealers, and for John Ford's long-established Holyrood Glass Works, Edinburgh. A number of large goblets engraved with Scottish views – notably the Scott Memorial in Edinburgh – have been reasonably attributed to the Millar workshop, most made at the Holyrood Glass Works. There were also foreign engravers in Glasgow, notably Vincent Keller who, although recorded at James Couper's Flint Glass Works, also worked for other firms. Many of the Bohemians appear to have been essentially freelances working to commission.

The curving forms of decanter and wine-glass which developed early in Victoria's reign lent themselves to wheel-engraving at the expense of cutting. In an intermediate phase the two techniques co-existed as they had done in Baroque Central Europe, designs being engraved over the flat surfaces offered by broad, vertical flutes. By 1851 all-over engraved designs had become common, especially on the thin hemispherical bowls (Pl. 60d) of the new champagne-glasses (first mentioned by Disraeli in 1832),[29] and on the trefoil-lipped jug based on the classical *oinochoë*, now becoming widely popular as part of the move towards classical forms. A particularly fine example was shown at the 1851 Exhibition by the London firm of J. G. Green, the body engraved with *Neptune*, but the shoulder, neck and handle decorated with rows and swags of pearls in a formalised style which was to recur in the 1860s in the work of the London firms Apsley Pellatt and James Powell & Sons, and of others in the Midlands.[30] Most of the ornaments and much of the figural decoration were classical in inspiration, a mainstream joined in the 1870s by other historic styles – Renaissance, Baroque, Medieval, Arabian and Egyptian. A reaction against this eclectic tendency inspired in some quarters a partial return to the simpler, naturalistic, mid-century themes, with flowers and birds and the ubiquitous fern designs. These last were particularly suited to the straight-sided, tapering jug which became popular in the 1860s.

Amid this bewildering plethora of styles, the Stourbridge firm of Thomas Webb & Sons played a dominant role, mainly through their Artistic Director, James O'Fallon, himself a skilled engraver. Webb's spanned the whole repertoire, and O'Fallon himself not only excelled in Celtic-style ornament but developed a new genre of animal subjects humorously treated in a characteristic Victorian vein. Their most distinguished engraver was probably Frederick E. Kny, who worked in many styles, often on the thin-blown, ovoid-bodied decanter with trefoil lip and hollow globular stopper – the counterpart of the trefoil *oinochoë* – which reached peak popularity after 1870. Kny, together with his countryman William Fritsche, was also a pioneer in a new style destined to dominate the 1880s and to last into the twentieth century. This was 'rock-crystal' engraving, deep intaglio cutting into a solid crystal glass, the cuts being polished throughout.[31] Much use was also made of relief ornaments, the inspiration coming in equal parts from the Far East and Baroque Silesia. About 1875 Kny engraved a vase with a relief zone copied from the Parthenon frieze, accompanied by typical 'Grecian' ornaments, in intaglio. This may have been an answer to the 'Elgin' vase, with similar relief-engraved central zone, begun in 1864 and finished in 1873 by the important English engraver and technician, John Northwood of Stourbridge. These two exceptional pieces, although epoch-making in their technique and use of relief-engraving, did not strictly exemplify 'rock-crystal' engraving, a term first used in 1878, although Japanese-inspired glass recalling 'the highest qualities of Chinese engraving on pure rock crystal' was mentioned in 1874. Kny was associated with 'rock-crystal' from the beginning, and was one of its greatest exponents; but of comparable importance was William Fritsche, of Meistersdorf, who in 1886 completed a masterpiece of the style in a ewer with ornaments in polished relief and intaglio based on the theme of water (Pl. 55b). It was directly influenced by the true rock-crystal engraving of Baroque Central Europe, whereas the most characteristic 'rock-crystal' engraving of the 1880s was inspired technically by Chinese hardstone carving and thematically by Japanese art, so popular at this time. This influence is particularly strong in the work of Stevens & Williams of Brierley Hill, near Stourbridge, for whom worked talented engravers such as the Bohemian Joseph Keller, and the Englishmen John Northwood and John Orchard. The Stevens & Williams work tended to a panelled style with fields outlined by strong relief- or intaglio-cuts, while at Thomas Webb's the Baroque character of Fritsche's ewer continued into the 1890s with swirled and curvilinear designs. In this period, to mitigate the high cost of this ware, some of the relief elements were mould-blown; and efforts were made towards 1900 to accommodate neo-classical and Art Nouveau themes. These were alien to the spirit of 'rock-crystal', however, and the failing style did not survive 1914. In this last phase, some attractive work was done by the Stour-bridge firms of Webb Corbett and Stuart and Sons, both firms assisted by William and Ludwig Kny, sons of Frederick.[32]

A method of cutting glass somewhat resembling the earlier 'obscured glass' (p. 200) emerged about 1890, being first cultivated by John Northwood for Stevens & Williams. This method, confusingly called 'intaglio', employed the glass-cutter's small stone wheel like the engraver's copper wheel, producing bold cuts which could be brilliantly polished. The technique lent itself well to simplified curving designs, and was widely used at Stevens & Williams, whose talented engraver, Joshua Hodgetts, brought it to a high degree of perfection. It was also taken up by other Stour-bridge firms.[33]

The need for economy which had encouraged intaglio work also brought out another weapon in the glass-maker's armoury – etching by means of hydrofluoric acid. Isolated instances of acid etching glass are known from the seventeenth century onwards, but consistent success with it dates only from around 1800. At this time methods of masking glass with varnish, scratching through this with a point, and then exposing the glass to hydrofluoric acid fumes, were published in several learned journals. The earliest known English acid-etched glass is dated 1783, but it is a far cry from this amateur essay to a commercial application of the process.[34] In 1835 the firm of Thomas Hawkes is recorded as producing a plateau engraved and etched by William Herbert (p. 203), but this piece is lost. As late as 1849 Apsley Pellatt wrote in his *Curiosities of Glassmaking*, 'Etching by fluoric acid has been introduced, but its bite is not sufficiently rough, and is not found effective for general purposes' (p. 127). In the 1850s, however, Benjamin Richardson, who was manager of the great Stourbridge firm of W. H., B. and J. Richardson, and who had been trained in the Hawkes glasshouse, was experimenting with the technique. In 1857 he patented a process which involved mixing hydrofluoric with sulphuric acid to obtain a bright finish, and the use of gutta percha or india rubber as the protective resist. His patent also covered coloured cased glass, and a wine-glass with a blue diaper design in Broadfield House Glass Museum, is inscribed: 'Mr. B. Richardson, Wordsley, 1857' – evidently an experimental piece.

In this work Benjamin Richardson was helped by John Northwood, but in 1859 Northwood set up an independent decorating shop in Wordsley, first in a partnership of four, and from 1860 in association with his brother Joseph, as J. and J. Northwood (Pl. 55a) his other erstwhile partners setting up as Guest Bros. These two decorating shops executed most of the etching work in the district, particularly for Richardson's and Webb's. Northwood's etched designs followed in the main the naturalistic, classical and other eclectic ornaments of the wheel-engravers, but Northwood soon introduced a range of technical innovations. The first, in 1861, was the template etching machine, which substituted a form of stencilling for handwork in painting on resists. The geometrical etching machine followed in 1865, reproducing mechanically various repeat borders, such as key-frets, intersecting loops and simple floral repeats. He then discovered a means of matting glass by means of 'white acid' – hydrofluoric acid modified by a neutralizing carbonate to etch the surface of the glass without biting deeply. First used commercially in 1867, this was eagerly taken up on the Continent.[35]

Further refinements followed, mainly directed to the production of effective masks by the transfer printing process, using lithographic stones. The resist was applied to an etched stone and then transferred to paper in a press, the paper being transferred to the glass. These processes were apparently developed by Richardson's during the early 1870s, although similar perhaps more primitive techniques may have evolved in France slightly earlier. A comparable process was also used at Stevens & Williams, who apparently showed interest in acid etching before 1850 (Pl. 54d).[36] Transfer printing was particularly appropriate for mass production and was much employed for the cheap commemorative glass popular towards 1900.

Perhaps the greatest break which the nineteenth century made with the eighteenth was in the predilection for coloured glass above colourless lead-crystal. Coloured glass – deliberately coloured by metallic oxides – had, of course, been used down the ages, but sparingly. The eighteenth century certainly witnessed an extension of its use, particularly latterly, but this was as nothing compared with the explosion which followed. The extensive use of gilding on blue, manganese-purple and copper-green glass has already been mentioned (pp. 189–91). Although this decoration was certainly practised in London, the only concern of which we have any details is that of the Jacobs family in Bristol. Michael Edkins may have done work of this kind on glass made at Lazarus Jacobs' Temple Street Glasshouse (p. 187). Lazarus Jacobs died in 1795 and was succeeded by his son Isaac, who prospered and, in 1805, established the Non-Such Flint Glass Manufactory in Great Gardens. In 1806 he entitled himself 'Glass Manufacturer to His Majesty' and referred to 'specimens of the Dessert set which Isaac Jacobs had the honour of sending to their Majesties in burnished gold upon royal purple coloured glass.' None of this service has survived, but a rum decanter and several finger-bowls and stands survive with gilt decoration and mark $^{I.\,Jacobs}_{Bristol}$. The decoration is invariably simple – a Greek key-fret (Pl. 44b), an armorial crest, etc. – and most marked pieces have been in blue glass.[37] Lightly gilt coloured glasses (mainly spirit decanters) continued to be made well into the nineteenth century. On a distinctly lower plane were the lightly enamelled and gilt glasses produced in the workshop of William Absolon at Yarmouth (p. 202). Absolon decorated opaque-white and blue, as well as colourless, glass with artless representations of ships, masonic insignia, and the like; and although he himself died in 1815, his workshop apparently continued, for a blue bowl exists with the arms of Yarmouth, inscribed in gold: 'A Trifle from Yarmouth July 1820'.[38] If Absolon's 'best clients were the East Anglian farmers', the same stratum of society further north was provided for by the 'milk and water' opaque-white and the blue milk jugs and sugar bowls inscribed 'Be canny with the sugar', or the rolling-pins with 'Forget me Not', attributed to the Tyneside glasshouses but probably not exclusive to them. The painting is often worn and was apparently rendered in fugitive colours stoved on, rather than in fired enamels.[39]

Probably even further down the social scale were the jugs (Pl. 56d), flasks, tankards and rolling-pins made in blackish glass decorated with flecks or threads of opaque-white, and sometimes also coloured, glass marvered into the surface. Always called 'Nailsea', they must in fact have been made in the bottle-houses where this dark green or brown metal was used. The Nailsea glassworks made mainly window-glass, although there does appear to have been a bottle-house there possibly between 1815 and 1836. A flask with white arcaded threading dated 1809 must therefore have been made elsewhere.[40] A jug with coloured flecking in the Victoria and Albert Museum is believed to have been made in the Donnington Wood glasshouse, Shropshire,[41] and a number of pieces have been attributed to the Alloa glassworks in Scotland, a tradition given force by a bottle dated 1827, bearing owner's initials and the name of nearby Stirling (Pl. 56b).[42] At Alloa too was practised a rough type of point-engraving, executed according to one authority by 'chipping . . . with a sharp-pointed hammer'. A surviving bottle with the motto 'Speed the Plough' is signed 'Engraved by D. Erskine, Alloa 1840',[43] and another is inscribed 'A Present to Mr. and Mrs. Watt from Alloa 1878'.[44] A number of solid rolling-pins also are decorated in this way with maritime subjects, often with named ships, and inscriptions such as 'Look out for Squalls Jack 1847'.[45] Not infrequently a bridge is depicted, and some were probably made and decorated on the Tyne or Wear. An early example commemorates Queen Victoria's Coronation in 1838, and a date as late as 1867 is recorded. Most seem to have been made as gifts to wives and sweethearts.

As for 'Nailsea', objects other than windows were certainly made of the pale green glass used in the window-houses – notably large milk pans (easily made by a crown-glass blower) for setting cream, preserving jars, jugs, cloches, cucumber glasses, rolling-pins and inkwells. Some were fancy glasses presumably made at the workman's whim from the glass left in the pot at the end of a shift, such as mock Derby hats and twisted 'walking-sticks' which were hung up in houses to ward off disease.[46]

A second type of 'Nailsea' glass may equally be dissociated from that centre. This comprises flasks (Pl. 56c), carafes, hollow rolling-pins, large pipes, beakers and mugs of colourless metal decorated with loops of usually pink (sometimes blue) glass; opaque-white is also used, sometimes as the body-glass. One or two pieces, however, of a faintly greenish tinge have circumstantial – perhaps correct – attributions to Nailsea; on the other hand, some examples are associated by strong traditions with other centres such as Warrington or Gateshead.[47] The great predominance of ruby glass is noteworthy. During the eighteenth century only one manufacturer of ruby glass made with colloidal gold is known. This was Mayer Oppenheim, a Jew from Pressburg (Bratislava), who in 1756 obtained, and in 1770 renewed, a patent for making 'Transparent Red Glass' on a lead-glass base. By 1762 at the latest Oppenheim was established in a glasshouse at Snow Hill in Birmingham, and was advertising: 'The Red Transparent Glass is to be had at the above Glasshouse, either in a light rose or deep ruby colour.' In 1777 he was bankrupted and languished in the King's Bench Prison between July 1778 and February 1780. He then disappeared to France.[48] Although Mayer Oppenheim almost certainly did exploit his patent, very few putative English ruby glasses of eighteenth-century date have been identified, and of these none seems to conform very satisfactorily to Oppenheim's patent specification. Oppenheim's ruby glass was probably mainly used by the Birmingham 'glass-pinchers', who made small pressed objects such as buttons; or possibly by the Birmingham enamellers in the preparation of their pigments. In short, ruby glass seems to have been rare in eighteenth-century England. When therefore – no doubt owing to Bohemian influence – it began about 1830 to be used for glass decoration, it probably struck the English public with the full force of novelty.

It has been surmised that it was mainly the Excise which paralysed the English glass-maker and inhibited him from following more speedily the trend towards colour which was gathering momentum on the Continent. In Bohemia the stone-like 'Hyalith' and 'Lithyalin' glasses were evolving in the 1820s, and cased coloured glasses were well developed by 1828.[49] In France opalescent white and tinted glasses *(opalines)* were well established before 1830.[50] A surviving English price list apparently of the mid-

1830s, however, shows a number of coloured glasses in use, often for casing, and demonstrates that some more enterprising firms were abreast of foreign developments, despite the Excise. After 1845 other Midlands firms entered the field. In particular, Benjamin Richardson, of W. H., B. & J. Richardson, proved himself a notable innovator and, in 1845 itself, showed opaline and cased coloured glasses at an exhibition in Manchester. In the Birmingham Exhibition of 1849 almost all the well-known Birmingham glass firms, as well as Richardson's, exhibited glasses in the same categories. The trend was firmly established by the time of the Great Exhibition in 1851, when nearly all British glass-makers showed coloured glasses, the firm of Rice, Harris & Son of Birmingham having on exhibition 'opal, alabaster, turquoise, amber, canary, topaz, chrysoprase, pink, blue, light and dark ruby, black, brown, green, purple, etc.'. The range rivalled that of the Bohemian glass in the exhibition.[51]

The classic use of coloured glass in Bohemia – particularly of the universal translucent ruby, but to a lesser extent of translucent blue, green and yellow – had been in cased glasses cut or engraved, or both, through the coloured layer to the underlying crystal. Occasionally more than one overlay was used, opaque-white being a favourite. Before long various stains analogous to the translucent enamels used by stained-glass painters replaced the more expensive coloured glasses; these could be cut and engraved in just the same way. When, in addition, enamelling and gilding were used, results of the utmost richness and complexity (and sometimes ugliness) were achieved. All these effects were used to the full in England, the main exploiters being the firms in the Midlands, at Birmingham and Stourbridge, and in London (Pl. 57a, b, c).

The semi-opaque opaline glasses mainly French inspired, whether white or coloured, did not lend themselves to cutting or engraving, but might be enamelled or gilt, or occasionally embellished with applied decoration. They tended to be made in the flowing curved forms naturally produced by blowing, and not in the angular shapes suitable for cutting. In England the preferred shapes were inspired by Greek pottery – the amphora and the oinochoë – and the enamel-painted, and sometimes enamel-printed, decoration also frequently drew on classical sources, although some attractive overall floral painting in polychrome enamels was executed by the Richardson firm. Other important concerns in this field were the Birmingham firm of Bacchus, J. F. Christy of Lambeth, and Davis, Greathead and Green of Stourbridge. Both styles were also applied to colourless glass, the polychrome floral designs being particularly effective (Pl. 57d). This work too was done by the concerns mentioned, some designs by the painter Richard Redgrave for Christy's being especially successful.[52]

A distinctive surface treatment of crystal glass stands to the credit of the Longport (Staffordshire) firm of Davenport, famous for its ceramics, but also important in the glass-making field. In 1806 John Davenport patented 'a method of ornamenting all kinds of glass in imitation of Engraving or Etching', the process consisting of an application of finely ground colourless frit in a medium of 'double refined loaf sugar dissolved in two parts of water . . . and about one third part of common writing ink.' This light grey coating was scratched away with a point as desired and finally fired. A number of glasses decorated in this way survive, usually marked 'PATENT' on the base (Pl. 58c). The designs are mostly sporting scenes and landscapes (Pl. 58c), with clumsy classicising borders, used on jugs and rummers.[53] An important royal order of 1807, involving 'A Service of Glass Etch[d] Grecian border' and running to over 250 pieces, was probably of this glass. The bill was rendered by John and James Davenport and the decoration is described as 'Etch[d] Feathers' and 'Etch[d] His Royal Highness Arms in full'.[54] The repeated word 'Etch[d]' is virtually decisive for this identification, for acid etching was not established as a commercial process by this date (p. 208), whereas 'etched' could equally refer to the scratched designs. Apparently not much was made, probably because the handwork involved made it expensive. A similar process for decorating flat glass is described in Dionysius Lardner's *Cabinet Cyclopaedia* of 1832 (pp. 300–1). This prescribes that 'a pattern must be drawn upon paper, having its lines sufficiently strong to be visible through the powder; and this being fixed upon the reverse side, the artist with a blunt wooden implement scrapes off the composition in lines accordant with those of the pattern.' The general appearance of the Davenport glasses suggests that prints were pasted behind the glass to guide the artist.

One other innovation independent of continental inspiration was also due to a Midlands firm. This was the 'gold enamel' ware introduced by Thomas Hawkes of Dudley (Pl. 58a). This designation too was a misnomer, for the technique with which it is identified seems essentially to have called for a double-walled vessel, the outer skin decorated by cutting and the inner by applied gold and colours. A plate decorated in this way, but with no external protective glass, bears the Royal Arms printed on a ground, and may have been part of a service which Hawkes made for a dinner given to

Queen Victoria by the Corporation of London after her Corona-tion (1837).[55] These pieces are of extreme technical complexity and were presumably too expensive to have been made in quantity. The same was probably true of the 'gem enamelled' glasses made by Apsley Pellatt and others, including probably F. & C. Osler, of Birmingham. Here coloured glass 'jewels' were combined with gilding in rich patterns, no doubt inspired by the contemporary enthusiasm for 'jewelled' Sèvres porcelain.[56]

The general scheme of glittering decoration represented by Hawkes's double-walled gilt glasses may have suggested a further type of glassware which emerged about the mid-century. This was the double-walled silvered glass for which Frederick Hale Thom-son and Edward Varnish took out a patent in 1849. The process involved precipitating silver over the internal surface by a solution of silver nitrate and glucose. The silver layer was protected by a cement covering, the air being excluded by a plug fixed in the hole in the foot through which the solution had been poured: this plug sometimes bore the name of the patentee. These vessels were often left plain to gleam like silver, but were sometimes cased in a transparent coloured glass which could then be cut or engraved (Pl. 58b). Perhaps the most ambitious piece is the ruby-overlay goblet engraved with heads of Queen Victoria and Prince Albert, now at Osborne House; but a cut green-overlay goblet is known with the engraved arms of Thomas Farncombe, Lord Mayor of London in 1849–50. It bears the Varnish mark and was shown in the 1851 Exhibition. These glasses were probably made by James Powell and Sons, Edward Varnish & Co. being retailers. A patent for the same technique was also claimed by W. Lund, whose mark occasionally appears; and several other patents for silvering vessel- and flat-glass, sometimes with en-graving, were taken out about this time.[57]

A development which may perhaps be treated as an independent episode, hovering equivocally between engraved glass and coloured glass, was cameo-glass. This wholly English phenomenon is no doubt due to the historic accident that the Barberini-Portland vase, probably the single most famous work of classical applied art, found a final home in England. In 1845 it had acquired the additional notoriety of being smashed in broad daylight in the British Museum, to which it had been lent by the 4th Duke of Portland.[58] It inevitably interested and puzzled the glassmen of the day, influenced as they were by contemporary classicising tend-encies, and intrigued by the vase's technical complexities. Among them was Benjamin Richardson, who reportedly offered £1,000 to the man who could reproduce it accurately in glass. John North-wood (pp. 207–8), fired by the same enthusiasm, seems to have experimented with cameo carving methods. His first essay, a vase with an Amazon attacked by a lion, in white on a blue ground, was subsequently smashed.[59] His second work was the crystal 'Elgin' vase (p. 207). In 1873 Northwood and his cousin Philip Pargeter, Benjamin Richardson's nephew and owner of the Red House Glass Works at Wordsley, agreed to collaborate in copying the Portland vase. Despite initial failure with the casing process, a suitable blank was finally produced, and worked on by Northwood for three years.[60] Some of the initial work was done with acid etching and the engraver's wheel, but the main work was apparently done with hardened steel burin-like tools sharpened to a triangular point.[61] The successful completion of this enterprise established cameo-carving as an important feature of Stourbridge glass-making, and Northwood went on to make for Pargeter a 'Milton' vase with themes from *Paradise Lost* and a set of three tazzas with busts of Flaxman, Newton and Shakespeare.[62]

In the mid-1870s Thomas Wilkes Webb, of Thomas Webb & Sons at Stourbridge, commissioned Northwood to decorate perhaps the most striking of his cameo glasses, the 'Pegasus' vase now in the Smithsonian Institution in Washington.[63] This was a white-on-blue vase some 54.6 cm (21½ in.) tall, with opaque-white horse-head side handles, and a three-dimensional winged horse finial, while round the body was a frieze representing Neptune and Amphitrite. The vase was shown unfinished at the Paris Exhibition of 1878, where Richardson's also exhibited cameo-glass, mainly by Alphonse E. Lechevrel, but including an unfinished Portland vase by Joseph Locke.[64] The Pegasus vase was not finished until 1882, and by this time other firms had entered the field, notably Stevens & Williams. John Northwood became Art Director there in the early 1880s and his firm, J. & J. North-wood, devoted much of its output to cameo work for the con-cern.[65] At Thomas Webb's the cameo workshop had been taken over by Thomas and George Woodall, originally with North-wood's. Cameo-glass was now being made commercially, and inevitably economic pressures were changing its character. Much of the work was done on the wheel or even by acid etching, and occasionally the design was in colour on a light ground. The classical figure style tended to give way to floral decoration (Pl. 59b) echoing the contemporary 'rock-crystal' engraving (p. 206), often made in the same workshops. The Woodalls at Webb's continued to produce figural subjects, often on ambitious large plaques, in the sentimental, and sometimes mildly erotic, taste of the 1890s (Pl. 59a).[66] The trade, meanwhile, was being undermined by cheap Bohemian substitutes with thick, white enamelling on a tinted glass. The quality of cameo work declined, and about 1906 Webb's closed down their cameo department, although work continued at Stevens & Williams as late as the 1920s, its chief practitioner being Joshua Hodgetts (1857–1933).[67]

A whole new strand was introduced into the already complicated texture of English nineteenth-century glass-making with the growing awareness of Venetian glass, past and present.[68] Felix Slade, whose bequest forms the backbone of the British Museum's collection of post-medieval glass, was ahead of his time when in the second quarter of the century he started collecting Venetian glass of the fifteenth to seventeenth centuries. Selected pieces were first put on show in the Society of Arts' Exhibition of Ancient and Medieval Art in 1850.[69] A growing consciousness of Venetian style and techniques was, however, evident before this, for Apsley Pellatt (*Curiosities of Glass-Making*, 1849) described and reconstructed several Venetian techniques, occasionally incorrectly. These included 'filigree', or decoration by means of opaque-white and coloured canes (Pl. 60d); 'vitro di trino', extending the filigree technique to produce vessels with a net-like thread-decoration; 'mille-fiore'; 'Venetian diamond-moulded', which Pellatt proposed should be produced by blowing into a diamond-patterned mould; and 'Old Venetian Frosted Glass', more properly 'ice-glass', made by dipping the hot paraison into water and re-working it so that the resultant cracks widened into fissures. Examples of Pellatt's ice-glass are known, and he showed pieces in the 1851 Exhibition (Pl. 60c). His lead was followed by other manufacturers, of whom George Bacchus and Sons of Birmingham went further by embellishing their ice-glass with marvered-in patches of coloured glass and gilt bands. Pellatt's 'Venetian diamond-moulded' glass also survives, some of it incongruously decorated partly by wheel-engraving. The technique was later extended to produce air pockets trapped below an outer layer of transparent glass of a contrasting colour – a process patented by Richardson's in 1858 (p. 221). Pellatt certainly also made filigree glass, used mainly in the stems of drinking-glasses, apparently under the mistaken impression that this was a Venetian speciality. In this too he was followed by Bacchus (Pl. 60d), who gave some of his stems a double loop, in a vague reminiscence of seventeenth-century wrought stems, then attributed indiscriminately to Venice. As early as 1849 Richardson's exhibited a glass with 'threaded Venetian stem', and elaborate looped stems were made by Lloyd and Summerfield of Birmingham. True Venetian 'filigree', however, seems to have been best mastered in the 1870s in Alexander D. Jenkinson's glasshouse, Edinburgh, his men apparently inspired by the historic glasses recently acquired by the Edinburgh Museum of Science and Art (now the Royal Scottish Museum). During the 1850s a collection of Venetian glass had also been begun in London in what was to become the Victoria and Albert Museum.

The Venetian influence was further strengthened by the opening of a branch of the Anglo–Venetian glass-making company headed by Dr Antonio Salviati, one of the leading figures in the Venetian glass-making revival begun at Murano before 1850. The London branch was established about 1866–7, and showrooms were opened at 30 St James's Street in 1868. Already by 1867 the London firm with the most sensitive response to Venetian style – as opposed to Venetian technique – had been exhibiting Venetian-style glass at the Paris Exhibition of that year. The firm was James Powell & Sons, of the Whitefriars glasshouse (Pl. 62a), whose directors were fascinated less by the tricks of Baroque technique than by the classic poise and lightness of the sixteenth century. Not surprisingly, Powell's was to be the firm *par excellence* which catered for the tastes of the Arts and Crafts Movement (p. 224). There is a world of difference between the confident attitude of Apsley Pellatt in 1849 and the critical approach of the commentators of the 1870s. Pellatt (*Curiosities of Glass-Making*), having described the Venetian decorative techniques, could write:

> It appears, however, that the English manufactures were for a considerable time much inferior to the Venetian. . . . Our Glass-manufacture has since made rapid progress; and the white crystal Glass-works of England indisputably excel . . . those of any other country.
> The essential and distinguishing qualities of good Glass are . . . its near resemblance to real crystal in its brilliant, pellucid, refractive and colourless transparency. In all these respects, the productions of the British Glass-houses are at present unrivalled. It only remained for them to evince their superiority in the ornamental branches of the art.

With this may be contrasted Charles Eastlake's sentiments in *Hints on Household Taste* (1868), where he writes of Salviati's glass: 'Of course, the smooth perfection and stereotyped neatness of ordinary

English goods are neither aimed at nor found in this ware. But if fair colour, free grace of form, and artistic quality of material, constitute excellence in such manufacture, this is the best modern table glass.'[70]

If Powell's, often by the use of natural green or opalescent glass, came nearest to masking the fatal brilliance and perfection of English crystal and to emulating the Venetian *leggerezza*, there were other manufacturers who were content to mimic the tricks of Venetian technique on glasses which had little enough of the Venetian spirit. Towards 1850 twisted handles and other decorative adjuncts began to appear. A decade later close twisting supervened, and in the 1860s close sharp ribbing on handles, feet and decorative 'shell' accessories became almost universal. With this frequently went applied drops of (often turquoise) glass, either plain or stamped to produce raspberry prunts (Pl. 60b). Venetian-inspired horizontal trailed threading was also much used in the later 1860s and 1870s, and in 1876 a patent for a threading machine was taken out by W. J. Hodgetts, of Hodgetts, Richardson & Son, Stourbridge.[71] The resultant mechanical close threading produced quite different effects, especially when the free 'combed' patterns of the Venetians were imitated mechanically by a 'pull-up' machine devised by John Northwood (patented in 1885).[72] Other Venetian techniques popularised at this time were the waving and crimping of rims (Pl. 60a), and the application of strips of glass which could be corrugated with a rigaree, or tooled into the forms of leaves and even fish.

These basically plastic effects found their most ambitious, and most characteristically Victorian, expression in the table centre-pieces with flower vases which to some extent replaced the dessert layouts of the eighteenth-century tradition. Mrs Beeton's *Household Management* (revised edition 1888) refers to 'The important subject of table decorations' recording that, 'The decoration of tables at the present time is almost universal . . . Hostesses in the season vie with each other as to whose table shall be the most elegant, and are ready to spend almost, if not quite, as much upon the flowers as upon the dinner itself.' The table centre-piece, therefore, should never be visualised without its complement of flowers or plants (fig. 24). Great effort went into the production of an unending series of novel table-centres, and a London firm of dealers such as Dobson and Pearce registered a whole string of designs at the Patent Office in the 1860s. Daniel Pearce, its leading exponent, ended up twenty years later at Thomas Webb's as head of the department producing table-centres. The first designs were appar-

3062. *Flowers for decoration* should be those which are not very strongly scented. To some the perfume of such flowers as gardenias, stephanotis, hyacinths and others is not offensive, but to others the strong scent in a heated room, especially during dinner, is not to be borne. Otherwise, there is no dictating what the flowers should be.

RUSTIC FERN STAND.

It is well to avoid many colours in one decoration, for, even if well grouped, they are seldom as effective as one or two mixed with white and green. It is a fashion to have a single colour for a dinner-table decoration, this being often chosen of the same tint as the hostess's dress or the hangings of the room, though these are sometimes varied to suit the flowers. Again, all white flowers are very often employed, relieved by plenty of foliage.

3063. *Vases and Flowers.* — If there are vases of all kinds to select from, then almost any kind of flower can be used, but few people have many sets for dinner-table decorations. Some prefer low decorations, others high ones, but there is one rule that should always be in force, and that is, that the flowers and their receptacles should never interfere with the line of vision, but be above or below it. The great objection to the epergnes of olden days was that they hid the guests from one another.

If the vases be coloured ones, of glass or china, let the flowers, if they cannot be had of a corresponding tone, be white only, mixed with foliage. If the vases

CACTUS VASE.　　　　　RUSTIC GLASS BASKET.

be of white china, use coloured flowers. If they are high stands, use those flowers which are naturally of high growth, with long stems ; if low, the reverse. Roses look always best in low stands or bowls, or in specimen tubes where only a single flower is placed.

Fig. 24　Page showing table centres in porcelain and glass from Mrs Beeton's *Household Management.*

ently for trumpet-shaped flower vases rising from footed bowls. These were soon elaborated with subsidiary flower vases, and subsequently with hanging flower baskets. The central feature might be a mirror plate, and the general decorative effect might be enhanced by the use of tooled glass leaves replacing, or alternating with, the subsidiary vases (Pl. 62b). Whereas some of the earliest examples were in engraved crystal glass, in due course all the Venetian tricks were exploited, and in the 1870s when coloured glass became popular the flower-centres too began to appear in green and ruby. They continued well into the twentieth century and were a favoured product of the one-pot 'cribs' operating in the Worcestershire–Staffordshire area. The almost infinite variations of this type of table ornament have been studied in detail by Hugh Wakefield and Barbara Morris.[73] According to *Household Management*, however, small flower stands 'are preferred by many people to large ones, as it is so easy to arrange a few blooms, the vase itself lending beauty' (p. 1347). Some stands illustrated show tubs and troughs made up, in rustic style, of glass rods simulating logs, the whole confection standing on a mirror plate. Similar stands are shown in a catalogue dated 1889 issued by Silber and Fleming, a London firm of wholesalers.[74] Some of these individual flower stands were considered by *Household Management* 'more suitable for drawing-room than dining-room' (p. 1347).

An adjunct of the flower stand was the fairy lamp, itself often adapted to hold flowers.[75] The holder was designed to take one of Samuel Clarke's Patent 'Fairy Lights', and consisted of an inverted thimble-shaped shade set on a bowl, often with crimped edge. Opal glass was often used and the shades were not infrequently enamelled. Of these lamps *Household Management* says, 'Fairy lamps of different kinds, being a cheap and easy mode of decoration, find favour with many, but, for ourselves, we prefer no light, however faint, below the line of vision' (p. 1347).

Two types of Venetian glass were not so readily accommodated within the general development. The first was *millefiori*, where sections of canes were embedded in a colourless matrix. In Venice itself the manufacture of canes, ancillary to the bead industry, had never died and with the nineteenth-century revival of glass-making the canes, considerably elaborated in design, began to be put to new uses to decorate cane heads, knife handles, and so on. In 1845 Pietro Bigaglia produced a paperweight with a *millefiori* ground beneath a crystal dome, a style probably already anticipated in France. France thenceforward led the field, but English glass-makers had ventured into it by 1848 at latest. The first firm was

Bacchus, closely followed in 1849 by another Birmingham concern, the Islington Glass Works of Rice Harris. Understandably, the firms which made coloured canes for wine-glass stems (pp. 216–17) also made paperweights and inkwells with *millefiori* decoration. At this time paperweights were not particularly valued, and were bought, like any other writing accessory, in stationers' shops. English weights are relatively rare.[76]

The second type of Venetian glass which lay outside the main development of 'fancy' styles was marbled opaque glass, revived in Venice by Lorenzo Radi and others earlier in the century, and now taken up in a number of variations by Alexander D. Jenkinson of Edinburgh (Pl. 60a). The shapes used were relatively sober and simply decorated. Only during the 1880s and later, it seems, were the marbled and mottled glasses made in *outré* shapes with lavish applied decoration.

The onset of colour in the late 1870s and 1880s was mainly confined to body glasses, often shading from one colour to another as a result of heat treatment. The names were as exotic as the colours – 'Amberina' (amber shading to deep ruby), produced under licence from the USA by Sowerby's Ellison Glass Works, Gateshead; 'Crushed Strawberry', with apricot overlying an ivory lining, advertised in 1883 by John Walsh Walsh, Birmingham; 'Sunrise' (yellow tones shading to pink), and 'Uranium' (probably resembling Webb's 'Burmese'), produced by Burtles, Tate & Co. of the Victoria Glass Works, Bolton, the former from 1892 onwards; 'Peach Glass' (with an outer layer shading from pink below to red above, the inner layer being a greenish cream) perfected by Webb's in 1885; 'Peach Blow', a similar glass by Stevens & Williams; 'Alexandrite' (shading from amber through pink to blue), first advertised by the same firm in 1887; 'Queen's Burmese Ware' (shading from greenish-yellow to deep pink), produced by Webb's to an American formula. These shaded semi-opaque glasses were used mainly for vases with crimped or foliate rims, but the material was particularly popular for fairy lights. The favoured forms of decoration were mould blowing and enamelling, mainly with Japanese-inspired floral motifs, but also with Kate Greenaway children's figures.[77]

Parallel to these shaded glasses ran the plain opal glasses, some doubled with clear coloured overlay and decorated in a bewildering variety of techniques, some exploited for their resemblance to ivory or porcelain. With the former much use was made of mould-blown ribbing and diamond diaper between the layers, with air-trap effects (p. 216, Pl. 61a, b).[78] These glasses were frequently embellished with a *sharawadgi* decoration of applied stems, leaves and flowers in crystal. The Japanese influence was pervasive and when, in 1884, John Northwood patented a machine for shaping the flowers in such decorations he invented the name 'Matsu-no-kee' for his glasses, produced by Stevens & Williams.[79] The cased glasses were often given a slightly matt satin finish by acid treatment, a process perfected in the 1880s (Pl. 61a, b). Occasionally an outer coloured layer was etched away to leave a spray of flowers in slight relief above the satin ground; alternatively the surface might be enamelled and gilt.[80]

Enamelling was also the favoured decoration of the plain opalines, which were given the usual fanciful names – Webb's 'Ivory' (from 1884), Richardson's 'Ivorine' (1884), Edward Webb's 'Worcester Ivory Glass' (1883) and 'Dresden Cameo' (1885). The enamelled and gilt decoration for Webb's was mainly done in the workshop of Jules Barbe, who was associated with Webb's from about 1880 (Pl. 61c) but later executed commissions for other firms too (e.g. Richardson's). For Stevens & Williams this work was done by another Frenchman, Oscar Pierre Erard (Pl. 61d), who also exploited a silver deposit process patented as 'Damascened' (1885). This left on the glass a silver coating which was subsequently engraved. To Erard also is probably due the same firm's 'Tapestry' glass, in which a painted design was overlaid by mechanical trailing to give a broken effect suggesting the texture of a woven fabric. Erard's decoration had a pronounced Oriental character.[81]

Erard's silver deposit had been anticipated by other metallic surface treatments. Iridescent glass, inspired by continental models, had been patented by Webb's as 'Bronze Glass' in 1878. An adaptation of this combined a green iridescent surface with the cracked ice technique to produce 'Scarabeous Glass', which was also occasionally gilt. The mode was soon copied by other firms such as Alexander D. Jenkinson of Edinburgh, Henry Greener & Co. in Sunderland, and Richardson's at Stourbridge.[82]

Actual metal foils were also incorporated between layers of glass. In 1883 Edward Webb's White House Glassworks at Wordsley was producing 'Argentine' from silver, and 'Oroide' from gold – used sometimes with coloured and sometimes with crystal glass – the foil occasionally being 'shattered' like the gold leaf of sixteenth-century Venetian glass. Towards 1900 Stevens & Williams used solid silver foil embedded in crystal and decorated with applied threads of coloured glass, calling it 'Silveria'.[83]

The marbled and mottled glasses soberly used by Jenkinson's

(p. 221) were now exploited in the fancy shapes, and with all the applied embellishments, typical of the 1880s. Fanciful names were given to match: 'Carrara' (1888), imitating marble; 'Marmara', similarly streaked; and 'Balzarine', marbled in blue, pink and other colours. 'Coralene' involved firing tiny fragments of glass on previously enamelled designs, and a variant called 'Snowflake' (1886) imitated the effect of fallen snow. A more enduring mimicry of nature was the 'moss agate' of Stevens & Williams, introduced by John Northwood about 1888. Here the natural stone was imitated by a layer with green and red colorants encasing an internal paraison fissured by the cracked ice technique, the whole cased in crystal. The technique was no doubt inspired by the great French artist Eugène Rousseau, who was producing such glasses by 1885 at latest.[84]

The energy and initiative which drove the leading Victorian glass-makers on to invent or adapt such a bewildering variety of ornamental techniques were naturally not accompanied by the balance and restraint which might weld the whole into a coherent style. Where techniques lent themselves to adaptation and combination in almost infinite permutations, it is hardly surprising that monsters should result – a trefoil-lipped classical jug with a clumsy tooled Venetian dragon for the handle, the whole enamelled and gilt with vaguely Japanese birds on sprays; or the vase made by Webb's: 'Amber body 4 flint feet 2 puce reptiles on body and 1 on cover Puce flowers Brown leaves'.[85] One cannot but feel wonderment, however qualified, at the breathtaking exuberance and vitality of late Victorian fancy glass.

From this broad path another Venetian-inspired faction had diverged some two decades earlier.[86] Ruskin's theories, encouraged perhaps more by his distaste for cut glass and his love of Venice than by his actual knowledge of Venetian glass, were swallowed whole by the intellectuals of the day, including William Morris and Sir Charles Eastlake. Another theoretician, however, Dr Christopher Dresser, was also a practical designer with a possibly better insight into the nature of applied art. Whilst accepting the Ruskinian doctrine that a work of art should be faithful to the nature of its material, he emphasised the functional notion of fitness for purpose, and showed a real appreciation of the nature of cut glass. William Morris himself did not design for glass, but the first glasses of the Aesthetic Movement were produced at his instance. They were designed in 1860[87] by the architect Philip Webb (1831–1915), who also designed Morris's Red House at Bexley Heath. The service seems to have disappeared completely but the designs survive. They show strong medieval influence and some were enamelled. They were executed by James Powell & Sons' Whitefriars glasshouse and anticipated the glasses subsequently made by Powell's, to Webb's designs, for Morris's retail outlet, Morris, Marshall, Faulkner & Co. These glasses show characteristically a bulged outline, the wine-glasses often having stems of four- or six-lobed section (Pl. 62c). The spiral thread decoration of the Red House glasses and the use of prunts were Venetian features readily assimilated into the repertoire of Powell's. In 1862 the firm successfully showed Venetian-style glass at the London International Exhibition.[88] Webb continued for many years to design simple table-glass to be made by Powell's for Morris's company, and in 1874 Powell's themselves commissioned the architect T.G. (later Sir Thomas) Jackson to design a comparable range of glasses. These display a number of Venetian-inspired decorative tricks as well as the waved profiles initiated by Webb. In 1875 Harry J. Powell (1853–1922) joined the family firm, and in 1880 took control of it, continuing active in its affairs until 1920. He never abandoned Powell's 'aesthetic' style, even though the tide turned against it towards 1900. Both he and James C. Powell took a positive interest in historic glass and devoted much effort to copying excavated glasses – whether Roman or Renaissance[89] – and glasses represented in paintings. These pastiches apart, Harry Powell assimilated much of the spirit of the early glass, as is shown by many of his original designs, such as his 'Tear service', where shapes of eighteenth-century flavour are decorated with applied vertical strips recalling Venetian glasses of about 1500, or perhaps Roman pillar-moulded bowls (Pl. 62d). In 1862 Powell's had exhibited 'Venetian opal' glass but this was overshadowed by a predilection for pale green, reflecting innate sympathy for the 'natural' glass of Roman and medieval times. Its use in Venetian styles is not without irony. Threading was often executed in blue, and opaque-white threads were 'combed' in arcaded designs. Soft mould-blown ribbing showed a sure instinct for the light-catching quality of glass. Like Christopher Dresser, Harry Powell even understood the proper function of cutting, devoting a whole chapter to it in his *Glass-making in England*: 'Cutting applied in such a way as to proclaim the brilliancy of glass, without obscuring or cloaking the form given by the glass-blower's breath, helps to illustrate an essential quality of the material, and should no longer be regarded as barbarous.'[90] He had a comparable sympathy with wheel-engraving, which was sensitively used in spiralling, flowing plant-motifs in Art Nouveau style on tall elegant shapes.

The firm's chief engraver was a Mr Hillebauer. Powell even had a feeling for diamond-point engraving – a medium neglected virtually since the seventeenth century.[91]

Christopher Dresser himself also contributed directly to the development of 'aesthetic' glass, being commissioned to design for the 'Clutha' glass of James Couper and Sons of Glasgow (Pl. 64a). This was a deliberately bubbled normally pale green glass, occasionally streaked in pale pink and other colours, for which Dresser designed forms inspired by Roman or Near Eastern glass, or occasionally drawing on less obvious sources such as South American pottery, all with an Art Nouveau inflection. From about 1896 Couper's commissioned designs from the Glasgow architect George Walton (1867–1933), and in these the glass was normally enlivened by patches of glittering 'aventurine'. Walton later also produced Venetian-style designs which were probably executed by Powell's.[92]

James Boardman, an Englishman who toured the USA in 1829, and subsequently retailed his experiences in *America and the Americans*, in October of that year visited the Fair of the American Institute of the City of New York. He commented superficially on the 'cut and beautifully moulded glass', but went into more detail with the pressed glass, 'which was far superior, both in design and execution to anything of the kind I had ever seen either in London or elsewhere. The merit of its invention is due to the Americans.'[93] This statement may not be literally true, but its general tenor is undeniably correct. It has often been pointed out that English glass comports, rummers, salt-cellars, etc. of the years about 1800 have pressed 'lemon-squeezer' feet; and Deming Jarves, a pioneer of pressed-glass manufacture in the USA, recorded in his *Reminiscences of Glass Making* (1865) that fifty years previously he had imported from England articles 'with pressed square feet, rudely made, somewhat after the present mode of molding glass.'[94] Apsley Pellatt, however, a glassman of equal eminence, insisted that: 'The invention of pressing Glass by machinery has been introduced into England from the United States of America.'[95] His account of mould-pressing is illustrated by an engraving showing a press which by that date was distinctly primitive, being hardly more than an extension of the 'glass-pincher's' tongs, used primarily for chandelier-arms and drops.[96] The American superiority probably lay in the improvement of the press, the introduction (probably under patent of 1827) of the 'cap mould' which controlled the finish of the rim, and the use of increasingly elaborate composite moulds.[97]

Apsley Pellatt himself, when applying in 1831 for a patent for a
method of mould-assembly, illustrated a 'machine for pressing
glass by the mode lately introduced from America' which was at
least as complex as his 1849 illustration.[98] By 1827 Deming Jarves
was pressing salt-cellars and small cup-plates, and probably also
tumblers in two- or three-piece moulds.[99]

In America, with its enormous unsatisfied demand for domestic
utensils, pressing was the obvious route to economic expansion. In
the more sophisticated countries of Europe, however, the process
appeared crude. Apsley Pellatt voiced a salient criticism in his
Curiosities of Glass-Making:[100] 'It has not, however, realized the
anticipations of manufacturers; for, by the contact of the metal
plunger with the Glass, the latter loses much of the brilliant trans-
parency so admired in cut Glass; hence, it is now chiefly used for
common and cheap articles. The process of rewarming or fire
polishing, after the pressure, has somewhat remedied this defect.'
Despite this drawback pressed glass gained wide popularity among
the poorer classes, not least when it imitated the expensive cut-glass
– 'it added a domestic luxury to every poor home, however
humble.'[101]

Despite Apsley Pellatt's prominence as a commentator, he does
not seem to have contributed greatly to the development of press-
moulded glass.[102] This occurred mainly in the Midlands. Besides
wares imitating cut-glass, a number of plates depicting Queen
Victoria were presumably also made there. A plate with a crown
and VR bears the mark 'WR', initials once thought to stand for
Webb Richardson but now thought possibly those of the
Birmingham die-sinker William Reading. The mark appears also
on pieces which have close affinities with known work of continental factories and like most of the commemorative plates have
the stippled background which in America characterises the 'lacy'
style of pressed-glass decoration, and which usefully conceals
bubbles and stone in the glass, as well as the dulling effects of
mould-chilling mentioned by Apsley Pellatt. The first of the
manufacturers to use the Patent Office Design Registry (established in 1839) was Rice Harris of Birmingham. Significantly his
first registrations in January 1840 relate not to flat forms but to
drinking-glasses, including tumblers, with flute decoration imitating the broad-flute style of contemporary cut glass (p. 199). Some
sixty years after the event a writer in the *Pottery Gazette* asserted
that pressed tumblers had first been produced by Rice Harris in
1834 or 1836, from moulds made by a Birmingham die-sinker
named James Stevens. Stevens had apparently already made

PLATE 49

a. Jug, one of a pair, cut glass. About 1780–90. H. 26 cm (10¼ in.). Private Collection.

b. *Epergne*, cut glass with metal mounts. About 1770. H. 48.9 cm (19¼ in.). Wadsworth Atheneum, Hartford, Connecticut.

c. Tankard, cut glass. About 1760–70. H. 11.8 cm (4⅝ in.). Christ Church, Oxford.

d. Decanter and stopper, cut glass. About 1760. H. 30.5 cm (12 in.). V.A.M.

PLATE 50

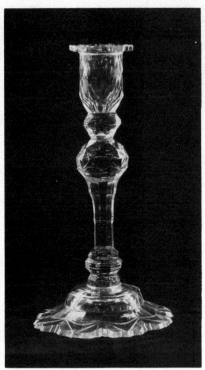

a. Goblet, cut glass with wheel-engraving. Inscription: 'Fari quae Sentio. Prosperity to Houghton'. Made for a member of the Walpole family. About 1740. H. 19 cm (7½ in.). Museum of London.

b. Candlestick, cut glass. About 1760. H. 24 cm (9⅜ in.). V.A.M.

c. Wine-glass, cut glass. About 1770. H. 18.5 cm (7¼ in.). V.A.M.

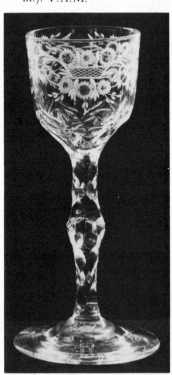

d. Cordial- or wine-glass, cut glass with wheel engraving. About 1760. H. 14.5 cm (5¾ in.). V.A.M.

e. Decanter and stopper, cut glass. About 1750. H. 30.5 cm (12 in.). V.A.M.

f. Cordial- or wine-glass, cut glass with wheel-engraving. About 1760. H. 15 cm (5⅞ in.). V.A.M.

PLATE 51

Chandelier, cut glass. From the parish chapel of Thomastown, Co. Kilkenny, Ireland. Probably made in London; about 1765. H. 140 cm (55 in.). V.A.M.

PLATE 52

a. Cruet, cut glass with silver stand and mounts, hallmarked for London; about 1820. Private Collection.

b. Decanter and stopper, cut glass with wheel-engraved crest. Probably London; about 1820. H. 30.5 cm (12 in.). Corning Museum of Glass.

c. Covered bowl and stand, cut glass, with silver-gilt mounts by John Emes, with London hallmark for 1805.

d. Decanter and stopper, and jug, cut glass. Allegedly supplied by the Dudley firm of Badger (presumably Thos Badger & Co.) for cutting in the 'Stourbridge Warehouse' of W. T. and J. Powell, Bath Parade, Bristol. About 1830. H. 26.4 cm (10⅜ in.). Bristol Museum & Art Gallery.

PLATE 53

a. Jug and claret glass, cut glass, supplied by Perrin and Geddes, of Warrington, to R. Wright in 1809. H. of jug 17 cm (6¹¹/₁₆ in.). Private Collection, on loan to V.A.M.

b. Plate, cut glass with enclosed sulphide of a stag's head crest. Probably by Apsley Pellatt, Falcon Glasshouse, Blackfriars; about 1820. D. 16.2 cm (6⅜ in.). Corning Museum of Glass.

c. Decanter and stopper, cut glass, acquired in Birmingham about 1820. H. 25.5 cm (10 in.). Conservatoire National des Arts et Métiers, Paris.

d. Scent-bottle and stopper, cut glass, with 'crystallo-engraving' medallion-portrait of William IV. Marked 'Pellatt & Co. Patentees'. Apsley Pellatt, Falcon Glasshouse, Blackfriars; about 1834. H. 11 cm (4¼ in.). V.A.M.

PLATE 54

a. Jug, cut and wheel-engraved glass, commemorating Lord Nelson and signed: 'John Williams Engraver Newcastle'. Newcastle upon Tyne; second quarter of nineteenth century. H. 16 cm (6¼ in.). Monmouth District Council.

b. Claret-jug, cut and wheel-engraved, signed 'W. Herbert' (of Dudley) and inscribed 'The Road', 'The Wonder, Birmingham–Stourbridge–London'. Stourbridge area; dated 1833. H. 29.5 cm (11⅝ in.). Private Collection.

c. Vase, wheel-engraved glass 'arranged' by J. Jones and signed by Paul Oppitz (1827–94) as engraver. Commissioned by W. T. Copeland & Sons Ltd and shown at the Universal Exhibition of Vienna in 1873. H. 28.3 cm (11.1 in.). V.A.M.

d. Vase, acid-etched crystal. 'The Death of Socrates'. Brierley Hill (Stevens & Williams Ltd); about 1865. H. 30 cm (12 in.). V.A.M.

PLATE 55

a. Vase, acid-etched crystal. Decorated by J. and J. Northwood, and shown at the Paris Exhibition of 1878. Stourbridge; 1878. H. 21.6 cm (8.5 in.). Broadfield House Glass Museum, Kingswinford.

b. Ewer, with 'rock crystal' engraving by William Fritsche (1853–1924). Stourbridge (Thomas Webb & Sons); completed 1886. H. 38.5 cm (15¼ in.). Corning Museum of Glass.

c. Decanter and stopper, cut glass. Brierley Hill (Stevens & Williams Ltd); designed 1887. H. 35.6 cm (14 in.). Messrs. Stevens & Williams Ltd.

d. Decanter, cut glass. About 1840–5. H. 33 cm (13 in.). Broadfield House Glass Museum, Dudley.

PLATE 56

a. Bottle, dark green glass, with contents, cork and wiring intact. From the Goodwin Sands. About 1720. H. 15.1 cm (6 in.). Corning Museum of Glass.

b. Bottle, dark green glass with incorporated white splashes and applied rigaree bands. Seal inscribed: 'J.S. J.M. Stirling 1827'. Perhaps Scottish; 1827. H. 29.5 cm (11.6 in.). V.A.M.

c. Flask, colourless glass with incorporated combed threads of opaque-white and ruby. 'Nailsea type'. Second quarter of nineteenth century. H. 21.5 cm (8½ in.). V.A.M.

d. Jug, dark green glass with incorporated white splashes. 'Nailsea type'. Early nineteenth century. H. 19.7 cm (7¾ in.). V.A.M.

PLATE 57

a. Toilet-bottle, cut through blue casing on crystal. Blackfriars, Falcon Glasshouse (Apsley Pellatt); 1851. H. 18.3 cm (7¼ in.). Conservatoire National des Arts et Métiers, Paris.

b. Vase, cut through opaque-white casing on ruby, and gilt. Probably Stourbridge (W.H., B. & J. Richardson); about 1850. H. 30.5 cm (12 in.). V.A.M.

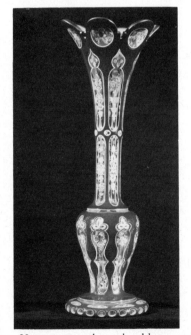

c. Vase, cut through blue and opaque-white casings on crystal, enamelled and gilt. Probably Stourbridge (W.H., B. & J. Richardson); about 1848. H. 40.6 cm (16 in.). Broadfield House Glass Museum, Dudley.

d. Jug, enamelled in colours. Stourbridge (W.H., B. & J. Richardson); design registered in 1848. H. 23.5 cm (7¼ in.). V.A.M.

PLATE 58

a. Vase, doubled crystal glass cut externally and decorated internally with gilding and painting in colours, with ormolu finial. Probably Dudley (Thomas Hawkes); about 1830–40. H. 37.2 cm (14⅝ in.). V.A.M.

b. Standing bowl, doubled glass cut through external ruby casing and silvered internally. Marked 'E. VARNISH & CO./PATENT/LONDON'. Probably London, Whitefriars (James Powell & Sons); about 1850. H. 18.5 cm (7¼ in.). V.A.M.

c. Goblet, cut stem, the bowl decorated by Davenport's 'Patent etched' process. Longport, Staffordshire (Davenport factory); about 1810. H. 15 cm (5⅞ in.). V.A.M.

PLATE 59

a. Plaque ('Venus and Cupid'), cameo-glass, opaque-white on deep amethyst. Signed 'Geo. Woodall'. Stourbridge (Thomas Webb & Sons); about 1890. D. 46 cm (18 in.). Corning Museum of Glass.

b. Vase, cameo-glass, opaque-white on yellowish-brown, designed by Thomas Woodall. Stourbridge (Thomas Webb & Sons); 1884. H. 18.7 cm (7.4 in.). V.A.M.

c. Busts of Queen Victoria and Prince Albert, moulded crystal with roughened surface and some cutting. Inscribed: 'Published by F. and C. Osler, 44 Oxford St., London, May 1st 1845'. Birmingham (Broad Street, F. & C. Osler); about 1845. H. 24.5 and 25 cm (9⅝ and 9¾ in.). V.A.M.

PLATE 60

a. Vase, mottled brown glass with wrought and applied decoration. Edinburgh (Norton Park Glass Works, Alexander D. Jenkinson); about 1880. H. 18 cm (7 in.). Royal Scottish Museum.

b. Jug, with applied turquoise drops and wheel-engraved decoration. Stourbridge (Richardson's); about 1870–5. H. 12.7 cm (5 in.). Broadfield House Glass Museum, Dudley.

c. Finger-bowl, ice-glass. Blackfriars, Falcon Glasshouse (Apsley Pellatt); 1851. H. 10 cm (4 in.). Conservatoire National des Arts et Métiers, Paris.

d. Champagne-glass, with filigree stem and wheel-engraved decoration. Birmingham (George Bacchus & Sons); about 1850. H. 12.7 cm (5 in.). V.A.M.

PLATE 61

a. Bowl, opaque-white glass mould-blown to form a diamond 'airlock' pattern cased with coloured glass, satin-finished. Brierley Hill (Stevens & Williams); about 1885–90. H. 12.7 cm (5 in.). Broadfield House Glass Museum, Dudley.

b. Bowl, opaque ivory glass mould-blown to form a ribbed pattern cased with pale ruby glass, satin-finished. Brierley Hill (Stevens & Williams); about 1885. H. 14 cm (5.5 in.). Broadfield House Glass Museum, Dudley.

c. Goblet-vase, crystal glass with gilt decoration by Jules Barbe. Stourbridge (Thomas Webb & Sons); about 1890. H. 24.8 cm (9¾ in.). Broadfield House Glass Museum, Dudley.

d. Jug, crystal glass with engraved silver deposit decoration by Oscar Pierre Erard. Brierley Hill (Stevens & Williams); dated 1886. H. 14.6 cm (5¾ in.). Messrs. Stevens & Williams.

PLATE 62

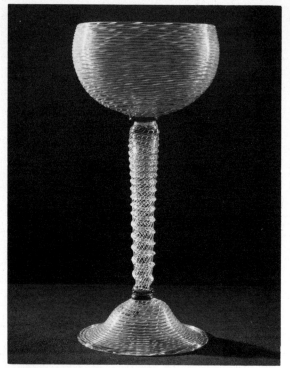

a. Goblet, bluish-green glass with incorporated white threads and external trailing, made by Joseph Leicester. London, Whitefriars (James Powell & Sons); 1869–70. H. 21.6 cm (8½ in.). V.A.M.

b. Flower-stand, crystal glass decorated with ruby trailing. Stourbridge (Hodgetts, Richardson & Son); design dated 1878. H. 63.5 cm (25 in.). Broadfield House Glass Museum, Dudley.

c. Goblet, crystal glass, designed by Philip Webb. London, Whitefriars (James Powell & Sons); about 1865–70. H. 12.7 cm (5 in.). V.A.M.

d. Goblet, crystal glass with applied green ribs. London, Whitefriars (James Powell & Sons); about 1895–1900. H. 20.6 cm (8⅛ in.). Museum of London.

PLATE 63

a. Bowl, opaque-white pressed glass ('Patent Queen's Ivory Ware'). Gateshead (Sowerby's Ellison Glassworks); pattern registered 6 June 1879. D. 13 cm (5⅛ in.). V.A.M.

b. Sugar bowl, colourless pressed glass, inscribed: 'GLADSTONE FOR THE MILLION'. Sunderland (Henry Greener); registered 1869. H. 11.7 cm (4⅝ in.). Private Collection.

c. Bowl in the form of a coal-waggon, colourless pressed glass. Newcastle upon Tyne (W. H. Heppell); registered 1880. H. 8.9 cm (3½ in.). V.A.M.

d. Pair of candlesticks, black pressed glass, marked 'Queen Anne Candlestick. J. Mortlock & Co., Oxford Street and Orchard Street, London'. Gateshead (Sowerby's Ellison Glassworks); 1886. H. 26 cm (10¼ in.). Private Collection.

PLATE 64

a. Vase, yellow-green and red glass with silver flecks, designed by Christopher Dresser. Marked 'Clutha Designed by C.D. Registered'. Glasgow (James Couper & Sons); about 1885–90. H. 49 cm (19¼ in.). V.A.M.

b. Vase, furnace-worked glass. London, Whitefriars (James Powell & Sons); about 1934. H. 31.8 cm (12½ in.). V.A.M.

c. Bowl, cut glass, designed by Keith Murray for Stevens & Williams, Brierley Hill; 1939. H. 20.5 cm (8⅛ in.). V.A.M.

d. Vase, crystal glass wheel-engraved, on a black foot, designed by Keith Murray for Stevens & Williams, Brierley Hill; about 1935–40. H. 19.7 cm (7¾ in.). V.A.M.

moulds for salts for a visiting American glass-maker, and others in various shapes for Rice Harris. Stevens and his family were to remain influential in this field over a long period. The importance of the mould-maker in this branch of the industry was paramount, the operative skill required being very slight. Designs were jealously guarded – in 1828 Deming Jarves wrote to an associate, 'Be careful no one gets a clay impression from the new mold . . . Better take the plunger away.'[103]

If Birmingham–Stourbridge was the first main focus of the mould-pressing technique during the 1840s and 1850s, with John Gold's, George Bacchus & Sons and Lloyd & Summerfield competing with Rice Harris to patent designs, by 1850 a number of glassworks in the Manchester area had taken up the technique. Sherwood and Company, of the Eccleston Flint Glass Works at St Helens, in early 1850 registered designs copying hobnail cutting, and other firms involved were Robinson & Boulton, and Alderton Higginbottom & Company, both of Warrington. In Manchester itself worked two important firms: Molineaux Webb (1827), manufacturing high-quality cut and engraved glass[104] and already engaged in glass-pressing at Ancoats by 1848, and James Derbyshire & Brothers at Hulme and Salford. Other firms were Percival Yates & Vickers, Ancoats (founded 1844); and Burtles Tate & Co. of Manchester and the Victoria Glass Works, Bolton. All registered pressed-glass designs. By the 1860s, cut glass being in decline, the demand for pressed-glass copies presumably also diminished, and the Manchester glasshouses turned to a tasteful vein of classical ornamentation such as key-frets and anthemion panels, executed in an alternation of rough and polished surfaces somewhat recalling intaglio engraving on 'obscured' glass (p. 200).

Somewhat later in taking up press-moulding were the glasshouses of the north-east. The prime mover was apparently John Neville, a one-time apprentice of the Bacchus concern. Neville joined John Sowerby at Gateshead about 1857, in a factory destined to become the most productive pressed-glass centre in the country, operating eight furnaces in 1880. Other important firms were Angus and Greener, of the Wear Flint Glass Works in Sunderland, a partnership set up in 1858 and including Henry Greener (1820–82), son of the glass-engraver (p. 203); George Davidson & Company, of the Teams Glass Works, Gateshead (established 1867 or 1868); and W. H. Heppell, of Newcastle upon Tyne. The registered designs of Sowerby's Ellison Glassworks and Davidson's Gateshead company only begin in the 1870s and tend to echo styles already evolved in Lancashire. These included classical motifs and naturalistic themes of leaves, etc. on a wide range of tablewares, sometimes exploiting the alternation of bright and 'obscured' areas. Technical advances in the 1870s enabled objects of a sculptural character to be pressed. Apart from figures in solid glass (p. 229), much of this work consisted of vessels in unexpected forms, answering the demand for novelty paramount in this period. Many of these receptacles were intended to hold flowers in a table decoration, trinkets on a dressing table, or spills on the mantelshelf. Already in 1866 Robinson and Bolton of Warrington had registered a barrel-shaped tumbler, and in 1872 Hodgetts, Richardson and Son, Stourbridge, registered a swan which was much copied by rivals. More bizarre, but inexplicably popular at the time, was the theme of an armless hand, sometimes as a mantel ornament (registered by Burtles, Tate & Co., Manchester, 1871), sometimes as a flower vase (J. J. & T. Derbyshire, Manchester, 1874); while a pair of hands, the truncation decently concealed by a vine spray, provided a dish, presumably for dessert (registered by John Ford, Edinburgh, 1876). Other equally incongruous containers included a wheel-barrow or a pit-waggon (W. H. Heppell, 1889) (Pl. 63c), a lady's boot (John Derbyshire, 1875) or a lifeboat (Henry Greener, Sunderland, 1887).

In 1879 Sowerby's introduced an opaque-white material dubbed 'Patent Queen's Ivory', for which a range of shapes was designed 'corresponding with carved ivory' (Pl. 63a). Twenty of these were illustrated in the *Pottery Gazette* (1 November 1879) and included pieces in classical style, and others showing Japanese influence or using floral, bird and nursery-rhyme themes in harmony with the mood of the 'Aesthetic' Movement. Some of their designs are probably attributable to John G. Sowerby, a painter of some note in his day. The firm of John Derbyshire used an almost black-purple opaque glass for a spill-vase shape which had been registered in 1876, and Sowerby's followed up their 'Ivory Ware' with an opaque 'Vitro-Porcelain' glass in a number of colours, often given fancy names, such as the marbled 'Green Malachite', 'Brown Malachite', the plain black 'Jet' (Pl. 63d) and the white 'Blanc de Lait'. Other colours included plain turquoise or olive-green, and purple. These 'slag' glasses were made by other firms in the north-east, such as Greener & Co., George Davidson & Co. and W. H. Heppell, whose moulds were bought by Davidson's in 1884. In 1889 Davidson's registered a patent 'Blue Pearline' on which differential tones of turquoise were obtained by heat treatment. Similar effects were obtained in a greenish-yellow 'vaseline' glass, the closely ribbed designs popular about 1890 lending themselves well to this type of glass.

In the 1880s the revival of cut glass (p. 201) naturally brought with it a recrudescence of pressed-glass imitations. Some of these reflected the current 'Brilliant' cutting, but others harked back to the styles of the mid-century. Thus Davidson's produced about 1885 a celery vase with fields of relief-diamonds enclosed in curvilinear panels in an unmistakable mid-century style. Its sinuous curves however, harmonised well enough with the mood of the nascent Art Nouveau.

The most obvious use of the pressing technique was for commemorative glass, a popular demand being almost instantly met by a flood of topical objects, all made from a single mould (Pl. 63b). The makers had grasped these possibilities at the very outset, with the glasses celebrating Queen Victoria's Coronation; and with the Jubilees of 1887 and 1897 immense quantities of souvenir glasses were produced. The cheaper glasses, with their simple emblems and inscriptions, were diversified by a profuse use of dots, recalling the ground-fillers of the 'lacy' period. More expensive pieces might be in opaque glass, such as Greener & Co.'s white sugar basin celebrating Disraeli's success at the Congress of Berlin in 1878.

A final development made possible by pressing was the creation of three-dimensional solid sculptures.[105] This had been anticipated in the mid-century by F. & C. Osler and Lloyd & Summerfield, of Birmingham, who made a series of figures, allegedly by mould-blowing.[106] The former concern in 1845 put out busts, some 24.8 cm (9¾ in.) high, of Queen Victoria and Prince Albert (Pl. 59c), with a matt surface apparently produced by abrasion.[107] In this they were followed by Lloyd & Summerfield, who exhibited their versions in 1851. In the mid-1860s John Ford of Edinburgh produced a pair of tazzas supported by figures of a fisher-boy and girl, and in 1874 John Derbyshire of Manchester made a 'lion after Landseer'. This, although registered as a paperweight, could be used as a chimneypiece ornament, as could the same maker's 'Sphinx' (1875),[108] which elicited a response a year later from the rival firm of Molineaux Webb, in the form of a 'Winged Sphinx'. On the whole this extension of the mould-pressing technique seems not to have been particularly successful. It certainly offered no challenge to the supremacy of the contemporary Parian ware figure-sculpture which probably inspired it.

Epilogue: 1900–1939

In the sphere of domestic and fancy glass the early years of the twentieth century seem more like the running down of the nineteenth century than the beginning of a new era. Some of the lines which had been developed with distinction in England – cameo-glass, for example, or 'rock-crystal' engraving – survived into the twentieth century, but were already on their last legs (pp. 207–216). Although one or two pieces in clear glass with green trailed decoration were made by A. Stanier for Stuart & Sons about 1905,[1] the Stourbridge makers seem to have fallen back on their traditional lines of cut glass, and only Whitefriars, under the direction of Harry J. Powell, appears to have kept alive the flame of 'Art glass'. No particular new lines seem to have been developed there although a glass coloured with selenium was shown at the Arts & Crafts Exhibition in 1906.[2] In general, the industry was depressed under the impact of cheap imports encouraged by Free Trade. With the outbreak of the First World War the British glass industry was speedily reshaped to meet war needs, even firms such as Stevens & Williams, Stuart & Sons and Thomas Webb & Sons going over to the making of electric light bulbs, tubing and rod for various chemical and industrial uses, and so on.[3] A Department of Glass Technology was set up under Professor W. E. S. Turner at Sheffield University to disseminate the necessary technical knowledge in, for example, the optical field, and in association with it a Society of Glass Technology was created (1916) to promote technical co-operation within the industry.

Despite this technological support, the post-war era was a particularly difficult one for the British industry. Whitefriars, which during the war had also gone over to making X-ray bulbs and thermometer tubing,[4] resumed manufacture of domestic glass much in its old vein of unpretentious furnace-worked wares in coloured and crystal glass. Harry Powell died in 1922, in which year also the factory was moved to Wealdstone in Middlesex; but the tradition continued under Barnaby Powell (1891–1939) and James Hogan (1883–1948). Their style produced simple well-proportioned vessels in which mould-blowing and reticent tooling

(Pl. 64b) created satisfying nuances of light and shade in crystal and gradations of tone in coloured glasses – green, amethyst and amber. Light cutting was also on occasion tactfully employed.

The notion of the designer in industry was now gradually gaining general acceptance, an acceptance accelerated in the glass industry by the dramatic international success of the Swedish Orrefors concern with its two artistic Directors, Simon Gate and Edward Hald. The first important designer of this kind in England was Keith Murray (b. 1893), a New Zealander trained as an architect, who looked at English glass, old and modern, with a fresh eye and made critical comparisons. After tentative essays at Whitefriars, Murray began work as a part-time designer in 1932 for Stevens & Williams at Brierley Hill. After a period of adjustment to the realities of factory work in glass, Murray's ideas began to flower in a series of simple shapes, sometimes in crystal, sometimes in green, which owed more to Whitefriars than to contemporary continental developments, although occasionally he might fall for the modish use of the opaque black glass then favoured abroad (Pl. 64d). Above all, he understood the virtues of cutting, returning to the broad, shallow flutes and facets of the eighteenth century with great success (Pl. 64c). His engraved designs too – occasionally in a broad 'intaglio' style – were sympathetically conceived for the glass material (Pl. 64d).[5]

One other designer who approached glass in a thoroughly professional spirit was Clyne Farquharson, who produced a number of straightforward vases and other forms for John Walsh Walsh of Birmingham, and who displayed a restrained feeling for cut and engraved designs.[6] He later worked for Stevens & Williams. Somewhat less professional were the designs by Graham Sutherland, Dame Laura Knight and other contemporary painters for Stuart & Sons of Stourbridge. As with some of the artists of the Omega Workshop, they had not had the discipline of factory floor experience to which Keith Murray had submitted himself. All these artists showed their work at the Exhibition 'British Art in Industry' organised by the Royal Society of Arts in Burlington House in 1935. Their glasses, taken as a whole, convey an unmistakable flavour of their period, and represent a characteristically toned-down version of the international Art Deco. By then, however, the political situation was darkening. When war came in 1939, Keith Murray gave up his work in glass and a hopeful decade in English artistic glass-making was brought to an end. As in 1914, the industry was gradually turned over to war purposes.

Abbreviations in the Notes and Bibliography

A.J.	*Antiquaries Journal*
AJA	*American Journal of Archaeology*
Annales	*Journées Internationales du Verre* (later Association Internationale pour l'Histoire du Verre), *Annales*, Liège (1959–)
Ant. Coll.	*Antique Collector*
Arch.	Archaeology or archaeological
Arch. J.	*Archaeological Journal*
BM	British Museum
Bull.	Bulletin
Burl. Mag.	*Burlington Magazine*
Cat.	Catalogue
C.G.C.	Circle of Glass Collectors (later Glass Circle)
Chr.	Christie's
C.L.	*Country Life*
Coll.	Collection
Conn.	*Connoisseur*
C.S.P.	*Calendar of State Papers*
C.S.P. Ven	*Calendar of State Papers . . . in the Archives and Collections of Venice* (ed. Allen B. Hinds), London
D.N.B.	*Dictionary of National Biography*
ed.	editor or edition
Exh.	Exhibition
G.C.	*The Glass Circle* (occasional publication of the society of the same name)
GEC Journal	*General Electrical Company Journal* of Science and Technology
G.N.	*Glass Notes* (publ. Arthur Churchill Ltd, London)
Gl. Tech.	*Glass Technology*
JGS	*Journal of Glass Studies* (publ. Corning Museum of Glass, Corning, New York)
Med. Arch.	*Medieval Archaeology*

Mus.	Museum
Post-Med. Arch.	*Post-Medieval Archaeology*
Proc.	Proceedings
pt.	part
Riv. della Staz. Sper.	*Rivista della Stazione Sperimentale del Vetro* (Murano, Venice)
Soc.	Society
Soth.	Sotheby's
S.P.Dom.	State Papers Domestic
Surrey Arch. Coll.	*Surrey Archaeological Collections*
Trs. E.C.C.	*Transactions of the English Ceramic Circle*
Trs. S.G.T.	*Transactions of the Society of Glass Technology* (Sheffield)
VAM	Victoria and Albert Museum

Notes and References

CHAPTER 1

Bibliographical Note

The most up-to-date work on the subject matter of this chapter is Harden (1956), 132–67, supplemented by Harden (1972), 78–117, and Harden (1978), 1–24. Earlier essays in classification included those in Hartshorne (1897), 111–23, and Thorpe (1961), 43–74. The present chapter is essentially based on these publications, and the facts rehearsed here may be traced in them; other statements are substantiated by individual references. Continental parallels are most readily studied in Rademacher (1942), 285–344, and Arbman (1937).

For window-glass, see Harden (1961), 39–63.

References

1   Chambon/Arbman, 199–211.
2   Harden (1951), 263, fig.9.
3   Chambon/Arbman, 211–13, fig.3, nos.4–7.
4   Chambon/Arbman, 215, fig.3, no.10.
5   Evison (1972).
6   Chambon/Arbman, 222–9.
7   For an alternative suggestion, see Fremersdorf, 13–17.
8   Fremersdorf, figs.1–3.
9   Evison (1955) and (1975).
10 Evison (1975), 79–80, fig.15, no.49.
11 Warhurst, 25–8, fig.2.
12 Leiden, no.333, fig.42.
13 Harden (1951), 262, fig.6.
14 Chambon/Arbman, 217, fig.5, no.19.
15 Chambon/Arbman, 215, fig.3, nos.11–13.
16 Arbman, 36–47, Pls.4–5.
17 Arbman, 53–6, Pl.10,1.
18 Arbman, 52–3, Pl.8,1.
19 Arwidsson, 261–4, Pl.XIV.
20 Arbman, 27 ff., Pls.1–2.
21 Cramp (1969) and (1970).
22 Barrelet (1953), 20, Pl.XIV,b.
23 Hawthorne/Smith, 54–5, 57.
24 Harden (1954).
25 Barrelet (1953), Pl.X,b.
26 Rademacher (1933), Pl.31,c–d.
27 Hawthorne/Smith, 59.
28 Cramp (1970), 330–3, Pl.LIV,g–i.

29 Bimson, 427 ff.
30 Cramp (1971), 52.
31 Hammond (1975).
32 Colyer/Jones, 60–1.

CHAPTER 2

Bibliographical Note

Medieval glass has only relatively recently emerged as a possible field of study, thanks to modern archaeology. For the earlier part of the period the reader should consult Harden (1972), 98–107; Harden (1978), 11–19; Harden (1972), 97–111; and 'Table-Glass in the Middle Ages' (1975). Specifically for England, see Charleston (1980a), 65–76.

For window-glass the reader should consult Harden (1961), 54–8, and Salzman (1952), 173–86; for the early glass industry in England, Kenyon (1967).

References

 1 Huggins, 89, 117.
 2 Chambon (1950), 123–4; Barrelet (1953), 15, 28.
 3 Gasparetto, 43.
 4 Barrelet (1953), 15, 28.
 5 Barrelet (1953), 29–30.
 6 Barrelet (1953), 30–1
 7 Charleston (1980), 66–8.
 8 Barrelet (1953), 48–51, Pls.XXV–XXVI.
 9 Harden (1966), 70–8; Whitehouse, 177–8.
10 Davidson (1940), 297–324; Weinberg, 136–41.
11 Charleston (1975b), 101–7.
12 Charleston (1975), 204, 216–9.
13 Charleston (1980), 66–8.
14 Harden (1966), 70–8; Whitehouse, 177–8.
15 Barrelet (1953), 48–51, Pls.XXV–XXVI; Renaud; Chambon (1975), 151–7; Isings/Wijnman, 77–82.
16 H. Maryon, 'The King John Cup at King's Lynn', *Conn.* (May, 1953), 88.
17 Lightbown, 91–2, Pl.LXIX.
18 Charleston (1975), 218–9, no.1513.
19 *Mille Anni di Arte del Vetro a Venezia*, 70, no.51.
20 Charleston (1975), 216–7, nos.1488, 1490–5.
21 Davidson (1952), 114, no.746.
22 Charleston (1974), 68–9.
23 Harden (1966), 71; Davidson (1952), 114, no.744.
24 Kojić/Wenzel, 91, fig.18.
25 Charleston (1972), 45–6.
26 Kojić/Wenzel, 86–7, fig.16,b.
27 Harden (1975), 39.
28 Charleston (1980), 69.
29 Harden (1966), 71–2; Davidson (1952), 107, no.694, 109, no.699, etc.
30 Charleston (1975), 216–7, no.1489.
31 Beresford, 138–9, fig.42, no.35.

32 Charleston (1976), 326–35.
33 Lamm, 77–99.
34 Charleston (1980), 68–9.
35 Whitehouse, 177, fig.30, no.4.
36 Zecchin (1969), 39–42.
37 Charleston (1975), 216–7, no.1498.
38 Colvin, 90.
39 Cook, 173–7.
40 Cook, 177.
41 Charleston (1980), 68.
42 Weinberg, 131–3.
43 Harden (1975), 38–9, fig.10.
44 Barrelet (1959), 207–8, fig.3, Pl.7.
45 Harden (1975), 38, fig.9.
46 Charleston (1975), 218–9, nos.1512, 1513.
47 Harden (1975), 40, fig.15.
48 Barrelet (1953), 48–51, Pls.XXV–XXVI; Renaud; Chambon (1975), 151–7; Isings/Wijnman, 77–82.
49 Rider, 137.
50 Charleston (1980), 70.
51 Charleston (1980), 70.
52 Crossley (1967), 49–51.
53 Dodwell, xxxiii.
54 Hawthorne/Smith, 57–8.
55 Barrelet (1953), 30–1, Pl.XVIII.
56 Oakley/Hunter, 298–9, no.GL 53.
57 Rademacher (1933), 75–90, Pls.18,a,b,19–20.
58 Crowfoot/Harden, 196–208.
59 C. Zigrosser, *Ars Medica*, Philadelphia Museum of Art (1959), 6, 47, 50, 55–6, 59.
60 Zigrosser, 27, 51.
61 Nesbitt, lxxii.
62 Harleian Ms.1419, folio 147,v.
63 Charleston (1980), 72.
64 Wood (1965), 65–7.
65 Charlesworth (1969), 85–6, nos.36–8.
66 Hume (1957), 104–8; Charleston (1980), 72.
67 Charlesworth (1967), 83–6, fig.12.
68 Wood (1965), 65.
69 Rademacher (133), Pl.6,a–c.
70 Nesbitt, cxxxii.
71 Hartshorne, 134.
72 Hume (1957), 107–8.
73 Hartshorne, 134.
74 Rademacher (1933), Pl.7c.
75 Rademacher (1933), Pl.6,e–m.
76 Neugebauer, 110, fig.21.
77 Hume (1957), 107, fig.7.
78 Hume (1956), 99, fig.4,c–d.
79 *The Canon's Yeoman's Tale*, lines 791–4.
80 Winbolt, 49.
81 Moorhouse (1972), 91–5.

82 Rademacher (1933), Pl.B,4.
83 Haevernick/Haberey, 130–8.
84 Holden, 163–4.
85 Newstead, 35; Ridgway/Leach, 133–40.
86 Lafond, 37–8.
87 Harden (1961), 40, Pl.V; Gasparetto, 150–1, 157.
88 Wood (1965), 65.
89 Harden (1961), 55.
90 Harden (1961), 56–7.
91 Harden (1961), 56.
92 Harden (1961), 56.
93 Harden (1961), 57.
94 Ashdown, 16.
95 Kenyon, 28.
96 Kenyon, 28.
97 Rackham, 16–17.
98 Rackham, 12–19.
99 Salzman, 185.
100 Rackham, 17–19.

CHAPTER 3

Bibliographical Note

Hartshorne published many of the original documents relating to this period, supplemented by Thorpe (1929), who also added further material in *English Glass* (1935, 1949, 1961). To these was added in 1976 Eleanor S. Godfrey's indispensable *The Development of English Glassmaking 1560–1640*, the most intensive discussion of this period published to date. It has been used as the main source of the earlier part of this chapter, almost exlusively in some passages (pp. 60–2, 71–8), although the author's conclusions do not always agree with hers. (Detailed references have in the main not been given in the text for these basic sources.) Kenyon remains a useful source for the forest industry, and many aspects of glass-making in this period are illuminated by Vose (1980).

References

1 Zecchin (1967), 20–3.
2 Zecchin (1968), 25.
3 Zecchin (1969a), 25–6; (1970), 27–8.
4 One *inghistera* base illustrated Holdsworth, fig.IV.
5 Charleston (1975), 206–7, 218, 220, nos.1522, 1531–2, 1536; numerous examples in the City Museum.
6 Charleston (1975), 218, 220, no.1528.
7 In the King of Sweden's Collection.
8 Holdsworth, fig.VI.
9 Zecchin (1968a), 22–5; (1977), 175–9.
10 Charleston (1956), 84, Pl.46,B; H. S. Stannus, *Richard Weoley*, priv. print (n.d.).
11 Holdsworth, fig.VII; Charleston (1975), 218, 220, no.1526.
12 Holdsworth, fig.V and cover.

13 R. J. Charleston ed., *World Ceramics* (London, 1968), fig.398; Harden (1975), fig.22.
14 Holdsworth, back cover; Charleston (1975), 221–2, no.1548.
15 Harleian Ms.1419, fol.143,v.
16 Clarke, 22 ff.
17 Clarke, 52, fig.C 6.
18 Hartshorne, 141–2, fig.154.
19 Harleian Ms.1419, fol.149,r.
20 *Mille Anni di Arte del Vetro e Venezia*, 26, fig.X and 83, no.72.
21 Harleian Ms.1419, fol.143,r; 143,v; 144,r.
22 Zecchin (1968b), 105 ff.
23 In British Museum.
24 Charleston (1975), 208, 218, 220, no.1523. London fragment in Mus. of London.
25 Zecchin (1968c), 110; (1971), 2–3 of offprint.
26 Charleston (1975), 209–10; Polak (1976), 270–3.
27 Glanville, 147–50, Pls.XIII–XVI.
28 British Museum, *Masterpieces*, 142, no.186.
29 Glanville, 151, Pl.XX.
30 Glanville, 154, Pls.XVIII–XIX; Charleston (1956), 80–2, Pls.41–2, 45.
31 Harleian Ms.1419; Zecchin (1968c), 113.
32 Girouard, 46–51.
33 F. J. Furnivall ed., *Early English Meals and Manners* (London, 1868), 15–16.
34 *Shakespeare's England* (Oxford, 1916), II, 120.
35 Harleian Ms.1419.
36 E.g. the Duke de Berry's banquet, *c*.1410 (Girouard, Pl.I).
37 *House and Farm Accounts of the Shuttleworths*, Chetham Society (1856), III, 659.
38 *House and Farm Accounts of the Shuttleworths*, Chetham Society (1856), III, 659.
39 Harleian Ms.1419, fol.148,r.
40 Harleian Ms.1419, fol.150,r.
41 Barrelet (1953), 63.
42 Lightbown, 43–5.
43 Chambon (1951), fig.3; (1955), Pl.O(b).
44 G.N., 7 (Dec., 1947), 22.
45 'Fêtes de la Palette' (Isaac Delgado Museum Catalogue), New Orleans (1963), Pl.1, no.15.
46 R. A. M. Stevenson, *Rubens, Paintings and Drawings* (London, 1939), Pl.137.
47 'The Court and Country' in U. Kentish-Wright ed., *A Mad World My Masters* (London, 1929), I, 214.
48 E. Stone, *Chronicles of Fashion* (London, 1845), I, 39.
49 N. Williams, *Henry VIII and his Court* (London, 1971), 80.
50 W. E. Mead, *The English Medieval Feast* (London, 1931), 250.
51 Hartshorne, 149; Thorpe (1929), 61–2; Powell, 27–9.
52 Hartshorne, 151, 393; Thorpe (1929), 58, 62.
53 Godfrey, 17; cf. Thorpe (1961), 94.
54 Thorpe (1961), 95.
55 Thorpe (1961), 96–7.
56 Godfrey, 26.
57 Full text in Hartshorne, 399–401.
58 Thorpe (1961), 98–9; Godfrey, 30–1.

59 Sutton/Sewell, 190–2.
60 Buckley, W. (1929), 9–13.
61 Zecchin (1966), 27.
62 Buckley, W. (1929), 7, 14, 17–19, Pl.26.
63 Thorpe (1948), 110–17; Fitzwilliam Museum (1978), 77–8, no.171.
64 Barrelet (1953), 198, Pl.XXXVI,B.
65 Charleston (1975), 211–12, 221–2, nos.1557–60.
66 Sold Christie's 3.10.1971, Lot 113.
67 Thorpe (1935), 150–7.
68 British Museum, *Masterpieces*, 166–7, no.231.
69 Thorpe (1935), 155–6.
70 Sold Sotheby's 16.5.1966; illus. Thorpe (1961), Pl.XVI(a).
71 Chambon (1955), Pls.O,P.
72 Hume (1962), 271–2, no.11.
73 Thorpe (1961), 110; Wine Trade, 71, no.265, frontis.
74 Cecil Higgins Art Gallery, 6; Thorpe (1961), 111.
75 Thorpe (1929), 87.
76 Oswald/Phillips, nos.XV, XVI.
77 Cf. Tait (1967), figs.25–6.
78 Tait (1967), figs.1–17.
79 Oswald/Phillips, nos.XV, XVI.
80 Honey (1946), Pl.30,A.
81 Oswald/Phillips, 34–5, no.XIV.
82 Thorpe (1961), 103, 121.
83 Hudig, 17–18, 26–7; Thorpe (1961), 121–4.
84 Thorpe (1961), 123.
85 Gasparetto, 110–11; Barrelet (1953), 79, 95–6, 104–5, 120–1.
86 Schuermans, XXIX, 131; Gasparetto, 108–9.
87 Thorpe (1961), 123, 126.
88 Thorpe (1961), 121, 123; Godfrey, 97.
89 Godfrey, 125,*n.*
90 Godfrey, 188.
91 Hartshorne, 431, 433, 435–6; Godfrey, 215–6 (a different interpretation).
92 *Verney Memoirs*, I (1907), 54.
93 Hume (1962), figs.7–8.
94 Charleston (1978), 285–7.
95 Charleston (1978), 288.
96 Lewis, 141, 147, fig.4, no.G 1.
97 Oswald/Phillips, 31–2, no.IV; Charleston (1978), 288, fig.3,d–e.
98 Moorhouse (1971), 63–5, nos.1–3, 10.
99 Oswald/Phillips, 31–2, no.III.
100 Oswald/Phillips, 32–3, no.VI; Charleston (1978), figs.l,g and 3,c.
101 Oswald/Phillips, 33, nos.VII–VIII.
102 Oswald/Phillips, no.VII,a; Charleston (1978), 288–9, fig.3,a–b.
103 Marston Hall Inventory, 1605 (Ralph Creyke).
104 Cf. Oswald/Phillips, no.VII,c.
105 Charleston (1969), 88, fig.31, no.2.
106 Moorhouse (1971), 65–6, no.18.
107 *C.S.P., East Indies* (1513–1616), no.455.
108 Moorhouse (1971), 64–6, nos.16–7.
109 Moorhouse (1971), 65–6, no.21.
110 Marston Hall Inventory, 1605 (Ralph Creyke).

111 Hartshorne, 413–14.
112 Hartshorne, 178.
113 Hartshorne, 431.
114 Godfrey, 19–20.
115 Crossley (1967), 46, 62.
116 Wood (1982), 19–22, 44.
117 Godfrey, 211.
118 Godfrey, 56.
119 Kenyon (1967), 90.
120 Godfrey, 85, *n.*7.
121 Hartshorne, 431.
122 Godfrey, 212.
123 Godfrey, 202–4.
124 Salzman, 184.
125 Salzman, 177.
126 Rackham (1936), 119–20.
127 Rackham (1936), 120–1; Armitage, 50–1; Woodforde (1951), 12–13; Woodforde (1954), 42–3; Kirby, 117–21.
128 H. Walpole, *Anecdotes of Painting in England*, II (London, 1782), 28.
129 Archer, 1563.
130 Archer, 1454, figs.1, 8.
131 Salzman, 185.
132 Godfrey, 207–8.
133 D. Gardiner ed., *The Oxinden Letters, 1607–42* (London, 1932?), 288 (1663).
134 Godfrey, 93; Crossley (1981), 2–7.
135 Godfrey, 92–3; Hogan, 24–5; Vose (1980), 143–6.
136 Daniels, 19–20.
137 Daniels, Pl.XVII.
138 Vince, 15.
139 Thorpe (1929), 67.
140 Daniels, 9; Vince, 15–17.
141 Godfrey, 62–3, 192.
142 Daniels, 6.
143 Daniels, 20.
144 Daniels, *passim.*
145 Bridgewater, 300–15.
146 Pape (1933), 172–7.
147 Horridge, 29; Fox, 14–15.
148 Pape (1933), 177.
149 Horridge, 27, 29; Crossley (1967), 47.
150 Crossley (1967), 60.
151 Godfrey, 36, 115.
152 Godfrey, 53–4, 84–5; Kenyon, 128, 137–9.
153 Godfrey, 36.
154 Godfrey, 93.
155 Pape (1933), 175.
156 Godfrey, 63.
157 Hurst, 26–9; Vose (1972), 138–9.
158 Hogan, 24–5; Vose (1971), *passim*; Vose (1972), 139–44; Personal communication, Mrs Vose.
159 Vose (1980), 110, 142–3.
160 Crossley/Aberg, 107–159.

161   Cf. Daniels, Pl.VII, 58a.
162   Hejdová, 146–7, fig.14.
163   Rademacher (1933), 104, Pl.33.
164   Hume (1962), 270, nos.1–4; Hume (1968), 259–61, nos.1–5.
165   Daniels, Pl.VI, 45, 47.
166   Fragments in VAM.
167   Crossley/Aberg, fig.61, nos.24–5; fig.64, nos.68–71, 73, 75, 78–81.
168   Kenyon, 203–6, Pl.XVI, 5.
169   Daniels, Pls.I–III, etc.
170   Chambon (1955), Pls.N,a,c,d; V,19–21.
171   Kenyon, Pl.XI.
172   Crossley/Aberg, fig.60, nos.18–22.
173   Fragments in Gloucester Mus. (Daniels, Pl.VI, 46).
174   Vince, fig.2, 14.
175   Hogan (1969), fig.l,h.
176   Daniels, Pl.IX, 77–9.
177   Bridgewater, fig.4, no.15.
178   Crossley/Aberg, fig.67, nos.111–12.
179   Hurst, fig.1,a.
180   Kenyon, 183.
181   Wood (1982), 22–4, fig.10, no.12.
182   Daniels, Pl.VI, 43; cf. Pl.XI, 11.
183   Crossley/Aberg, fig.67, nos.115–17.
184   Fragments at VAM.
185   Crossley/Aberg, fig.61, no.41.
186   Daniels, Pl.IX, 80–1.
187   Rademacher (1933), Pl.9.
188   Kenyon, Pl.XIV,a; Daniels, Pl.IV, 25.
189   Daniels, Pl.VII, 50, 52.
190   Crossley/Aberg, fig.66, nos.100–1.
191   Hogan (1969), fig.2,d.
192   Crossley/Aberg, fig.61, no.36.
193   Fragments in VAM and Ashmolean Mus., Oxford.
194   Oswald/Phillips, 34, no.XI,a.
195   Oswald/Phillips, 31, no.II.
196   Fragments in Gloucester Mus.
197   Rademacher (1933), 56, Pl.8c,e.
198   Daniels, Pl.VI, 41.
199   Pape (1933), 177, fig.III,a.
200   Crossley/Aberg, figs.60, nos. 11–12; 63, nos.44, 57.
201   Kenyon, Pl.XIV,b; XVI,3.
202   Hogan, fig.2,b.
203   Crossley/Aberg, fig.63, no.48.
204   *Epistolae Ho-Elianae*, 10th ed. (London, 1737), 206.
205   Halliwell, 74.
206   Halliwell, 11.
207   *House and Farm Accounts of the Shuttleworths*, Chetham Society (1856), I, 53.
208   Charleston (1969), 87–9, fig.31, nos.5–8.
209   Godfrey, 231.
210   Hume (1956), 100–3, nos.4, 14.
211   Crossley/Aberg, fig.60, nos.5(?), 8, 9.
212   Moorhouse (1971), 69–70, no.65.

213 Godfrey, 228–30; Hume (1961), 93.
214 Hume (1961), 98, 102, fig.3, 1.
215 D. Gardiner ed., *The Oxinden Letters, 1607–42* (London, 1932?), 164; Charleston (1954b), 157–9.
216 Ruggles-Brise, 26.
217 Thorpe (1938), 193.
218 McKearin (1971), 120–7.
219 Charleston (1959), 159, 161; Barrelet (1953), 101–2; Godfrey, 230–2.
220 Thorpe (1961), 135.
221 F. Buckley (1914), 18.
222 De la Cam agreement (18.8.1660), Ms. in BM, Dept. of Medieval and Later Antiquities; Thorpe (1961), 137–9.
223 Hudig, 71–2.
224 Thorpe (1929), 102.
225 *D.N.B., s.v.*
226 Hartshorne, 437–9.
227 S. P. Dom. C 66/3038, no.9.
228 Hartshorne, 439–40.
229 Young, 15.
230 H. J. Powell, 37.
231 Hartshorne, 449–51.
232 F. Buckley (1928), 150; Bill, Bellingham *v.* Ducem Bucks. (24.11.1676), Ms. in VAM Library.
233 Hudig, 55, 74–5.
234 C.S.P. Ven., XXXVIII (1940), 265.
235 F. Buckley (1915), 36; Bowles, 7, both based on J. Nichols, *History of Lambeth* (1788).
236 C.S.P. Ven., XXXVIII (1940), 272.
237 P.R.O. Chancery Proceedings, 1682, Ravenscroft *v.* Bellingham, C 7. 295 59, kindly communicated by Mr R. Walker.
238 Thorpe (1932), 361–2; Charleston (1957), 230–1.
239 Charleston (1954b), fig.1.
240 In the Toledo Museum of Art, Ohio, USA.
241 Charleston (1969), 86–8, no.1.
242 Thorpe (1961), 142.
243 Charleston (1957), 231–2, figs.3–4.
244 Thorpe (1961), 143.
245 Charleston (1957), 231.
246 Bles, 19–21, Pls.1–2.
247 Thorpe (1929), 106, Pl.VII, 1; Charleston (1957), 232, fig.6; British Museum, *Masterpieces*, 171–2, no.239.
248 Theuerkauff-Liederwald, 153–4, fig.63.
249 E.g. Corning Museum of Glass *Guide* (1974), 67, no.84.
250 Young, 13–15.
251 Young, 16–20.
252 Young, 40.
253 Young, 31.
254 Hartshorne, 228–33, 440–54, Pls.30–2; Thorpe (1929), 113–15; Thorpe (1961), 172–3.
255 Zecchin (1960), 27, 46, 51; (1965), 1162–3; (1980), 257–62; Gasparetto, 99.
256 Zecchin (1971a), 77–83.
257 Hartshorne, 449–51.

258 Hartshorne, 451.
259 Young, 31.
260 Young, 31.
261 C.S.P. Ven., XXXVIII (1940), 2, 195, 264–5.

CHAPTER 4

Bibliographical Note

The main sources of this chapter are inevitably Hartshorne, Young, F. Buckley (1925) and Thorpe (1929 and 1961), supplemented by the articles of the two last-named, quoted below in their appropriate contexts. In the post-war period Haynes (1948 and 1959) anatomised the forms of English eighteenth-century glasses, a process foreshadowed and continued in many articles listed in the bibliography; and in a series of surveys of individual wine-glass types published by Messrs Arthur Churchill under his direction (in *Glass Notes*). Hughes (1956) furnished many details of the social background to glass, a contribution marred by numerous errors and a failure to identify sources. Guttery provided a background history of the important Midlands area, and R. Wilkinson contributed a number of insights into technical aspects of English glass. A lavishly illustrated survey of drinking-glasses, and an invaluable bibliography, are provided by Bickerton.

In the early part of the chapter our knowledge of George Ravenscroft has been expanded and modified by the researches of Rendel (1976 and 1975a), Watts, Charleston (1968), and Walker (ref. 3 below).

References

1 Hartshorne, 457.
2 Thorpe (1929), 118–9.
3 Rendel (1975 and 1975a); personal communication, Mr R. Walker.
4 C.S.P. Ven., XXXVIII (1940), 265.
5 Thorpe (1961), 154.
6 Young, 67, no.4.
7 C.S.P. Ven., XXXVIII (1940), 116.
8 Thorpe (1929), 121, *n.*1(3).
9 Hartshorne, 454–6.
10 Young, 65, no.1.
11 Hudig, 17, 67; Charleston (1959), 156.
12 Thorpe (1929), 122.
13 Hudig, 71.
14 Hartshorne, 451.
15 Hartshorne, 451.
16 Thorpe (1929), 122, as corrected by Watts, 73, 83.
17 Watts, 73–4.
18 F. Buckley (1914), 36, no.21.
19 F. Buckley (1914), 37, no.23.
20 Thorpe (1938), 168–9, 185.
21 Young, 67, no.4, corrected.
22 F. Buckley (1914), 38, no.24.
23 Thorpe (1929), 116 ff.; Watts, 75 ff.
24 Hartshorne, 438.

25 Thorpe (1929), 108–9; F. H. Garner, 'John Dwight, some contemporary references', *Trs. E.C.C.*, I, Part 5 (1937), 35.
26 Thorpe (1938), 182–5.
27 Hartshorne, 451.
28 Watts, 71 ff.
29 Charleston (1968), 156 ff.
30 Thorpe (1938), 180.
31 Thorpe (1938), 204.
32 Anon (1949), 17.
33 Thorpe (1938), 190.
34 Charleston (1968), 163–5.
35 Thorpe (1938), 189.
36 Thorpe (1929), 129, fig.17.
37 Rendel (1975), 68–9.
38 Young, 71, no.7.
39 F. Buckley (1914), 38, no.24.
40 Hartshorne, 452.
41 Hartshorne, 452–3.
42 Young, 69, no.6.
43 F. Buckley (1914), 57–8; H. J. Powell, 88; Thorpe (1929), 132, 137, 140.
44 F. Buckley (1914), 49; Young, 72; Thorpe (1929), 132, 137, 140–1.
45 Hartshorne, 220; F. Buckley (1914), 40; Thorpe (1929), 137–8.
46 F. Buckley (1914), 41; H. J. Powell, 87; Thorpe (1929), 138–9.
47 F. Buckley (1914), 41.
48 H. J. Powell, 89; Thorpe (1929), 139.
49 F. Buckley (1914), 46.
50 Thorpe (1929), 69, 139–40; Sun Insurance policy, 1720, kindly communicated by Miss N. Rothstein.
51 Thorpe (1929), 138.
52 Watts, 75–7.
53 Charleston (1968), 161.
54 F. Buckley (1925), 29.
55 Alvey, 70–1, no.4.
56 Hartshorne, 457.
57 Thorpe (1929), Pl.XI,2.
58 Thorpe (1929), Pl.XIII.
59 Thorpe (1929), Pl.XIV,2.
60 Thorpe (1929), Pl.XXI,3.
61 Watts, 83, fig.6.
62 Thorpe (1929), Pl.XXIII,B.
63 Thorpe (1938), 190.
64 Thorpe (1929), Pl.XXXVI,B,3.
65 Thorpe (1929), XXXV,3; LV,A,3.
66 Thorpe (1929), Pl.XLII.
67 Thorpe (1938), 205, fig.14.
68 C. Oman, *English Domestic Silver* (London, 1949), 129.
69 Soth. 29.7.1947, 197.
70 Bickerton, fig.16 (1703); Soth. 20.5.1963, 34 (1706); W. Buckley (1939), 162, no.486 (1711); Jackson-Stops, 30.11.1959, 245 (1713).
71 Soth. 28.4.1980, 11.
72 F. Buckley (1925), Pl.VI.
73 Thorpe (1929), Pl.XXXI,2; cf. F. Buckley (1925), Pl.VIII (Chequers).

74 Charleston (1954), figs.1, 4.
75 Toledo Museum (1969), 61; Soth. 29.7.1947, 200.
76 C.G.C., Exh., no.122.
77 Charleston (1975), 225, nos.1600, 1603.
78 Thorpe (1938), 184–8.
79 Fitzwilliam Museum (1978), no.190; C.G.C., Exh. no.131.
80 Bickerton, fig.15.
81 Bles, Pl.85.
82 Soth. 20.5.1963, 31.
83 Soth. 30.6.1980, 156; Crompton, Pl.46.
84 Bles, Pl.5, no.9.
85 E.g. Bles, Pl.59, nos.86–7.
86 W. H. Quarrell & M. Mare, *London in 1710: from the Travels of Zacharias Conrad von Uffenbach* (London, 1934), amended translation based on Z. C. von Uffenbach, *Merkwürdige Reisen*, III, Ulm (1754), 239–41.
87 Landman, no.44.
88 Chr. 9.3.1964, 174.
89 Soth. 25.2.1947, 18.
90 Chr. 9.3.1964, 171.
91 Bles, Pl.19, no.26.
92 Graham, 10 (based mainly on Thomas Somerville, *My Life and Times, 1741–1814* (Edinburgh, 1861)).
93 Graham, 10.
94 Graham, 78.
95 *Amiable Renegrade: the Memoirs of Capt. Peter Drake, 1671–1753* (Stanford, 1960), 56.
96 *Amiable Renegade*, 324.
97 Plant, 44.
98 *Amiable Renegade*, 214.
99 Horridge/Haynes, 47–50; *G.N.*, 12 (Dec., 1952), 11–13; Wallis, 105.
100 Soth. 25.2.1947, 18.
101 Polak (1953), 329–30, Pl.71, no.169.
102 Ash (1962), 87.
103 H. W. Thompson ed., *The Anecdotes and Egotisms of Henry Mackenzie, 1745–1831* (London, 1927), 81.
104 Hughes, 231.
105 F. Buckley (1925), 145, no.109.
106 Vydrová, 205–15.
107 S. C. Roberts, *A Frenchman in England, 1784* (Cambridge, 1963), 30–1.
108 Girouard, 254–5, Pls.158–9.
109 Raines, Pl.5.
110 Bosc d'Antic, I, 158.
111 F. Buckley (1925), 146–7, no.118.
112 Schmidt, 391–2.
113 F. Buckley (1925), 119, no.3.
114 Hughes, fig.32; see Treglown/Mortimer, 46–8.
115 Polak (1969), fig.38.
116 W. Buckley (1930), Pl.12.
117 Rush, Pls.28, 33,b, 34–5.
118 W. Buckley (1930), Pl.22.
119 W. Buckley (1931), Pl.8,A.
120 Bles, Pl.44.

121 Thorpe (1929), Pl.XLVII,1.
122 Fitzwilliam Museum (1978), no.296.
123 Bles, Pls.23, 89.
124 Wills (1968), 11.
125 Bickerton, fig.694.
126 Bickerton, fig.188.
127 Hartshorne, 358, n.1.
128 Fitzwilliam Museum (1978), no.205,b.
129 Thorpe (1929), 212.
130 F. Buckley (1925), 53–4.
131 McKearin (1954), 15.
132 Thorpe (1929), 308.
133 E.g. Thorpe (1929), Pl.XCV,1.
134 Thorpe (1929), 212.
135 R. Wilkinson, 27–9, fig.8.
136 R. Wilkinson, 30–2, figs.10–11.
137 Thorpe (1929), 213.
138 F. Buckley (1925), 58.
139 Smith, 54.
140 F. Buckley (1925), 61.
141 F. Buckley (1925), 59–60.
142 B. Cozens-Hardy (ed.), *The Diary of Silas Neville* (Oxford, 1950), 38.
143 F. Buckley (1925), 151, no.139.
144 F. Buckley (1927).
145 Guttery, 83.
146 F. Buckley (1925), 151.
147 Smith, 53.
148 Anon (1948), 29–48.
149 Hartshorne, 291; *G.N.*, 14 (Dec., 1954), 7; Soth. 22.7.1968, 164 &
      7.10.1980, 162.
150 Horridge/Haynes, 47–50.
151 Honey (1946), 109.
152 Matcham/Dreiser, 15–52; Charleston (1964), 83–100.
153 Thorpe (1961), 212.
154 Honey (1946), 107.
155 Bles, Pl.44.
156 Francis, Pl.XXXVI.
157 Wills (1965), 46, 152, Pls.20, 22; Thorpe (1972), 11–12, 15.
158 Wills (1965), 152–6, Pl.21; P. Macquoid & R. Edwards, *Dictionary of
      English Furniture* (London, 1960), see under *Mirrors*.
159 Wills (1965), Pl.21.
160 *C.L.*, 22.3.1946, figs.11–12.
161 Wills (1965), 148.
162 F. Buckley (1925), 120.
163 Young, 7.
164 Westropp (1920), 49.
165 MacLeod, 125.
166 Charleston (1982), 4.
167 F. Buckley (1925), 120.
168 F. Buckley (1925), 120; F. Buckley (Sept., 1928), 392–3.
169 A. Oliver ed., *The Journal of Samuel Curwen, Loyalist* (Cambridge, Mass.,
      1972), I, 168, kindly communicated by Arlene Palmer-Schwind.

170   Seddon, 40–78.
171   Trubridge (1972), 46–57; Trubridge (1965), 26–36.
172   Simon (1948), 67 ff.
173   Hughes, figs.30, 156.
174   Simon (1926), 16, 54.
175   Simon (1948), 77.
176   Simon (1926), 75.
177   Thorpe (1929), 106.
178   Thorpe (1929), 308.
179   Hughes, 210, figs.162, 167.
180   Westropp (1920), 57.
181   Haynes (1959), 200.
182   F. Buckley (1925), 117.
183   E. & F. Ancon ed., *Mary Hamilton* . . . (London, 1925), 171.
184   F. Buckley (1925), 124.
185   Charleston (1975a), 7.
186   F. Buckley (1925), 128, no.25; Westropp (1920), 57.
187   Hughes, 185.
188   Merrett, 225–6.
189   Thorpe (1972), 13.
190   Simon (1926), 73.
191   Thorpe (1929), Pl.CLIII.
192   Hughes, 189.
193   John Macdonald, *Memoirs of an 18th century Footman* (London, 1927), 70.
194   E. K. Waterhouse, *Painting in Britain 1530–1790* (London, 1953), 137, Pl.107.
195   F. Buckley (1925), 132, no.49.
196   Hartshorne, 470–1.
197   Hughes, 341.
198   F. Buckley (1925), 122–5.
199   Churchill, 18, no.78.
200   Hughes, 340.
201   Simon (1926), 27.
202   Simon (1926), 27–8.
203   *The Letters and Journals of Lady Mary Coke*, I (1889–96, repr., Bath, 1970), 190.
204   *The Letters and Journals of Lady Mary Coke*, III, 253.
205   Hughes, 226.
206   Lady Mary Wortley-Montagu, *Letters*, Everyman ed. (London, 1934), letter dated Sept., 1727.
207   F. Buckley (1925), 126, no.23,c.
208   Charleston (1977), 42–3.
209   Delomosne (1978), 37, no.55.
210   Simon (1926), 28–38.
211   Simon (1926), 266–7.
212   A. P. Herbert, *Mr. Gay's London* (London, 1948), 9–10.
213   McKearin (1954), 15.
214   Watson (1951), 27.
215   Thorpe (1929), 318–21; Thorpe (1929a), 196 ff. & 271 ff.; Bacon (1939), 13–15; Sanctuary, 113 ff.; Hughes, 257–83.
216   F. Buckley (1925), 120, no.9,c.
217   F. Buckley (1925), 132, no.48.

218 F. Buckley (1925), 133, no.51.
219 F. Buckley (1925), 124, no.17,1.
220 Cf. Barrelet (1953), Pl.LIV; Gasparetto, fig.143.
221 *The World*, 8.2.1753.
222 F. Buckley (1925), 107.
223 Westropp (1920), 43.
224 *Quarterly Bull.*, National Gallery of Victoria, Vol.2, no.4 (1947).
225 Hughes, 298.
226 Hughes, 286.
227 *Proc. Soc. Antiquaries of Newcastle upon Tyne*, IV, 4 (1929–30), 310–11.
228 F. Buckley (1925), 120, no.9,a.
229 Westropp (1920), 99.
230 F. Buckley (1925), 132, no.48.
231 E. Smith, *The Compleat Housewife* (London, 1753; repr., 1968), 191.
232 R. Bradley, *The Country Housewife and Lady's Director* (London, 1732), Part II, 168.
233 Hartshorne, 471.
234 Charleston (1966), 100, 181.
235 F. Buckley (1925), 144, no.102.
236 F. Buckley (1925), 132, no.48.
237 Thorpe (1929), 321–2, Pls.LXVII–LXXVII; Hughes, 285 ff., figs.230–43.
238 Haynes (1941), 75–7.
239 Hughes, fig.27.
240 F. Buckley (1925), 123, no.17,d,e.
241 F. Buckley (1925), 135, no.169.
242 F. Buckley (1925), 132, no.46.
243 W. B. Honey, *Dresden China* (London, 1934), 126, 191, *n.*174.
244 McKearin (1955), fig.3.
245 F. Buckley (1925), 130, no.39.
246 S. C. Robert, *A Frenchman in England, 1784* (Cambridge, 1933), 29–30.
247 Tobias Smollett, *Travels through France and Italy*, ed. F. Felsenstein (Oxford, 1981), 34.
248 Thorpe (1929), 332.
249 F. Buckley (1925), 121, no.12.
250 F. Buckley (1925), 122, no.17,a.
251 F. Buckley (1925), 132, no.49.
252 F. Buckley (1925), 128, no.26.
253 F. Buckley (1925), 124, no.17,j,m.
254 F. Buckley (1925), 137, no.76.
255 *Sophie in London* (Diary of Sophie von la Roche), tr. & ed. C. Williams (London, 1933), 207.
256 A. C. Powell, 239; F. Buckley (1925a), 43, 58; Josephs (1977), 110 ff.
257 Hughes, 307.
258 Hughes, 306.
259 Hughes, fig.245.
260 Hughes, 306.
261 F. Buckley (1931), 586.
262 F. Buckley (June 1928), 247.
263 Young, 7.
264 F. Buckley (June 1928), 247.
265 F. Buckley (1925), 122, no.17,a.
266 F. Buckley (1925), 83.

267 F. Buckley (1925), 42–3, 119, no.1.
268 *The Plate-Glass Book*, by a Glass-house Clerk (London, 1764), p.xi.
269 Cf. G. B. Hughes, 'Silver Casters and Cruets', III, *Apollo* (July 1954), 12–14.
270 Charleston (1966a), fig.3.
271 F. Buckley (1925), 119, no.4.
272 F. Buckley (1925), 43.
273 F. Buckley (June 1928), 248.
274 F. Buckley (June 1928), 248.
275 Thorpe (1929), Pl.CIV,3.
276 Thorpe (1929), 308–9.
277 Bills dated 25.5.1767 to Sir Lynch Cotton, and 2.7.1781 to the Revd. Thomas Moore, in Winterthur Museum, Del., USA.
278 Thorpe (1929), Pl.CXXXIX.
279 Charleston (1965), 46 ff.
280 Guttery, 108.
281 Cf. Thorpe (1929), 313–4, Pls.LIV, ff.; Hughes 315 ff., figs. 247–60.
282 C. Oman, *English Domestic Silver* (London, 1949), 171–4, figs.114–7.
283 Thorpe (1929), 313–4, Pls.CXLIII–CXLIV; Hughes, 319 ff., figs. 261–6.
284 F. Buckley (1925), 119, no.5.
285 F. Buckley (1925), 120, no.9,c.
286 F. Buckley (1925), 101.
287 F. Buckley (1925), 101.
288 Fowler/Cornforth, 221.
289 Fowler/Cornforth, 223.
290 Fowler/Cornforth, 222.
291 Fowler/Cornforth, 222.
292 Fowler/Cornforth, 222.
293 Wills (1965), fig.27.
294 F. Buckley (1925), 43.
295 Perret (1939), 101–4; Mortimer (1970), 172–4.
296 F. Buckley (1936), fig.1.
297 Perret (1939), 101–4; Perret (1938), 187–92.
298 F. Buckley (Sept., 1928), 393.
299 F. Buckley (1925), 124, no.17,k.
300 Perret (1938), 187–92, 334.
301 Perret (1939), 139.
302 Powell, 63.
303 Perret (1939), 101–4.
304 Mortimer (1972), 107–11.
305 Charleston (1954), 297.
306 Rooksby, 25; Charleston (1959a), 63.
307 Thorpe (1961), 201–2.
308 Watney/Charleston, 59–60.
309 Watney/Charleston, 72.
310 Charleston (1954a), 8.
311 Mallet, 142–3, 153.
312 Watney/Charleston, 80.
313 Westropp (1920), 43.
314 Charleston (1954a), 3–16.
315 Charleston (1953), 13–20.
316 Watney/Charleston, 74–6.

317   Benton, 137–163.
318   Delomosne, 1–31.
319   Charleston (1966), 96.
320   Charleston (1966), 100, 181.
321   Charleston (1966), 176 ff., and Delomosne, 32–9.
322   Charleston (1963a), 320–3; Rush, *passim*; Delomosne, 40–5; Newcastle
         (1980), *passim*.
323   Watney/Charleston, 60–9, 78–80, 82–107.
324   Charleston (1979), 16–30.
325   F. Buckley (1926), 43, no.25.
326   F. Buckley (1926), 44, no.36.
327   F. Buckley (1926), 42, no.16.
328   C. Morris ed., *The Journeys of Celia Fiennes* (London, 1947), 279.
329   Barrelet (1953), 81.
330   Douglas/Frank, 143 ff.
331   Wills (1965), 48 ff.
332   Wills (1965), 49; VAM, *Osterley Park* (London, 1977), 36.

CHAPTER 5

Bibliographical Note

The most influential event which brought Victorian glass to serious attention was
the Exhibition of Victorian and Edwardian Decorative Arts at the Victoria and
Albert Museum in 1952. It brought together two main groups of early and late
Victorian glass and a number of pieces associated with individual designers; and its
Catalogue remained the chief work in the field until Hugh Wakefield's *Nineteenth-
century British Glass* appeared in 1961 (2nd ed. 1982). Wakefield had played a main
role in organising this exhibition, and two of his collaborators subsequently
published books on the subject – Barbara Morris with *Victorian Table Glass and
Ornaments* (1978), and Betty O'Looney with the slighter VAM production
Victorian Glass (1972). Other contemporary works in the general field included
A. C. Revi's *Nineteenth-century Glass* (1959 & 1967). On particular areas may be
cited J. Northwood's book on his father, John Northwood (1958) and G. W.
Beard's *Nineteenth Century Cameo Glass* (1956); more recently, the Dudley Art
Gallery's Exhibition Catalogue *English 'Rock Crystal' Glass* (1976), and Colin R.
Lattimore's work on the increasingly popular subject of *English Nineteenth-
century Press-moulded Glass* (1979).

References

 1   Westropp (1978), Pls.X–XIV; figs. on pp.232–3.
 2   Sunderland Museum, 10–12.
 3   C.L. (15.4.1976), 966.
 4   Pellatt (1849), 118–19.
 5   *Wrightson's Triennial Directory.*
 6   Morris, 18.
 7   Wakefield (1969), 50–4; Wakefield (1982), 33.
 8   Morris, 21.
 9   Pellatt (1849), 126.
10   Pellatt (1849), 118–19.

11   Pellatt (1849), 119–21.
12   Morris, 42–3.
13   Morris, Pl.4.
14   Churchill, 19–21, 26 ff.
15   Charleston (1982), 4–19.
16   Morris, 78.
17   Morris, 78; Sunderland Museum, 8.
18   Charleston (1982), 8.
19   Churchill, no.172, Pl.39; Guttery, 113.
20   Charleston (1982), 8.
21   Davis, fig.65; Wakefield (1978), 426; private communication, H. Wakefield.
22   Wakefield (1982), 86, Pl.83.
23   Morris, 79.
24   Charleston (1982), 9.
25   Pazaurek, 58–60, figs.38–9; Pellatt (1849), 126.
26   Wakefield (1982), 92–102; Morris, 83, 89–95.
27   Pazaurek, 142.
28   Pazaurek, 143.
29   Thorpe (1929), 314.
30   Morris, 79–83, Pls.44–7; Rose (1979), 7 ff., figs.7 ff.
31   Dudley (1976), *passim*; Wolfenden (1982), 20–45: for Webb's generally, see
        Woodward (1978).
32   Dudley (1976), *passim*; Wolfenden (1982), 20–45.
33   Wakefield (1982), 98, 102–3; Morris, 104–6.
34   Charleston (1979a), 31–9.
35   Wakefield (1982), 102, 104–6; Morris, 113–26: for J. Northwood, see
        Northwood, *passim*.
36   Wakefield (1982), 102.
37   Josephs (1977), 110–13; Josephs (1978), 98–101.
38   Kiddell, 60–3.
39   Wakefield (1982), 53–4; Morris, 71 ff., Pl.41; Sunderland Museum, 20–2.
40   Wakefield (1982), 48 ff.; Morris, 69 ff.; Vincent, *passim*; Chance (1969),
        33–9.
41   Wakefield (1982), 48, 53, fig.37; Chance (1964), 1–8.
42   Wakefield (1982), Pl.36.
43   Wakefield (1982), 86, Pl.82; Fleming, 125–7, Pl.XXIX.
44   *G.N.*, 15 (Dec., 1955), 10.
45   C.G.C. Exh. *Cat.* (1962), no.370.
46   Vincent, 9, figs.12–13, 67–71, 76.
47   Wakefield (1982), 48, 53, Pls.38–48; Morris, 71–5.
48   Josephs (1977), 113–19.
49   Pazaurek, 257, 262 ff.
50   Barrelet (1953), Pl.LXII.
51   Wakefield (1982), 57, 60 ff.; Morris, 31 ff.
52   Wakefield (1982), 60 ff., Pls.56–68; Morris, 52 ff.
53   Wakefield (1982), 53, 57, Pl.49; Barraud, 187.
54   Warren (1981), 225, *n*.1.
55   Wakefield (1982), 57, 60, Pl.A; Morris, 61–2, Pls.36–7.
56   Morris, 63.
57   Wakefield (1961), 34, Pl.A; Wakefield (1982), 74, Pl.D; Morris, 35–9,
        Pls.14, 16; *G.N.*, 8 (Dec., 1948), 30.
58   D. E. L. Haynes, *The Portland Vase* (London, 1964), 7–13.

59 Beard, 12–13.
60 Beard, 15 ff., Pl.II; Morris, 106–7.
61 Beard, 5–6.
62 Beard, 20–1, Pls.II–III; Morris, 109.
63 Beard, 22–4, Pl.IV; Wakefield (1982), 106, Pl.106.
64 Wakefield (1982), 111.
65 Wakefield (1982), 111.
66 Wakefield (1982), 111; Beard, 35 ff., Pls.V ff.; *G.N.*, 8 (Dec., 1948), 22–3; Morris, 110, Pl.65.
67 Beard, 30–1, 50; Morris, 110.
68 This phase is best studied in Wakefield (1982), 68, 74–5, 77, 112–24; Morris, 127–48; Wakefield (1972), 293–7.
69 Morris, 130–1; Tait (1979), 7–8.
70 Wakefield (1972), 294.
71 Morris, 224.
72 Morris, 229–30.
73 For table centre-pieces, see Wakefield (1982), 112–13, 117, 119–22, 124, 130–2; Morris, 149–62; Wakefield (1968), 200–5.
74 Morris, Pl.108.
75 Wakefield (1982), 124; Morris, 156, 161, 229, 241–3; Godden (1965), 55–7.
76 Wakefield (1982), 74, 77; Morris, 47–8; Elville (1967), 39 ff.; Corning Museum (1978), 155.
77 Wakefield (1982), 124–5; Morris, 237–43.
78 Wakefield (1982), 124.
79 Morris, 234–5.
80 Wakefield (1982), 124; Morris, 226–9.
81 Wakefield (1982), 124; Morris, 65–8, 224–6.
82 Morris, 217–20.
83 Morris, 221–2.
84 Morris, 231–2.
85 Morris, Pl.38; Wakefield (1982), 122.
86 For the Arts and Crafts Movement, see Wakefield (1982), 133–9; Morris, 163–84.
87 H. J. Powell, 43, gives the date 1859.
88 H. J. Powell, 160.
89 H. J. Powell, 22–3; Honey (1946), 125.
90 H. J. Powell, 152.
91 H. J. Powell, figs.30, 34.
92 Corning Museum (1971), 15, no.13.
93 McKearin (1941), 332.
94 McKearin (1941), 333.
95 Pellatt (1849), 31.
96 Pellatt (1849), 121–3.
97 Innes, 258.
98 Wakefield (1982), 142.
99 McKearin (1941), 334.
100 Pellatt (1849), 31.
101 Quoted in Morris, 190.
102 For pressed glass generally, see Wakefield (1982), 140–59; Morris, 185–216; Lattimore, *passim.*
103 Innes, 259.
104 Dodsworth (1982a), 66–7.

105 Morris, 202.
106 Morris, 45, 47.
107 Wakefield (1982), 74.
108 Corning (1971), 13, no.8.

EPILOGUE

1 VAM (1952), 12–13.
2 H. J. Powell, 165.
3 H. J. Powell, 171.
4 H. J. Powell, 167.
5 Polak (1962), 59–61.
6 Polak (1962), 61.

Bibliography

ALVEY, R. C., 'A Cesspit Excavation at 26–28 High Pavement, Nottingham', *Trs. Thoroton Society of Nottinghamshire*, LXXVII (1973), 53–72.

ANGUS-BUTTERWORTH, L. M., *British Table and Ornamental Glass* (London, 1956).

ANON. (1947) 'Sixteenth-Century Pageantry', *G.N.*, 7 (Dec., 1947), 22.

(1947a) 'A Check List of the Air Twist Glasses', *G.N.*, 7 (Dec., 1947), 32–40.

(1948) 'A Check List of the Opaque-White Twist Stem Glasses', *G.N.*, 8 (Dec., 1948), 29–48.

(1949) 'Annus Mirabilis', *G.N.*, 9 (Dec., 1949), 11–19.

(1951) 'The Traquair Amen Glass', *G.N.*, 11 (Dec., 1951), 12–13.

(1951a) 'The Empty Bud', *G.N.*, 11 (Dec., 1951), 18–21.

(1951b) 'A Check List of Glasses with Composite Stems', *G.N.*, 11 (Dec., 1951), 38–43.

(1953) 'More Ravenscroft Glass', *G.N.*, 13 (Dec., 1953), 21–3.

(1953a) 'A Check List of Glasses with Balustroid Stems', *G.N.*, 13 (Dec., 1953), 34–60.

(1954) 'A Check List of the Baluster Glasses', *G.N.*, 14 (Dec., 1954), 35–48.

(1955) 'A Check List of the Plain Stem Glasses', *G.N.*, 15 (Dec., 1955), 43–7.

(1956) 'Sarah Siddons? A Study in Identity', *G.N.*, 16 (Dec., 1956), 19–20.

(1956a) 'The Portrait Glasses of Prince Charles Edward in Enamel Colours', *G.N.*, 16 (Dec., 1956), 21–6.

(1956b) 'A Check List of Glasses with Hollow Stems', *G.N.*, 16 (Dec., 1956), 46–7.

(1956c) 'A Check List of Glasses with Incised Twist Stems', *G.N.*, 16 (Dec., 1956), 48–9.

ARBMAN, H., *Schweden und das Karolingische Reich* (Stockholm, 1937).

ARCHER, D. M., '"Beest, Bird or Flowre": stained glass at Gorhambury House – I', *C.L.* (3.6.1976), 1451–4; 'Elements and Continents; Glass at Gorhambury – II', *C.L.* (10.6.1976), 1562–4.

ARMITAGE, E. LIDDALL, *Stained Glass* (London, 1959).

ARWIDSSON, GRETA, 'Some Glass Vessels from the Boat-grave Cemetery at Valsgärde', *Acta Archaeologica*, III (1932), 251–6.

ASH, D. (1962) *How to Identify English Drinking Glasses and Decanters, 1680–1830* (London).

(1975) *Dictionary of British Antique Glass* (London).

ASHDOWN, C. H., *History of the Worshipful Company of Glaziers* (London, n.d. ?1918).

BACON, J. M., 'Bottle-decanters and Bottles', *Apollo*, XXX (1939), 13–15.

'Baluster', 'Ale and Ale-Glasses', *G.N.*, 6 (Dec., 1946), 17–23.

BARRAUD, RONALD, 'John Davenport; a Nineteenth-Century Glass Decorator', *Conn.* (Mar., 1970), 186–8.

BARRELET, JAMES (1953) *La Verrerie en France* (Paris).

(1959) 'Le Verre de Table au Moyen Age', *Cahiers de la Céramique*, 16, 194–225.

BEARD, GEOFFREY W., *Nineteenth Century Cameo Glass* (Newport, Mon., 1956).

BEATSON, CLARK & CO., *The Glass Works Rotherham, 1751–1951* (Rotherham, 1952).

BENTON, E., 'The London Enamellers', *Trs. E.C.C.*, 8, pt. 2 (1972), 137–63.

BERESFORD, G., 'The Medieval Manor of Penhallam, Jacobstow, Cornwall', *Med. Arch.*, XVIII (1974), 90–139.

BICKERTON, L. M., *Eighteenth-Century English Drinking Glasses* (London, 1971).

BIMSON, MAVIS, 'Coloured Glass and Millefiori in the Sutton Hoo Ship Burial', *Annales*, 7, Liège (1978), 427–33.

BLES, JOSEPH, *Rare English Glasses of the 17th and 18th Centuries* (London, n.d. ?1925).

BOSC D'ANTIC, P., *Oeuvres: contenant plusieurs mémoires sur l'art de la verrerie*, 2 vols. (Paris, 1780).

BOWLES, W. H., *History of the Vauxhall and Ratcliff Glasshouses and their Owners* (London, 1926).

BRIDGEWATER, N. P., 'Glasshouse Farm, St. Weonard's: A Small Glassworking Site', *Trs. Woolhope Naturalists' Field Club*, XXXVII (1963), 300–15.

BRITISH MUSEUM, *Masterpieces of Glass*, by D. B. Harden *et al.* (London, 1968).

BUCKLEY, F. (1912) *English Baluster-Stemmed Glasses of the 17th and 18th Centuries* (Edinburgh).

(1913) *Old London Drinking Glasses* (Edinburgh).

(1914) *The Glass Trade in England in the 17th Century* (London).

(1914a) *The Taxation of English Glass in the 17th Century* (London).

(1915) *Old London Glasshouses* (London).

(1924) 'Cruet Bottles of the 18th Century', *Glass*, I, 489.

(1924a) 'The Development of English Cut Glass in the 18th Century', *Burl. Mag.* (July–Dec. 1924), 299–304.

(1924b) 'Lancashire Glasshouses of the 18th Century', *Glass*, I, 537–8.

(1924c) 'Note on the Glasshouses of the Leeds District in the 17th, 18th and 19th Centuries', *Trs. S.G.T.*, 8, 268–77.

(1925) *A History of Old English Glass* (London).

(1925a) 'The Early Glasshouses of Bristol', *Trs. S.G.T.*, 9, 36–61.

(1925b) 'Glasshouses on the Wear in the 18th Century', *Trs. S.G.T.*, 9, 105–11.

(1926) 'Glasshouses on the Tyne in the 18th Century', *Trs. S.G.T.*, 10, 26–52.

(1926a) 'Cumberland Glasshouses', *Trs. S.G.T.*, 10, 384–6.

(1926b) 'Old Nottingham Glasshouses', *Trs. S.G.T.*, 10, 270–3.

(1927) 'Notes on the Glasshouses of Stourbridge, 1700–1830', *Trs. S.G.T.*, 11, 106 ff.

(1927a) 'The Birmingham Glass Trade, 1740–1933', *Trs. S.G.T.*, 11, 374–86.

(1927b) 'Glasshouses of Dudley and Worcester', *Trs. S.G.T.*, 11, 287–93.

(1928) 'Great Names in the History of English Glass', *Glass*, V: I (Mar.) 'Cassilari', 103–4; II (April) 'John Bellingham', 150; III (May) 'Sir Robert Mansell', 199–200; IV (June) 'John Akerman', 247–8; V (July) 'Thomas Betts', 299–300; VI (Aug.) 'The Duke of Buckingham', 341–2, 366; VII (Sept.) 'Jerom Johnson', 392–3; VIII (Nov.) 'Jackson', 488–9; IX (Dec.) 'Bowles', 540, 548.

(1928a) 'Old Decanters', *C.L.* (Dec., 1928), 94–8.

(1929) 'Old Lancashire Glasshouses', *Trs. S.G.T.*, 13, 229–42.

(1929a) 'Old Glass Lamps and Candlesticks', *C.L.* (Apr., 1929), 492–4; (May, 1929), 710–12.

BUCKLEY, F. (1929b) 'West Country Glasshouses', *Trs. S.G.T.*, 13, 124–9.

(1930) 'Notes on Various Old Glasshouses', *Trs. S.G.T.*, 14, 30–6.

(1930a) 'Old London Glasshouses: Southwark', *Trs. S.G.T.*, 14, 137–49.

(1931) 'Documentary Old English Glasses', *Ant. Coll.* (Oct., 1931), 585–8.

(1935) 'Some Jacobite Relics: a newly discovered glass inscription', *Ant. Coll.*, 56–8.

(1936) 'Old Cut Glass Chandeliers . . . George I to the Regency', *Ant. Coll.*, VII (June 1936), 178–81.

(1936a) 'Seventeenth-Century English Table Glass from pre-Ravenscroft Fragments to Early Flint Glass', *Ant. Coll.*, VII, 150–2.

(1937) 'Earlier Cut Drinking Glasses', *Ant. Coll.*, VIII, 78–80.

(1938) 'The Jelly Glass and its Relations', *Ant. Coll.*, IX, 298–300.

(1938a) 'The London Glass-Sellers', *Ant. Coll.*, IX, 112–14.

(1939) 'Old English Glass Salts', *Ant. Coll.*, X, 44–6.

(1939a) 'Seventeenth- and Eighteenth-Century Ribbed Glasses,' *Ant. Coll.*, X, 138–40.

(1940) 'The Cycle Club and Jacobite Hunts and Some Commemorative Glasses', *Conn.* (Jan.–June, 1940), 57–62.

BUCKLEY, W. (1926) *European Glass*, London.

(1928) 'Anglo-Dutch Glasses of the 18th Century', *Old Furniture*, 151.

(1929) *Diamond Engraved Glasses of the 16th century* (London).

(1930) *Notes on Frans Greenwood and the Glasses that he engraved* (London).

(1931) *Aert Schouman and the Glasses that he engraved* (London).

(1939) *The Art of Glass* (London).

(1939a) 'Anglo-Dutch stem glasses of the 18th century', *Arts and Decoration* (Sept., 1939), 10–11.

BUNGARD, G., 'Men of Glass': a Personal View of the De Bongar Family in the 16th and 17th Centuries', *G.C.*, 3 (1979), 79–86.

C.G.C. Exh. (1962) Circle of Glass Collectors, Commemorative Exhibition, 1937–62, *Catalogue* (London).

CECIL HIGGINS ART GALLERY (BEDFORD), *Glass* (Bedford, 1969).

CHAMBON, R. (1950) 'Pour l'Histoire de la Verrerie en Belgique', *Silicates Industriels*, XV, 6 (June–July, 1950), 122–4.

(1951) 'Note Relatif à Deux Chefs-d'Oeuvre en Verre . . . au Milieu du XVIe Siècle', *Silicates Industriels*, XVI, 7 (Aug.–Sept., 1951), 1–3.

(1955) *L'Histoire de la Verrerie en Belgique du IIme Siècle à nos jours* (Brussels).

(1975) 'La Verrerie entre Rhin et Loire au 14e Siècle', *JGS*, XVII, 151–7.

CHAMBON R. & ARBMAN, H., 'Deux Fours à Verre d'Époque Mérovingienne à Macquenoise (Belgique)', *K. Humanistiska Vetenskapssamfundets i Lund Årsberättelse,* VII (1951–2), 199–232.

CHANCE, SIR HUGH (1964) 'The Donnington Wood Glasshouses', *C.G.C. Papers*, 140 (London, Nov., 1964).

(1969) 'The Nailsea Glassworks', *Studies in Glass History and Design* (ed. R. J. Charleston, *et al.*), Sheffield, 33–9.

CHARLESTON, R. J. (1953) 'A Painter of Opaque-white Glass', *G.N.*, 13 (Dec., 1953), 13–20.

(1954) 'English Eighteenth-Century Opaque-White Glass', *Antiques* (Oct.–Dec., 1954), 294–7, 487–91.

(1954a) 'Michael Edkins and the Problem of English Enamelled Glass', *Trs. S.G.T.*, 38, 3–16.

(1954b) 'Bottles, mainly Glass', *The Pennant*, IX, no. 5, 155–9.

CHARLESTON, R. J. (1956) 'Pottery, Porcelain and Glass' in ed. Edwards, R. & Ramsey, L. G. G., *Conn. Period Guides: the Tudor Period, 1500–1603* (London), 79–88.

    (1957) 'Dutch Decoration of English Glass', *Trs. S.G.T.*, XLI, 229–43.

    (1958) 'A Notable Collection of Glass', *Conn.* (July–Dec., 1958), 238–41.

    (1959) 'English Glass-making and its Spread', *Annales*, I, 155–72.

    (1959a) 'Souvenirs of the Grand Tour', *JGS*, I, 63–82.

    (1962) 'Twenty-five Years of Glass Collecting', *Conn.* (May–Aug., 1962), 121–4.

    (1962a) 'Le verre blanc opaque anglais du 18e siècle à décor polychrome', *Cahiers de la Céramique*, 28, 260–77.

    (1963) 'The Glass Circle Commemorative Exhibition of 1962. Pt. I: Some Important Early English Glasses', *Antiques* (Jan., 1963), 92–4.

    (1963a) 'The Beilby Glasses', *Antiques* (March, 1963), 320–3.

    (1964) 'Wheel-engraving and -Cutting; Some Early Equipment', *JGS*, VI, 83–100.

    (1964a) 'Medieval and Later Glass', in Cunliffe, B., *Winchester Excavations, 1949–60*, Winchester, I, 145–51.

    (1965) 'Wheel-engraving and -Cutting: Some Early Equipment, II, Water-Power and Cutting', *JGS*, VII, 41–54.

    (1965a) 'English Glass in the Reserve Collection at the Rijksmuseum', *Conn.* (July–Dec., 1965), 236–8.

    (1966) 'James Giles as a Decorator of Glass', I and II, *Conn.* (June–July, 1966), 96–101, 176–9.

    (1966a) 'Apropos of Tea-Caddies in Cut-Glass', *Ant. Coll.* (Aug., 1966), 151–5.

    (1968) 'George Ravenscroft: New Light on the Development of his "Christalline Glasses"', *JGS*, X, 156–167.

    (1969) 'Glass', in P. J. Huggins, 'Excavations at Sewardstone Street, Waltham Abbey, Essex, 1966', *Post-Med. Arch.*, 3, 47–99.

    (1972) 'Glass', in Moorhouse, S., 'Finds from the Excavations in the Refectory at the Dominican Friary, Boston', *Lincs. History & Archaeology*, I, no. 7, 45–8, 52–3.

    (1974) 'The Glass', in Neal, D. S., 'Excavations at the Palace and Priory, King's Langley', *Herts. Arch.*, III, 67–9.

    (1975) 'The Glass', in C. Platt and R. Colman-Smith, *Excavations in Medieval Southampton 1953–69*, II, *The Finds*, Leicester, 204–26.

    (1975a) 'A Glassmaker's Bankruptcy Sale', *G.C.*, 2, 4–16.

    (1975b) 'Some English Finds of Medieval Glass with Balkan Analogues', *Verre Médiéval aux Balkans*, Belgrade, 101–7.

    (1976) 'A 13th Century Syrian Glass Beaker excavated in Lübeck', in O. Ahlers, *Lübeck 1226*, Lübeck, 321–37.

    (1977) *The James A. de Rothschild Collection at Waddesdon Manor – Glass and Enamels* (with D. M. Archer & M. Marcheix), Fribourg.

    (1978) 'Some Aspects of 17th Century Glass found in England', *Annales*, 7, 283–97.

    (1978a) 'I. Glass Furnaces through the Ages: II. A Gold and Enamel Box in the form of a Glass Furnace', *JGS*, 20, 9–44.

    (1979) 'Decoration of Glass, pt. 4: Printing on Glass', *G.C.*, 3, 16–30.

    (1979a) 'Decoration of Glass, pt. 5: Acid-etching', *G.C.*, 3, 31–9.

    (1980) 'Glass of the High Medieval Period (12th–15th century)', *Bull. de l'Association Internationale pour l'Histoire du Verre*, 8 (1977–80), 65–76.

CHARLESTON, R. J. (1980a) '16th–17th Century English Glass', *Bull. de l'Association Internationale pour l'Histoire du Verre*, 8 (1977–80), 77–99.

(1982) 'Some English Glass Engravers: late 18th–early 19th century', *G.C.*, 4, 4–19.

CHARLESWORTH, DOROTHY (1967) 'Glass', in G. Jobey, 'Excavation at Tynemouth Priory and Castle', in *Archaeologia Aeliana*, 4th Series, XLV, 36 ff.

(1969) 'Glass Flasks', in Rahtz, P. A., *Excavations at King John's Hunting Lodge, Writtle, Essex, 1955–7* (London).

CHURCHILL, ARTHUR, LTD, *History in Glass* (London, 1937).

CLARKE, T. H., '*Lattimo* – a Group of Venetian Glass Enamelled on an Opaque-White Ground', *JGS*, XVI (1974), 22–56.

COLVIN, H. M., 'Excavations at Dale Abbey: Interim Report', *Derbyshire Arch. and Natural History Soc. J.* (1938), 87–90.

COLYER, CHRISTINA & JONES, M. J., 'Excavations at Lincoln. Second Interim Report', *A.J.*, LIX, pt. I (1979), 60–1.

COOK, JEAN M., 'A Fragment of Early Medieval Glass from London', *Med. Arch.*, 11 (1958), 173–7.

CORNING MUSEUM OF GLASS, *Glass from the Corning Museum of Glass: a Guide to the Collections* (Corning, 1955, 1958, 1965, 1974).

(1963) *English 19th century Cameo Glass from the Collection of Mr. and Mrs. Albert Christian Revi* (Corning).

(1971) *Victorian Glass . . . from the Victoria and Albert Museum* (Corning).

(1978) *Paperweights: 'Flowers which clothe the Meadows'* by Paul Hollister & Dwight P. Lanmon (Corning).

CRAMP, ROSEMARY (1969) 'Glass Finds from the Anglo-Saxon Monastery of Monkwearmouth and Jarrow', *Studies in Glass History and Design* (ed. R. J. Charleston, *et al.*), Sheffield, 16–19.

(1970) 'Decorated Window-Glass and Millefiori from Monkwearmouth', *A.J.*, L, pt. II, 327–35.

(1971) 'Excavations at the Saxon Monastic Sites of Wearmouth and Jarrow, Co. Durham: an Interim Report', *Med. Arch.*, XIII, 21 ff.

(1975) 'Window Glass from the Monastic Site of Jarrow: Problems of Interpretation', *JGS*, XVII, 88–96.

CRELLIN, J. K. & SCOTT, J. R., 'Glass and British Pharmacy 1600–1900', *G.C.*, 1 (1972), 33–45.

CROMPTON, SIDNEY (ed.) *English Glass* (London & Melbourne, 1967).

CROSSLEY, D. W. (1967), 'Glassmaking in Bagot's Park, Staffordshire, in the 16th century', *Post-Med. Arch.*, I, 44–83.

(1981) *Kimmeridge Excavations*, 1980 (Sheffield?).

CROSSLEY, D. W. & ABERG, F. A., 'Sixteenth-century Glass-making in Yorkshire: Excavations at Furnaces at Hutton and Rosedale, North Riding, 1968–71', *Post-Med. Arch.*, 6 (1972), 107–59.

CROWFOOT, GRACE M. & HARDEN, D. B., 'Early Byzantine and later Glass Lamps', *J. Egyptian Arch.*, XVII (1931), 196–208.

DANIELS, J. STUART, *The Woodchester Glass House* (Gloucester, 1950).

DAVIDSON, G. R. (1940) 'A Medieval Glass-factory at Corinth', *AJA*, XLIV, 297–324.

(1952) 'Glass Vessels', in *Corinth, XII: Minor Objects*, Princeton, 76–122.

DAVIS, DEREK C. (1964) *English and Irish Antique Glass* (London).

(1972) *English Bottles & Decanters, 1650–1900* (London).

DAVIS, D. C. & MIDDLEMAS, K., *Coloured Glass* (London, 1968).

DAVIS, FRANK, *Early 18th-century English Glass* (London, 1971).

DELOMOSNE & SON LTD, *Gilding the Lily* (London, 1978).

DODSWORTH, ROGER (1982) *Glass and Glassmaking* (Princes Risborough).

(1982a) 'The Manchester Glass Industry', *G.C.*, 4, 65–84.

DODWELL, C. R., *Theophilus, de Diversis Artibus* (London, 1961).

DOUGLAS, R. W. & FRANK, S., *A History of Glassmaking* (Henley-on-Thames, 1972).

DUDLEY ART GALLERY, *English 'Rock Crystal' Glass, 1878–1925* (Dudley, 1976).

EBBOTT, REX, *British Glass of the 17th and 18th centuries* (Melbourne, 1971).

ELVILLE, E. M. (1951) *English Table Glass* (London & New York).

(1953) *English & Irish Cut Glass, 1750–1950* (London).

(1954) *Paperweights and other Glass Curiosities* (London).

(1967) *Paperweights and other Glass Curiosities* (London).

EVISON, VERA I. (1955) 'Anglo-Saxon Finds near Rainham, Essex, with a Study of Glass Drinking-horns', *Archaeologia*, XCVI, 159–95.

(1972) 'Glass Cone Beakers of the "Kempston" Type', *JGS*, XIV, 48–66.

(1975) 'Germanic Glass Drinking Horns', *JGS*, XVII, 74–87.

(1982) 'Bichrome Glass Vessels of the 7th and 8th Centuries', *Studien zur Sachsenforschung*, 3, 7–21.

(1982a) 'Anglo-Saxon Glass Claw-beakers', *Archaeologia*, CVII, 43–76.

FITZWILLIAM MUSEUM, CAMBRIDGE, *Glass at the Fitzwilliam Museum* (Cambridge, 1978).

FLEMING, A., *Scottish and Jacobite Glass* (Glasgow, 1938).

FOWLER, JOHN & CORNFORTH, JOHN, *English Decoration in the 18th Century* (London, 1974).

FOX, RUSSELL & LEWIS, ELIZABETH, *William Overton and Glassmaking in Buriton*, Petersfield Monographs, no. 1 (Petersfield, 1982).

FRANCIS, GRANT R., *Old English Drinking Glasses, their Chronology and Sequence* (London, 1926).

FREMERSDORF, F., 'Zur Geschichte des Fränkischen Rüsselbechers', *Wallraf-Richartz-Jahrbuch*, NF, II/III (1933–4), 7–30.

GABRIEL, RONALD, *English Drinking Glasses* (London, 1974).

GASPARETTO, ASTONE, *Il Vetro di Murano* (Venice, 1958).

GEDDE, W., *Booke of Sundry Draughtes* (London, 1615).

GIROUARD, MARK, *Life in the English Country House* (New Haven & London, 1978).

GLANVILLE, PHILIPPA, 'The Parr Pot', *Arch. J.*, CXXVII (1971), 147–55.

GLASS MANUFACTURERS' FEDERATION, *Catalogue . . . of Stourbridge Glass covering three-and-a-half centuries* (Stourbridge, 1951).

GLASS-HOUSE CLERK, *The Plate-Glass-Book*, 4th ed. (London, 1764).

GODDEN, GEOFFREY A., 'Fairy Lamps for Collectors', *Antique Dealer and Collector's Guide* (Dec., 1965), 55–7.

GODFREY, ELEANOR S., *The Development of English Glassmaking, 1560–1640* (Oxford, 1976).

GRAHAM, HENRY GREY, *The Social Life of Scotland in the 18th century* (London, 1928).

GUTTERY, D. R., *From Broad-Glass to Cut Crystal* (London, 1956).

HADEN, H. J. (1949) *Notes on the Stourbridge Glass Trade* (Brierley Hill).

(1953) 'The Richardson Bequest of Stourbridge Glass', *G.N.*, 13 (Dec., 1953), 24–6.

(1971) *The 'Stourbridge Glass' Industry in the 19th century* (Tipton).

HAEVERNICK, TH. E. with HABEREY, W., 'Beiträge zur Geschichte des Antiken Glases. XII. Glättsteine aus Glas', *Jahrb. des römisch-germanischen Zentralmuseums, Mainz*, X. Jahrg., 130–8.

HALL, W. D., 'The Collection of Glass in the City Art Galleries, Manchester, *JGS*, III (1961), 131–3.

HALLIWELL, J. O., *Ancient Inventories* (London, 1854).

HAMMOND, NORMAN, 'Repton: Saxon glass workshop', *The Times* (27.8.1975).

HARDEN, D. B. (1950) 'Glass Vessels in Anglo-Saxon Britain', *Archaeological News Letter*, 3, no. 2 (July, 1950), 21–7.

(1951) 'Saxon Glass from Sussex', *Sussex County Magazine*, 25 (June, 1951), 260–8.

(1954) 'A Glass Bowl of Dark Age Date and some Medieval Grave-finds from Shaftesbury Abbey', *A.J.*, XXXIV, nos. 3, 4, 188–94.

(1956) 'Glass Vessels in Britain and Ireland, AD 400–1000'. *Dark-Age Britain* (ed. D. B. Harden), London, 132–67.

(1959) 'New Light on Roman and Early Medieval Window-Glass', *Glastechnische Berichte*, VIII, Sonderband 32K, 8–16.

(1961) 'Domestic Window Glass: Roman, Saxon and Medieval', *Studies in Building History* (ed. E. M. Jope), London, 39–63.

(1966) 'Some Glass Fragments mainly of the 12th–13th Century AD, from Northern Apulia', *JGS*, VII, 70–8.

(1972) 'Ancient Glass, III: Post-Roman', *Arch. J.*, CXXVIII, 78–117.

(1975) 'Table-Glass in the Middle Ages', in (ed. J. G. N. Renaud) *Rotterdam Papers* II (Rotterdam), 35–45.

(1978) 'Anglo-Saxon and later Medieval Glass in Britain: some Recent Developments', *Med. Arch.*, XXII, 1–24.

HARTSHORNE, A., *Old English Glasses* (London & New York, 1897).

HAWTHORNE, J. G. & SMITH, C. S., *On Divers Arts: the Treatise of Theophilus* (Chicago, 1963).

HAYNES, E. BARRINGTON (1941) 'Fringed and looped Sweetmeats', *Apollo* (Sept., 1941), 75–7.

(1942) 'Rummers', *Apollo* (Dec., 1942), 165–6.

(1959) *Glass though the Ages*, rev. ed. (Harmondsworth, 1959).

HEJDOVA, DAGMAR, 'Types of Medieval Glass Vessels in Bohemia', *JGS*, XVII (1975), 142–50.

HOGAN, D., 'The Du Houx and the Haughton Green Glasshouse', in (ed.) R. J. Charleston, *et al.*, *Studies in Glass History and Design* (Sheffield, 1969), 24–5.

HOLDEN, E. W. 'Excavations at the deserted Medieval Village of Hangleton', in *Sussex Arch. Collections*, CI (1963), 163–4.

HOLDSWORTH, P., *Luxury Goods from a Medieval Household* (Southampton, n.d., 1976?).

HOLLISTER, PAUL JR. (1969) *The Encyclopaedia of Glass Paperweights* (New York).

(1974) 'The Glazing of the Crystal Palace', *JGS*, XVI, 95–110.

HONEY, W. B. (1946) *Glass: a Handbook for the Study of Glass Vessels of all Periods and a Guide to the Museum Collection* (London: Victoria and Albert Museum).

(1946a) *English Glass* (London).

HORRIDGE, W., 'Documents relating to the Lorraine Glassmakers in North Staffordshire', *G.N.*, 15 (Dec., 1955), 26–33.

HORRIDGE, W. & HAYNES, E. B., 'The "Amen" Glasses', *Conn.*(Sept., 1942), 47–50.

HOWARD, ALEXANDER L., *The Worshipful Company of Glass-Sellers of London* (London, n.d.).

HUDIG, F. W., *Das Glas* (Vienna, 1923).

HUDSON, J. PAUL, 'Seventeenth century Glass Wine Bottles and Seals excavated at Jamestown', *JGS*, III (1961), 79–89.

HUGGINS, P. J., 'Excavations . . . at Waltham Abbey, Essex, 1969–71', *Med. Arch.*, XX (1976), 47–99.

HUGHES, G. BERNARD, *English, Scottish and Irish Table Glass* (London, 1956).

HUME, I. NOEL (1956) 'A Century of London Glasses', *Conn. Year Book*, 98–103.

    (1957) 'Medieval Bottles from London', *Conn.* (Mar., 1957), 104–8.

    (1961) 'The Glass Wine Bottle in Colonial Virginia', *JGS*, III, 91–117.

    (1962) 'Tudor and Early Stuart Glasses found in London', *Conn.* (Aug., 1962), 269–73.

    (1968) 'A Find of Elizabethan Ale Glasses', *Conn.* (Dec., 1968), 259–61.

    (1969) *Glass in Colonial Williamsburg's Archaeological Collections* (Williamsburg, Virginia).

HURST, RUTH, 'The Bickerstaffe Glasshouse', in (ed.) R. J. Charleston, *et al.*, *Studies in Glass History and Design* (Sheffield, 1969?), 26–9. (See also under: VOSE, RUTH HURST.)

INNES, LOWELL, *Pittsburgh Glass 1797–1891* (Boston, 1976).

ISINGS, CLASINA & WIJNMAN, H. F., 'Medieval Glass from Utrecht', *JGS*, XIX (1977), 77–83.

JOKELSON, PAUL, *Sulphides. The Art of Cameo Incrustation* (New York, 1968).

JOSEPHS, ZOE (1977) 'Jewish Glass-makers, *Trs. Jewish Historical Soc. of England*, XXV, 107–119.

    (1978) 'The Jacobs of Bristol, Glassmakers to King George III', *Trs. Bristol and Glos. Arch. Soc.,* XCV, 98–101.

KENYON, G. H., *The Glass Industry of the Weald* (Leicester, 1967).

KIDDELL, A. J. B., 'William Absolon Junior of Great Yarmouth', *Trs. E.C.C.*, 5, pt. 1 (1960), 53–63.

KIRBY, H. T., 'The van Linge Window at Wroxton Abbey, Oxfordshire', *J. Br. Soc. Master Glass Painters*, XIV, no. 2 (1965), 117–21.

KOJIC, LJUBINKA & WENZEL, MARIAN, 'Medieval Glass found in Yugoslavia', *JGS*, IX (1967), 76–93.

LAFOND, J., 'Was Crown Glass discovered in Normandy in 1330?', *JGS*, XI (1969), 37–8.

LAMM, C. J., *Oriental Glass of Medieval Date found in Sweden* (Stockholm, 1941).

LANDMAN, HEDY B., 'Glass from the Museum's Collections', *Bulletin of Rhode Island School of Design, Museum Notes* (Jan., 1974), 5–144.

LARDNER, DIONYSIUS, *Cabinet Cyclopaedia* (London, 1832).

LATTIMORE, COLIN R., *English 19th-century Press-moulded Glass* (London, 1979).

LEIDEN, RIJKSMUSEUM VAN OUDHEDEN, *Glas uit de Oudheid* (Leiden, 1962).

LEWIS, J. M., 'The Excavation of the New Building at Montgomery Castle', *Archaeologia Cambrensis* (1968), 127–56.

LIGHTBOWN, R. W., *Secular Goldsmiths' Work in Medieval France: a History* (London, 1978).

LLOYD, WARD, *Investing in Georgian Glass* (London, 1969).

LONDON MUSEUM (1965) *The Garton Collection of English Table Glass* (London).

    (1970) *Glass in London* (London),

MCKEARIN, GEORGE S. & HELEN, *American Glass* (New York, 1941).

MCKEARIN, HELEN (1954) 'Eighteenth Century Advertisements of Glass Imports into the Colonies and the United States, I', *G.N.*, 14 (Dec., 1954), 13–21.

    (1955) 'Eighteenth century Advertisements of Glass Imports into the Colonies and the United States, II', *G.N.*, 15 (Dec., 1955), 15–25.

    (1955a) 'Sweetmeats in Splendor', *Antiques* (Mar., 1955) 217–25.

    (1971) 'Notes on Stoppering, Bottling and Binning', *JGS*, XIII, 120–7.

MCKEARIN, HELEN & WILSON, KENNETH M., *American Bottles and Flasks and their Ancestry* (New York, 1978).

MACLEOD, CATRIONA, *Irish Glass* (Tallaght, Co. Dublin, 1980).

MALLET, J. V. G., 'John Baddeley of Shelton', *Trs. E.C.C.*, 6, pt. 2 (1966), 142–66.

MANCHESTER CITY ART GALLERIES, *Glass* (Manchester, 1959).

MATCHAM, JONATHAN & DREISER, PETER, *The Techniques of Glass Engraving* (London, 1982).

MEIGH, EDWARD, *The Story of the Glass Bottle* (Stoke-on-Trent, 1972).

MERRETT, CHRISTOPHER, *The Art of Glass* (translated, with notes added, from A. Neri's *L'Arte Vetraria*, Florence, 1612; London, 1662).

MILLE ANNI DI ARTE DEL VETRO A VENEZIA (Venice: Comune di Venezia, 1982).

MOORHOUSE, S. (1971) 'Finds from Basing House, Hampshire, Part Two', *Post. Med. Arch.*, 5, 35–76.

　　(1972) 'Medieval Distilling-Apparatus of Glass and Pottery', *Med. Arch.*, XVI, 79–120.

MORGAN, ROY, *Sealed Bottles* (Southampton, 1980).

MORRIS, BARBARA, *Victorian Table Glass and Ornaments* (London, 1978).

MORTIMER, MARTIN C. F. (1970) 'Dating an Early Glass Chandelier', *Conn.* (July, 1970), 172–4.

　　(1972) 'English Glass Candelabra', *Antique Dealer and Collector's Guide* (Dec., 1972), 107–11.

NESBITT, A., *A Descriptive Catalogue of the Glass Vessels in the South Kensington Museum* (London, 1878).

NEUGEBAUER, W., 'Die Ausgrabungen in der Alstadt Lübecks', in (ed.) J. G. N. Renaud, *Rotterdam Papers* (Rotterdam, 1968), 93–113.

NEWCASTLE, TYNE AND WEAR MUSEUMS AND ART GALLERIES, *The Decorated Glasses of William and Mary Beilby, 1761–78* (Newcastle, 1980).

NEWSTEAD, R., 'Glasshouse in Delamere Forest, Cheshire', *J. of the Chester and N. Wales Architectural, Arch. and Historical Soc.*, N.S., XXXIII (1939), 32–9.

NORTHWOOD, J. JR., *John Northwood* (Stourbridge, 1958).

OAKLEY, G. E. & HUNTER, J., 'The Glass', in J. H. Williams, *St. Peter's Street, Northampton Excavations 1973–6* (Northampton, 1979), 296–302.

O'LOONEY, BETTY, *Victorian Glass* (London: Victoria and Albert Museum, 1972).

OSWALD, A., & PHILLIPS, H., 'A Restoration Glass Hoard from Gracechurch Street, London', *Conn.* (Sept., 1949), 30–6.

PAPE, T.(1933) 'An Elizabethan Glass Furnace', *Conn.*, XCII (Sept., 1933), 172–7.

　　(1933–4) 'Medieval (and later) Glassworkers in North Staffordshire', *Trs. N. Staffs. Field Club*, LXVIII, 74–121.

　　(1947–8) 'The Lorraine Glassmakers of North Staffordshire', *Trs. N. Staffs. Field Club*, LXXXII, 111–15.

PAZAUREK, G. E., *Gläser der Empire- und Biedermeierzeit* (Leipzig, 1923).

PELLATT, APSLEY (1821) *Glass Manufactures* (London).

　　(1845) *Memoir on the Origin of Glassmaking* (London).

　　(1849) *Curiosities of Glass Making* (London).

PERRET, BERNARD J. (1938) 'The 18th century Chandeliers at Bath', *Conn.* (July–Dec., 1938), 187–92, 334.

　　(1939) 'The Evolution of the English Glass Chandelier', *Apollo*, XXX (1939), 101–4, 139.

PLANT, M., *The Domestic Life of Scotland in the 18th century* (Edinburgh, 1952).

POLAK, ADA BUCH (1953) *Gammelt Norsk Glas* (Oslo).

　　(1962) *Modern Glass* (London).

POLAK, ADA BUCH (1969) 'The "Ip Olufsen Weyse" Illustrated Price-List of 18th-Century Norwegian Glass', *JGS*, XI, 86–104.

    (1975) *Glass: its Makers and its Public* (London).

    (1976) 'Venetian Renaissance Glass: the problems of dating *vetro a filigrana*', *Conn.* (Aug., 1976), 270–7.

POWELL, A. C. 'Glass-making in Bristol', *Trs. Bristol and Gloucester Arch. Society*, XLVII (1925), 238–40.

POWELL, H. J., *Glass-making in England* (Cambridge, 1923).

RACKHAM, B. A Guide to the . . . Stained Glass (London: Victoria and Albert Museum, 1936).

RADEMACHER, F. (1933), *Die Deutschen Gläser des Mittelalters* (Berlin).

    (1942), 'Fränkische Gläser aus dem Rheinland', *Bonner Jahrbücher*, 147, 285–344.

RAINES, ROBERT, *Marcellus Laroon* (London, 1966).

RAMSEY, W., *The Worshipful Company of Glass Sellers of London* (London, 1898).

RENAUD, J. G. N., 'Un Verre à boire du 14e siècle', *Proc. International Congress on Glass, Brussels* (1965), Paper 267.

RENDEL, ROSEMARY (1975) 'Who was George Ravenscroft?', *G.C.*, 2, 65–70.

    (1975a) 'The true Identity of George Ravenscroft, Glassman', *Recusant History*, 13, no. 2 (Oct., 1975), 101–5.

REVI, A. C., *Nineteenth-Century Glass*, rev. ed. (New York, 1967).

(RIDER, D.), 'The earliest recorded glassmaker in England', *Gl. Tech.*, I, no. 4 (Aug., 1960), 137.

RIDGWAY, M. H. & LEACH, G. B., 'Further notes on the Glasshouse Site at Kingswood, Delamere, Cheshire', *Cheshire Arch. Soc. J.*, 37 (1948), pt. 1, 133–40.

ROOKSBY, H. P., 'Opacifiers in Opal Glasses through the Ages', *G.E.C. Journal*, 29, no. 1 (1962), 20–6.

ROSE, J. A. H., 'The Apsley Pellatts', *G.C.*, 3 (1979), 4–15.

ROYAL ACADEMY OF ARTS, LONDON, *Victorian and Edwardian Decorative Art: The Handley-Read Collection* (London, 1972).

ROYAL SCOTTISH MUSEUM, *English Glass* (Edinburgh, 1964).

RUGGLES-BRISE, SHEELAH, *Sealed Bottles* (London, 1949).

RUSH, JAMES, *The Ingenious Beilbys* (London, 1973).

SALZMAN, L. F., *Building in England down to 1540* (Oxford, 1952).

SANCTUARY, C. T., 'The Evolution of the Decanter', *Apollo* (Nov., 1949), 113–15.

SCHMIDT, ROBERT, *Das Glas* (Berlin & Leipzig, 1922).

SCHUERMANS, H., 'Lettres sur la Verrerie', *Bull. de la Commission Royale sur l'Art et l'Archéologie*, XIX–XXXI (Brussels, 1883–91).

SEDDON, G. B., 'The Jacobite Engravers', *G.C.*, 3 (1979), 40–78.

SIMON, ANDRE (1926) *Bottlescrew Days* (London).

    (1948) *Drink* (London).

SMITH, SHEENAH, 'Glass in 18th century Norwich', *G.C.*, 2 (1975), 49–64.

SUNDERLAND MUSEUM, *The Glass Industry of Tyne and Wear*, I: *Glassmaking on Wearside* (Sunderland, 1979).

SUTTON, ANNE F. & SEWELL, J. R., 'Jacob Verzelini and the City of London', *Gl. Tech.*, 21, no. 4 (Aug., 1980), 190–2.

TAIT, HUGH (1967) 'Glass with Chequered Spiral-Trail Decoration', *JGS*, IX, 94–112.

    (1979) *The Golden Age of Venetian Glass* (London: British Museum).

THEUERKAUFF-LIEDERWALD, ANNA-ELISABETH, 'Der Römer, Studien zu einer Glasform', *JGS*, X (1968), 114–55.

THORPE, W. A. (1925) 'The Rees Price Collection of English Glass', *Apollo* (July–Dec., 1925), 250–8.

(1926) 'Drinking Glasses commemorative of William III', *Apollo* (Jan.–June, 1926), 165–70, 210–16.

(1927) *English and Irish Glass* (London).

(1928) 'The Beilby Glasses', *Conn.* (May–Aug., 1928), 10–23.

(1928a) 'The Henry Brown Collection of English Glass. I. Preference for balusters; II. Decline and Decoration', *Apollo* (July–Dec., 1928), 141–8, 208–14.

(1929) *History of English and Irish Glass*, 2 vols. (London).

(1929a) 'The Evolution of the Decanter' and 'The Evolution of the Decanter pursued', *Conn.* (April–June, 1929), 196–202, 271–81.

(1930) 'The Beginnings (and rise) of English Cut Glass', *Conn.* (July–Dec., 1930), 226–34, 307–13.

(1930a) 'Development of cut-glass in England and Ireland', *Antiques*, 300–3, 408–11.

(1930b) 'A newly discovered Verzelini glass', *Burl. Mag.* (Jan.–Jun., 1930), 256–7.

(1932) 'The Scudamore Flute and other Glasses in the Collection of Sir Richard Garton', *Ant. Coll.* (Oct., 1932), 361–4.

(1932a) 'Towards a classification of Nailsea glass', *Antiques*, 13–16.

(1933) 'The Dagnia Tradition in Newcastle Glass', *Conn.* (July–Dec., 1933), 13–25.

(1933a) 'Some Types of Newcastle Glass', *Antiques*, 206–9.

(1935) 'An Historic Verzelini Glass', *Burl. Mag.*, LXVII (1935), 150–7.

(1935a) 'The Roscoe Collection of English Glass', *Conn.* (July–Dec., 1935), 205–9.

(1937) 'English glassware in the 17th century', in A. Churchill Ltd, *Cat. of Old English Glass*, 13–22.

(1938) 'The Glass Sellers' Bills at Woburn Abbey', *Trs. S.G.T.*, 22, 165–205.

(1938a) 'Memorable Glass in the Cecil Higgins Collection', *Burl. Mag.* (July–Dec., 1938), 155–62.

(1948) 'The Lisley Group of Elizabethan Glasses', *Conn.*, CCXXII (Dec. 1948), 110–17.

(1949) *Collections of Glass at Brierley Hill Public Library: a Handlist*, Brierley Hill.

(1956) 'English glassware in the 17th century', *G.N.*, 16 (Dec., 1956).

(1961) *English Glass*, 3rd ed. (London, earlier eds. 1935, 1949).

(1972) 'The Hoare Bills for Glass', *G.C.*, 1, 10–17.

TOLEDO MUSEUM OF ART, *Art in Glass* (Toledo, Ohio, 1969).

TREGLOWN, G. L. & MORTIMER, M. C. F., 'Elegant and Elusive: wine-glasses of the Kit-Cat Club', *C.L.* (2.7.81), 46–8.

TRUBRIDGE, P. C. (1972) 'The English Ale Glasses, 1685–1830', *G.C.*, 1, 46–57.

(1975) 'The English Ale Glasses, Group 3. The tall Baluster and Flute Glasses for Champagne and Ale', *G.C.*, 2, 26–36.

(1979) 'The English Ale Glasses Group 4. Ale/Beer Glasses in the 19th century', *G.C.*, 3, 87–96.

TRURO, COUNTY MUSEUM, *The English Glass Bottle, Catalogue* (Truro, 1976).

VICTORIA AND ALBERT MUSEUM (1952) *Catalogue of an Exhibition of Victorian and Edwardian Decorative Arts* (London).

(1968) Exhibition of English Glass, *Catalogue* (London).

(1968a) *English Glass*, by R. J. Charleston (London).

VINCE, ALAN G., *Newent Glasshouse* (Bristol, 1977).

VINCENT, KEITH, *Nailsea Glass* (Newton Abbot, 1975).

(VOSE, RUTH HURST) (1971) *The Denton Glass Excavation* (Liverpool).

    (1972) 'Bickerstaffe and Haughton Green Excavations', *Annales*, 5, 137–44.

    (1980) *Glass* (London).

VYDROVA, JIRINA, 'Les Débuts de la différenciation des Types de Verre de Table en Bohême', *Annales*, 5 (1972), 205–15.

WAKEFIELD, HUGH (1961) *Nineteenth Century British Glass* (London).

    (1965) 'The Development of Design for Pressed Glassware, as exemplified in British Sources', *Proceedings of International Congress on Glass, Brussels*, Paper 208.

    (1965a) 'Glasswares by Apsley Pellatt', *Antiques* (Jan., 1965), 85–8.

    (1967) 'Richardson Glass', *Antiques* (May, 1967), 632–5.

    (1968) 'The Development of Victorian Flower-stand Centrepieces', *Annales*, 4 (?1968), 200–5.

    (1969) 'Early Victorian Styles in Glassware', *Studies in Glass History and Design* (ed. R. J. Charleston, *et al.*), Sheffield, 50–4.

    (1970) 'Victorian Flower Stands', *Antiques* (Aug., 1970), 232–6.

    (1972) 'Venetian Influence on British Glass in the 19th Century', *Annales*, 5, 293–7.

    (1978) 'Glasswares at the Great Exhibition of 1851', *Annales*, 7, 421–6.

    (1982) *Nineteenth Century British Glass*, rev. ed. (London).

WALLIS, W. CYRIL, 'An Unrecorded "Amen" Glass in the Royal Scottish Museum, Edinburgh', *Conn.* (Oct., 1952), 105.

WARHURST, A., 'Two Anglo-Saxon Glass Vessels from Lyminge, Kent', *G.N.*, 14 (Dec., 1954), 25–8.

WARREN, PHELPS (1970) *Irish Glass* (London).

    (1973) 'Glass relating to William III', *JGS*, XV, 98–134.

    (1981) *Irish Glass*, rev. ed. (London).

WATNEY, B. & CHARLESTON, R. J., 'Petitions for Patents concerning Porcelain, Glass and Enamels', *Trs. E.C.C.*, 6, Part 2 (1966), 57–123.

WATSON, ROWLAND, *Merry Gentlemen* (London, 1951).

WATTS, D. C., 'How did George Ravenscroft discover lead crystal?', *G.C.*, 2 (1975), 71–84.

WEEDEN, CYRIL, 'The Ricketts Family and the Phoenix Glasshouse, Bristol', *G.C.*, 4 (1982), 85–102.

WEINBERG, GLADYS DAVIDSON, 'A Medieval Mystery: Byzantine Glass Production', *JGS*, XVII (1975), 127–41.

WESTROPP, M. S. DUDLEY (1920) *Irish Glass* (London, n.d. ?1920).

    (1978) *Irish Glass*, revised by Mary Boydell (Dublin).

WHITEHOUSE, D. B., 'Ceramiche e vetri medioevali provenienti dal Castello di Lucera', *Bolletino d'Arte*, III–IV (1966), 171–8.

WILKINSON, O. N., *Old Glass* (London, 1968).

WILKINSON, R., *The Hallmarks of Antique Glass* (London, 1968).

WILLS, GEOFFREY (1965) *English Looking-Glasses* (London).

    (1966) *Glass* (London).

    (1968) *English and Irish Glass* (London).

    (1971) *Antique Glass for Pleasure and Investment* (London).

    (1976) *Victorian Glass* (London).

WINBOLT, S. E., *Wealden Glass* (Hove, 1933).

WINE TRADE LOAN EXHIBITION, Vintners' Hall, *Catalogue* (London, 1933).

WOLFENDEN, IAN, 'English Rock Crystal Glass, 1878–1925', *G.C.*, 4 (1982), 20–45.

WOOD, ERIC S. (1965) 'A Medieval Glasshouse at Blunden's Wood, Hambledon, Surrey', *Surrey Arch. Coll.*, LXII, 54–79.

(1982) 'A 16th century Glasshouse at Knightons, Alfold, Surrey', *Surrey Arch. Coll.*, LXXIII, 1 ff.

WOODFORDE, CHRISTOPHER (1951) *The Stained Glass of New College, Oxford* (Oxford).

(1954) *English Stained and Painted Glass* (Oxford).

WOODWARD, H. W., *Art, Feat and Mystery: the Story of Thomas Webb & Sons, Glassmakers* (Stourbridge, 1978).

YOUNG, S., *The History of the Worshipful Company of Glass Sellers of London* (London, 1913).

ZECCHIN, L. (1959) 'Le prove per il passaggio a maestro', *Note di storia dell' arte vetraria Muranese*, Venice, 27–51.

(1959a) 'L'Arte muranese fra il 1525 e il 1615', *Note di storia dell' arte vetraria Muranese*, Venice, 81–105.

(1960) 'L'Arte Vetraria Muranese dal 1618 al 1753 . . .', *Giornale Economico* (May 1959–March 1960), 7–96.

(1965) 'Il Libro d'oro dei Muranesi', *Giornale Economico*, Venice, 1159–65.

(1966) 'Antiche Insegne Vetrarie: Leon, Pigna, Gallo', *Vetro e silicati*, X, no. 60 (Nov.–Dec., 1966), 24–7.

(1967) 'Nascita del Cristallo Veneziano', *Vetro e silicati*, XI, no. 66 (Nov.–Dec., 1967), 20–3.

(1968) 'Il Barovier e il vetro cristallino', *Vetro e silicati*, XII, no. 67 (Jan.–Feb., 1968), 23–6.

(1968a) 'Cristallini dorati e smaltati', *Vetro e silicati*, XII, no. 68 (Mar.–Apr., 1968), 22–5.

(1968b) 'Maria Barovier e le "rosette"', *JGS*, X, 105–9.

(1968c) 'Fortuna d'una Parola sbagliata', *JGS*, X, 110–13.

(1969) 'Un decoratore di vetri a Murano alla fine del duecento', *JGS*, XI, 39–42.

(1969a) 'Denominazioni antiche dei Prodotti Muranesi', *Vetro e silicati*, XIII, no. 74 (Mar.–April, 1969), 25–8.

(1970) 'Cesendelli, Inghistere, Moioli', *Vetro e silicati*, XIV, no. 80 (Mar.–Apr., 1970), 25–8.

(1971) 'Una fornace muranese all' insegna della Sirena', *Riv. della Staz. Sper. del Vetro*, I, 2 (Mar.–Apr., 1971).

(1971a) 'I muranesi Miotti, vetrai all' Insegna del Gesù', *JGS*, XIII, 77–83.

(1977) 'Decoratori di vetri a Murano dal 1480 al 1500', *Riv. della Staz. Sper. del Vetro*, VII, 4 (July–Aug., 1977), 175–9.

(1980) 'I Morelli, vetrai muranesi all' insegna della Colombina', *Riv. della Staz. Sper. del Vetro*, X, 6 (Nov.–Dec., 1980), 257–62.

Index

Abbots Bromley 76, 78
abrasion 80
Absolon, William, Junior 202, 209, 210
acid-etching 203, 208–9, 213, 215, 222;
    Pls 54d, 55a
Ackermann, *see* Akerman
Acqua, Giovanni Maria dall' 65–6, 70
Adam style 179
Aesthetic Movement 223, 228
Aetna Glass Works 199
air-trap effects 221; Pl. 61a
air-twist stems 144, 146–7, 150, 169, 178;
    Pl. 38a–d
Akerman, John 174
alabaster 212
albarello 93–4; fig. 19
Albert, Prince 214, 229; Pl. 59c
Alberti, Girolamo 108, 110–11
alchemy 53; *see also* laboratory equipment
Alconbury, Huntingdon 110
Aldersgate, London 117; fig. 22
Alderton Higginbottom & Company 227
ale-glass 154–6, 173; Pls 27b, 40c, e, 43a;
    see also beer-glass, 'short ale'
Alemayne, John 29
alembic 36–7; Pl. 19c; fig. 10
Aleppo 26; Pl. 7a
Alexandrian glass 26
'Alexandrite' 221
Alfold, Surrey 71–2, 78, 90
Alfriston, Sussex 8
'Al Gesù' glasshouse 107
Alicante 64
Alken, Henry 174
Allan, David 158
'alla porcellana' 46
Allen & Moore 201
Alloa glassworks 210
Alnwick Castle 59, 170
Altare 111
amber-coloured glass 11, 12, 212, 221, 223,
    231; *see also* brown
'Amberina' 221
'Amen' glasses 139, 150
America 201, 226
Amphitrite 215

amphora 212
Amsterdam 99
Ancoats 227
angelica 160
Anger 18
Angles 2
Anglo-Saxon 1, ff.; Pls 1–5
'Anglo-Venetian' 132; *see also* Venetian style
Angus and Greener 227
'an Honest True Blue' 189
animal subjects 206
Anne, Queen 134, 137, 150–1; Pl. 32a
annealing furnace 13–14
Anstey Church, Hertfordshire 35
Antwerp 53, 59, 111
apothecary's glassware 92–3
Appel, Peter 71–2
apple-tree Pl. 39d
apricot 221
Apthorpe, Thomas 113
Apulia 23–4
arabesques 55–7
Arbroath Pl. 39b
arcaded designs 4–5, 7
'Argentine' 222
armorials 26–7, 80, 193
army 202
Arras 53
arsenic 185
Art Deco 231
Art of Glass 107; *see also* Neri, Äntonio
'Art glass' 230
Art Nouveau 207, 224–5, 229
Arts and Crafts Exhibition 230
Arts and Crafts Movement 201, 217
Arundel, Earl of 66
Ascot Doilly Castle, Oxfordshire 39
ash 85; *see also* beech, bracken, potash
Ashburton 145
Ashford, Kent Pl. 4b
Ås-Husby 11
'assay' 49
Aston, Warwicks. 186
Audnam, near Stourbridge 149
Augsburg 153
Austin Friars, London 64